Wealthy Masters – 'provident and kind'

The Household at Holkham 1697-1842

Mary Anne Garry

Dec 2012

For
K.J.M.G.
1937–1986

PUBLISHED BY LARKS PRESS
Ordnance Farmhouse, Guist Bottom
Dereham, Norfolk NR20 5PF
01328 829207

Printed by Mimeo, Huntingdon, Cambridgeshire
November 2012

British Library Cataloguing-in-Publication Data.
A catalogue record for this book is available
from the British Library.

ISBN 978 1904006 64 0

Designed by Dominique Lorenz
Typeset in Bembo

Front Cover: The two Earls of Leicester as Roman senators.
Thomas Coke by Loiuis-Francois Roubilliac and
Thomas William Coke by Sir Francis Chantrey.

Back Cover: Corridor, Holkham Hall.

Bell drawing: Loretta Schauer.

Wealthy Masters – 'provident and kind'

The Household at Holkham 1697-1842

MARY-ANNE GARRY

LARKS PRESS

Acknowledgements

Above all my thanks to Holkham; without the kindness of the Earl of Leicester and Viscount Coke in allowing me access to the archives, this book would not have been written. It remains for them to judge whether their generosity was justified.

Also at Holkham I owe an immense debt to Christine Hiskey the archivist who over the years never tired of discussing servant related issues, and has been kind enough to read the script and make suggestions. It is thanks to her that there should be few, if any, errors of fact. Those that do occur are entirely mine. Other private houses with archives were equally welcoming and I must thank the Duke of Bedford and Anne Mitchell at Woburn, the Marquess of Salisbury and Robin Harcourt-Williams at Hatfield, the Marquess Townshend at Raynham and Lord Walpole at Wolterton. Thanks are also due to the following record offices: the Centre for Kentish Studies, Berkshire Record Office, Dorset Record Office, East Sussex Record Office, Hertfordshire Record Office, Leicestershire Record Office, Lincolnshire Archives, London Metropolitan Archives, Norfolk Record Office, Northampton Record Office, Nottinghamshire Archives and Nottingham University Library Nottinghamshire Archives and Nottingham University Library, Sheffield Archives, Staffordshire Record Office, Suffolk Record Office Bury St Edmunds branch, West Sussex Record Office and Wiltshire and Swindon Archives. In addition the British Library, Swaffham Library, the Huntingdon Library and the New York Public Library. The Eastern Daily Press in Norwich allowed me to read their eighteenth century copies of the Norwich Mercury at a time when the Record Office was closed after the fire.

Dr David Edwards of Wingerworth in Derbyshire was kind enough to give me valuable information about the Hunloke family, and Max Green also of Derbyshire supplied me with a copy of the Longford census for 1841. Trevor Fawcett of Bath told me many interesting facts about Bath in the early eighteenth century and John Smith of Stamford did the same for Culverthorpe in Lincolnshire. The late Mr Squire enlightened me as to what sort of a garment an Alburness is and the late Pamela Clabburn explained the characteristics of Norwich crepe. Dr Edwina Ehrman of the London Museum and Dr Gilly Lehman of the University of Franche-Comte, Besançon, France, helped me with the eighteenth century diet and explained exactly how French food of the time differed from English. David Turner of Narborough, Norfolk, allowed me to quote from unpublished correspondence in his ownership. I owe thanks to Gwen Agna of Massachusetts, to the parish priest of St Giles in the Fields, London who allowed me to study the parish registers in situ over two days and to Mary Clow for nobly transcribing Jane Coke's correspondence held in New York.

Lastly to those who read the script at its various stages, Christine Hiskey as already mentioned also Rachel Young, Jean Joice, Professor Richard Wilson and Susan Yaxley my editor. To them I am immensely grateful.

Finally, a piece about Sarah Staniforth has appeared in the Holkham Newsletter and a longer account of Charlotte Edwards was included in my article 'Seduced by the Devil' Divorce in 18th Century Norfolk, Norfolk Archaeology Vol.XLIV Part IV 2005.

Picture credits

The family portraits are reproduced by kind permission of Lord Coke and the Trustees of the Holkham Estate, as is the plan of the house, and the page from the account books. Cover photographs by Colin Shearer. Additional photographs are by Dominique Lorenz assisted by her niece Ottoline Lorenz.

Abbreviations

HA – Holkham Archives.
NRO – Norfolk Record Office.
TNA – The National Archive.

Foreword

The great estate of Holkham boasts two major distinctions. Its centrepiece, the hall itself, is generally reckoned to be the finest Palladian house in Britain. Its estate was in the van of important changes in agricultural practices in the eighteenth and nineteenth centuries. The house and its contents were essentially the lifetime's work of Thomas Coke [1697-1759], created Earl of Leicester in 1744; the much trumpeted improvement of the estate during its sixty-six year ownership was the work of his great-nephew, T.W. Coke [1754-1842] himself advanced to the earldom of Leicester in 1837 but much better known to posterity and a vast band of students studying the industrial and agricultural revolutions as Coke of Norfolk. Both the building of the house over thirty years, the remarkable result of the contributions of the Earl of Burlington, William Kent and Matthew Brettingham, all refined and driven forward by Thomas Coke's great passion for architecture; and the fame of the estate made known by T.W. Coke's gift of publicity amongst his fellow agriculturists have been extensively studied by architectural and economic historians. Obviously, given their agendas, neither breed was much interested in the servants at Holkham.

Yet as Mary-Anne Garry shows in this welcome addition to the subject of domestic service – hitherto particularly thin on the eighteenth century – servants underpinned every aspect of life at Holkham. Her researches throw new light on family, house and estate alike. In the pre-factory age, before the 1790s, the great country houses of the peerage were amongst the largest employers of labour, the largest economic units (although seldom driven by strict considerations of profit and productivity) in the country. In the thirty years after 1734 when the house was being built Thomas Coke employed a small army of people: almost forty indoor staff, besides gardeners and estate workers and scores of labourers and highly skilled craftsmen building the house itself.

The basis of the book is the Holkham household accounts – the best were those kept by Lady Margaret, Thomas Coke's competent wife and after his death the chatelaine of Holkham for fifteen years – in which Mrs Garry has immersed herself for many years. It is a remarkable reconstruction of the Holkham 'family' from 1697 to 1842. There are many riches. From the account of numbers, duties and wages fascinating vignettes emerge: the challenges of running a menagerie; the logistics of moving the household to London each year; the routine servicing of the twenty-seven chimneys at the London house in Bloomsbury and the seventy-five at Holkham; the purchase of the grand service of plate from Paul de Lamerie which must have weighed close on a quarter of a ton. Unsurprisingly, also with big purchases of land and the cost of maintaining semi-regal show on their appearances in London and Norwich, the Cokes borrowed heavily.

Nevertheless, they were good employers. Wages, in comparison with those paid by the Norfolk gentry and professional classes, were generous. Annuities were arranged on retirement; a top rate of interest rewarded those servants who placed their savings with the Cokes. Medical care was provided for those who were ill. On a lighter note, visits to the Opera in London and the little theatre in Walsingham were organised. Yet there was always a large turnover of staff especially of cooks, house and laundry maids, possibly accounted for by the practice of employing non-local indoor staff where possible. Considering that no servant correspondence survives and there is no recourse to oral history in the years the book covers, the lively detail which emerges from the account books is most impressive. Any producer, exploiting the general interest in upstairs-downstairs themes and contemplating a successor to Downton Abbey might profitably turn to this book for a genuinely realistic account of the great households of two remarkable men across almost a century and a half.

Richard Wilson

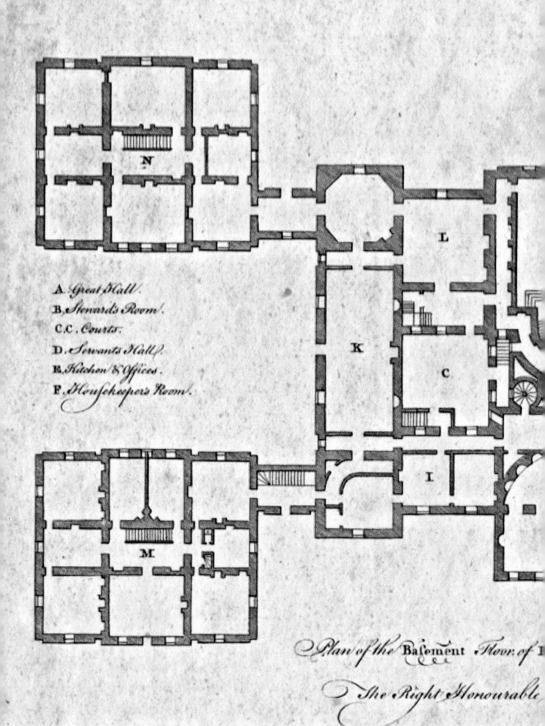

A. *Great Hall*.
B. *Steward's Room*.
C.C. *Courts*.
D. *Servants Hall*.
E. *Kitchen & Offices*.
F. *Housekeeper's Room*.

Plan of the Basement Floor of

The Right Honourable

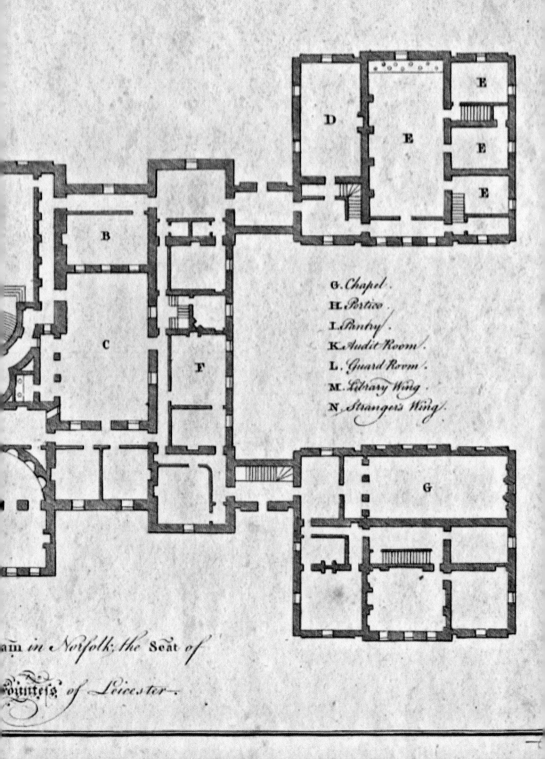

G. *Chapel.*
H. *Portico.*
I. *Pantry.*
K. *Audit Room.*
L. *Guard Room.*
M. *Library Wing.*
N. *Strangers Wing.*

...ain in *Norfolk; the Seat of*
...ountess *of Leicester.*

List of illustrations

Contents

Wealthy Masters – 'provident and kind'

The Household at Holkham 1697-1842

Introduction

There was something in the air during the 1990s. As country house visiting declined in popularity the servants quarters were looked at afresh as being areas of the house which could potentially interest visitors every bit as much as the salons, dining rooms and bedchambers. At about the same time historians, who had, with the exception of J. Jean Hecht in the 1950s, largely ignored servants, responded and began to research, to write and to publish. Since then a plethora of books on every aspect of domestic service has appeared. Can yet another be justified?

The starting point for this one began when researching the history of Castle Acre, a parish which forms part of the Holkham estate in Norfolk. In the course of discovering much about the people who inhabited the village in years past there was one found of particular interest, Thomas Boyce the tenant landlord of the Ostrich Inn, Castle Acre's premier hostelry. What marked him out was that for many years prior to his arrival at the inn in 1802 he had been coachman to Thomas William Coke at Holkham Hall. He must have been a valued servant for on leaving Holkham he was given two separate annuities, one each from Mr and Mrs Coke, giving him an additional income of £15 a year. This led to wondering what happened to the Cokes' servants in general. Was it customary for the older ones to retire, be rewarded with pensions and move on to other occupations as Boyce had done? How many were employed at Holkham in the first place, who were they and where did they come from? To answer these queries a casual examination of the material available proved irresistibly tempting. The Household Accounts in the Holkham archives are particularly rich, especially for the early eighteenth century and it soon became apparent that to answer satisfactorily would require detailed study.

Holkham Hall on the north Norfolk coast was built in the mid-eighteenth century by Thomas Coke, Earl of Leciester and made famous some years later by his heir, Thomas William Coke, as a centre of agricultural innovation. The great and good, and the not so good, from the Prince of Wales downwards visited to discuss improved farming techniques and to enjoy the many marvels the great house had to offer. Set in a large park, no expense was spared in the building of the house, yet for all its grandeur it was intended to be a comfortable home to the Coke family, which it became and still is today. Largely unaltered the house continues to be cared for, polished and admired.

For centuries servants formed a large percentage of the population and in some households outnumbered their employers, yet they have hardly left a mark. When servants were immortalised in plays it was almost always to their detriment. With few exceptions (the nurse in Romeo and Juliet) they were portrayed as faithless gossips ready to denounce their employers at the drop of a hat. Or as lazy, ungrateful creatures, yes creatures, hardly human, and a trial to anyone who had the misfortune to employ them. During the eighteenth century they were scarcely if ever mentioned in the correspondence of the employer class and when they were it was all too often in an impersonal way, unnamed. In fact servants were not all lowly people needing to be tamed and trained, but came from a variety of social levels. With limited employment choices for those no longer needed at home, or of necessity obliged to support themselves, setting out to work as a servant and live in a stranger's house was daunting. However, service had its attractions. It could be a positive experience for some if they wished it to be and were fortunate enough to enter a prosperous and well-run household. In a good house, and many were, it provided a degree of security and the opportunity for improved living conditions, both highly valued, and as will be seen not all servants were miserable or demeaned. A good servant was always in demand, for above all they were needed.

Until the twentieth century, with the advent of electricity and the invention of labour-saving devices, in households where the master and mistress wished to be freed from domestic drudgery and could afford to be so, a number of servants were essential to perform the multitude of tasks required for comfortable living. From getting out of bed in the mornings, 'rising', to retiring at night, daily tasks were more time consuming than they are today. To begin with, how were they to know what time it was on waking? Before the late eighteenth century timepieces were rare, hence the need for the town, or village, crier. In the house the absence of running water and central heating, meant non-stop labour. To keep the worst of the cold at bay

2

fires needed to be laid, lit and attended to at least once every hour. Cooking was done over non-adjustable heat. Food was strictly seasonal with a short shelf life and sometimes contaminated. Cleaning agents were efficient but the lack of running water, and the need to heat it for washing, hampered those with the best intentions. Day-to-day chores were a struggle, alleviated only by the presence of help, either in the form of family members or in the case of the better off, servants. Almost everyone who could afford it employed a servant. Some took the presence of a servant for granted; others employed them for limited spells only, as their fortunes and circumstances fluctuated.

In the late seventeenth and eighteenth centuries, the period this book covers, those households where more than one or two servants were employed can be divided into three. The first was the peerage group, the very grandest households, though having a title was not necessary for membership, since some commoners were landowners on a similar scale. The second were the gentry and the third the professionals. The households of the peerage group invariably employed between twenty-five and thirty indoor servants and were characterised by the presence of one or two male cooks, very often foreign ones, and it is to this group that the Cokes of Holkham belonged. The second group, the gentry, had around ten servants with no man cook but a cook maid and, sometimes, but not necessarily, a full-time footman. While in the third group, the servants employed by a clergyman, merchant, doctor, lawyer or prosperous farmer, would number no more than four or five.

Apart from having sufficient disposable income, that is simply being able to afford it, the reason why so many servants were employed may also be explained by the times. This was an age when a household reflected its master and a family who aspired to be courtiers, such as the Cokes, needed to demonstrate that they were able to support a peerage lifestyle. Prior to 1728 the Cokes had no title, but they were large scale land-owners. Their income derived from the land in the form of rent and their estate was comparable in size to many of the greatest ennobled families. Land-based wealth was regarded as the most socially acceptable and was far preferable to that accumulated by other means such as banking or merchant trading. In common with other families of the land-owning classes the Cokes owned estates in more than one county and consequently had more than one residence. Minster Lovell in Oxfordshire, an ancient house on the banks of the Windrush, was one, the most favoured; while others such as Knightley in Staffordshire were let to tenants and only visited occasionally. At the time of Thomas Coke's birth in

1697, his parents Edward and Cary, when not at Holkham, rented a house in London and another at Tittenhanger in Hertfordshire.

The master of an eighteenth-century household was head not only of his immediate family, his wife and children, but also of those he employed as servants. The whole was referred to, and seen, as a 'Family'. And as head of the 'Family' the master was concerned with all aspects of the servants lives, often recording in detail exactly what each servant was expected to do, when and how often. The servants wages were paid by him, they were fed, housed and clothed by him. He listened to their grievances and judged their complaints, and to their master servants were expected to be loyal. Servants represented those they worked for and though they might be largely silent when on display, their appearance and demeanour were important. The wearing of liveries by the male servants presented a united front to visitors as they stood in their matching suits made up in the family colours. Female servants were kept out of sight and consequently had no need for livery. Almost all domestic work was performed manually, some unlucky dogs ran in wheels to turn the kitchen spit and donkeys similarly turned cogs to draw water from wells, but generally there was a complete and entire reliance on human muscle for cleaning, cooking, washing and sewing. And the larger the house the more hands were needed to keep it in good order.

The concept of a household as a 'Family' is derived from earlier times when many of the upper servants, or officers, were just that, cousins or distant relatives of the family employing them. Others might claim ties with the family, living on the estate as yeomen, or were the sons of gentry neighbours. [1] Until the seventeenth century in great households most of the servants were men. They did all the cooking and serving, much as they would continue to do, but also all the cleaning. These male servants, whether related to the family or not, wore livery to denote their kinship (in the widest sense) and could present a united, semi-military presence. Only with the increase of maid servants, laundresses in particular (all that lace and silk), did the housekeeper and her domain gradually emerge. Economic considerations had a hand in this; maids were cheaper than men. Households reduced in size again and the need for fewer male servants came about largely due to the removal of the country house from its agricultural context to a freestanding one. Holkham is a good example of this. Where previously the Cokes' house had been at the centre of a farm, the new build was a pleasure dome. It was far removed from any direct association with farming, emphasised by its setting in the surrounding park, land which they could afford not to cultivate. [2] Despite these changes the concept of servants as members of a family persisted. The sense of belonging to a family, if in name only, provided companionship and encouraged loyalty. Even today the concept of employees as members of a family survives in places. [3]

By the early eighteenth century servants in elite households were drawn from many different parts of the country and on arrival had little or no traditional ties to the house in which they were to serve. In the steward's room, the servants hall and corridors in between, a range of accents would have been heard, a good percentage of which were foreign. This disparity could be a recipe for tensions and disputes. It should be noted however, that most employers, while ambivalent as to how far they could trust their servants, did their best to be fair and considerate. It was in their interest to do so. They aimed at control, but tempered with kindness and reason. The eighteenth century gentleman strove to be recognized by the four aims of the age, Politeness, Improvement, Progress and Reason which he endeavoured to carry into every sphere of his life. Religion was equally important. Family prayers were said morning and night when, as many of the 'Family' as could be gathered in the same room, came together. Servants were expected to attend church on Sundays. Prayer books and bibles were supplied for them, and improving texts such as *Aesop's Fables* given out as reading matter. However, despite the care and concern for their welfare, the gulf that separated master from servant must never be crossed. Intimacy and occasional affection could be shown and shared, but the fact remained that a domestic servant was a person at a master's or mistress's beck and call at most times of the day and night. No matter the hour, he or she could be commanded to perform duties and expected to carry them out without any show of visible complaint. A sense of duty and service was not confined to the servant class but came down from those who employed them. Children of the elite were drilled with the need for obedience and responsibility from their earliest years.

Opportunities for servants to air grievances (and make requests) are recorded in one household and doubtless took place in many another. The accounts of the Duke of Chandos in the early 1720s show him presiding over a weekly audit board where, for example, an enquiry came from the Steward's Room. Who exactly was allowed to drink tea there? At present: 'all who come are seemingly welcomed'. The answer was no-one who does not dine at table. Next, the footmen's request for extra lanterns in the corridors to light the servants carrying his Grace's supper, was granted. The Duke agreed to provide iron scrapers for cleaning shoes. He also agreed to a grill against the window of the butler's room, where the silver was kept, and a grate at the dairy's sink to stop the rats getting in. Not every request was sanctioned. When the house porter said his duties did not allow him enough time to look after the poultry the Duke replied 'Nonsense'. Had he not got a boy to help him? [4]

To be engaged as a servant in a peerage household, provided you agreed to the rules by which the house was run, was to enjoy the security of receiving a regular wage, provision of warmth, clothing, light and food, medical care when ill, with the added possibility and excitement of travel and a pension in retirement. However for many, domestic employment was often no more than a transient stage in their lives brought about by necessity rather than choice. Most expected to change occupations several times during their working lives and periods working as a servant were frequently short, especially among the more menial servants who tended to be very young. For others it was time spent at a training ground, a chance to acquire skills and knowledge which would enable them to apply to other households in hopes of promotion to a higher post. To 'better oneself' was a constant spur. For those who aspired to independence, the experience was an opportunity to learn at first hand the style of gentry life. It allowed them an insight into the habits and tastes of the elite, which would prove to be an invaluable asset when setting up a shop or other service industry.

Servants do present certain conundrums, not least the perceived imbalance of labour. Boswell famously asked Dr Johnson why women servants, who were paid less and had to provide their own clothes, worked so much harder than the males. Answer came there none. [5] Expectations of how domestic labour was viewed and carried out in the eighteenth century tends to suggest footmen were more ornament than use. Dressed in their livery and waiting on their master and mistress they were often seen to be doing very little, simply hanging about. But it can be argued that the long hours of apparently not doing very much belied the manual work they would have performed earlier in the day. All servants earned their wages.

Domestic innovation advanced at a snail's pace not least because there was no apparent need; apart from inventing a better apparatus to turn the spit, dogs not being very reliable, Holkham was to be ahead of most in water supplies and heating, but for the elite of generations past the concept of any form of 'labour-saving' devices was quite alien. It simply did not occur to them.

The presence of servants meant there was always a plentiful fund of hands to call upon. And up to the late nineteenth century there was no shortage of people willing to apply for servant positions in well-to-do households. Even then, the hey day of the servant registry office, it was not until after the second world war (1939-1945), when 'mod cons' came into general use, that servant numbers seriously begin to decline. Even now servants have never entirely disappeared. In the 1950s English servants were replaced by Italian and Spanish couples; today the circle is complete and cooks and butlers are once again English, though most maids are not.

Next comes the question of who should and who should not be included in this narrative. Domestic servants yes, but what about the household as a whole, for to define precisely what constituted a household is itself a challenge. A simple interpretation could be those who slept under the same roof, but this would exclude a number of servants who lived out, such as coachmen and postillions, part-timers, casual help and the occasional specialists who served the household but lived elsewhere. When a family owned a house in town and more than one in the country, it is difficult to view a household as a fixed number of people, but one that expanded and contracted as circumstances dictated. For the purposes of this account a household may be defined as those people a master paid to perform tasks of a domestic or service nature, either daily, on trial, or on a fixed or long-term basis.

Many studies have been made of servants in general, taking examples from a variety of sources. The purpose of this book is to focus on a sole household, recording, as far as possible, those who worked as servants and also to breathe some life into the elusive beings, who all too often have left no mark behind but their names. The wealth of material for the eighteenth century at Holkham made this an attractive prospect, for much has been written about domestic service in the nineteenth century, but comparatively little about the eighteenth. In discovering the origins, functions and conditions of the servants, light is also cast upon the lives of their masters.

The book is divided into two parts. Part One covers the lifetime of Thomas Coke 1st Earl of Leicester, of the first creation and the builder of Holkham Hall. It begins with a brief look at the last years of the seventeenth century and then follows Thomas Coke as a child at school, his Grand Tour and his servants while abroad, his marriage on inheriting Holkham in 1718 and the building of the new house, known as the mansion. It ends with his death in 1759.

Part Two is the period of his great nephew and heir Thomas William Coke who reigned at Holkham from 1776 to 1842, and for whom the title of Earl of Leicester was re-created in 1837. An epilogue briefly discusses the household after the death of Thomas William Coke.

NOTES

1. Alice T. Friedman, *House and Household in Elizabethan England, Wollaton Hall and the Willoughby Family,* Chicago and London 1989 p43.

2. Friedman p.48 and she continues p.49 'Thus, while the creation of the country house helped to place domestic work and family life directly under women's control, it also opened up the possibility for an identification of women with the home and for the virtual exclusion of women from public life.'.

3. In a conversation with the author in September 2011 Maurice Bray an estate worker at Holkham spoke of his satisfaction of working there 'I have never wanted to work anywhere else. It is like a big family here.'.

4. Huntingdon Library Stowe MS. ST44 folio 25.

5. James Boswell *Life of Samuel Johnson* London 1791, Penguin Classics 2008, p.375.

Part One:

In the time of Thomas Coke,
the builder of Holkham Hall,
1697-1759

CHAPTER 1

Childhood

The present house at Holkham known as Holkham Hall was built in the mid-eighteenth century by Thomas Coke, created Earl of Leicester in 1744. It was probably conceived, if not while Coke was on his Grand Tour in the early 1700s, then shortly afterwards, but building did not begin until the early 1730s and it was only fully completed in 1764.

The house was designed to emulate a classic Palladian villa, so much in favour at the time. Not the least of its functions was to create a suitable home for the paintings, statues, books and other works of art Coke had purchased. It was to impress all who saw it by its grandeur: the marble hall, the gilded windows, the precious objects within, and the park without, yet on a more domestic level the arrangements for the household were to be equally notable. The servants quarters and their work places were also to be admired. The state-of-the-art kitchen was designed to be as much a show place as the state apartments.

Previously the Cokes had lived in Hill Hall, a Tudor manor house since demolished, which stood on a site to the south-west of the present Hall. It had been in the family since John Coke, the fourth son of the wealthy and eminent lawyer Sir Edward Coke, inherited it on marriage to Meriel Wheatley in 1612.

No pictures of Hill Hall have survived, though a map of 1590 shows it to have been a typical Tudor manor house surrounded by a small enclosure wherein were a number of trees. The location was a village one. The proximity of several neighbouring houses point to this; the whole was set in a farming landscape of pasture and arable fields. By the mid-seventeenth century John Coke had enlarged and altered the house to suit his sizeable family and twenty-three servants. At the time of his death in 1661 the central hall of the house still functioned as the servants eating room (which it continued to do until the building of a new servants hall in 1729) but he had added a spacious new dining room capable of seating forty-five people. Throughout this period the house was first and foremost the centre of a working farm. The myth that subsequently grew up of Holkham land being barren and infertile is quite erroneous. The great deer park that surrounds the present house was still far in the future; prior to its creation the land was farmed most profitably.

After John Coke's death in 1661 the house changed very little, for, until the advent of Thomas Coke, the intervening masters at Holkham were in possession for short periods only. Despite having had five sons John Coke was survived by only one of them, also John, who died unmarried in 1670. Holkham then passed to his cousin Robert Coke, who died just eight years later aged only twenty-three, though leaving a son, Edward. This child grew to manhood and married, but he too died young at thirty-one in 1707, in the same year as his wife Cary. Even in an age of frequent mortality, a marked feature of the seventeenth century including the well-to-dos, the Cokes were seen as a family doomed, fated to die to out, ' ... I am very sorry Mr Coke is so ill ... as if the fate of the family was coming upon him, not to outlive thirty'. [1]

However, Edward and Cary Coke left five children all of whom lived to adulthood, and the eldest of these was Thomas.

1697-1707

When Thomas Coke's parents Edward and Cary married in 1696, they had a household of twenty-six indoor servants plus a kitchen boy and Tom Aaron, an unwaged foot or page boy. As newlyweds they had submitted to the custom of an older woman supervising their household during their first year together. In their case this was Edward Coke's mother, Lady Anne Walpole. Lady Anne was the daughter of Thomas Danby, the Lord Treasurer and first Duke of Leeds. Ambitious to become M.P. for King's Lynn, Robert Coke, her husband, was short of cash and borrowed a considerable sum from his father-in-law in order to achieve this goal. He succeeded in being elected but died soon afterwards leaving an only child, a son, Edward. Some years later Lady Anne married again, this time to Horatio Walpole, uncle to Sir Robert, and a 'heavy drinking' man of uncertain temper. By the time of her son's marriage Lady Anne was living at Beck Hall in Norfolk, twenty miles from Holkham, but moved into the London house the newly-weds had taken, 'my Lady to have the management of it'. [2] The sixteen-year-old bride whose own mother was long dead could not be expected to control a large household without guidance. Edward and Cary appear to have been fortunate in their mutual affection for each other; it was a happy marriage and one that pleased both sides of the family.

The house they rented in London was in the north east corner of St James's Square, adjoining York Street, a most fashionable address. The St James's development, built between 1665 and 1676 on Pall Mall Field, aimed from the start to attract the Quality, with its convenient shopping centre adjacent (the extensive St James's market) and a church in Jermyn Street built in 1684 to designs by Sir Christopher Wren. In this church Edward Coke paid £25 a year for seats marked 5, 4 and 3 in the South Gallery (the third seat was for his mother Lady Anne Walpole) and in this church the rector Dr Wake christened the Coke children. [3]

Besides spending part of the summer at Holkham, the Cokes rented a country house more convenient for London at Tittenhanger in Hertfordshire, which still stands today. Built in 1655 in the then entirely new form of a stubby H, it was three storeys high above a basement and with attics. On the first floor landing were four doorcases with pediments, two of which were triangular, very similar to those Thomas Coke would later choose for Holkham. [4] The rent was £90 a year and the landlord Sir Thomas Pope Blount. This house was much used by the young Coke family in the years to 1707. The accounts for Tittenhanger include several entries for 'play things for Master Tommy' and a fiddler hired to entertain for his sister Cary's second birthday.

At the head of the servant tree was the house steward who kept the accounts and dealt with matters deemed too trivial to warrant his master's attention. The man employed by Edward Coke for this post was Charles Wright, referred to as 'cousin'. Cousin was a generic term used to include people both closely and distantly related; it was still common at this period to employ relatives as servants. It is not clear how Charles Wright was related, but he may have been a member of the Wright families of Eyam and Great Longstone in Derbyshire, who in turn were relatives of Sir John Newton, Edward Coke's father-in-law. [5] As steward Charles Wright was paid £20 a year to run the household. He also had to collect the rents of Coke properties in the City of London and to travel 'into ye West' (Oxfordshire and Somerset) to collect rents there, journeys which lasted up to six weeks. His duties did not extend to Holkham itself which was the responsibility of the Norfolk steward, Humphrey Smith.

After Charles Wright came a valet de chambre, a housekeeper and her maid, four footmen (two each for the master and mistress), a butler, under-butler, a house porter who opened the door to visitors and dealt with the post, one or two male cooks, a cook's maid, at least two laundry maids, a still-room maid and a number of housemaids. For the children there were nurses and nurse maids and, when the boys of the family were old enough, a tutor. In addition were several 'invisible' servants whose names do not appear on the wages list, the lady's maids and pages; lady's maids were usually paid for by the mistress of the house from her own allowance. There were two grades of lady's maid, the first known as her mistress's 'woman' who was an assistant/companion, and the other a chambermaid who saw to her mistress's clothes and personal needs. There was usually a small foot boy, e.g. Tom Aaron in service, an apprentice. His clothes and board appear in the household accounts to indicate his presence, but no wages. He was there to learn the ways of a great household.

Various gentlemen were attached to the household and in the country would expect to eat dinner each day in the hall. At Holkham these were the chaplain who ate at the family table, the secretary and head gardener. The latter lived in a cottage on the estate. [6]

Out of doors were four more liveried servants, two coachmen and two postillions. In the country there were a number of stable and hunt servants who saw to the welfare of the horses and dogs; at least four grooms, a dog feeder, and three stable helpers. All of these were in full-time employment and appear in the lists of servants wages. Part-timers included the brewer and his boy, a man to bake bread, charwomen, washer-women and on occasion extra help in the kitchen. Garden workers, both male and female, are listed separately in the Country Accounts under the heading of day labourers and are not individually named.

Provision for this large number of people was needed fifty-two weeks a year no matter where the family was, either in London or the country, and in both places there was a stream of visitors. At Holkham tradesmen, carriers, workmen and others who had often travelled a considerable distance to get there expected to be refreshed with at least a drink, at best a meal. In London many might ask but the only ones who could count on a meal were the servants of the family's visitors and chairmen. In London chairmen were engaged by the season. They usually carried the lady of the house while the master made do with a chair hired at a stand. Chairmen were never servants per se, though they might wear an emblem of livery and have some semi-permanent connection to the household. For instance when the family were out of town chairmen were often engaged to 'watch the London house'. [7]

Edward Coke paid his servants wages twice a year, at Christmas and mid-summer. Occasionally the upper servants were given a bonus, such as in December 1699, a Christmas treat of going 'to the Play'. This was both a reward for loyal service, a gesture of appreciation and an education. Education was important in the master–servant relationship. Edward and Cary Coke paid generous wages and it is recorded that Cary laid out money for 'teaching the Footmen'. [8] Female servants who showed the same good service could expect to receive gifts of cloth with which to make gowns. These were given at the discretion of their mistress and paid for from her pin money.

Living-in servants provided their employers with a comfortable life, but their presence was not without a certain risk, for they were no more immune to illness and death than other people. During the four year period 1698-1702 three of the Cokes' servants died. Two were housemaids and more worryingly the third was the children's nurse. The first of these deaths was recorded as simply 'burying a maid'. The second, Alice Palmer, had wages owing to her of £2 which were sent to her mother. The third was Mrs Page the nurse who had care of the precious children. Her funeral was paid for by her master, and two guineas was spent on hatbands and gloves for the servants mourning. Mrs Page's outstanding wages of £20 were paid to her husband.

The causes of servants deaths were a very real anxiety to the rest of the family. In the early days of her marriage Cary Coke received a letter from her step-mother Lady Newton alerting her to the fact that living in a house with a good many servants meant that illness among *them* was as much a source for concern as it was among the immediate family.

' ... the same illness your sarvants have had is in all places. Mr Newton's sarvant that waits of him [a valet] is now of it in Lincolnshire ... ' [9]

There was little the family could do before illness struck, except keep everything as clean as possible. But when it did strike, servants were often sent away to be nursed elsewhere, especially if they fell ill in London. In July 1700 Cary's personal footman became ill and was sent away at once. A nurse was paid £1. 4s. 0d. for keeping him for four weeks. He received a further £1. 7s. 0d. for board wages.

Illness or the threat of it was ever present. This was an age when every ailment, no matter how mild, was seen as potentially serious, if not fatal. When Jack Lee, who worked in Coke's stables, was sent away for two weeks to be nursed by a Mrs Forster, the accountant noted he had been 'in a Distemper supposed to be the Chicken Pox, but first thought to be the small pox'. This illustrates how prompt the re-action to danger was, better to act fast whatever the monetary cost than risk spreading disease.

Despite this the Coke children were often unwell. As their grandfather Newton remarked, 'your family are so sickly particularly the children of the ague, the frequent returns of which I can not but attribute to ye situate of the place [Holkham] lying so open to the sea'. [10]

Ague, which laid everyone low from time to time, was defined as burning fever, with hot and cold fits, probably malaria. Opinions about the benefits of sea air were of course to undergo a complete change-about over the course of the next fifty years.

However it was not the Coke children who succumbed to a fatal illness, but their parents. In 1707 both Edward and Cary Coke fell ill and died, aged thirty and twenty-seven respectively. Edward Coke died in April and Cary in early August, and with their eldest son Thomas aged only ten years old, the household was broken up. Aside from the very natural grief and distress that must have accompanied these events, the servants had no cause to worry about their immediate future. The fact that Edward had left an heir, Thomas, with two more sons Edward and Robert waiting in the background, was a positive factor for the servants. It meant that the *estate* would continue in the family's ownership and some of them might hope to be kept on during the heir's minority, or at the very least have their wages paid, with perhaps a legacy to tide them over. For those who expected to be pensioned off the presence of an heir was also good news, since it suggested the estate would continue long enough to pay their pensions. [11]

Events moved swiftly following the funerals. Thomas's great-grandfather the Duke of Leeds assumed his role as head of the family, and by rights and the law, he wrote that the orphaned children should live with their paternal grandmother, his daughter Lady Anne Walpole. However in view of her bucolic husband, known by his family as 'the black Colonel', together with her distinct lack of enthusiasm, he decided they would be better cared for by their maternal grandfather, Sir John Newton, who had a young family by his second wife. Lady Anne Walpole offered no word of protest. On the contrary she pleaded ill health and doubted the children could bear the long journey to Norfolk, 'thus late of the year'. Though of course, she added hastily, in future she would welcome them for short visits. The prospect of caring for five grandchildren alarmed her. It was only the previous year that she had been obliged to welcome young Dorothy Walpole, her husband's exuberant niece into her care, after Dorothy's behaviour had made it impossible for her to remain in London. [12]   Next, four guardians were appointed to care for the estate and the children. These were all relations: Sir John Newton, the children's grandfather, Sir Charles Bertie of Uffington in Lincolnshire, Lady Anne Walpole's uncle on her mother's side, a Derbyshire cousin, Sir Edward Coke of Longford, a Derbyshire cousin, and John Coke, a much younger man not yet thirty, a lawyer. Fifty-eight-year-old Sir Edward Coke was a great-grandson of his namesake Lord Chief Justice Coke, the founder of the family fortunes who had bought the Longford estate for his favourite son Clement, the grandfather of Sir Edward. It was one among many manors outside Norfolk that the Lord Chief Justice purchased for his sons. The reasons for his choices have not survived and these estates were possibly not even visited by him. However, the motivation for buying Longford can be seen. When the last owner, Nicholas Longford, died without a male heir, his trustees agreed to sell the estate for £5,000. This was in 1616 and Longford's *female* heir, his great niece, was married to Clement Coke. A further inducement was that Longford lies adjacent to the parish of Trusley where another Coke family lived. Despite what might, at first glance, seem to be an apparent kinship, the two families do not appear to have been related, though close ties were kept between them and they referred to each other as 'cousin'. It was from the Trusley Cokes that young John Coke, the guardian, was descended. [13] Lady Anne wrote from distant Norfolk that she was happy to do whatever the guardians thought best, confident in the knowledge that she had been relieved from the burden of their care: 'I have so much tender regard for every one of them than for pleasing myself'. [sic] [14]

Hardly had the burials of Edward and Cary taken place in the family mausoleum at Tittleshall (Norfolk) than the house in St James's Square was given up, its contents sold and the Tittenhanger lease disposed of. It seems unlikely that the children visited Holkham again for some years, for that house was also emptied. A sale of goods was held there early in September 1707 barely a month after Cary Coke died. On 3rd September Mrs Windham of Felbrigg wrote to her son John: 'Mr Cooks Goods at Holcom are to be sold and I am going thither for a penniworths … know not if you want any'. [15] The sale of house contents on the death of their owners was common practice, even among families of the elite, although in this case every 'penniworth' was needed to pay off the debts left by Edward Coke. Cary Coke née Newton was said to be worth £40,000 on her marriage which, together with Edward's not inconsiderable income, should have made them very comfortable. But an extravagant lifestyle, mortgages, the debt owed by Robert Coke at the time of his election and possibly some questionable dealings, soon ate it up. As early as 1700 they seem to have been in difficulties and by the time of Edward Coke's death the amount owed was £22,000. Only the very rare or valuable items mentioned in his will were destined to continue in the family as heirlooms. Even if there had been no necessity to sell up, most objects inherited from previous generations tended to have no more than a curiosity value for the young. Fashion played a paramount role. Jewels were kept in the family, but only to be reset; silver retained only to have it melted down and remade in the latest style. [16] Seventeenth century furniture and furnishings were rapidly falling out of date by 1707, as were many ornaments and paintings. Portraits were thought fit for displaying only in country houses. In town 'landskips' and still lifes were preferred. 'Old and inconvenient' was a much used descriptive phrase at this time.

After selling the household goods at Holkham, the more valuable items were brought to London to be auctioned there. These included the collection of family paintings, which gives some indication of the guardians' determination to raise every penny they could, however unfashionable such paintings might have been. Fortunately one of them, Sir John Newton, spent £50 of his own money buying '48 family pictures great and small as came from Holkham'.

The family lawyer Peniston Lamb was engaged to pay off the outstanding household bills in London. His first act was to hire a coach and carry the family strong box and the money it contained from the house in St James's Square to Sir Richard Hoare's the goldsmith in Fleet Street for safe keeping. A week later Lamb purchased a bag into which he put all the outstanding tradesmen's bills and the following day with Humphrey Smith, the steward from Holkham, and an unnamed servant 'examined' them. Over the next three and a half days Lamb and Smith set forth in a coach each morning taking with them the unnamed servant who showed them the houses of the various tradesmen to whom money was owed. This was a necessary exercise for in 1707 there were few street names in situ and no street numbers. Shops and warehouses were described as being for example 'At the sign of the Three Chairs and Walnut Tree the east side of St Pauls Churchyard near ye school'.

Over the course of the three days Lamb, Smith and the servant dined at inns, spending 3s. 6d. on the meal, rather more than the cost of 'an ordinary', a set meal with no menu, which was a shilling. Four days later, after all the tradesmen had been paid, a publication called The Postman carried an advertisement, 'For Sale the coach and horses belonging to the late Edward Coke Esquire'. In October the house itself was put up to let. Each advertisement cost three shillings. On 1st December 1707, another Sale by Auction was held of 'The Plate of the Hon Mrs Coke deceased'. This had a printed catalogue three pages long: everything from dishes to coffee pots, candlesticks, an egg stand, a travelling cup with spoon and fork and salt box, to more personal items such as powder boxes, patch boxes and pincushions.

As the houses were cleared and the furniture, plate and pictures sold, so too the servants were given their final wages. The expectation that they might be retained for the sake of the children evaporated. In some cases their treatment appears quite harsh, but the need to economise was uppermost in the guardians' minds and they did not intend to pay for an entire household when not strictly needed. Old Richard Pulleyn the butler was given an annuity of £10 as he was almost blind and would be unable to find another situation. The house porter, another Richard, was also given an annuity of £10. Offered a post on the Holkham estate as a woodward (a sort of gamekeeper) this employment would add a further four pounds a year to his salary if he accepted. Nurse Smith was to receive an annuity of £10 but only as long as Thomas Coke remained a minor. As the guardians recorded: 'it was the Custom of the Family to make allowances to their nurses and that the late Mr Coke on his death bed had recommended her as having been Nurse to three of his children'. The provision for the daughter of Mrs Page, the nurse who had died, was to be continued; this girl named Sarah had already begun an apprenticeship as a seamstress paid for by Cary Coke. Jane Chaplin was kept on; her exact status is unknown, she may have been a governess. At any rate it fell to her to continue caring for the two little girls, Anne and Cary, keeping them in the mourning clothes they had put on for their father until 'they grew too tall for them'. Following his help with paying the London bills, Humphrey Smith the Holkham agent was to return to Norfolk to care for the house and estate there. The guardians decreed that he should live at Hill Hall 'in the offices – and to have the use of no part of the house but the Kitchen, pantry and rooms above'. Since the house was more or less unfurnished this would be no hardship. Just twice a year on the Audit Days the house was opened up to welcome visitors; these were the Norfolk tenants bidden to Holkham to pay their rents, exchange news and views and eat and drink at their landlord's cost. They were entertained in the pantry, the great hall and steward's room, a tradition which continued until 1757, after which the purpose-built Audit Room came into its own.

In London the remainder of the servants had their wages paid and were dismissed, and it is to be hoped given some help in finding employment in the wider family. The most dependable way of finding a new situation was by word of mouth and this applied as much to the employers as to the servants. Networking was the accepted method and London was the best place for it. The death of a master or mistress could be a precarious time for those servants who had money invested with the family as several would have done. The competition to secure a good position within a household of the elite was often fierce and since the number of servants seeking positions was generally greater than the vacancies, an extra incentive was offered when possible. On being taken into a household many servants offered their savings as proof of their serious intent. In an age before banks it was an opportunity for those servants who had savings to invest them and at the same time make themselves attractive to prospective employers. Lord Ashburnham looking for a footman in 1695 advertised for one who could dress a peruke well, arrange for his laundry to be done 'out of the house and ... give £200 for his honesty'. [17] Most male servants from footmen upwards, even when on trial, were expected to give a 'good security'. This was then 'invested' with their master for their master's use. In theory interest was paid each year to the servant and the original investment returned to the servant when he left, though there was always the risk that this money might no longer be available if their master died intestate or without funds.

1707-1712

With the servants dispersed and the house at Holkham standing largely empty for the next eleven years until Thomas Coke came of age, there was, strictly speaking, no 'household'. From the guardians' viewpoint this was a considerable and desirable economy, but for the five children, two girls and three boys, who had lost both their parents in the same year and their home, the price paid was heavy. Taken in by their kindly grandfather Sir John Newton, his equally agreeable second wife and their children known to the young Cokes as Uncle Mike and Aunt Sue, the young orphans would have had new homes in London and the country. Sir John had a Lincolnshire house at Culverthorpe, of which Thomas Coke was to be very fond, and another near Bristol. In town they lived in Soho Square (still fashionable in 1707) where they spent most of the year, with visits to a fourth house in Richmond.

However Thomas, the ten-year-old heir, was to sent to board at a school in Isleworth, an establishment run by a Mr Ellis and his sister. A fore-runner of a prep school, Mr Ellis's was just the sort of educational establishment to which delicate sons and heirs were sent in preference to the rough and tumble of the two great schools of the period, Westminster, if you were from a Whig family, or Eton if Tory. Small schools were preferred by many families. The widowed Mrs Sacheverell, sister to Sir John Newton and Thomas's great aunt, had made such a choice a few years previously. She preferred to send her sons to a small school where she understood that the master: ' ... studies the temper of his boys and has made many good scholars, and his wife so good a manager of children'. [18]

Whether the school at Isleworth had already been chosen by Thomas's parents or whether it was a decision taken by the guardians is not known. At all events it was thought advantageous for him to be in a suitably homely atmosphere where a close eye would be kept on him in view of his supposed propensity to illness. The guardians' accounts for 23rd August 1707 state 'Agreed to send Mr Coke to Isleworth School under the care of Mr Ellis'. Previously Thomas had been taught by a tutor at home, a man of the cloth the Rev'd Mr Brooks, who was now promised the first living that should fall vacant in the gift of the estate.

For the duration of his years at school Thomas's expenses were administered by Matthew Longstreth who had once been in the service of his grandmother as a footman. He was judged to be suitable as by 1707 he was a married man with children. Despite this qualification the choice of Longstreth had not been unanimous. At one of the guardians' monthly meetings John Coke made it clear that he considered Longstreth to be over officious and far from softened by fatherhood. Since John Coke was unmarried and might have been inclined to be stricter than the others, being still young himself, this shows Longstreth in an even more unfavourable light. [19] However, Longstreth was duly appointed 'to wait on' Thomas. For this he was paid £20 a year with a further £20 for board and lodging in London. Longstreth's orders were to ride out to Isleworth at least once a week and to keep Thomas's accounts. This actually meant listening to Thomas's requests and granting them or not. His account book opens in September 1707 and the first entry is for school expenses: 'four servants £1'. This has been interpreted by C.W. James, author of a Coke family history, as four servants accompanying the boy to school and remaining there. It is more likely to have been money paid out in tips, or vails as they were known, that is £1 divided between four of the school's servants. Longstreth recorded a payment of seven shillings and six pence to 'the Maid that looks after my Master's room at Mr Ellis', which suggests Thomas had a room of his own, but not his own maid. This is further confirmed by there being frequent entries in the accounts for vails (tips) to servants but none for servants wages.

The £30 a year school fee included board, lodging and schooling, plus washing (linen, that is, not the boy). A further £2 a year was paid to a French master, £4 to a dancing master and £6 to a fencing master. A deposit was required for the latter two of £1 and thirty shillings known as Entrance money. All bills and accounts were examined and then paid by the guardians by 'drawing upon Mr Gibson's account', the family cashier and auditor.

The employment of a non-resident upper servant, in this case Longstreth, to oversee the welfare of his charge who was attending a school at some distance, was customary. A fellow pupil at Mr Ellis's school was Charles Mordant, the future sixth baronet and landlord of an estate in Norfolk, whose father had arranged for his London steward to fulfil this role. Collins writing to Mordaunt père, shows that he kept a watchful eye on Charles in the same way as Longstreth did on Thomas Coke. Like Longstreth, Collins visited the school regularly and at the start of a new term in 1710, reported that young Mordaunt 'hath the same Bedfellow as he used to have and lyes in the same Roome ...' but was in need of more shirts and some cravats. There may even have been a degree of co-operation between these men, suggested by Longstreth's entry for May 1708 when he gave five shillings to Sir John Mordaunt's servant. [20]

Inevitably Longstreth's accounts tell us more about the living conditions at the school than about the boy's studies. We learn for example that a carpenter was paid for making a partition in one of the cellars, that a caldron of coals was purchased and kept there with the kindling wood 'Chips to kingle his fire' [sic] and that a basket was bought for carrying the coals and wood to his room.

During his time at the school Thomas periodically went 'across the water' (the Thames) to visit his great-grandfather the Duke of Leeds at his house in Wimbledon and his Newton relations at Richmond.

At the end of his first term, the Christmas holidays were spent with Mr Casey in Wood Street, Westminster, where his younger brothers were now lodging. [21] Soon after Thomas started at the Isleworth school the guardians decided that, after all, Edward and Robert Coke, aged just three and four years old, should leave the Newtons and lodge instead with Mr Casey and his wife. The two little girls would remain with their grandparents. Casey was a relation of the children's Nurse Smith, probably a first cousin, [22] and an agreement was drawn up between him and the guardians 'that Mr Casey does agree for sixty pound to board the two little Master Cokes and their Nurse [Nurse Smith] and that they shall have the Back Parlour wherein they now lodge and that Mr Casey is to find coals for a fire there and Candles, and wash the two young Masters [laundry again]. Note Mr Casey is to teach the two young Gentlemen their Books into this bargin and that they are to dine above stairs with the other boarders, and it is desired by Sir John Newton, they are in Summertime to have a room to lodge in above stairs'. [23]

This was not quite as grim as it sounds. The little boys had a kind nurse in Sarah Smith whom they had known since birth and for whom they retained a lifelong affection. [24] It is to be hoped that the Back Parlour opened onto a garden. Whether Nurse Smith was related to Humphrey Smith, the steward at Holkham, as seems probable, it has not been possible to discover.

The arrangement was not unusual, especially in large families where the young children were known as The Nursery and frequently lodged for long periods apart from the parents, though within visiting distance. While the parents stayed in central London, their children's lodgings were generally chosen for their healthy situation, such as Chelsea or Hampstead. [25] In the holidays, when Thomas joined them, he was treated like a lodger and charged rent: £3. 18s. in 1708 and £4. 16s. in 1709, with an additional 2s. for a lantern that he broke. While lodging with Casey the Coke children enjoyed a reasonable amount of entertainment in the holidays. That first Christmas Thomas went 'to the Play' several times, (the theatre soon became a passion of his), and together with his brothers saw the 'strange Birds and Beasts' at the Tower of London. The following Christmas there was an outing to view the 'Drummedare' (dromedary?) and when their sisters visited Wood Street Thomas paid out 2s. for oysters and cheesecake 'to treat them'.

In June 1708 Thomas celebrated his eleventh birthday at school in Isleworth with a dinner costing £1, 'mousick' 10s. 6d. and wine 7s. 6d. The following year, when he was twelve, he was taken to see the Lord Mayor's Show. By now his appearance was that of a young adult: he wore buckles on his shoes, muslin ruffles on his shirt front and cuffs, black worsted stockings, slippers

or pumps on his feet and in the evening a night gown that cost £1. 15s.
A night gown was evening not bed wear, though it may be seen as a fore-
runner of the dressing gown. Worn instead of a coat it suggested a degree
of informality and could be made of silk or on colder evenings, wool. [26]
As a young boy his hair had been cut five times during the first year at school,
but by the time he was twelve his head was shaved by a barber in preparation for wearing a wig and soon, to the concern of his guardian Sir Charles
Bertie, he 'is gott into a Perriwig like a Young Beau'. Fortunately for him
another of the guardians, Sir Edward Coke, disagreed with Bertie: 'There is
no harm in a perwig or ruffles or his new Clothes, his estates set him above
the consideration of these things'. [27] Thomas bought packs of playing cards
at 4d. a pack, played at shuttlecock and battledore, took dancing and fencing
lessons, acquired the rudiments of the French language in preparation for life
at court, bet at bowls at Islington Green and in April 1710 probably fell in
love, or at any rate was smitten by the beauty of an actress as he went to the
theatre five nights on the trot. That year in London he went to the theatre
a total of twenty-one times during the Christmas holidays.

Longstreth's accounts show Thomas to be a spirited boy, but like many
young men he gave cause for concern when it came to school work. 'Mr
Coke is not a studious boy' his headmaster Mr Ellis reported and worse still
he was absent for long periods due to ill health. These were heartily regretted by Mr Ellis, not merely from his concern for his pupil's welfare, but the
absences he believed created 'in young Gentlemen an aversion to school'. [28]
Schools, even the smaller more caring variety such as Mr Ellis's, strove to
enforce rigorous attendance and to instil the virtues so highly valued in the
eighteenth-century.

Dr Radcliffe, a most highly esteemed doctor after whom a number of
landmark buildings in Oxford were named, notably the Radcliffe Camera,
Infirmary and Observatory, was currently physician to the Queen. He was
also called upon to attend Thomas in his illnesses and on each visit Radcliffe's
servant was given 1s. in vails. There is some evidence for believing Isleworth
was not a healthy location. Malaria is known to have survived in the more
marshy parts of south-east England well into the nineteenth century but for
some reason schools often chose to set up in these areas. Hackney marshes
was another.

In early 1711, when he was thirteen, Thomas wrote to his cousin and
guardian, Sir Edward Coke of Longford, informing him that after a long

bout of illness he had taken a purge and was greatly improved in health. On receiving this news Sir Edward was concerned and suggested that the boy could benefit from the purer air of Derbyshire. He put the case to his fellow guardians who agreed. Accordingly Mr Ellis the headmaster was informed and Thomas's desk, cupboard and books were 'rapped with Cords' and sent by water (barge) down stream to Wood Wharf, the nearest quay to Wood Street where Mr Casey took them in. Among the final bills that Longstreth paid at Isleworth was one for the care of Thomas's fighting cocks. Thomas's health must have taken an almost instant turn for the better after leaving Isleworth, for once away from the class room he went to the theatre and the opera several times before setting off for Derbyshire.

Thomas was to travel north in the company of his guardian, John Coke, and Humphrey Smith, the Norfolk steward. Like many of the Coke household, Smith was Derbyshire born and bred. They were accompanied by a groom, William Holland, also from Derbyshire. Matthew Longstreth remained in London; 'having a Wife and Children makes it inconvenient for him to attend Mr Coke' the guardians recorded, and agreed to pension him off at £20 a year. His duties brought prematurely to an end, Longstreth's book of accounts was passed to Humphrey Smith who recorded the details and expenses of the journey to Derbyshire and continued to act as accountant for the following month until the arrival of Dr David Wilkins, a tutor. [29]

The journey was slow, partly due to bad weather and partly to the lumbering coach in which they travelled. It would not have been suitable for a person of Thomas Coke's status to travel on horseback, except for short periods, though it would have been quicker and easier. Instead a coach, coachman and postillion were hired at a cost of £14.

It was the coachman's task to drive and control the horses and the postillion's to know the way and act as a look-out. The postillion, riding one of the lead horses, was in pole position to spot vehicles approaching from the opposite direction. This was especially important when the roads were narrow for there were strict rules of etiquette when passing. He should also be alert to the dangers of pot holes, deep ruts, overhanging branches and any number of other hazards. Hired coaches were drawn by post-horses which were changed for fresh ones at post stages, on average every twenty-five miles. A post boy came with each set of horses; he was needed to return the horses when the next changeover was reached. Often he was an asset and helped the postillion by doubling as a guide. In this way a coach could travel night and day if needed, which negated the need and expense of the passengers staying at an inn. However the Coke party was affluent enough to afford overnight accommodation. They also had with them four saddle horses. This was a welcome alternative to constant travelling inside the coach, for coach travel was well known to make people feel seasick. The party would change to saddle horses when the ruts in the road prevented the heavily laden coach getting through, or when a steep hill presented itself.

The sight of a coach on a country road in 1711, even a hired one, was rare. It indicated a wealthy traveller and this in turn attracted small clusters of people. The number of those waving, cheering or straightforwardly asking for alms as the coach passed was recorded by Humphrey Smith in the accounts. Servants in the various inns where they stopped were likewise eager for vails. It should be noted that country inns on main routes were often found to be superior to London inns for the simple reason that elite families travelling between town and their country estates were likely to use them. [30]

As they grew near to their destination Thomas Coke's arrival was signalled in the villages by the ringing of church bells. This practice occurred whenever a landowner approached his estate. The ringing of bells served not only to alert the tenantry it also meant the traveller could not sneak by unnoticed. Smith's accounts list payments both to the bell-ringers and to the poor of the various villages they passed through. The master arrives, the master gives alms. Doubtless on arrival at Longford Sir Edward Coke's servants came out to greet young Master Coke and were also rewarded with vails.

It was during Thomas's stay at Longford (which was to last over a year) that some of the servants who were to form the household at Holkham first appear. Sir Edward Coke's household was not large. He was a bachelor and lived in modest gentry style, with no more than ten servants. Unlike Thomas's parents Sir Edward had no male cook but a cook maid, according to the Christmas boxes Thomas handed out in December 1711. There were four male servants plus a groom, one resident housemaid, a dairy maid and a washerwoman. Abraham Thomas, who headed Sir Edward's list of servants, was to transfer to Thomas's household in 1719 as valet de chambre and, with one short gap, would remain in his service until his death in 1744.

Having safely delivered his young master to the care of Sir Edward, Humphrey Smith remained at Longford for a month before returning to Holkham after a farewell party: 'paid for Ale at the New Inn at parting with Mr Smith'. [31]

A week or two later, in a letter to his grandfather Newton dated 10th June 1711, Thomas makes a reference to 'my Valet'. [32] The date, a week before his fourteenth birthday, poses the question at what age were young members of the elite allocated their own servants, grown men and women to whom they could give orders? Of course children such as Thomas were usually reared by a wet nurse until they were old enough to be weaned, which could take place at any age from a year to three years old and then cared for by nurses and nurse maids. But later came a subtle shift between servants who looked after the children and were in a position of some authority, to servants who were primarily employed to attend to their young masters. In some elite households children of ten or even younger were allocated their own footmen. [33] For the daughters of the family their lady's maids were often well known to them having graduated from nursery maid, but in the case of footmen and valets, these men were generally brought in from outside. The dichotomy between a young person growing up, subject to the confines of the school room and tutors, to being presented with the knowledge that another human being's primary duty in life was to serve him and wait on his needs and orders is a difficult one to digest in the twenty-first century. There is a vast difference between being brought up to respect servants as workers in your house, keeping your bedroom relatively tidy and being on time for meals, and having it within your power to make a person happy or miserable.

Thomas had yet to have a footman of his own, but it was a mark of his status that he was allocated a valet. Unlike a footman, who was essentially a carrier of messages and a liveried servant, a valet wore no livery but dressed as finely as his master. His duty was to look after his master's person from the most intimate services such as shaving him, both head and beard, dressing his wigs, seeing that all his clothes were clean and in good repair, to accompanying him when he went out, often in the role of quasi companion. A valet would make sure his young master was always dressed in a manner suitable to his station in life. Footmen, by contrast, when not engaged in housework, waiting at table or delivering messages, did not enjoy the same degree of personal contact. In Thomas's case as someone soon to embark on the Grand Tour, as the guardians had already suggested that Thomas might, a valet could be seen as preferable to a footman.

The valet Thomas referred to in his letter was Edward Jarrett, whose wages are recorded as commencing 28th May 1711 at £20 per annum. This was a handsome wage and remained consistent throughout Thomas's lifetime, his valets were always paid £20 a year. For the next eleven months, while Thomas continued at Longford, Jarrett travelled with him on the numerous outings they took, together with the tutor Dr Wilkins and a groom.

The third servant who appeared at this time was the groom William Holland. He had been employed by Thomas's father at Holkham, although born in Derbyshire at Thurvaston in 1690 and baptised at Longford. When at school in Isleworth Thomas kept a horse which may have been cared for by William Holland although there is no documentary evidence to substantiate this. However it seems probable that he did, as he accompanied Thomas on the journey from London to Longford.

Meanwhile Sir Edward Coke soon found his young cousin a handful and quickly realised that his quiet household was not altogether suited to the presence of an exuberant youth. Derbyshire air did indeed agree with the boy. Sir Edward had remarked how thin Thomas had been on arrival, but that he soon began to fill out and grow; with no further mention of illness. The one blot at Longford, as far as Thomas was concerned, was his tutor, the highly recommended Dr Wilkins. The guardians had gone to great lengths to choose him: 'the character given of him is very great ... the sooner [Thomas] has a Governor the better, now he is from schole,' Sir Edward wrote, probably counting the days until one would be sent. Wilkins had been interviewed in London by Sir John Newton and brought with him a glowing reference from Edward Bedingfeld who had recently returned from eight years abroad, some of it in the company of Wilkins. 'You can't pay too dear for him' enthused Bedingfeld from Bath in a long letter to Sir John 'I do not know of any body so greatly qualified ... gentilely behaved and of good Morals with as sweet temper so he comes represented by me a very sincere and intelligent Person ... ' [34] That among several other recommendations clinched it, but from the start Thomas and Wilkins did not get on, and Thomas spent as much time absenting himself as he could manage.

Whenever possible he escaped three miles down the road to Hilton where Mr Vernon lived. Vernon was a great hunting man and a breeder of the increasingly fashionable fox hound. At Hilton Thomas found a pastime that absorbed him. Cock fighting was another attraction, also bowling and shooting, though the latter frightened Mrs Chaney (possibly Sir Edward's housekeeper) so much that he was told not to shoot within a mile of the house. Even then he complained there was nothing better to aim at than sparrows. In July 1711 he had to pay 2s. 6d. out of his own pocket for breaking a window pane in the parish almshouse. [35]

Not surprisingly Sir Edward yielded some months later when the fourteen year old Thomas, perhaps conscious that his continuing presence was not altogether welcome, pleaded to see something of his own country before embarking on the next stage of his education. For once he found support in Dr Wilkins. It was agreed that two or three short tours would be beneficial, and so a few weeks later, accompanied by Wilkins, the valet Edward Jarrett and groom William Holland, the party set out for Chatsworth. This spectacular house, set in extensive formal gardens, was in sharp contrast to the surrounding wild countryside of 'ye Peak' and had recently been re-built by the first Duke of Devonshire. After admiring this place, they visited Thomas's great-grandmother Newton at Renishaw, returning by Bolsover Castle Hardwick Hall and the lead mines at Wirksworth. On a second expedition in the autumn they went further afield, first to Cambridge, with a possible view that Thomas might attend the university, and then to Kimbolton Castle, where work was in progress rebuilding the castle to designs by Sir John Vanburgh, following a collapse some years previously. The following day they travelled to Boughton, the Duke of Montagu's house in Northamptonshire, which Thomas was to revisit many times in future years and finally to Burley on the Hill, another recently completed county seat. Its builder was Daniel Finch, Earl of Nottingham whose wife was first cousin to Thomas's future wife. The sight of these great houses, many of which were 'new' may have set Thomas thinking of what, in time, he might do at Holkham.

Kedleston, just a few miles from Longford, was also visited. Here Wilkins paid vails to the cook, butler and groom. It was of course the old house, not the present one which owes much to the designs later used at Holkham. The payment of vails recorded by Wilkins are a guide to Thomas's movements and activities at this time. For example he was bought a new suit of clothes costing £5. 2s. 6d. and a few days later attended a summer ball in Derby in company with young Mr Budworth, the son of Longford's vicar. Derby in the early eighteenth century was a town with many large houses, more gentry than trade as Daniel Defoe was to write, but the ball appears to have been a public one, in a series of Assemblies, for Thomas paid a £4 entrance fee for himself and young Mr Budworth. [36] They were well prepared for the evening's entertainment and had for some time been taking weekly dancing lessons. The inevitable bell-ringers at Derby were given 10s. on their arrival in the city and their horses were stabled at the inns, a major expense of £1. 3s. 8d. The young men were provided with a pair of new gloves each 2s. 6d. and paid

11s. 6d. for wine at the ball and supper at the tavern afterwards. They spent 3s. on 'Sweetmeats for ye Ladies' (who were they?) Thomas lost £1. 1s. 6d. at cards and paid vails to the porter of 1s. Mr Godwin's servant (unknown) got 10s. and the same amount was given to the Dancing Master at the Ball. Vails paid to the musicians £1. 1s. 6d. and 2s. 6d. to the Dancing Master's maid. Perhaps she found them partners. Altogether going to the Derby Ball cost £10. 17s. 1d., an enormous sum.

The references to Thomas's character in the small amount of correspondence that has survived from the early 1700s show him to have had 'a passionate and violent nature' while continuing to be 'cool towards his studies'. These observations were made by Sir Edward Coke [37] while the tutor Dr Wilkins managed to criticise Thomas and at the same time flatter him. Wilkins had a way with words that is reminiscent of Mr Collins. [38] The guardians' attitude towards Thomas was to temper affection with discipline. Their aim was to make him an accomplished gentleman but at the same time there is a certain undercurrent of awe in their correspondence as if they were aware of how he might consider *them* when he reached adulthood. Thomas required restraint and direction, but the luxuries of life were not to be denied him. From an early age young men of his generation were highly aware of their future inheritance. It soon became apparent that, while Thomas benefited from the Derbyshire air, as his guardians had hoped, growing tall and strong, he needed more than Dr Wilkins and Longford could offer. What were they to do with him next? While this was being decided Humphrey Smith the Holkham steward wrote of the dilemma for Thomas: University or the Grand Tour? Smith's anxieties were quoted in a letter from Sir Edward Coke to Sir John Newton, an insight into the servant-master relationship, for not only did Smith feel free to express his views, but they were acknowledged, quoted and considered by all the guardians. [39] Before long the idea of entering Thomas at Cambridge was rejected as being unlikely to engage the young man, and instead a Grand Tour was proposed. But before this could begin Thomas made a journey to Holkham, as a reminder, if one were needed, of where his future lay. He travelled to Norfolk in April 1712 where he entertained his tenants at Wells and the people of Wells came to Holkham 'with Drums and fire Arms to salute Mr Coke'. He visited Tittleshall where his ancestors, and parents, were buried, his deer park at North Elmham where he gave a dinner, Beck Hall at Billingford where his grandmother Lady Anne Walpole received him, and lastly he dined at Hunstanton with his 'cosen' Sir Nicholas L'Estrange.

A slight cloud overshadowed this visit. While at his grandmother's the news arrived that her father, the old Duke of Leeds and titular head of the family, had died. Thomas wrote to Sir John Newton that, after some violent tears, Lady Anne was bearing up well and requested him to send a suit of mourning for himself and one his for valet Jarrett. Then, with these duty visits completed and with his last memories of England those of Norfolk, his party left for abroad, travelling directly to Gravesend and thence to Dover. [40]

NOTES

1. Gloucester Record Office D1844 C/11 – Thomas Headon to Lady Newton.

2. Lincolnshire Record Office, Monson 7/14 folio 83.

3. Paying to reserve seats in churches was common practice in the 18th and 19th century even in the country: the servants would have sat, or stood, towards the back.

4. J.Smith, *English Houses 1200-1800, The Hertfordshire Evidence* London 1992 p.68.

5. HA, F/G2 (2) folio 307. It is Sir John Newton who refers to Wright as 'cosen'. Among the entries in his general accounts for London and Tittenhanger HA F/EC 1 Wright includes several payments to his own brother, sister and mother. His brother was frequently paid 'for ye doctor' or for coach hire, and on one occasion *his* servant was paid for bleeding the Coke's servants. This suggests the brother may have been an apothecary; in 1700 he was paid 'in full' £115 and, in 1701, £124. Such large sums would not be unusual; apothecaries frequently earned more than doctors. Wright's sister and mother also received regular payments, sometimes for money they had 'laid out' or lent to Cary Coke, usually small amounts such as five shillings for 'Card Money', but once, in March 1701, £100.

6. In Thomas Coke's time this would also include the librarian.

7. HA. Richard Idle watched the London house, he was also 'one of my lady's chairmen'.

8. C.W.James *Chief Justice Coke his Family and Descendants at Holkham* London 1929, p.148.

9. HA, F/G2 (4) no. 65 Lady Newton to Cary Coke.

10. Lincolnshire Record Office, Monson 7/13 folio 13.

11. NRO – Lee Warner Archive, Box 10, 918x2, letter 9. In 1713 the Duc du Berry died leaving no children but a pregnant Duchess, all hopes were pinned on the child being a boy, but she gave birth to a daughter who lived only a few hours, 'a great loss to the Servants of the Dukes family who bought their places very dear, when in hopes it had proved a Son to have had their Pensions still continued but are now in a fair way of starving'.

12. Raynham Archives G1/12 and J.H. Plumb *Sir Robert Walpole, the making of a Statesman* London 1956, pp. 124-125. Dorothy Walpole [1687-1726] had scandalised society in London by associating with Lord Wharton, a notorious rake. A girl of spirit and temper she had also quarrelled with her sister-in-law, Sir Robert's wife, and was initially sent to stay with the Townshends. Lord Townshend the 2nd Viscount subsequently visited Dorothy when he was in Norfolk, reputedly teaching her to play the spinet. In 1713 after the death of his first wife, they were married.

13. TNA Prob 11/676, will of John Coke of Baggrave, Leics. John Coke was the younger brother of Thomas Coke of Melbourne – they were the sons of John Coke of Trusley 1653-1692. John Coke, the guardian, 1678-1736 d.s.p. and in his will left his large diamond ring to Lady Clifford wife of 'our' Thomas Coke showing a close friendship, but to date no relationship can be proved.

14. HA F/G2 (2) f.382.

15. NRO WKC 7/21/7.

16. This was to happen at Holkham some years later when a whole collection of Paul de Lamerie's plain but classic designs were remodelled to suit the more baroque taste of the age.

17. East Sussex Record Office Ashburnham MSS 4445,folio 137.

18. Lincolnshire Record Office, Monson 7/14 f.61.

19. HA F/G2 (4) f. 69. Letter of John Coke to Sir John Newton 1709.

20. Elizabeth Hamilton *The Mordaunts* London 1965 p.77 and passim to the end of chapter, and HA F/TC 2.

21. Wood Street, now Great Peter Street, ran north from Millbank up to the crossing with Tufton Street from whereon it became Peter Street.

22. TNA Prob 11/589. Mr Casey's will in which he leaves ten pounds to his uncle John Smith 'and to Mrs Sarah Smith my Silver Tankard and Silver Cup'. He left the bulk of his estate £450 to buy land in either Leicester or Derby, his executors to chose, the profits and rents of which were to pay for bread for the poor of the parish of Ashby de la Zouche, to be given to them on the first Sunday of each month. This suggests he was from the parish, and likely to have been related as well to Humphrey Smith who was a Derbyshire man.

23. HA F/TC 1 the Guardians Book and F/TC 3 the Guardians Accounts.

24. Suffolk Record Office, Bury St Edmunds branch, E 18/452/55 copy of Edward Coke's will of 1732, Thomas's brother.

25. Raynham Archives, G1/13 and G1/18.

26. Lesley Ellis Miller *An Enigmatic Bourgeois: Jean Revel Dons a Nightgown for his Portrait* , *Costume*, the Journal of the Costume Society no. 44 2010 pp. 46-55.

27. Wigs were not worn over a full head of hair but heads were shaved and a silk cap worn under the wig to prevent itching – correspondence between Sir Edward Coke, Mr Bertie and Sir John Newton, quoted by James p.168.

28. HA F/G2 (2) f. 409.

29. HA F/TC 1 Guardians Accounts and F/TC 2 Longstreth's accounts.

30. *The Diary of Sylas Neville 1767-1788* edited by Basil Cozens-Hardy London

1950 p.115.

31. HA F/TC 2.

32. HA F/G2 (2) f.424.

33. Thomas's son Edward got his first footman in 1724 when he was six.

34. Gloucester Record Office D 1844 C/11.The eight years Bedingfeld spent abroad is accounted for by his being a Catholic and educated in Belgium.

35. HA F/G2 (2) f. 425. and F/TC 2.

36. Daniel Defoe *A Tour through the Whole Island of Great Britain 1724-26* Penguin Classics 1971 pp. 458-459.

37. HA F/G2 (2) f.442.

38. HA F/G2 (2) f.422.

39. HA F/G2 (4) f.71.

40. HA F/G2 (2) f.450.

CHAPTER 2

The Grand Tour 1712-1718

In the early 1700s the Grand Tour had not yet evolved into the pleasure-seeking romp it was later to become, rather its purpose was to continue the education of those young noblemen who aspired to hold their own in the society of their peers and at court. French and Italian culture was highly esteemed and time spent at their Academies, which taught riding, dancing, singing and deportment and had no equivalents in England, was the choice of many. [1] A tour round France and Italy served as an educational rite of passage, one enjoyed by young men rather than their sisters. In addition to acquiring desirable accomplishments it offered these privileged youths an opportunity to see for themselves some of the antiquities they had studied at school. They were there purely for experience since these travels had no connection with commerce or diplomacy as would have been the case in earlier times.

The main requirement for travelling abroad, apart from having sufficient funds, had always been peace on the continent. Hostilities curbed some travels; nevertheless the Grand Tour with its opportunities to acquire knowledge by so many diverse means grew in popularity throughout the seventeenth century. Among the earliest participants from Norfolk were the two young sons of Sir Roger Townshend who, at the age of 18 and 16 respectively, set out for Rome in 1646. The elder one, also Roger, died at Geneva, but his brother Horatio returned safely to England after a tour of nearly three years. He was later to become the first Viscount. There are few surviving records of others, apart from those sent exclusively for schooling, such as the Bedingfelds of Oxburgh (as Catholics they were educated in the low countries) until those of Ashe Windham of Felbrigg who spent two years at Cambridge before embarking on his Grand Tour in 1693. Charles 2nd Viscount Townshend was also twenty years old when he and his tutor went to Italy via Holland in 1694. [2]

By 1700 a number of guides had been written. Guides with titles such as *Italy in its Original Glory, Ruin and Revival.* This, by Edmund Warcupp, was published in 1660. Others produced itineraries and directions suggesting where to go and what to see. Works of art topped the list, Roman antiquities, but visits to the studios of working artists were also recommended. The old cliché of travel broadening the mind was probably first made popular at this time, and it was true. The point was to expand knowledge, experience other cultures and report home to those who would never cross the channel. Were the French courteous, the Spanish lordly (actually hardly anyone went to Spain, the roads were notoriously difficult and the inns wretched), the Italians amorous and the Germans clownish as Jean Gailhard suggested in 1678? It was a chance to see for themselves. No one went to Greece either at this period, as it was still under Turkish rule, and even in Italy few ventured further south than Naples, though Thomas Coke would do so. The opportunity to buy works of art was plentiful and helped by them being surprisingly reasonable. It was the travelling which cost. Souvenirs in the form of coins, medals and curios were eminently portable. Books were packed into cases requiring separate transportation and customs clearance. Pictures and statues, purchased by the crateful, were sent to England in ships from Leghorn (Livorno), solid evidence as to taste the young tourist had acquired.

Tours varied in length from a year to three or more. There was with no fixed age at which the young gentlemen should embark on this adventure, some were in their twenties but most a good deal younger. Italy was the goal for the majority, necessarily passing through France en route (unless going by sea) and peeping into Switzerland, a refreshingly protestant country.

Thomas Coke was fifteen when he set out to travel 'Beyond the Seas'. His tour began in August 1712 and ended in May 1718, a month before he came of age. It lasted for a period of five years and nine months; almost twice as long as average. Such a protracted tour had not been planned, but when an extension was proposed it suited his guardians to agree. Several factors contributed to this, not least that keeping Thomas abroad was an excellent way of constraining a potentially extravagant young man. It allowed them more time to build up his resources in England, eliminating the expense of maintaining a household with its complement of servants, his absence they reckoned would make a saving of approximately £2,200 a year. A further factor was the changing times in England. When Thomas set out Queen Anne, the last Stuart monarch, was on the throne. Two years later she was dead and her successor, the untried Hanoverian King George, was, so reports had it, 'filling the English Court with German counts and barons'. On hearing this Thomas was content to stay away 'while things continue so troubled in England' as he wrote to his grandfather Sir John Newton. At that point, almost three years into his travels, his thoughts may have been straying towards returning home but his curiosity about Europe was far from sated. He was still only eighteen and more than happy to postpone his return to England in favour of more travel. [3] For those accompanying him however re-adjustments had to be made, for they had been engaged for three years only.

At the start of the tour, thankful to see the back of Dr Wilkins, Thomas was now in the care of Dr Thomas Hobart. Hobart, again carefully chosen by the guardians, was judged to be 'eminently suitable'. He had taken his degree as Doctor of Medicine at Cambridge in 1700, and by 1712 was an experienced tour governor or bear leader as they were later known. As both a scholar and medical man he was an ideal choice if the 'delicate' young Master Coke should fall ill. [4] Somewhat surprisingly he was no linguist but compensated for this by taking along Dr Ferrari, his Italian protégée, to act as co-governor and interpreter, at least when they reached Italy. Ferrari's grasp of French was shaky, and his self confidence was not helped by Thomas Coke nicknaming him Puncanello. [5]

Jarrett the valet was to go with them and keep the accounts, which would be inspected by Dr Hobart. To delineate his new financial responsibilities Jarrett headed the account book: 'An Account of the Money that I rec'd of Mr Hobart on acct of my Master Thomas Coke Esq vizt for cloaths necessaries Extraordinarys Travelling Expences and Other Paymts from August the 21, 1712'. [6] Two grooms completed the party, William Holland and John Cocks. Travel by coach and chaise, using post horses were to be the main means of transport, but as on all long journeys they also had several saddle horses. The anxious Humphrey Smith and his son Edward, travelled with them as far as Dunkirk in order to report back to the guardians that the channel crossing had been successfully negotiated.

The excitement of crossing the channel and setting foot on land 'beyond the Seas' cannot be over-estimated. The sea passage itself could be hazardous and it was. Even in August they were obliged to wait five days for a fair wind, but in a letter to his grandfather written from Dunkirk, Thomas recorded that once the ship left port the voyage was relatively smooth and how he was 'very little sea sick, for I stood on the deck all the while'. [7] This image reminds us of how thrilling the prospect was that lay before him. At that date the landmass of Europe had, at its limits, unknown countries where bears, tigers and lions roamed, wild creatures that in England were seen only at the Tower of London or in pictures. By the time the party reached Rome they would be nearer to the coast of north Africa with its pirate-infested waters than to Norfolk. [8] It is not known if any of the guardians had travelled in Europe and their views on the dangers of allowing Thomas to go have not survived. Doubtless he was on the receiving end of much good advice, some of which would have been Beware Women.

Contemporary opinions continued to regard Italy as an arcadia of landscape, climate, produce and culture, and France also worthy of serious regard, but no one had much good to say about the Swiss or the Germans. Mountains were not yet seen as romantic, more of an inconvenience. Greece continued to be dangerous. Despite its treasures it was; 'over run with robbers' as Lady Mary Wortley Montagu was told when she wished to visit the country on her voyage home from Constantinople in 1718. [9] Apart from risking the usual hazards when travelling there was also a morbid fear among the English at this date of what might befall them in a Popish country, not the least of which was of being converted. Even educated people harboured a distinct terror of dying abroad for they feared the possibility of being buried without the reassurance of an Anglican funeral. Dr Hobart was a case in point. Despite, or perhaps because of his experiences on the continent, Hobart had a horror of dying in a Catholic country: ' ... tho' my body may meet with ill usage if I dye in a popish Country' he wrote in his will, fearful of the fate of his mortal remains; quite what he had in mind can only be guessed at. [10]

For servants the way ahead was a challenge indeed. An important perk of serving in households of the elite was of course the opportunity to travel. Accompanying their master and mistress either to London or to the houses of his friends in different parts of England, gave their lives variety. To travel abroad for a prolonged visit of several years and be expected to negotiate with foreign people and foreign ways was, however, only offered to a few. If the chance did come their way the servant could see this as an opportunity for self improvement, for there were a considerable number of European domestic servants working in England, especially French ones, and French *fashion,* food, clothes and manners, were prized by English society. A servant who learnt French customs at first hand and acquired the skills of French servants, would be to find his prospects greatly enhanced. [11] The servant most likely to improve himself on this occasion was of course the valet/accountant Edward Jarrett; but he does not appear to have taken much advantage of the opportunity. Over the years of the tour his handwriting certainly did *not* improve and he seems to have been impervious to both French or Italian ways, writing everything in English whenever he could. He almost always recorded the names of the inns where they lodged in English, and his spelling of French names suggests he did not spend any time learning the language. Was there really a *White Horse Inn* at Montpellier and a *Golden Mountain* in Rome? No. However this anglicisation may have been an accepted custom for the benefit of the guardians back home. Richard Creed, who travelled with the fifth Earl of Exeter in 1699, did the same in his journal when going through Italy, but not always in France. On arriving in Boulogne his party stayed at the *Golden Deer* and the *Bull's Head* at Abbéville, but at Fontainebleau it was the *Lion d'Or*, suggesting his readership could cope with a few French names but not Italian ones. [12]

Once in France and having bade farewell to the two Smiths, father and son, the party went on to Paris where they took lodgings. Here their landlady had a maid who cleaned the rooms, but she did not provide meals. Thus daily entries appear in the accounts for bread, butter and coffee or chocolate bought in for their breakfasts. Dinner was eaten out, very often at 'the Alliance'. [13] On rare occasions, possibly when entertaining, a roasting cook was hired to cook meals in the landlady's kitchen. Nor did the landladies provide any laundry services, for weekly bills for washing were recorded by Jarrett.

In Paris the two grooms William Holland and John Cocks were bought new clothes, black suits and blue greatcoats. The black suits may have been for mourning for the Duke of Leeds, but equally the choice of black would render the wearers discreet. Dressed in black, rather than livery, they attracted less attention which would have been beneficial as they lodged separately from the main party, near to the stables. Their lodgings were paid for direct by Jarrett but they ate in places of their own choosing, paying for it out of their board wages. Board wages was money given to servants when the family were absent from home, a weekly allowance to cover the cost of their food. As lower servants the two grooms would not have expected to dine with their master in France any more than they would have done at home in England. It says something for them that they appear to have managed without too many difficulties in a foreign country at a time when the handling and exchange of money on the continent was always a challenge. The French franc, which preceded the euro by some two hundred years, was not introduced until the time of Napoleon, at the end of the eighteenth century. In 1712 French money was made up of livres and sous. When Jarrett changed £82. 19s. of English money into French livres he received 1,389 or approximately 176 to the pound. A rough guide to the cost of items bought in Paris was a pound of sugar five livres, a groom's greatcoat eighteen, and seven weeks lodgings 180.

Thomas enjoyed enormously his time in Paris which was enhanced by the presence of his half-uncle Mick. This was Michael Newton the son of Thomas's grandfather Sir John Newton by his second wife. Thomas was especially fond of Uncle Mick who was only five years his senior and an exuberant sports lover with a passion for horses matching Thomas's own. Uncle Mick does not appear in Jarrett's accounts again, but he must have spent more time with them, for two years later in May 1714 Thomas, writing from Rome, says he is 'glad to hear my uncle arrived safely in England, all his acquaintance on this side of the water very much regret the loss of his company'. [14]

On 17th November, after approximately two months in the capital, Dr Hobart moved the party on to Angers in western France. At this juncture the groom William Holland left to return to England, travelling to Calais by stage coach. This was pre-arranged and it was not a dismissal, since he was sent to Holkham. In his place a French groom known simply as Jean-Baptiste was engaged and bought a new greatcoat. The obvious advantage of engaging a French groom when in France needs no further comment.

The fun was now at an end. At Angers Thomas entered the Academy where his days were filled with French language lessons, mathematics and the basis of civil law. It was back to school. Simple accountancy was also taught, and put into practice. Every six months Dr Hobart encouraged Thomas to examine Edward Jarrett's accounts before they were sent off to the guardians in England. He was taught to play the trumpet and the flute. All in all lessons much as he had had at Isleworth. Rather more to his taste were the riding, fencing and dancing sessions.

The riding instructions took place in the Academy's indoor school and set out to teach highly skilled manoeuvres, the art of manege, that is making horses circle, leap or kneel, much like the Spanish Riding School in Vienna does today. This had been made fashionable in the seventeenth century by William Cavendish, whose Riding House survives at Bolsover Castle, a place Thomas had visited from Longford. The floor of the riding house was covered with soft sand and the horses tied to tall posts to train them to move in tighter and tighter circles. William Cavendish listed the names of his fifty-four horses which included ones from Turkey and Barbary in North Africa, the finest money could buy. [15] It is a slight surprise then to learn that Thomas

Coke owned a fine 'Barb' himself, two new horses had been purchased for him in Derbyshire £8 and 13gns respectively and another in Dunkirk but with no descriptions. A Barb was the Harley Davidson of its day.

During the weeks spent in Angers the grooms, Cocks and Jean-Baptiste, would have been kept busy caring for Thomas's horses. In addition to daily riding lessons and studying the finer points of horsemanship, Thomas often hunted. Wild boar was the quarry, and sometimes deer. There were shooting parties for which the groom John Cocks bought gunpowder and shot, 'oyle' for the guns and on one occasion paid for a 'dinner a-shuting'. There were also dogs to be cared for, both hounds and pets. At one house they visited on the journey from Paris to Angers compensation was paid for 'the dogs fouling a silk carpet'.

In addition to his duties as a valet, Jarrett had the extra challenge of language, and in his capacity of accountant, of paying the masters at the school, the landlord (a Mr Fagan) and daily entering a multitude of small expenses into the account books.

By early 1713, after a few months in Angers, the young student grew impatient to move on and see more of the continent. Lessons, he said, took up every moment of his day. He had no time for himself. Angers itself was unpleasantly low-lying and foggy, and the masters, Thomas claimed, were second rate. Soon he knew enough French to know that they spoke with a regional accent. [16] Neither Dr Hobart nor Dr Ferrari were able to judge this: '[they] always speak English to me ... not being able to pronounce French'. Finally Thomas complained of having only one companion at Angers, the son of Sir Strensham Masters who had been his school fellow at Isleworth – a nice enough fellow but limited. [17] Dr Hobart was now experiencing something of the difficulties that Dr Wilkins had encountered and found that to try and keep 'so young a man, of such, temper and fire' in a place he didn't care for was not easy. [18] A rumour that many young Englishmen and Scotch were due shortly to descend on Angers provided the excuse needed and Dr Hobart prepared a move south.

A chaise was purchased and painted, its doors decorated with Thomas's coat of arms. For travelling a chaise was preferable to a coach as it was lighter. Later a second one was bought for the servants. Hobart had already bought 'fusils' and a pair of double barrelled pistols in Paris. The fusil may have been for sport, but the pistols were for protection. He had also thought fit to buy a demycircle [sic], a pedometer and a rule. As Lady Mary Wortley Montagu was to write in 1751 criticising the general concept of a Grand Tour, governors, even the most learned, were really only interested in 'Situations and Distances'. [19] Certainly governors were under an obligation to justify their every decision to the family at home. When posting off Jarrett's account books Hobart was at pains to inform the guardians of how much more expensive France had become than the last time he had been there, yet 'when I look back, I don't see how we could have spent less'. [20]

Once they left Angers they were never to spend more than a few weeks in any one place for the entire duration of the tour. Dr Hobart led them south to Bordeaux and then, following the Garonne valley, down to the shores of the Mediterranean. This being an age before maps were readily available, guides were hired and post horses used, just as in England. Only in France the posts were closer together, on average just ten miles apart. In theory this made for an easy journey, however the unbridling and changing of horses could be a protracted business. Payments to postillions and their horses, plus purchases of oil and grease to repair the chaise, fill pages of Jarrett's account books. Their own saddle horses travelled with them, including we must assume Thomas's prized Barb. In order to have ready cash to pay the travelling expenses and lodgings along the way there was no need to carry large amounts of coins, for there existed a network of English agents at Nantes, Bordeaux and Montpellier; each in receipt of funds from Mr Waters in Paris, the guardians' banker.

It is at Montpellier that the first entry for hiring a footman appears: 'paid a Servant for nine days as a Footman'. The man is not named nor are there any details other than the amount of his wages, ten livres. Hiring a footman in a foreign town had many self-evident advantages. As a native of the place his local knowledge was useful whether acting as a simple guide or arranging introductions. By September they had moved on to Aix. After so much leisurely travelling and sightseeing Hobart wrote to the guardians explaining why they had taken their time, apart from 'our curiosity and some little accidents having retarded out voyage'. He described how Thomas had visited the governor of each province they travelled through 'and been well received by ym'. [21] Though there is little documentary evidence to enlarge on this, either in the accounts or surviving letters, it would have been the case that Thomas was furnished with letters of introduction to the most important personages that he might encounter. In Paris he was to attend the royal court at Versailles and in Italy the courts of the Grand Dukes. In the same letter Hobart explained that illness was the reason they had not stayed longer in Toulouse, a place the guardians had recommended. After a poor harvest and 'ill air' caused by the Garonne flooding, the subsequent mortality was so serious that the even the Jesuits had closed their schools. If this had not been the case Dr Hobart would have entered Thomas at the Academy in Toulouse. He did so instead at Aix, for a refresher course. Hobart explained that the purpose was for Thomas: 'to remember what he has formerly learnt, and may help a little to fix his mind, ... he rides and vaults twice a day, takes two lessons on ye flute, continues his civil law ... '. [22]

None of these stops lasted long. Two weeks later they were in Lyons where preparations were made to cross the mountains into Italy before the snows arrived. The two grooms were bought new waistcoats, breeches, hats, stockings and shoes, and Jarrett noted that enough cloth was purchased to make three livery coats. All but two of the horses they had brought with them were sold, the remaining two, including perhaps the Barb, were put into the care of John Cocks who had instructions to ride them home to London. For this he was given two hundred livres, about £12, and dressed in his new clothes he set off. John-Baptiste meanwhile accompanied Thomas boar hunting.

The journey south over the Alps was reckoned to be almost more perilous than crossing the Channel. It was not a journey to be undertaken on horseback, far less in a chaise, for when Henry Lee Warner of Walsingham set about it a couple of years later he described going up the mountains by mule and down in 'chairs carried by two men, it is amazing how custome makes them walk a good pace from stone to stone down places I should be afraid to crawl'. [23]

At the far side of the Alps was the Piedmonte. Here Italian was spoken and Dr Ferrari settled them in Turin before he, for reasons unknown, turned back for Paris. In Turin a footman was engaged, if nothing else he would be useful for dealing with the 'money of Piedmont'.

Italy in 1713 was divided into small kingdoms, each with its own currency. In Genoa, where they went next, it was pauls, worth about ten pence each in English money, slightly less than a shilling. Dr Hobart made a note in the accounts book, 'The value of money in Italy changing very often according as one passes thro the dominions of several princes I think it fit for the Ease of our accounts and that they may be better understood by any that Read them to make use only of the donomination of money which is incurred through all Italy that is the old french Louidors or Spanish pistols which by Reason of universal reception seems to be the only General Standard tho to be so Exact as we could wish in Edward Jarrett's account of expenses in details will be seen how many livres and louidors consists of in Each dominion'. After reading and digesting Dr Hobart's note one can appreciate the appeal of the euro.

Each time they crossed a border in Italy and re-adjusted their finances a different footman was engaged. Although in the course of the tour Thomas Coke, and perhaps Dr Hobart too, learnt Italian, a local man engaged as a footman continued to be a useful appendage. For Thomas with his many letters of introduction to local 'great men' a footman was an essential go-between and equally useful for gaining permission to visit the many abbeys, churches and even convents. Convents held a particular fascination for the English and it was usual for tourists to visit them. Generally they were disappointed to find that far from beautiful women being held against their will, the women inside were content and unremarkable. In Catholic families at least one son was expected to become a priest, and therefore would not marry, thus surplus daughters were often ready to believe they had a vocation and accept life as a Bride of Christ. Women of lower status also entered convents to work as servants. Within living memory the difference between them were their titles, elite nuns were addressed as Mother, and the lower ones as Sister. On his Grand Tour Henry Lee Warner, Thomas's Norfolk neighbour, visited at least two convents, and wrote of one in 1714 where he knew an English nun called Turner (probably one of the Turners of Norfolk) and of how the Abbess had entertained him with sweetmeats, fruit, cakes and pasties. Here, he said: 'They discourse of heaven. A charming nun sung a divine hymn and like other married people they told us they would not change their condition for the world, we are at liberty to believe them for it is too late for them to say otherwise'. [24]

Next Hobart led Thomas to Venice where they stayed at the *White Lyon* for a month arriving on New Year's Day. Venice was considered the most elegant city in Europe, but was also renowned for its libertine ways and numerous courtesans. It was a place that invited intrigues, being the custom to wear masks almost whenever you liked, men and women, except in church, convents (!) or when wearing religious clothes. Sometimes they were de rigueur, any woman going to the theatre without a mask and a cloak would be letting down her family honour. On the other hand, a law was passed in 1703 banning the wearing of masks in casinos where hitherto they had provided a perfect means of avoiding creditors. [25] Thomas attended a masquerade the very day they arrived and on 8th January Jarrett records buying six 'masques' and a further six on the 20th. Stefano the boatman was hired for the month and by boat (gondola) Thomas went to the opera several times, wearing a new scarlet cloak, and on at least one occasion dined with Lady Baltimore. This woman was separated from her husband and about to marry the sometime consul at Leghorn. She was thirty-six in 1714. The stay in Venice was not wholly given over to pleasure, for there were lessons in arithmetic, ancient history (Titus Lucius) and Italian grammar.

A month later they were in Rome, to enjoy the carnival and observe the Easter celebrations, and here a named footman, Carmagnole was hired. On first arrival it was still only February and a licence was needed to eat 'flesh in Lent'. For dealing with bureaucracy the services of a Roman was essential, though obtaining this particular licence presented no difficulty. [26] These jobbing footmen were paid every fifteen days and like footmen in England were occasionally given extra 'for several small things'. Carmagnole wore livery and Thomas gave him an allowance for shoes. In Rome Dr Hobart installed the party at the *Golden Mountain,* and they were to return there several times after various journeys to Naples (the city only; it would be another twenty years before Pompeii was excavated) and Florence, paying Carmagnole the footman a retainer in their absence.

Almost as soon as they had arrived in Rome this first time, Thomas met William Kent whom he later commissioned to buy works of art on his behalf. William Kent [1685-1748] a talented painter had been sponsored by several Englishmen, convinced of his potential, to study in Rome under the celebrated Giuseppe Chiari. Chiari was the most fashionable contemporary artist and an obliging one who undertook commissions. Sir Andrew Fountaine, a Norfolk man, advised many on the Grand Tour what and what not to buy, and when in Rome was known to suggest suitable subjects for Chiari to paint, even down to size. (It was not unknown for paintings to be cut to fit expensive frames). However Fountaine's name does not feature in Jarrett's accounts – it appears to have been Kent who opened Thomas's eyes to an appreciation of painting as art. For after meeting Kent Thomas wrote to his grandfather Newton explaining how he felt transformed by what he had seen: 'I have become since my stay in Rome a perfect virtuoso and a great lover of pictures'. [27] Up until this time, May 1714, Thomas had been fairly confident in his choice of manuscripts and books to be purchased, far less so when it came to paintings; but now he asked his guardians for a separate allowance to buy works of art. It seems they refused this initial request as in September he wrote that he had made a note in his pocket book of several pictures in Rome which he would have liked to have bought, and intended to do so when he came of age. [28] Some idea of the joy of collecting can be seen when contrasting the prices of comestibles. The cost of living and travelling was considerable. Three weeks at the *Golden Mountain* with meals came to 500 pauls, a footman cost forty-eight pauls a month, two weeks of washing thirty-one, a pound of Naples soap eighteen and a pair of black silk stockings bought new twenty-one. Yet a folder of antique paintings was only ninety. Consequently the temptation to purchase works of art was irresistible and Thomas 'seeing such a number of fine things ... could not hinder myself from making free with more money than my allowence'. [29]

During the summer of 1714 some time was spent in Florence where a different unnamed footman served Thomas. During this stay John Cocks the groom returned from England and was given his year's wages, £8 in English money, 304 pauls in Florentine. In November while at the *Three Kings* in Milan Cocks had his greatcoat relined and four linen shirts made for him. The coldest months of the winter of 1714–15 were spent in Turin. In contrast to the summer when leather covers had been fixed across the chaise windows against the heat, the party was now extremely chilly. This time they did not stay at an inn but in lodgings, described as being two furnished chambers, though it was necessary to buy another table. They paid for several cartloads of wood, a warming pan, a good supply of candles, a frying pan and even hired blankets 'at five ould livres a month'. Other domestic items bought were a milk pot, drinking glasses, white plates, towels and the customary daily amounts of chocolate, milk and bread. Vails given to the servants of the kitchen and the hall suggests that these lodgings were small flats with communal dining rooms.

At Turin Thomas was bidden to spend the mornings at the Turin Academy which, despite the riding and fencing lessons, he did not enjoy, maintaining he was treated like a child although he was now seventeen and a half. Travelling to the Academy each day in a sedan chair should have been warm work for the chairmen but the weather was so intensely cold that extra coats were hired for them. Turin did offer some attractions, for here was the Royal Palace of the Duke of Savoy and Piedmont and here the English had an embassy. Thomas went to the opera and playhouse, and several times to watch the rope dancing, a form of acrobatic spectacle.

The footman engaged at Turin was called Jerro, and before they left at the end of January 1715 a second footman appeared in the accounts named Joseph. Both were bought suits of black clothes, gloves and shoes.

April 1715 was spent in Milan, here the accommodation and food cost 188 livres and 'the Rest' another 125 livres went on servants, 'antiquerys and Curiousitys [sic] of my Masters, plus his Pocket Money'. In Milan a new footman was engaged who broke the pattern of the previous jobbing footmen. The two from Turin, Jerro and Joseph, had been left behind in that city as was the custom, but Abraham, taken on in Milan, must have agreed to a longer contract for not only was he bought clothes, plus shoes and stockings, but two months later Jarrett records buying him a hat with silver lace, a livery waistcoat and breeches. Unlike the previous foreign footmen who were engaged only for the duration of the stays in the different cities, this man was to be permanent, travelling with Thomas Coke and his party for the remainder of the tour and even to England. His full name was Abraham Blaumer; hired in Milan he can hardly have been a native of that city, more likely a Protestant Swiss from the Savoie.

By now the tour was winding down, the end was in sight, and thoughts and plans turned to home. The next journey was a return over the Alps and back to France, stopping at Chambéry on the way for two weeks. Here Edward Jarrett the accountant was unwell and needed the services of a surgeon before they could proceed to Lyons. In Lyons a second footman was hired, but only for six days.

It was now May 1715 and if they were to continue north by the time they reached Dunkirk they would have been on the tour for three years, the agreed term for which Hobart had been released from his position as a fellow of Christ's College 'to go along with Mr Coke, the Duke of Leeds' Grandson'. [30]

At Lyons there is an increase in the volume of letters and postage entered in the accounts book, it was not merely that letters awaited them at that place needing to be answered, but many were received during their stay. Among them must have been some important queries and decisions, for after two weeks the party did indeed set off, but not north to Paris, Dunkirk and eventually England, but south, a return to Chambéry, where lodgings were taken with Madame Rossett.

What exactly occasioned this change of plan cannot be known for sure, other than the guardians writing to Dr Hobart asking him to prolong the tour. The previous September Thomas had informed his grandfather Newton that the death of Queen Anne had resulted in many young Englishmen cutting short their tours to return to England, but in his case Thomas felt differently and was in no hurry to go back. [31] The rumours he heard of life in the English court under the Hanoverian king made him curious to see Germany for himself. He also asked to spend 'one more winter in Italy'. [32]

It is unclear how Thomas Coke spent the next few weeks at Chambéry during this unplanned séjour. Only that he went fishing, took the waters at Aix les Bains a few miles to the north, and drank quantities of champagne and Rosele, a tea made from an infusion of flowers. There was no attending the Academy, although Thomas had been a pupil there briefly on the previous visit and no other lessons are recorded. The Duke of Savoy and Piedmont lived in the Chateau de Chambéry but Jarrett makes no mention of this. It was a time of idleness passed in the mountains among the spring flowers and simple pleasures. Nothing of any significance was purchased and there were no expenses other than Joseph one of the Turin footmen who came to help out. Money was spent only on housekeeping. At this time the new foot-man Abraham Blaumer took on some of the valet's role. Over the next five months there are regular entries for shaving 'My Master' and dressing wigs, even mending his master's clothes; a barber was paid for 'Abraham's larning'. This visit to Chambéry seems to have been spent happily for when they left at the end of July 1715 Madame Rossett was paid an extra sixty livres for her 'Great Care and kind yousage'.

The destination this time was Switzerland. Dr Hobart installed them at Lausanne where Thomas met up with his 'cousin' Mr Hamon L'Estrange of Hunstanton and Mr Lee Warner of Walsingham, both of whom were a little older than Thomas Coke and enjoying far shorter tours. [33] It was agreed the three young men should travel together through Switzerland to Germany. Having had the chaise mended for the umpteenth time, Hobart purchased eight pounds of Swiss tea and hired a boat to transport Thomas's chest of books before the party set off.

A gap, the first and only one, then occurs in the accounts from the 10th to the 16th of August while the party was in Basel. The account of what happened between those dates is filled by Lee Warner's letters home which tell of the illness and death of Hamon L'Estrange from the smallpox. He was twenty-five years old. [34] Dr Hobart, Lee Warner wrote, took all possible care while L'Estrange was ill and afterwards arranged the burial. It must have given Dr Hobart a degree of satisfaction that the interment could take place in a Protestant country. Thomas and Lee Warner went on together for a while, but parted soon after arriving at Frankfurt.

Thomas Coke's Grand Tour was to continue for a further three years. He found he disliked Germany and as soon as could be arranged turned south again to France and in January 1716 embarked from Marseilles for Sicily. Abraham the footman was given a New Year's gift of a blue greatcoat lined with red. Four months were spent in Sicily with a short visit to Malta. It was not usual for either of these islands to be included on a grand tour, especially Malta. The purpose of going there may have been a visit to the 'Prince' of Lorraine whose servants were given vails.

In Sicily Thomas acquired a new dog, a mastiff, very probably the one that appears in his portrait painted in Rome by Trevasini which now hangs at Holkham. Shortly after the dog was purchased there is an entry for curing it of the mange and it being trained by a 'dog master'. After an extensive tour of Sicily and then to Malta the party returned to the mainland disembarking at Naples. Here it was the turn of Abraham Blaumer to become unwell, he stayed behind for two weeks until he was recovered enough to rejoin the party in Rome.

Back in Rome Carmagnole the Roman footman, whom they had not seen for two years, was engaged once more and Thomas stayed in lodgings where meals were cooked for him with the occasional supper sent in from the *Black Eagle*. Unlike previous visits the footmen and grooms lived out on board wages. Thomas took architecture lessons from Signor Giacomo, who also acted as a guide to the city, and flute lessons from Signor Valentino. William Kent was again in Rome and so too was Lord Harrold, the eldest son of the Duke of Kent, who was to become Thomas's brother-in-law. Lord Harrold had been sent to Italy with the specific purpose of finding approval for and improving his father's plans for a Palladian house to be built at Wrest their estate in Bedfordshire. Both he and Thomas purchased paintings from Chiari and shared a mutual interest in architecture. [35]

Thomas and Dr Hobart left Rome at the end of the summer to spend the winter months in Turin as they had done before, returning to Rome in early 1717. Once again the Roman footman Carmagnole was engaged. But this time he did not last long and was replaced first by Domick and then Anthony. By now Thomas Coke was fluent in Italian, although Dr Hobart and Edward Jarrett were not. It is conceivable that with the advantage of understanding the language better it was found that the Italian footmen who hired themselves to the young Englishmen were less dependable than first thought.

The most common reasons for dismissing servants in England were 'sawciness', drunkenness, or their inability to get on with their fellow workers. Jobbing or temporary footmen had even less reason to be loyal and honest than those hired with a surety and the opportunity to exploit foreign 'milords' when they could must have tempted many. Equally their masters would show little tolerance towards these servants when things went wrong. The poor light in which servants were often held had been highlighted the previous year when Thomas received news from England of the elopement of his sister Anne with a neighbour, Major Philip Roberts. Frustrated by distance and anxious to redeem the honour of the family, his furious response was to blame the servants who he was certain had connived at the arrangements. Loyalty to individual members of the family was not enough, servants were expected to be loyal to the family as a whole – in this instance Thomas would have suspected the servants to have been bribed. When things went wrong servants were a convenient scapegoat. [36]

Thomas enjoyed his extra year in Italy, but in the autumn of 1717 prepared to leave Rome for the last time. Heading north Dr Hobart led the party to Venice and thence to Austria. After Italy, Thomas found Vienna dull. The Wortley Montagus, whom Lord Harrold had met there the previous autumn, had recently left for Constantinople. There were operas almost every night but the Court lacked excitement. What did catch Thomas's attention however were the continuing hostilities in Hungary where the Austrian army was making impressive gains over the Turks. At this particular juncture the fighting centred round Belgrade no great distance from Vienna and Thomas conceived the idea of joining the action himself. He began preparations by buying maps of Belgrade and hiring a room 'to put the Campaign baggage in', filling it with tents, bottles, gunpowder, a trunk and other necessary equipment. A second footman was taken on in addition to Abraham Blaumer and a cook, all of whom who were to accompany him; with two new grooms to care for the horses and porters to carry the campaign baggage. Meanwhile Dr Hobart wrote post haste (in the literal sense) to the guardians. The precious heir was just that, too precious to be risked. Naturally the guardians agreed with Hobart, who took his own effective, if drastic, action. The night before Thomas was due to depart for Belgrade, Hobart arranged, at some expense, for the governor of Austria to have him arrested! Then the next day, surely by pre-arrangement, Hobart got him released and hurried him off, protesting, to Prague. From this place Thomas wrote to his grandfather Newton somewhat disingenuously 'I thought you might be unwilling to let me expose myself at a campaign ...' knowing full well that Sir Edward Coke had already flatly refused. [37]

This episode was the nearest any of Coke's servants came to becoming involved in a war or any military action. Had they got to Belgrade the camp would have been well behind the lines and their lives would not have been in danger, nevertheless the prospect is an intriguing one.

Prague was followed by Dresden and Berlin. Though Thomas never felt as comfortable in Germany as he had in Italy and France, it was politic to visit in view of the new Hanoverian king occupying the English throne. By way of compensation Thomas soon found to his pleasure that Germany was able to provide better hunting than he had hitherto enjoyed on the continent. Hobart then led him to Hamburg and Hanover, hiring occasional extra footmen for a few days at a time. At Hanover they inspected the Elector's kennels and even took time out for the odd flute lesson. In late 1717 they left Germany and arrived in Antwerp where Hobart engaged two new footmen, making three with Abraham. It was now December and here they spent Christmas.

In January 1718 they moved on to Paris, the last stop before home. Like Rome, Paris was full of friends and acquaintances including Thomas's younger brother Edward at the start of his Grand Tour. The two brothers with two French footman and Jean-Baptiste, the erstwhile groom, went around together. Thomas and Edward rode on horseback to Versailles, attended masquerades, and Edward found, as Thomas had before him, that little fun could begin until the French language was 'acquired'. Frequent entries appear for payments to roasting cooks, for the new fashion of drinking beer and for a footman named Andrew, who may have been Andrew Griffiths (of whom more later). Thomas arranged for his brother Edward to enter an Academy in Luneville in Lorraine where Dr Ferrari would oversee his studies. Edward was happy with this arrangement and wrote to Sir Edward Coke enthusiastically, and in a hurry: ' ... there are but two English [there] can't write more for the horses stay for me at the door, pray to Excuse the Blots'. [38]

For himself Thomas ordered a new Berlin coach and Jean-Baptiste prepared to drive it to Calais. A first move towards the parting of the ways. Over the five years and nine months of the Grand Tour Dr Hobart had been with Thomas Coke the entire time apart from five weeks in Holland when he was unwell. In England they were only to meet on one more occasion. Hobart continued to be employed as a governor and lead young men on their Grand Tours until, fulfilling his worst fear, he died in France in 1727. [39]

Thomas Coke stayed away on his Grand Tour nearly twice as long as most of his contemporaries. The advantages for his guardians were obvious, not only were they able to keep a check on his spending, but they were also relieved of the problem of what to do with him had he returned earlier while still a minor. From the surviving letters of the period it is clear that while his travels consumed the greater part of his life and interests, he was always privy to events at home. His status as heir and his future duties and responsibilities were never far from his thoughts.

In common with the majority of his peers he never went abroad again, though he continued to add to his art collections using agents to purchase works on his behalf. Thomas Coke returned to England fluent in French and Italian, long accustomed to foreign servants, footmen, coachmen, postillions and cooks, foreign ways, and most importantly foreign food.

His Grand Tour was to have a profound influence on the household at Holkham, from French cooks and French (and Italian) food prepared in the kitchens, to fruit and vegetables grown in heated greenhouses in an attempt to recapture the aroma and tastes of southern Europe, and to the employ-ment of foreign footmen and valets. His housemaids would dust the great works of art he had purchased, in particular the collection of statuary. The bookcases in his library would be home to many works in languages other than English. In the evenings at Holkham some of the servants would see him wearing his favoured leisure outfit, the Alburness, a loose fitting garment derived from Moorish wear and worn with a turban. Others would hear about it. All of this served to set him apart from the ordinary English squire immortalized by Squire Western.

For the duration of his tour his experience as a master of servants was almost entirely limited to male temporary servants; maids and washerwomen had worked for him but only at a remove. As far as we know he had neither engaged, dismissed nor paid a maid directly. Throughout his time away he had been (with one or two brief intervals) in the company of his tour guide or governor Dr Hobart a god-fearing Englishman and Edward Jarrett who kept the accounts, persisting to the end in his habit of recording as much as he could in English. The two other servants who accompanied him home to England were both foreigners, his footman Abraham Blaumer and groom John-Baptiste, one a Swiss, the other French.

NOTES

1. John Stoye, *English Travellers Abroad 1604-1667* Yale University Press 1989 p.38.

2. *The Complete Peerage*, Raynham Archives G1/10 and R.W. Ketton-Cremer, *Felbrigg, the story of a House* London 1982 Futura edition p.83.

3. HA F/G2 (2) f. 487.

4. James p.176.

5. HA F/G 2 (3) f.10. Thomas Coke to Sir John Newton: 'Dr Hobart and Mr Ferare always speak English to me, because they are not able to pronounce French ... '

6. HA F/TC 4. All material in this chapter is taken from this account book unless otherwise noted.

7. Gloucester Record Office D1844 C/11.

8. For more on this see Linda Colley *Captives* London 2002.

9. Isobel Grundy *Lady Mary Wortley Montagu* Oxford 1999 p.169.

10. TNA Prob 11/614. Will of Dr Thomas Hobart. Possibly he feared being buried in unconsecrated ground.

11. J. Jean Hecht *Continental and Colonial Servants in Eighteenth Century England* Massachusetts 1954, pp.5-6.

12. *Richard Creed's Journal of the Grand Tour 1699-1700* transcribed by Alice Thomas and published by the Oundle Museum, 2002.

13. The name of this place refers to the alliance between Scotland and France and was a meeting place for Jacobites. In 2010 a Scottish pub in Paris The Auld Alliance, 80 Rue Francois Miron, Paris 4.

14. HA F/G2 (2) f. 467. Thomas's sightseeing in Paris on this visit included Les Invalides built 1676, Notre Dame, the churches of St Denis, burial place of French royalty and St Jerome, the Palais du Luxembourg, St Cloud, Fontainebleau, the tapestry manufactory at Gobelines, but not Versailles.

15. Lucy Worsley *Cavaliers* London 2007 pp.59-60, pp.124-125 & pp.169-171, although Cavendish's favourite horse Le Superbe was Spanish not a Barb, also her English Heritage Guide to Bolsover Castle 2004 pp.6-7.

16. He may have had a point, as John Stoye says in *English Travellers Abroad* p.48. Thomas Wentworth later 1st Earl of Strafford in 1612 commented on the bad French spoken at Angers.

17. HA F/G2 (3) f. 10.

18. HA F/G2 (3) f. 84.

19. Lady Mary Wortley Montague, Penguin Selected Letters London 1997 p.359.

20. HA F/G2 (3) f. 84.

21. HA F/G2 (2) f.460.

22. HA F/G2 (2) f.460.

23. NRO Lee Warner Box 10, 918x2, letter 23.

24. Jeremy Black *The Grand Tour in the Eighteenth Century* Gloucestershire 1992 p.240 and NRO Lee Warner, Box 10, 918 x 2, letter 7. Lee Warner to his uncle Sir James Howe.

25. The oldest document pertaining to the use of masks in Venice dates back to 1268. The decree forbidding men entering convents dressed as women is dated 1458.

26. Stoye p.130.

27. HA F/G2 (2) f.467.

28. HA F/G2 (2) f.472.

29. Ibid HA F/G2 (2) f.472.

30. James p.177.

31. HA F/G2 (2) f. 472.

32. HA F/G 2 (2) f. 477.

33. HA F/G2 (2) f. 477 Thomas Coke writes of his 'cousin L'Estrange. According to C.W. James the cousinship was very distant, Maria the eighth daughter of John Coke had married Sir Nicholas L'Estrange.

34. NRO Lee Warner Box 10 918x2 letters 24 and 25 H. Lee Warner to his Uncle Sir James Howe.

35. Luton and Bedford Archives Lucas 30/8/33 and 30/8/28.

36. HA F/G2 (2) f. 489.

37. HA F/G2 (2) f.495.

38. HA F/G2 (2) f.493. ' ... [I] will take great pains to learn French for without being able to speak and understand no fun ... humbly beg you'l excuse the Blots ...' Edward Coke to Sir John Newton Paris May 1718.

39. Leicestershire Record Office DG7/Bundle 26 part two: July 17, 1723, Anne Countess of Nottingham writes to her son that Dr Ferrari 'goes abroad with Mr Mostyn' (her grandson) and the following year July 27, 1724, young Tom Mostyn wrote to his grandfather Daniel Finch Earl of Nottingham from Geneva about Dr Hobart who was bringing back a Caesar's head which he hopes his grandfather will approve of. See also PRO Prob 11/614. Will of Dr Thomas Hobart. Dr Ferrari re-appears in the Holkham accounts in March 1727 employed as librarian.

CHAPTER 3

Marriage and the First Household

Jarrett's book of accounts ends on arrival back at Dover. The last few entries are in 'English Money' payments for Humphrey Smith and his son Edward to travel from London to Boulogne (not Dunkirk after all) and meet the party there. The final ones were expenses at Calais and payments to Captains Gilbert and Waddington for crossing the channel. Jarrett then reverted to his role as valet and Edward Smith took over as accountant. He was fully prepared and had in his possession a brand new account book headed Tuesday 13th May 1718 in which he wrote:

' ... being the day that Mr Coke landed at Dover after near six years travails [sic] in France, Italy, Sicily, Germany, Malta, Holland and Flanders. The Account contains his Expences in London from that time to ye 17th June following which day ye said Mr Coke attained to ye Age of 21 Years. And upon Thursday ye 3rd of July following was married to ye Rt honble ye Lady Margaret Tufton 3rd daughter to Thomas Earl of Thanet a Lady of great Beauty, Singular Virtue and Goodness being 18 Years of Age, 16th June 1718'. [1]

So, within two short months of his return, Thomas Coke was to come of age, marry and acquire a household of servants. Such a rapid transformation from heir apparent to fully fledged master of his inheritance left little time to acclimatise, which may have been the guardians' intention. No correspondence relating to these momentous plans has survived.

Edward Smith records a payment made at Dover to Mr John Coke's man which indicates that one guardian at least was present to welcome the young heir home. It is not possible to know whether the other two surviving guardians, Sir John Newton and Sir Edward Coke, also came to greet him, but in view of his prolonged absence and the importance of imminent events, they probably did. Smith further recorded that two Berlin coaches took the travellers from Dover to London with four servants in attendance and that the cost of the two-day journey was £25.

During the eight weeks between his return to England and his wedding day Thomas Coke lodged in London. His landlady was a Mrs Cooley who charged him £26 for his stay. (A Mrs Eleanor Cooley appears amongst those who made Thomas Coke's wedding clothes as one of two seamstresses working on shirts, handkerchiefs and other linen for which she received £27). Despite not having a house of his own Thomas was to all intents and purposes already the head of a household and had a number of servants at his disposal. There were three footmen to wait on him as well as 'old John', a stableboy, two grooms, a postillion and a helper. The stablemen lodged at Hampstead where the horses were kept. The dogs, the mastiff and others, stayed at Thanet House. Thomas paid a London lodging bill for Mr Humphrey Smith the Holkham steward and his son Edward Smith the new accountant, and their man (their servant) for a total of eighteen weeks, cost 12gns. For the moment, Dr Hobart returned to Cambridge.

The first, and perhaps most important event, was Thomas's twenty-first birthday and coming of age which took place on 17th June just three weeks before his wedding. The usual custom was to honour the birthday of an heir with some splendour. Achieving *any* birthday in an age when smallpox and other illnesses could carry you off in a matter of days, was generally more marked than it is today. But there is nothing in Edward Smith's account to indicate that anything out of the ordinary happened as far as his 'household' was concerned, other than the servants being given a guinea to drink their master's health. An entry for a dinner at the tavern which came to £3 was recorded, but this was unexceptional. Dinners were often taken at the tavern, the only difference was that this one was recorded: 'with a Chicken'. It is not possible that the day of Thomas's majority passed unmarked. It can only be supposed that the guardians gave him some grand dinner the cost of which would appear in *their* accounts.

The arrangement of Thomas's marriage was the penultimate duty under-taken by the guardians. The last would be selecting and gathering together his complement of household servants. The wife they chose for him was Lady Margaret Tufton, the third daughter of Thomas Tufton 6th Earl of Thanet. In 1718 Thanet was a widower aged seventy-four with five daughters – his three sons all died as infants. Two of his daughters were already married, in 1708 the eldest to Edward Watson, Viscount Sondes, and in 1709 his second daughter Anne to James Cecil, 5th Earl of Salisbury. Now, after a gap of nine years, the next two daughters, Margaret and Mary, were to be married in the same year: Lady Margaret to Thomas Coke and Lady Mary, the younger of the two, to Anthony Grey, Lord Harrold, heir to the Duke of Kent. A year apart in age Margaret and Mary were each other's favourite sister. Lord Harrold it will be remembered and Thomas Coke had met in Rome.

Immensely wealthy, Lord Thanet had inherited the estates of his grand-mother Lady Anne Clifford and those of the earldom of Thanet following the deaths of his three elder brothers. His main residence was at Hothfield in Kent. According to Swift, Lord Thanet was a man of 'great piety and char-ity'. He was reputed by his grandson-in-law Lord Egmont to have given away £60,000 in his life time and left another £40,000 to different chari-ties. Physically he was described as thin, tall, with black hair and a red face, a good old country gentleman. [2] In his will he described himself as one who lived with little vanity and this is substantiated by his suits made from 'Ash coloured cloth' and 'Brown coloured cloth' with glazed holland to line the sleeves, modest indeed for a man of such great wealth. These clothes were probably made from Kentish cloth, an industry he supported; his footmen all wore shirts made of it. [3]

Lady Margaret was exactly three years younger than Thomas, almost to the day. She was born on 16th June 1700 and had spent her childhood divided between Hothfield and Thanet House in London. At the age of ten she caught smallpox, but there is no mention of scarring. The following year, 1711, she and her sister Lady Mary had the measles. She was bled several times as a child, the usual 'remedy' for illness, and in 1709 had her teeth cleaned by a 'French Surgeon'. [4] When in 1712 her mother died of the smallpox, with her older sisters already married, Lady Margaret was the eldest of the three daughters still at home.

Lord Thanet imbued in all his daughters the awareness of their power to do good, both in charitable gifts to the poor, practical assistance and education. It was a family with an above average sense of duty. While at Hothfield it is likely that Lady Margaret read the diaries of her great-grandmother Lady Clifford for in her later years, as will be seen, certain of her actions may be attributed to the influence of that redoubtable role model. [5] Lord Thanet, highly conscious of the duties that came with inheritance, supported many schools on his estates in the north of England and in Kent and Sussex, a favour-ite form of benevolence in the eighteenth century. In London he distributed coals to the poor of St Giles, the parish in which he had his town house. [6] Among his many records Lord Thanet kept a Book of Charity listing the numerous recipients of his benevolence and their changing circumstances. He preferred to choose these people himself rather than put money into the hands of the churchwardens and overseers of the poor to be distributed by them. In his will he went so far as to state this, reminding his children and executors to distribute charity by 'my usual Method'. In assisting the poor he had been aided in a practical way by his wife whose skills in the preparations of medicines he much admired. Lord Thanet made a particular request that the 'Druggs and Medicines and distilled Waters that I shall have at my death shall be removed to my said daughter the Lady Sondes' house at Lees Court [Kent] and be divided amongst my said five daughters not doubting but they will make the same good use of them as their Mother used to do in imploying such and the like Drugs and Medicines for the benefit of poor sick persons'. [7]

Arranged marriages between families of property was still the convention in the early eighteenth century. Lady Margaret brought no land with her but her dowry of £15,000, which Lord Thanet gave to each of his daughters, was large and her connections impressive. [8]

A surviving letter from the Earl of Thanet to the Duke of Kent, concerning Lady Margaret's younger sister's proposed marriage, provides a glimpse into how these affairs were conducted. It was a similar situation insomuch as the prospective husband, Lord Harrold, was still on his Grand Tour at the time of the agreement, and it appears that all was done sight unseen. For even when Lord Harrold returned to England Thanet merely sent a servant to the duke's house, Wrest Park in Bedfordshire, to assess his character on his behalf. The servant, in whom Thanet must have had a great deal of confidence, reported that Lord Harrold had 'all the desirable qualifications to make a wife happy'. Despite this Lord Harrold was refused a visit to Hothfield to meet his future bride: ' ... my Lord Sondes [Thanet's eldest son-in-law] will tell you,' wrote Lord Thanet 'my method was not to admit of visiting and access till the writings were more ready to be signed, for the lawyers are often so long in furnishing them, it may prove too tedious a trial upon a Lovers Patience'. In other words they were not to meet until it was too late for the arrangement to be rescinded, which in this case can only have been immediately before the marriage since the letter was written on 8th February and the wedding took place on the 17th. [9]

Thomas Coke was marginally more fortunate. In the weeks before his marriage he was allowed two visits to Hothfield, the first in the company of his guardians.

Weddings were a tremendous opportunity for displays of wealth and taste although those attending were few in number, close members of the family only. They were very much private ceremonies, especially if they took place in the country. Yet the splendour with which they were conducted, the huge amounts of money spent on outward appearances have gone largely unrecorded, except in household accounts. Marriage was regarded primarily as an honourable estate it being the duty of both families to demonstrate the high regard in which they held each other, and as confirmation of the young couple's commitment by shows of outward riches. It was usual for portraits of the bride and groom to be painted prior to marriage, but there are few if any paintings of actual weddings and at this early date there was no announcement in the newspapers.

Central to the pomp and display were the servants, kitted out in expensive new outfits chosen and paid for by their master, not only did they appear impressive and elegant, in number they far exceeded both families.

At Thomas Coke's wedding Mr Humphrey Smith, described as Mr Steward, was bought a suit costing the enormous sum of £33. His son Edward, now titled the Gentleman of the Horse, a high status position as the word gentleman implies, though he was still keeping the accounts, was even more splendidly attired in a suit costing £41. It was trimmed with gold lace, as was Mr Jarrett's, whose outfit cost £34. These three men were not liveried servants and therefore their suits would not have been owned, or loaned, by Thomas Coke but given to them as gifts. Livery suits were always the property of the master to be worn while in his service and returned to him on leaving. Meanwhile a further ten male servants who did wear livery had new greatcoats bought for them, new livery suits and hats with silver lace, buckskin breeches, boots, shoes and livery stockings. These servants are not named but would have included Abraham Blaumer the footman engaged at Chambéry in 1715, Andrew Griffiths also a foot-man, Francis Riggs coachman, John Large postillion, Robert Webster and John Walker both grooms, Jean–Baptiste the French groom and William Holland. The total spent on servants liveries for the wedding was £221, about double that which would be spent in a normal year. Not every item of clothing was provided, they were expected to pay for their own under–shirts, shirts, neckwear and wigs. A well made horse–hair wig cost in the region of £2. 10s. [10] and all liveried servants wore them, usually powdered. Only occasionally did Coke buy a new wig for the coachman as presumably his suffered more from the elements than did the others.

The Coke livery colours were blue with scarlet. Blue was a colour associated with calm and reliability and the most popular choice for liveries in an age when the choice of colours was relatively narrow. The main part of the Cokes' livery, the coat and waistcoat, was blue with scarlet collars and cuffs, blue breeches and scarlet stockings. In the splendour of their livery, servants were almost indistinguishable from their masters with one important difference; with the occasional exception of footmen, they did not wear swords. An edict of 1700 had declared that the wearing of swords by servants was no longer permitted, for a sword was seen as a symbol of gentility. The Swiss traveller de Saussure who visited and commented on England in the 1720s noted that any well-dressed person wearing a sword was treated as a gentleman. [11] The exception was footmen when out with their employers, when they were often equipped with 'servants pistols' as well as swords.

The female servants who attended the wedding came almost exclusively from the Hothfield household, they would each have been allowed new or embellished gowns. From time to time either livery or a badge of servitude was suggested as appropriate for female servants, but this never caught on. [12] Maid servants were at liberty to wear what they chose, funds permitting, and like their male counterparts the more affluent among them would have been almost indistinguishable from the family.

The cost of Thomas Coke's own clothes, bordered with gold and silver lace, came to a massive £215. He had two suits of silk, one for the marriage ceremony itself and the second for the dinner afterwards. Mr George Binkes was paid for 'Padefoy silk', and Mr Haines, Coke's tailor, £107 for making them and Mrs Gameron £87 for embroidering them. The entry for Mrs Gameron is intriguing, as it poses the question of how embroidered clothes were ordered and executed. In the weeks between Thomas Coke's return in May and his wedding in July there was hardly enough time for him to visit her, choose and order the embroidery, and for her (and her team?) to execute it. It would seem that she had work already done which could be made up to fit. A further £101 was paid to Mr Alexander the lace man, £3. 15s. to John Leek for hats and feathers, and another £41 for periwigs, swords and gloves. In portraits of this date Thomas Coke is shown wearing a modified full-bottomed wig, rather than large curls reaching down to waist level as his father would have done and which continued to be worn at court until the mid 1750s. The fashion in 1718 was for smaller tighter curls that reached only as far as the shoulders. This 'periwig' was made of real hair and he wore it powdered.

Almost as important as the finery worn on his back, and those of his servants, was the provision of new saddles. Here again large sums of money were laid out. Thomas Coke had a new saddle for himself in 'Rich Red Velvet Embroyder'd' cost £66, another in blue Genoa velvet with gold lace and a fringe, and for his bride a side saddle with embroidered green velvet cost £69. The upper servants and livery servants were also given saddles. The saddle for the Gentleman of the Horse came with saddle cloth, 'housing' and embroidered pistol cases. A new chariot had been purchased and fitted out lined with scarlet with a set of harness 'compleat for six horses' costing £179.

Mr Hooks the bit-maker was paid 4gns and Mr Hunton £4. 3. 6d. for two postillions' saddles, watering saddles and tail cases. [13] The purchase and giving of saddles was symbolic. Little or no riding took place on the actual day of the wedding, most of the participants walked to the church and back; but the giving of saddles represented Coke's new position of active management and guidance of affairs, and for the servants a readiness to work. There are many figurative sayings associated with this custom such as 'being in the saddle'.

The expenses did not stop with outfits and saddles; a costly though less visible part was the payment of servants vails – for on the occasion of a wedding servants collected vails on an exceptional scale. Previously, probably on his first visit to Hothfield, Coke had given Thanet's servants £31 to be shared amongst them; there were twenty-three of them, but now these amounts were increased considerably. Coke made a gift of 20gns to his bride's 'Woman' (lady's maid) Mrs Baker and to her chambermaid 6gns. He gave 10gns to Lord Thanet's housekeeper, 10gns to Thanet's steward and so on. In all he doled out £134 to his father-in-law's servants. Next were amounts given to the servants of those present at the wedding, his guardian Sir Edward Coke and his grandfather Sir John Newton (Mr Heydon the butler and two footmen) and to his grandmother Lady Anne Walpole for her servants. She had brought with her Tobias Quacco, probably 'a black', who received 2gns, and the same amount was given to a Mr Birch, to her footman, coachman and postillion. Next were the servants of his cousin and guardian Mr John Coke, and those of Mr Lamb the lawyer, plus Mr Lamb's nephew 2gns and to Mr Humphrey Smith's man 2gns. The list continues with the five musicians, of whom at least two were servants. One was Sir Edward's valet de chambre Ab.Thomas, the other a Mr Vincent in the employ of the Earl of Thanet. They each received either 3gns or 5gns. The Parson was given 5gns, his clerk 2gns, the poor of the parish 10gns and the bell-ringers 5gns. A passing poor man was given 5gns; this was thought to be lucky.

The servants at Lees Court, where Coke stayed for the days immediately before the wedding, the home of his about to be brother-in-law Lord Sondes, received 4gns and Coke gave his younger brother Bobby £5 to give to the Hothfield servants. The total number of servants who benefited from Coke on the occasion of his marriage was seventy-eight and the cost to him in vails came to £216.

Further it must be assumed that the servants received vails not only from Coke, but also from most of people present at the wedding, making it an extremely lucrative celebration.

Those present were Mr Robert Coke, that is the youngest brother Bobby to whom Coke gave a diamond ring and a new suit of clothes costing £105; the three surviving guardians, Sir Edward Coke, Mr John Coke and Sir John Newton; Mr Michael Newton (Uncle Mick) and Lady Anne Walpole on Coke's side; and Lord Thanet and Lord and Lady Sondes on Lady Margaret's. Coke's brother Edward was still in France with Dr Ferrari and neither of his sisters were present. By 1718 both were married, Anne to Philip Roberts living at Ampthill in Bedfordshire and Cary to a Yorkshire man, Sir Marmaduke Wyvill. Coke's great-grandfather the Duke of Leeds had died while Coke was abroad, as had his fourth guardian Sir Charles Bertie. However, Dr Hobart his Tour governor did attend, for the cost of his journey from Hothfield to London is recorded in the accounts. The number of family and guests was nine, plus Lamb the lawyer.

The day began with a wedding breakfast attended by all the family. Afterwards Lord Thanet, with Lady Margaret dressed in silver and white, led the party the short distance from the house to the church, walking through a line of tenants and groups of servants in their liveries. The servants then squashed into the tiny church behind the family group. Once the religious ceremony was concluded and the young couple were bound in matrimony, they returned to the house where the cake was cut. Tradition had it that the bride cut the first slice to ensure fertility, and that some of the cake was cut into small slivers and passed through the wedding ring, 'for the dreaming Emolument of many spinsters and batchelors'. These pieces were later put into paper and sealed up ready to be distributed. [14] The custom of sending morsels of wedding cake to friends of the young couple was followed at Hothfield, for an entry in the accounts records Mr Casey doing precisely that, a tradition that has lasted to the present day. On receipt of the gift many young people slept with it under their pillows hoping to dream of their future spouse. Another tradition that may have been followed at Hothfield was the handing of a silver cup of sack among the guests. The custom of a single cup being shared by those present went back to pre-Reformation days when wine was drunk at the end of the church service, often with a sprig of rosemary, flower of love and constancy, dipped in it. [15]

Next the party would have retired to dress for the Wedding Supper. This feast, for which Thomas Coke would have changed into his second silk suit, was likely to have been accompanied by music and followed by dancing. As one writer described a Coke wedding some years later: 'coffee and cards as usual', the servants also danced 'even to the Laundry in the Yard'. [16] At the wedding of his eldest daughter in 1709 Lord Thanet had hired Mr Patrick 'the franch cooke' to cook a 'weden supper' and 'the dinner the next day 24gns'. [17]

Rather than take a honeymoon it was the custom for newly-weds to pay visits by way of introducing the new family. Three weeks after their marriage the Cokes took a break at the fashionable spa of Tunbridge Wells where Coke (as Thomas Coke should now be named) played at cards and lost 5gns. He spent another 7gns on 'Gold Toys'. These were not for children, but were small costly items such as snuff boxes and pincushions. From Tunbridge Wells they went to Lord and Lady Fairfax at Leeds Castle and then visited Sir Robert Furnese before returning to Hothfield.

In mid-August they set off for London, entering that city to the sound of Drummers of the 3rd Regiment of Foot. Music was played in their honour on a kettle drum, six trumpets and a hautbois, plus the parish music of St Giles in the Fields, a fine old racket, somewhat more impressive than the mere ringing of church bells. Their destination was Thanet House in Great Russell Street, built in 1686 by Lady Margaret's father on land leased from the Bedford estate. While retaining the use of some rooms for himself, Lord Thanet made over the main part to his new son-in-law.

In 1718 Great Russell Street was still semi-rural as the land to the north was kept open by express purpose. Known as Southampton Fields, where cows grazed, it was also used for recreation and it appears that anyone was at liberty to walk there. This open aspect was attractive but made the houses backing onto it somewhat vulnerable to intruders. Thanet House was on the north side and like its neighbours, the grandiose houses of Bedford and Montague, looked out over fields towards Hampstead. [18] More modest in style, and more modern than they were, Thanet House was not set back with

a courtyard in front but opened directly on to the pavement. The garden
was a hundred and fifty feet deep but had no coach house or stabling. Great
Russell Street was a fashionable address warmly approved of by Strype who
wrote in 1720 for Stow's Survey of London that he regarded it as 'handsome,
large and well built,' consequently 'attracting the best class of inhabitants'. [19]
Thomas and Lady Margaret were to use it as their London base throughout
their married life. Another neighbour with a house on the south side was
Sir Hans Sloane, the foremost physician of his day and a famous collector of
antiquities which were later to form the basis of the British Museum.

Resident in Thanet House and waiting to welcome the bridal party were
four of Lord Thanet's servants, William Purden the butler and his wife, a
housemaid Sarah Howard and 'old John'. This first visit was brief, just seventeen days. Mr Farr, a cook, was engaged for precisely that length of time and
a house porter for twenty days; there appears to have been plenty to keep
the porter busy, opening the front door and keeping count of the comings
and goings. With friends and relations to entertain, £27 was spent on food
in the first week and £25 in the second, whereas in the future the average
would be closer to £18. Edmund Jarrett, who from 18th August was once
again doubling as accountant, recorded a bill for the purchase of three dozen
pewter plates, dishes, spoons and glasses and another for two dozen knives
and forks. The purchase of pewter would have served them adequately, for
the elite were quite used to eating off it. Pewter was not the dull grey stuff
generally seen today, but kept highly polished and at first glance indistinguishable from silver plate. China was still too rare for everyday use, earthenware
too clumsy and a set of silver plate had not yet been purchased by Coke.
Only the discerning might notice the difference as Lady Margaret's cousin
the Countess of Nottingham knew, writing to her husband in November
1718 'I hope you have your plate out and do not put the Ladys to eat upon
pewter'. [20] Below stairs pewter was not so popular, for it took many hours
of 'scowering' to keep it bright and shiny.

As for food, as Coke may have already found out, there were enough
cosmopolitan shops in London to meet any taste he might wish for after his
long time abroad; for during his formative years as a hungry adolescent he
would have eaten mainly Italian (in a largely pre-tomato age) and French
food. Fortunately for him almost everything he had enjoyed eating on the
continent was obtainable in London. Mr Pastacaldi and Mr Lucera were just
two of many shopkeepers whose stock came from Italy.

The time spent in London provided a brief glimpse into their future lives for the young couple, a taste of independence and living in a house with their own servants, for they had with them Mrs Baker, Lady Margaret's woman, and Jenny her chambermaid, three footmen, a coachman, a postillion, two grooms and a helper. Their coach and horses were lodged at the Blue Boar Yard at the east end of Great Russell Street where the outside servants, coachman, postillion and grooms slept in rooms above the stables.

Coke found time during those seventeen days to look over Thanet House and immediately executed his first commission. He paid the leading architect James Gibb three guineas for the design of a new staircase in a hall and a room to be added to the east end of the house, and asked for the work to begin at once. [21] The list of improvements that could and should be made to the house was a long one; in effect it was to be totally refurbished. In the kitchen area it was noted by Edward Smith that the water pipes needed forcing, which tells us that Thanet House was connected to the New River Water and later in the accounts there are many bills for this amenity. The New River was a man-made course which had supplied London with fresh water from Hertfordshire since 1613, and still does. An incredible feat of engineering for the times, the river terminated at Islington from where the water was distributed through wooden pipes to houses, which would otherwise have had to rely on wells or water carriers for their supply. New River Water was not fit, nor intended, for drinking, but it served for cooking, cleaning and washing and was free from the worst forms of pollution.

Then on 3rd September Coke and Lady Margaret, together with their entourage, left London for a tour, ending at Longford in Derbyshire where they were to stay until the following February, rather longer than they had intended. The servants who accompanied them were Edward Jarrett, the lady's and chambermaids, the three footmen, Abraham Blaumer, Andrew Griffiths and another unnamed, the coachman Francis Riggs, John Large postillion, Robert Webster groom and Robert Goodacre helper.

Mr Casey, into whose care the younger Coke boys had been delivered in 1707, was now appointed chief accountant in London. He moved into Thanet House to oversee the building works and keep the household accounts. By 1718 Mr Casey was a widower and the youngest of his charges, Bobby Coke, was fourteen and had followed his brothers to Mr Ellis' school in Isleworth. From this September day until his death in January 1723 four years later Casey kept a careful note of all that was spent on and in the London house.

The first entry was for ten shillings 'Given to the Poor at the Door the Day my Master went out of Town'. [22]

Thanet House, which the earl had loaned to Coke, was considered to be the prototype of a modern town house. Built on five floors it contained thirty-three rooms, including closets, kitchen and laundry. The rooms are recorded in an inventory written in her own hand by Lady Margaret in 1760 after the death of her husband. Naturally some changes must have taken place in the intervening years, but are likely to have been mainly decorative rather than structural. On the ground floor were the three principal rooms, dining, drawing and library, all lavishly furnished and containing many paintings mainly Italian. It was accepted that the best works of art should be displayed in a London house, not in the country and in the early years of their marriage this included the large set of silverware that Coke purchased. There was also a small dining parlour for use by the family when not entertaining. Being in the modern style the house had no great hall where the entire 'Family' ate together, but the servants had their own eating room large enough to accommodate all the household staff plus any visitors, whether tradesmen or the servants of visiting guests. Here the diners sat on benches at a communal table, it was not luxurious though it did have a fireplace. The cook's bedroom, with two beds in it, was also on the ground floor near the kitchen, everyone else slept upstairs.

On the first floor was a second, smaller library lined with bookshelves, a pair of steps and a globe. In earlier times libraries were almost always to be found upstairs; they were seen as rooms for private, even devotional use. A downstairs library, used as a public reception room as in Thanet House, was a new fashion. Between the main bedroom, where the master and mistress slept, and Lady Margaret's dressing room was one of seven closets in the house. A closet could vary from a largish room with a window and fireplace, armchairs and a desk such as in this one, to a semi-store room packed with chests of drawers, bookcases and cupboards. The closets in Thanet House are best described as spaces or small rooms between the larger rooms, and were found mainly on the upper floors. There were three further bedrooms on this floor for the use of family members and guests. The remaining rooms were for the servants, the valet de chambre and the house steward.

The footmen and maids all had bedrooms on the top floor. The housekeeper and steward's rooms were at the top of the back stairs, near to the butler's room. A back stairs was another newish invention, allowing servants to move between the floors of a house without being seen or heard. The servants bedrooms were well furnished. All had feather beds, a bolster, pillow, three blankets and a quilt. The valet and the steward each had a fireplace in their rooms, curtains around the bed and window curtains. It was a mark of wealth to have window curtains at this date when cloth of all kinds was expensive. Most people made do with wooden shutters. However, window curtains were not standard for all; the housekeeper had a stove in her bedroom and checked cotton curtains around her bed but none at the window and not all the bedrooms had fireplaces. Of the two maids' rooms, one had a fireplace and the other did not, and neither had window curtains. The footmen's room had no fireplace. One of the bedrooms, which had a bed with blue and yellow damask 'furniture' (curtains and valence etc.), would have been for Lady Margaret's woman. Her bed had four blankets and two mattresses, and two carpets (rugs) on the floor. The chambermaid had a more modest room with blue harrateen 'furniture', matching window curtains and some art work, four paintings and 'a Head in Plaister'. Harrateen was a stiff linen fabric imitating damask, very often used for bed hangings.

Outside, the garden was too small to allow an orchard or even a vegetable plot. However, there was a salting tub in the back yard and another in the kitchen with a lid, which suggests that meat was brought from Norfolk to be salted in London. Another part of the yard or garden was given up for a poultry run. Some members of the elite like the Duke of Bedford next door to Thanet House and Lady Margaret's sister Lady Salisbury, had estates near enough to London to allow perishable goods such as butter and vegetables to be sent from the country, but Norfolk was too distant. Venison and game and sometimes pork came from Norfolk and ale brewed at Holkham but little else.

As soon as Coke and Lady Margaret left for their tour to Derbyshire in September 1718, the builders moved in to begin work on the new extension. Mr Gibb the architect was paid £21 for overseeing this, giving directions and inspecting the finished results. The dust and upheaval may be imagined; straw was laid to catch the worst of the dirt. While the building work was in progress and the scaffolding in place, leaving walls and interiors exposed, Casey paid three men William Edwin, Thomas Edrington and Samuel Grimston a shilling each to watch the house at night. London in the eighteenth century was prey to opportunistic crime, theft or assault, just as it is today. Security was at all times a priority and one of Casey's first purchases was a strong padlock for the charcoal hole door. In fact all the doors in the house, as well as all cupboards and chests, had locks that worked and were used. As a further precaution, should an intruder manage to break in and enter the house, Casey had a blunderbuss ready and a pair of pistols kept in an anti-chamber next to the hall and, for more immediate use, a large sword by the front door.

It seems that problems with builders have changed little over the years for after some weeks Casey felt moved to give them vails of ten shillings: 'To the Joyners at their putting up the Stairs and Beausett [sic beaufet or sideboard] and *to Encourage their going forward with their work*'. [23]

As soon as that work was finished and the stone-cutter's men had earned an extra sixpence for cleaning the hall, waggon-loads of goods began to arrive, ninety-four tons from Hothfield and almost the same again from Longford. Unfortunately Casey did not record what these goods were; it was enough to know how much they weighed and he paid the carriers accordingly. New furniture was bought from London makers and one or two older pieces from Sir John Newton's house in Soho Square. Mr Wood the upholsterer furnished the main rooms in the house and provided curtains and covers for windows, beds and 'other'. He acted as an interior designer. £70 worth of new kitchen utensils were ordered and delivered, £127 worth of new glasses and chandeliers, as well as more new pewter and some china. Even more important, statues and other works of art began to arrive from the Custom House, the first fruits of the Grand Tour. Mr Vanstreton was hired to clean the paintings. Twenty-seven chimneys were swept and the house cleaned.

While the building and refurbishment work was going on, the only resident servants in Thanet House were the ancient butler Mr Purden and his wife; Mrs Purden was paid for sewing linen, perhaps part of the consignments from Derbyshire and Kent. 'Old John' who looked after the dogs, and two house-maids, Sarah Howard and Sarah Young, struggled with the dust and dirt. More help was needed to get the house into shape and Casey records taking on a number of charwomen and washerwomen who were each paid two shillings and three pence a day. Rather a generous amount, it was more usual to pay just a shilling. There was a temporary crisis in December when the housemaid Sarah Young caught the smallpox and was sent away to be cared for by Nurse Richardson. Her co-worker Sarah Howard may have taken fright at this for she left at the end of the month. After three weeks of illness and a further three of convalescence Sarah Young returned; no deduction was made in her pay dur-ing her six-week absence and all her medical expenses were paid for, it being the custom among the elite to care for servants when ill (see next chapter).

In January 1719 several new servants arrived. With the young master and mistress in distant Derbyshire it is not known who was in overall charge of choosing them, but it would seem to have been a combined effort by Coke's grandfather Sir John Newton, Lady Margaret's father the Earl of Thanet and the Countess of Salisbury, Lady Margaret's eldest sister. The first list of servants wages was recorded two months later on 25th March, Lady Day. This included of course the servants already in Coke's employ, Smith the accountant at Holkham, Abraham Blaumer and Andrew Griffiths footmen, as well as the coachman, postillion etc. Andrew Griffiths had already been hired in December 1717 while Thomas Coke was still abroad, and nothing is known about his origins though he may have been related to Mrs Griffiths, a milliner employed by the Coke family earlier in the century. Griffiths was to rise rapidly within the household; by 1720 he was butler and by 1726 accountant. In March 1719 Edward Jarrett received the accumulated wages due to him for his time on the Grand Tour a total of seven years which came to £140. In future his annual wage was to be £20 and he was to remain as accountant for a further two years in tandem with Mr Casey. Lady Margaret had her two maids with her, but who were these other new servants and where did they come from?

At least two came from Hatfield, William Shadbolt and James Davies both footmen who arrived at Thanet House on the same day, 1st March. Shadbolt had been footboy, later footman, in Lord Salisbury's service from 1711. The custom was to educate footboys, school in the mornings and household duties in the afternoon and this is confirmed in the Hatfield accounts where there are entries for Shadbolt's copy book and pens. Lady Margaret may even have remembered young Shadbolt as one of the Hatfield party who visited Hothfield. Davies is also a name which appears in the servants lists at Hatfield where a Henry Davies is described as Lord Salisbury's most faithful servant, John Davies was another, Prudence Davies kept the accounts for a brief period from 1712-1713 and one of Lady Salisbury's women was Hannah Davies. [24] Thus the Cokes began their married lives with three footmen each. Thomas's were Blaumer, Griffiths and William Holland promoted from groom, while Lady Margaret's came from her side of the family, Shadbolt, Davies and John Marson. The latter was from Kent where a James Marson was footman to Lord Thanet. To have three footmen each was extravagant, but not exceptional. [25]

William Tomley was engaged as house porter in mid–February 1719. Originally from Wales he had lived in London most of his life and was related to Alice Tomley a housemaid employed by Coke's parents and to Mrs Tomley from whom the family purchased stockings. Mr Casey continued as accountant in London and was paid an additional £21 for his trouble in overseeing the refurbishment of the house. Mr Purden the old butler was retired and his name does not appear in the wages list, although Coke paid his board wages. A cook named William Stephenson was engaged on 1st March at £30 a year, origins unknown. He stayed for nine months.

Mrs Johnson the housekeeper took up her post in January 1719 and it is probable that she too came from Kent, where Lord Thanet's valet de chambre was a William Johnson and Elizabeth Johnson one of his laundry maids. [26] But equally she may have been a Longford lass, for the name Johnson often appears in the registers there. Whichever was the case, or neither, it was customary for the housekeeper to have a maid of her own, in this instance Sarah Young, she who had had the smallpox and was already at Thanet House. Two new housemaids were engaged, Elizabeth Lish in January and Mary Strain in February; both came from Kent, as did Anne Baker the cook maid, but nothing is known about the origins of the two laundry maids taken on at this time, Jane Love and Mary George.

The coachman Francis Riggs, postillion John Large, grooms Robert Webster and John Walker were all from Norfolk. At Holkham there were a further six stablemen: Thomas Johnson farrier, William Pickford huntsman, Stephen Man dog boy, Robert Goodacre and John Wright helpers, and John Redfern stable boy. Jean-Baptiste from the Grand Tour appears in the list of the stable workers though his exact post is not recorded. Finally among the male servants and about to re-enter Coke's employ was Abraham Thomas. Since 1715 and his return to England from the Grand Tour, Ab. Thomas had been back in Derbyshire with Sir Edward Coke, but in February 1719 he left Longford to return to London with Thomas Coke, as his valet, replacing Jarrett.

Most servants would hope to stay for at least a year, the minimum time allowed for them to gain a 'settlement', which would entitle them to poor relief in the parish in which they served should they find themselves without work. [27] This first set was carefully selected, half being recruited from the groom's side and half from the bride's, nevertheless a mix that had potential for discord and competitiveness amongst them, a risk in all households. The amount they were paid in wages was unremarkable, virtually identical to the servants employed by the Duke of Montagu. Incidentally the three houses along Great Russell Street, Bedford, Montagu and Thanet all shared the same head gardener, Samuel Peniston, who lived round the corner at no. 3

King Street. A gardener of this sort was more of a designer and supervisor of labourers than one who did much physical labour himself. Samuel may have been related to Peniston Lamb the Earl of Thanet's lawyer. [28]

Other comparable households, insomuch as their surviving documents allow a reasonable comparison between the years 1719 and 1721, were the Duke of Richmond's whose servants were paid slightly less than Coke's, and the Duke of Chandos' who were paid the same. A list of wages for Lord Townshend's household of twenty-five servants in 1716 (a total that excluded stablemen), records marginally lower wages, his footmen and house porter were paid £6 per annum each, against Coke's who received £8 to £10, though the cook and the housekeeper were paid the same, £30 and £10 respectively. [29] Each of these households was similar in size and moved between the country and town. Servants employed in gentry families, as opposed to peerage households, were paid considerably less. Erasmus Earle of Heydon, a friend and Norfolk neighbour of Coke's, paid his footman John Barfield just £4 a year in 1718, but allowed him a further £1 for washing. [30] No comparison can be completely accurate, as different households were subject to different accounting methods. Coke's male servants had their liveries, including shoes and boots, paid for on top of their wages, while the Duke of Montagu usually included allowances for boots *within* the wages and sometimes beer money as well. Nor can servants wages be seen as a final total of their earnings due to the custom of vails. In some households the sums given by visitors in exchange for good treatment were pooled and divided among the whole staff. In others individual servants were allowed to keep whatever was given to them, thus a footman could soon pocket an amount far in excess of what a laundry maid might receive, though their basic pay was the same.

When leaving either the town or country house it was necessary for one or two servants to stay behind and look after it, but the idea that a complete set of servants inhabited each house owned is erroneous. Even the richest and most lavish members of the peerage group, the Dukes of Chandos and Newcastle, did not do this. It would have been far too expensive, wasteful and the numbers far too difficult to control.

Unlike many of his contemporaries, Coke does not appear to have had any black servants at this date. Black servants pose a problem, for by the nature of their position as slaves they would not appear in the list of wages. References to them must be looked for elsewhere, under clothing or travel

The house in Great Russell Street, London which Thomas Coke inherited from his father-in-law the Earl of Thanet. It was in this house that the Cokes' first household family was assembled at the time of Coke's marriage.

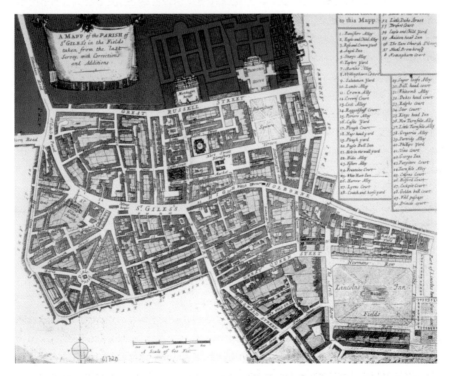

Map of London c.1720 showing Great Russell Street and its surroundings.

Lady Margaret with her son
Edward shortly after she
inherited her title of Baroness
Clifford. Edward was the only
one of the Cokes' children to
survive infancy.

Holkham Hall much as it would have appeared in the eighteenth century when
the majority of visitors approached from the south. The terraced gardens by
Nesfield are a nineteenth century creation.

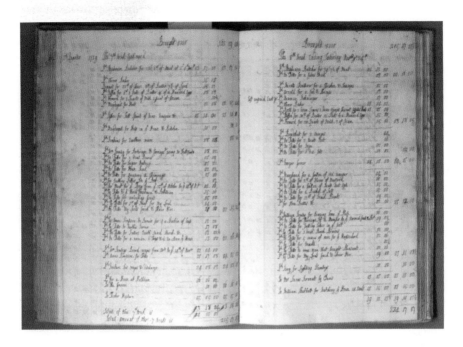

Lady Margaret's household account book for November 1739. The left hand page shows that the 'family' had just arrived in London. It includes an entry for board wages for the London servants and the discharge of Monsieur Faitcoeur the roasting cook who had travelled up from Holkham with the family. He had been employed since January.

The right hand page, the week ending Saturday 24th November lists food bought, William Tomley, the house porter, fetching home the plate (silver) from the bank and the purchase of a dozen birch brooms 2s. There is also an entry for William Shadbolt, the ex-footman, who was paid £1. 15s. for watching the London house while the Cokes had been in the country a period of fourteen weeks.

The ice house above the lake to the east of the mansion. In winter labourers cut slabs of ice from the waters of the shallow lake. The ice house was partially subterranean and used to store and preserve food, even ice cream, at least for a few hours. Eighteenth century ice cream was made in the morning and eaten later the same day, but meat, butter and other foods were stored for far longer.

A view of Kitchen Wing taken from the kitchen courtyard. The advantage of a kitchen in its own wing was that no noise or worse, cooking smells, would waft their way into the main rooms. A separate wing was considered a great improvement on a basement kitchen from where aromas inevitably rose filling the house, especially in an age when open roasting on the spit was almost a daily occurrence.

A servants staircase, one of the many corridors in the hall and a row of bells dating from the 1750s with the name of the room written beneath each one.

Thomas Coke 1697-1759 a portrait by Andrea Casali in 1744 the year he was made Earl of Leicester.

Lady Margaret 1700-1775 also by Andrea Casali in 1744. Casali portrays her in a rather simpering pose, an empty handed aristocrat, far removed from the capable manageress and dutiful employer we know her to have been.

expenses. Black page boys were a fashionable accessory but there is no evidence to support the presence of one at this time. There had been a John Carlo in the mid-seventeenth century where an entry reads: 'stockings for ye Black Boy' and in 1700 the Duke of Leeds 'owned' a boy named Caeser. [31]

Counting the stable workers and Lady Margaret's two maids, the total of this first household of servants was thirty-five. All these souls now became Coke's responsibility, is 'Family' for whom he must provide. They were remarkable insomuch as the place of origin of most can be traced with some degree of accuracy. Unfortunately this was not to last, for despite all good intentions the turnover was considerable and it is usually not possible to discover the origins of their replacements. If unable to find a servant within the family network, it was considered that servants hired in London were preferable to country ones, more likely to be conversant with the tastes and habits of the elite and less likely to run away home in times of stress. Equally, when the family left town and took up residence at their country seats it was better to have servants with no local connections who would not be tempted to run home, gossip about their employers in the locality or pilfer food to pass on to their relations.

At the time of hiring, servants were told about their duties and also that, in times of need, they might be asked to perform tasks which they 'must not refuse, tho' it may not be the particular business for which they were hired'. [32] They were expected to be flexible and to try their hand at all manner of different tasks, anything from 'airing' their masters' beds by sleeping in them, to looking after the dogs, helping with the harvest, or lending a hand in the laundry and kitchen. This could, and sometimes did, lead to promotion or even a complete change of role, as will be seen. It is no exaggeration to say that a co-operative attitude was desirable if servants wished to feel comfortable belonging to the greater 'Family'. At this period there was far less demarcation between their duties than there would be in the nineteenth century, although that did not stop many complaining. General rules for behaviour, especially at meal times, were often written up on a board (this is before the days of universal printing) and hung in the servants hall. One list of early eighteenth-century rules made it clear that boots and shoes were not to be cleaned on the dining table, if they were the culprit would be fined. Once the cloth was laid and the meal was about to be consumed it was a finable offence to swear or behave indecently and no male servant was to sit down to dinner with his jacket on. [33]

Many wrote down the duties they expected their servants to perform, the larger the household the more the need for this.

Now with the servants engaged and ready to 'do their duty' we can return to the spring of 1719 and making the house ready. The primary evidence we have for standards of cleanliness at this date is that recorded by visiting foreigners. Of these, the best known and more frequently quoted is the Swiss traveller César de Saussure who wrote in the 1720s that the English were: ' ... not slaves to cleanliness, like the Dutch, still they are remarkable for this virtue. Not a week passes by but well-kept houses are washed twice in seven days, and that from top to bottom: and even every morning most kitchens, staircase and entrance are scrubbed. All furniture, and especially kitchen utensils are kept with the greatest cleanliness. Even the large hammers and locks on the door are rubbed and shine brightly'. [34]

Yet, as Caroline Davidson rightly says in her book *A Women's Work is never Done,* this cleanliness was largely superficial. 'Bed-bugs, which thrive on filth, were ubiquitous'. [35] This was certainly true of London where Mr Southall the bugman was paid a guinea a year for keeping Thanet House clear of not only bugs, but moths in the hangings and various other infestations. He worked with his wife, and was later succeeded by Mr Bridges who charged two guineas. Cats are never mentioned in the accounts, though they were needed; rat traps were set near the kitchen and Mr Casey bought a couple of 'mouse-traps to set amongst the Books'.

An integral part of cleaning, as de Saussure noted, was washing the house. Being connected to the water supplied by the New River Water Company, as Thanet House was, allowed the washing of clothes, dishes and stone floors without too many hiccups. But when it came to washing the walls, ceilings and cornices a mixture of beer and sand was used. Casey notes buying beer 'to wash the Wainscot'. This entry tells us that the house had wainscoting, that is it was panelled. Today we might be more inclined to polish the wainscoting, or merely dust it, but 'washing' suggests it may have been painted, as would have been the fashion in the seventeenth-century. Had the wainscot been polished then Casey would have used the word 'rubbing'. The beer for cleaning was poured into buckets, fine 'Calais' sand was added and 'scowering', that favourite eighteenth century word so often used for cleaning, ensued. The wainscot was probably very dirty for Casey records bringing in a man to assist in scowering it, possibly from Montagu House next door where the Duke employed male cleaners known as 'rubbers'. [36] The cost of the beer, sand and brooms used by this man came to 1s. 1d. and his wages 2s.

In London, sand was bought by the bushel or cart load and came in two grades, Calais sand for cleaning the house and a finer variety, sometimes referred to as 'silver sand', for scowering pewter. A cart-load of house sand cost 3s. in 1719, and silver 4s. Even in Norfolk, despite the proximity of the sandy beach at Holkham, sand to clean the house and pewter was bought in from elsewhere.

Sand was employed to dry-rub wooden floors as this preserved the colour of the boards better than washing them with soap, which left a white appearance. [37] Sand mixed with Fuller's earth, known since at least the sixteenth century, was said to be the most effective cleaning agent. John Gay in the *Beggar's Opera* of 1727 referred to it with some irony claiming there was not a spot or a stain 'but what it [Fuller's earth] can take out'. [38] In some houses the more heavily used areas were kept sanded all the time; sand was liberally strewn to soak up grease and dirt, as well as any mud coming in from outside. At Thanet House this would have been at the tradesmen's entrance. In the main parts of the house sand was sprinkled through a sieve only prior to sweeping and was generally wetted or dampened to better absorb the dust and dirt. Occasionally ashes from the previous day's fires were added or even used as a replacement; they too needed to be sieved. Floors treated this way were left remarkably free of stains thanks to the sand's absorbent and abrasive action which made the scrubbing, with cold water, much easier than it would have been otherwise. [39]

Smoke from fireplaces and the large number of candles used, especially when entertaining, ensured the need for frequent cleaning. When beer was not employed vinegar and water were the main components to remove dirt from almost all surfaces. Lemon juice would have worked just as well, and smelt nicer, but lemons were expensive. Potatoes, another natural cleaning agent, were largely unknown in 1719, at least for this purpose. The housemaids were assisted by the footmen when ladders were needed for reaching the cornices. Climbing up ladders with buckets and cloths was a hazardous affair and it is surprising that no accidents or broken limbs feature in the accounts. Another cleaning agent was 'scowring oyl,' two quarts costing 3s. It is not known precisely what this was, but may have been linseed or some other vegetable-based oil used to clean leather. Black lead was purchased to clean the stoves and rotten stone for polishing copper and brassware. Rotten stone was a decomposed siliceous limestone, fine and soft in texture and particularly effective. [40]

The price of household cleaning utensils was relatively high; a list of goods purchased in London, show that a pail cost 2s., a mop 1s., a house broom 1s. 6d., a rubbing brush 1s. 3d., a dust basket and mop 2s. 2d., a scrubbing brush 1s., a hair broom 10d., a long sided brush 1s. 6d., a hearth broom and a dust shovel a 1s. each. The ladder needed by the housemaids to reach the cornices, mirrors and overmantles 4s. [41] Generally brushes were home-made but if fitted with wooden handles, rather than gathered and tied, then these were purchased from a wood turner, e.g. Mr Watkiss, turner, was paid 17s. for mops, brooms and brushes in 1740.

A high proportion of the floors at Thanet House, and Holkham, had some kind of covering. The main rooms may have had a carpet, though not a fitted one, or an oil cloth fixed to the floor and painted to look like a carpet. In other parts of the house straw matting was used, which was cheap and easily replaced when worn out. At Hatfield Lady Margaret's sister paid 14s. 6d. for fifty-eight yards of matting for a staircase and 12s. for a large mat thirty-six yards long for the pantry. [42]

The servants worked hard to get the house ready by February, for Coke and his wife were impatient to return. 'My house in town has taken much more time in altering than I had expected' Thomas Coke wrote in the January, [43] yet it was still only nine months since he had returned from abroad. But married and with Thanet House enlarged and improved, freshly decorated, every nook and cranny 'scowered', resplendent with fashionable furniture and fittings, art treasures and books arriving daily from abroad, and a line of servants to greet him, he was eager for his new life to begin.

NOTES

1. HA A/7

2. Quoted in *The Complete Peerage: Hist. MSS. Com.* Egmont Diary vol.i, pp.157-58 and Macky (*Characters* p.80) and Swift.

3. TNA Prob 11/635 and Kentish Studies ref: U 455 383 A/2.

4. Kentish Studies U 455 383 A/2.

5. See the *Diaries of Lady Anne Clifford* ed. by D.J.H. Clifford, Alan Sutton Gloucs. 1990 p. xii in which he states that the first Book of Record is known as part of the

Hothfield manuscripts, but on the following page says there is a question mark over the whereabouts of a large part of her diaries, 'it has been said' that the 6th Earl may have destroyed them but there is no hard evidence that he did.

6. The schools at Hothfield in Kent, Hartfield in Sussex, Skipton in West Yorkshire and Appleby in Westmoreland, are listed in the 1842 *Digest of Schools and Charities for Education*, a list of Non-classical Schools endowed or re-endowed during the eighteenth-century. M.G. Jones, *The Charity School Movement* London 1964, p.353.

7. TNA Prob 11/635.

8. R.A.C. Parker *Coke of Norfolk* Oxford 1975 p.12 and HA MS 472 Marriage settlement

9. Bedford and Luton Archives L 30/8/62

10. C. Willett Cunnington and Phillis Cunnington *Handbook of English Costume in the 18th Century* London 1957 p.95.

11. Quoted by Paul Langford *A Polite and Commercial People, England 1727-1783* OUP paperback 1992 p.66. His footnote for this Madame Van Muyden ed. *A Foreign View of England in the Reign of George I and George II: The Letters of Monsieur César de Saussure to his Family*, London, 1902 p.212.

12. J. Jean Hecht, *The Domestic Servant in Eighteenth Century England* London 1956 p.119.

13. Watering saddles – these were put on horses when they were taken down to drink at the river, traditionally used by cavalry regiments. A lighter type of saddle.

14. Christina Hole *English Tradition*, London 1940 p.21.

15. Christina Hole *English Home Life,* London 1947 p.61.

16. Berkshire Record Office D/EAH acc 6158.54, diary of the Rev'd. Abdy 1769.

17. Kentish Studies U 455 383 A/2

18. Gladys Scott-Thomson, *The Russells in Bloomsbury* London 1940 p.46. The lease on the house and land inherited by Thomas Coke in 1718 had been renewed at Michaelmas 1693 for a further sixty-two years. *LCC Survey of London* Vol V. Part II, St Giles in the Fields, London 1914 p.147.

19. Scott-Thomson p.173.

20. Leicestershire Record Office DG7/Bundle 25.

21. James Gibb [1682-1754] was an important Scottish architect, a friend and disciple of Wren and influential in spreading the Palladian style.

22. HA A/5.

23. HA A/5 and A/6

24. Hatfield Archives Accounts 132/19 no 52 Henry Davis 'my Lord Salisbury's faithful servant', and John Davis, Prudence Davis bill no. 454 and Hannah Davis bill no. 421.

25. Kentish Studies U 455 383 A/2 – as to the number of footmen many households had three each for the Master and Mistress at this date vizt the Earl and Countess of Nottingham Leicestershire RO DG7/1/119 book of wages 1683-1722, the Duke of Chandos Huntingdon Library, Stowe MSS ST44, Household Regulations for

Cannons 1721, and Coke's neighbour in Great Russell Street the Duke of Montagu, Northampton RO Mr Marchant's Accounts Box 2 no. 2, to Lady Day 1721.

26. Kentish Studies 1706-12 U 455 383 A/2.

27. Tim Meldrum *Domestic Service and Gender 1660*-1750 London 2000 p.23.

28. Northampton Record Office Mr Marchant's Accounts Box 2, no 2, to Lady Day 1721. And Woburn Archives household account book for 1742.

29. West Sussex Record Office Goodwood MSS no 229, Register of Servants at London and Goodwood 1727-1780, Huntingdon Library California Stowe MS ST44, and Raynham Archives G2/4.

30. NRO MF/R0 334.

31. Lincoln Record Office YARB 16/6/2.

32. Quoted by Christopher Simon Sykes in *Private Palaces* London 1985, p. 154, the Duke of Northumberland's Rules for a Family c. 1760. Alnwick. The Duke of Northumberland's Additional MSS (1973) C/21 a.

33. Rules for Servants, a board, shown to the author by the late Bryan Hall, part of his collection at Banningham, believed to have come from Narborough Hall where the Spelman family lived.

34. Quoted by Roy Porter in *English Society in the Eighteenth Century* Penguin paperback 1990 p.221.

35. Caroline Davidson, *A Woman's Work is Never Done* London 1986 p.115.

36. Northampton Record Office — Mr Marchant's Accounts Box 2 no.2 to Lady Day 1721.

37. *The Housekeeping Book of Susanna Wharton* National Trust edition, London 2000 p.37.

38. John Gay, *The Beggar's Opera* Act One, scene IX.

39. Davidson p.122.

40. Peter Brears, *The Compleat Housekeeper* Wakefield 2000 p.27.

41. Hatfield Archives Bill no 454 paid Jan 1714.

42. Hatfield Archives Bill no 45.

43. HA F/3 f.497.

CHAPTER 4

The Daily Round, Who did What and What they Wore

For the Elite:

The daily routine in eighteenth-century houses of the elite began each morning with the maids delivering a warm liquid drink to each member of the family, and to some of the upper servants, in their bedchambers, at approximately eight o'clock. (Possibly a little earlier for the upper servants). This beverage was invariably hot chocolate. Since the mid-seventeenth century chocolate had been regarded as not only a nourishing drink, but a stimulating one, suited to early morning consumption. While the family stirred, the servants were busy. Doors were unlocked, shutters opened, curtains drawn back, fires laid and lit in the downstairs rooms, hearths swept and any remnants of the previous day's meals and other clutter tidied away. Only at nine or even ten o'clock did the family emerge from their bedchambers and take breakfast in the dining room, where tea and coffee were served with rolls and butter. Breakfast 'rowls' were made from super fine flour. In town these were purchased from a baker, Mr King round the corner in King Street, and when in the country they were baked at home with flour sent from London. Often described as French rolls they were made with milk and eggs, a type of loaf which later was known as milk bread and the rolls as bridge rolls. Occasionally breakfast parties were given. In 1748 Lady Anson, whose husband the Admiral was abroad, described one of hers 'as Magnificent as any you ever gave in any part of the Globe ... piles of cakes, rolls, muffins ... fountains of coffee, chocolate, tea ... flowing into vases of the finest Dresden, Nanquin and old White China'. Her reputation she said, as a hostess, was now above reproach. [1]

At the conclusion of breakfast the long eighteenth-century morning began, broken sometimes by a dish of oysters or a slice of cake at midday. For the master and mistress of the house mornings were spent giving orders to the servants, reading the newspaper, writing letters, visiting friends and receiving them. The accepted hour for leaving the house to make visits was eleven o'clock; equally, visitors were not expected to call before this time.

Exercise was taken during the morning. In town this generally meant riding or walking in the park; in the country it might be hunting or riding, or merely strolling in the garden. Exhibitions and libraries were visited in the mornings, and in the summer there were outings such as trips on the river. Shopping was another morning activity, either visits to the shops or tradesmen coming to the house. While the purchase and fitting of garments, stays, shoes and gowns, took place in the privacy of the home, embellishments of all sorts, both for the figure and the home, were more often bought across a counter.

If going to Court, as Thomas Coke often did, then the correct hour for this was one o'clock. The King and Queen usually appeared at two. It was not done to walk to Court, almost any form of transport was acceptable, coach, sedan chair or even horseback, just so long as the foot did not touch the ground.

Dinner was taken at four o'clock. Unless entertaining, dinner was not a lavish meal, though a number of dishes were always prepared, nor was it a prolonged affair. A family eating alone or with just one or two guests would be finished within an hour. Dinner parties on the other hand lasted far longer and the guests were expected to stay on and enjoy further entertainments, generally card games and music. Invitations to dine were delivered by footmen.

For the elite, the evening, from after dinner until ten at night, was filled by card parties and musical entertainments, amateur dramatics, with the occasional ball, or visit to the opera or theatre.

As the drinking of tea became ever more fashionable this was served in the evenings at seven o'clock and developed into an opportunity to entertain informally as little preparation or outlay was needed. Evening tea parties were less elaborate than breakfast ones, but in common with them provided opportunities for women to entertain independent of their husbands. They were considered respectable since alcohol was not served. Seven o'clock became the hour when visitors could pop in casually without the need for an invitation. Visits to the gardens at Ranelagh or Vauxhall took place in the evenings and in town theatres and operas opened their doors at five o'clock. Theatrical performances consisted of a play, followed by a farce and country songs with acrobats or other amusements and were usually over by nine.

Supper was served at ten, a lighter meal than dinner but still meat-based (eggs and bacon was a favourite), followed by prayers and bed at eleven. The eleven o'clock bed time was kept by all but the most avid party-goers; it was known that the Royal family went to bed at eleven.

The Male Servants:

The servants fitted their duties in and around their masters. Except for the liveried servants they were to keep out of sight; some of the kitchen staff never saw beyond the green baize door, and yes, baize was around in 1720. If an encounter happened between master and servant formality was all important. Prior to his knighthood in 1722 Thomas Coke was always referred to as 'My Master', and afterwards for evermore as 'His Honour'. Or as one accountant, anxious to leave nothing out, wrote in 1726, 'His Honour Master Sir Thomas Coke'. As an earl's daughter Lady Margaret's status as her Ladyship remained constant. Modes of address for the servants were also strictly adhered to, for the upper servants the prefix Mr or Mrs was always employed, though it would not be unusual for Lady Margaret to address the housekeeper as Madam. Christian names were used for footmen and men lower down scale, often shortened to be made more familiar, as for instance Francis Riggs the coachman was known as Frank. Maids were called by their surnames.

The first named Upper Servants were the secretary and accountant. Thomas Coke employed a secretary from 1723 onwards at £30 a year; his duties need little description. The first was Edward Thomas who retired in 1728 due to ill health. A copy of all letters sent was always kept, both for reference and as insurance against the unreliability of the post. Unfortunately, the accumulation of so much paper meant that at least once a year, usually in January, there was often a grand clear out with most being thrown on to the fire. [2]

Mr John Casey was the accountant in London from 1718, in tandem with Edward Jarrett who had resumed his accountant's duties and kept a book of disbursements for both London and Holkham – and when travelling with Coke. Then, following the death of Casey in early 1723, and soon afterwards the departure of Jarrett, there was a general shake-up as Humphrey Smith, the Norfolk estate steward, also left Coke's employ at this time. The result was far from simple, for until 1726 there were now three, sometimes four, different but concurrent sets of accounts recorded. However, when Mr Williams, an accountant engaged in 1722, made a sudden unexplained exit on 22nd July 1726, the very next day Andrew Griffiths, the butler, was appointed to his position and from then on a more methodical record was employed.

His was an unusual promotion; already elevated from footman to butler, it is clear that Griffiths had a business mind, greatly needed after the confusing overlaps of the previous years. He was the first to keep comprehensive accounts week by week with headings in the margins, instead of merely listing items haphazardly as his predecessors had done. He also added up the amounts spent each quarter, again under headings, with a total at the end of the year. Griffiths continued as accountant until 1733 when he disappeared, having been in Coke's service for seventeen years. [3] Who had taught him is unknown, but he set the standard pattern used for the duration of Coke's lifetime. Despite certain items being duplicated in the garden or other account books, the Holkham household accounts are a model of punctilious record-ing compared with some other great households of the era. Each page was checked and initialled by Lady Margaret and for the first year, while Griffiths was accountant, by 'me' Thomas Coke and the lawyer Peniston Lamb.

Next in order of importance came the valet, Coke's personal servant, whose duties have already been described. They related to caring for his clothes, seeing that they were clean and if necessary mended. This was an age when fashions in dress changed frequently, although the three main components of a man's suit consisting of coat, waistcoat and breeches remained constant. The changes were in the detail of the cut and embellishments, which were important to a young man like Coke who was ambitious and highly social, and needed to be correctly and fashionably attired. [4] It was vital at this stage, and even more so a few years later when he was ennobled, for his valet to be au fait with the subtle changes in dress that his new position in society demanded. The valet made regular purchases on behalf of his master, he bought many items such as gloves, stockings, ribbons, washballs, powder and combs. Washballs were made from scented soap and dissolved in water, then frothed up to use for shaving. Jarrett had been Coke's first valet and was succeeded by Ab. Thomas who ran a myriad of errands, purchasing tea and coffee, pens, paper and making several visits to the Customs House on his master's business; he even lent his master pocket money. It was necessary therefore to trust the valet both in the matter of fashion and with finances. Although Coke had a secretary, Ab. Thomas wrote many business letters on his master's behalf, dealing with such matters as the dispatch of venison as gifts, keeping George Appleyard, the Norfolk steward, abreast of Coke's travel plans and many important matters to do with the surveying of outly-ing parts of the estate. It is also clear from the small amount of surviving correspondence that both Ab. Thomas the valet and Appleyard the steward were in constant written communication with each other and with Peniston Lamb, the London lawyer.

Then came the house steward, another upper servant who did not wear livery. His duties included buying the food and household necessaries such as candles and newspapers. He paid for these in cash, keeping the relevant vouchers and bills from the various trades people which he later passed on to the accountant. Every morning when in London, and on market days in the country, the house steward set out to select and order food for the day accompanied by the housekeeper. Having first consulted with the cook, the housekeeper did the actual selection and the house steward listed each purchase in his day book. Most purchases were delivered later by the shop-keeper's apprentice or boy; very little was carried home directly, an exception in town might be a cheesecake, pastry or a particular delicacy from the confectioner's. The list of Christmas boxes confirms the delivery of goods, for in December everyone, from the glazier's apprentice to the man who brought the bills from the Opera House, received a small sum of money, a reward for their services during the year.

In London Thanet House was within walking distance of Covent Garden where vegetables, fruit and flowers were sold, but not meat. Vegetables were offered for sale by the herbwoman and were extremely cheap, even the most fashionable, asparagus. The weekly bill for vegetables often came to no more than 4s. Far higher sums were spent on fruit. During the quarter of Lady Day to Midsummer 1719, £27 was spent on fruit compared to £23 on dry groceries. Some of this fruit would have been for distilling and bottling and some to cook in tarts and pies, but a large amount was eaten fresh. Thomas Coke was especially fond of apricots.

Nearer to Great Russell Street was the Bloomsbury Market. Like Covent Garden it was also owned by the Duke of Bedford and here meat and fish were sold. Unlike Covent Garden, and despite being promoted by the Duke, Bloomsbury Market, built between Hart and Hide Streets (today Bloomsbury Way and High Holborn), did not flourish beyond the mid-century, though it was still given as an address in the parish registers of St George's Bloomsbury as late as 1812.

The house steward was responsible for all aspects of household manage-ment; it was he who sanctioned the employment of extra help when needed and paid the daily wages of the char and washerwomen. He was in charge of all lighting in the house, and it was his duty to record the number of candles used, both wax and tallow, and to know and check how many were allowed and used in each part of the house. The house steward was the last to bed and first to rise, he saw to it that the fires and candles were extinguished each evening and made sure the doors and windows were locked. In the morning it was he who opened them again and supervised lighting of the fires. His remit included a certain amount of security; he purchased 'wyer against the larder window', padlocks for the garden gate and the tea canister, and saw to it that all locks were in working order.

After the house steward came the liveried servants, the most senior of whom was the butler. Although the butler wore livery he was still an upper servant and was therefore addressed as Mr. The butler's duty was to keep the buttery and cellars clean and refuse members of the greater family entry to either of these places except on legitimate business. It must have been a temptation for the servants to drop by the butler's domain on the off chance that they might be allowed an extra swig of ale, or something stronger, as they went about their work. The butler recorded the daily consumption of wine, beer and ale and washed the bottles as they were emptied and then replenished them. Some of the wine purchased was already bottled: ('Arthur's six dozen claret'), but most came in casks which were decanted and topped up from time to time to keep them airtight. Two of the butler's wine books from this period have survived. The first shows the amount purchased and the contents of the cellar and the second which wine was drunk, when and by whom. A resumé was then entered in the general household account books. An amount of small beer and strong ale was bought in London but some came from Holkham and transported to London as needed. These were the daily drinks for all members of the servant household as water was thought to be unsafe. There was however a flourishing trade in mineral water sold by the many spas that surrounded London, for example Epsom and Islington; the Cokes preferred mineral water from Bristol.

The butler was also responsible for looking after and cleaning the plate. Thomas Coke purchased a handsome set from Paul de Lamerie in the early days of his marriage, comprising sixty plates, twenty-one dishes, dozens of knives, forks and spoons, salvers, baskets, castors, ladles, candlesticks, basons, ewers, cream dishes and more, plus two large trunks with iron bars to keep it all in, and a further box for the brushes used for cleaning it. Included were twelve spoons for the steward's table. The cost was considerable, £2,218. 5s. 1d. As mentioned in the previous chapter the plate was used only in London at this date. When the family went to the country it was stored for safe keeping in Mr Snow's bank in the city. From 1720 to 1729 Coke's butler was Mr Griffiths, promoted from footman, and from 1729 to 1750 Mr James Davies who had come from Hatfield as lady's footman to Lady Margaret in 1718.

The last, but in many ways the most important of the male upper servants was the cook, classed as an upper servant by dint of his skill and commensurate salary. He was often the highest paid of all the servants. The cook suggested menus and wrote out lists of provisions needed. In the country he may have requested what vegetables should be grown. In town he dealt with the baker and the confectioner. Prior to 1700 many large town houses did not possess an oven, but sent out their pies and cakes to be baked. Thanet House however was 'modern' and the cook needed to be skilled 'in the art of pastry'. There were generally two cooks employed and they were supplied with dimity (stout white cotton) waistcoats, aprons, neckcloths and handkerchiefs.

The next in rank was the house porter, also a liveried servant, who was responsible for opening the front door to visitors, enquiring their business and receiving their 'admittance fee' or vail. If he judged them to have a legitimate reason for calling, he directed a footman to usher them to the correct destination and entered their names in a book kept for the purpose. His duties extended to paying the Sedan chairmen and receiving and sending all letters and parcels. Throughout the eighteenth-century letters and parcels were paid for by the recipient on arrival, not by the sender. There were no post offices or stamps in the modern sense, and the house porter kept money in his lodge for the receipt of any post. Each letter and parcel was recorded in his day book which he presented to the house steward once a month. He also dealt with tradesmen and the delivery boys who came to the back door, all goods delivered to the house were taken in by the house porter, including coal. The key to the coal cellar was in his keeping, this being a necessary precaution. In 1726 two boys were rewarded when they detected 'coal stealers'. The porter allocated prescribed amounts of coal to the different rooms in the main house, the kitchen and laundry. Coal was widely used both in London and the country as it gave out a far better heat than wood. The house porter also had a number of menial duties, he was responsible for keeping the front door clean and sweeping the steps. A lantern hung by the front door and it was his job to make sure it was in full working order as there was little or no street lighting and every house was encouraged to hang out a lantern. Another of his tasks was taking care of the poultry, seeing to their welfare when alive, and after their demise preserving and sorting their feathers.

The house porter stayed permanently in London during the major part of Thomas Coke's lifetime; it was not until 1755 that it was thought necessary to employ one for Holkham.

Footmen were next in the servant hierarchy. In the mornings they helped out with any household task that needed doing such as carrying coals to the numerous fireplaces, going to the still room to hack at the sugar which came in large conical pieces and needed breaking down before use, and to the laundry to turn the mangle or to the cellars to hold a barrel while the butler decanted the wine. In the country the lady's footman doubled as baker and often took charge of the brewing. The tradition of footmen as bakers continued well into the nineteenth century. [5] A footman was a versatile fellow. By mid-morning, with these more menial tasks behind them and changed into their livery, they were stationed in the hall ready to be summoned by their master or mistress. They stood to attention when anyone came by, but were not on sentry duty on either side of doors as so often portrayed in films and on television. They were better at lolling. Their duty was to deliver messages, run errands of every kind and accompany their employers on outings. In town this could simply be walking to the shops and carrying purchases home or, if going out with the Sedan chair walking ahead and carrying a staff to ensure people got out of the way. After dark, a footman lit the way by holding aloft a wax flambeau and was armed with a short sword and pistols. Lady Margaret had her own Sedan chair but when Coke needed one, a footman ran out to the nearest stand to call one over, for which he often received a vail of sixpence. Even in the country, footmen accompanied their masters and mistresses when they went out for exercise. [6] It may be remembered from Thomas Coke's journey from London to Longford in Chapter 1 that footmen acted as outriders on long journeys, deterrents against highwaymen and footpads. A servant could legitimately assault a third party in defence of his master, or mistress, though this was not always fully accepted as law until the end of the century. [7] Servant pistols are mentioned several times in the accounts and there are a few accounts of the servants, when travelling alone, being robbed on the road, but none when they were armed and accompanying the family.

The ideal footman was tall and athletic, good-looking and good-humoured. He was also expected to be a musician. So frequent are the references to footmen playing the fiddle at this period that it may have been part of a footman's remit to do so. When a Dutch footman Jeremiah Sommering was engaged in 1728 a fiddle was bought for him at a cost of £1. 6s. 0d. Equally popular was the French horn, also played by footmen. In the 1720s Christopher Bennet, a professional musician, was paid 3gns for teaching Philip Bender to play one. Over the lifetime of Thomas Coke thirteen French horns were purchased, all were for footmen to play and there are many entries for mending them and adding new silver mouthpieces. The French horn, along with the straight horn, is primarily associated with hunting, but it was also a much favoured instrument to be played during mealtimes. At first this may appear overly noisy and death to conversation, but in the summer the ideal was for the family to eat out of doors in the pleasure gardens, while the sound of a French horn wafted over the summer breezes from a distant wood. The inventory of 1775 lists 'a wheelbarrow with Partitions when dining in ye Garden'. In winter, music was played in an adjoining room or further along the corridor. Harps were popular especially in London. The fiddle was played more often for dancing. Footmen and many other servants, even down to gardeners, could expect to be dragged into taking part in family theatricals, sometimes simply to provide the music but often in speaking roles. Male servants were also called on to be dancing partners when the family entertained and there were not enough men to go round.

The coachmen and postillions also wore full livery. The short full dress jackets worn by postillions were heavily embroidered, sometimes with their master's arms emblazoned on the sleeve and on their heads they wore richly decorated caps. Postillions were provided with spurs, neckcloths and hand-kerchiefs and sometimes shirts.

Many households had their own buttons made with the family crest imprinted on them, these were worn by all livery servants. Thomas Coke paid for special buttons at the time of his wedding and though they are not mentioned again, new ones may have been included in the general livery bills under 'furniture' the term used for such miscellaneous objects.

Livery suits were given out annually. Each liveried servant received a jacket, waistcoat and breeches, stockings, gloves, hat, boots and shoes. New overcoats were provided every two years. Great care was taken over liveries, not only the general appearance, but the fit and correct manner of wearing them, i.e. what was deemed suitable to wear at times of mourning or celebration. Liveries were the direct concern of the master, including the pattern they should be cut to and the trouble of getting breeches to fit. [8] A telling entry occurs in 1739 for Mr Watkins, a London tailor, altering 'Liverys that were made in the country'. This suggests that country tailors did not always 'answer', although livery suits continued to be sourced from both country and London tailors. On leaving their employ servants were expected to leave their livery suits behind and it was always hoped that their successors would fit them, if in good condition, without requiring too many alterations. However for the greater part of the day, while working, livery servants wore a more simple outfit of leather breeches and loose fitting linen frock. Even after the accepted hour for visitors to call, eleven o'clock, it was not unknown for a visitor to find the house porter or even the butler 'out of livery', though this was more likely to happen in the country than in town.

At Holkham the huntsmen and later gamekeepers all wore livery. At this early date, the 1720s, there is no description of what it was, other than coats made of fustian cloth. Fustian was a thick hard-wearing cloth made from linen and cotton with parallel diagonal lines, supposedly an Egyptian cloth originating from Fostat, a suburb of Cairo. In lieu of livery the stable workers were given suits of clothes, and like the indoor servants, buckskin breeches, stockings and boots. The grooms had velvet caps. For working the stablemen wore an over-garment, a 'frock' made of kersey. Kersey was coarse woollen cloth, called after Kersey in Suffolk. Occasionally a clothing allowance was given, rather than the clothes being provided, as in the case of John Martin who worked at Holkham for seven months in 1728, and was given £5 for 'wearing his own clothes all that Time'.

Finally came the unwaged foot boys. These were usually the sons of local tradesmen or tenant farmers taken in to be educated in the three Rs and at the same time learn the ways of a great household. Some were charitable cases, others had their apprentice fee paid by their parents or guardians. The majority were about ten years old when they started and were trained in a variety of different ways. The first recorded is Tom Robinson, who in 1720 was clothed and fed, taught to read and write and play the straight horn at Coke's expense, in return for work over a seven-year period. A Mr Cowper taught him the French horn. When in the country Robinson worked with the huntsmen and was variously described as a whipper-in and groom's boy. He left in 1728 and his place was taken by John Pepper who also stayed for seven years. Pepper got through 'running stockins' at a fast rate, and numerous pairs of shoes. The list of clothes bought for him included wigs, but no livery. His talents seem to have been more for the domestic side of life and in 1733 he is described in one entry as under-butler. Like Robinson he received small gifts of money from time to time, and vails, but no wages. Other boys included William Talbot whose father had been the Holkham brewer; for four years he was clothed and fed under the heading Charity. [9] From 1736-1741 George Wintle appears as kitchen boy, with all his clothes paid for, at the same time as an unnamed lad described as 'the trufile boy'. William Overton, whose family farmed in the neighbouring parish of

Burnham, was with the household from 1736-1742 and on arrival was kitted out in all the splendour of a livery servant but again not waged. He was bought lace, gloves, buckles for his shoes and even supplied with a trunk for his clothes. During his first year in London Overton was put out to lodge with Mr Morrin a wig-maker at a cost of £35.14s., the equivalent of six years pay as a footman. Later he appears to have assisted the valet. When he left in 1742 Overton was given a gift of 5gns 'at his leaving the family'. He was succeeded by two more boys Will Woodward and Kouli-Khan of whom more in the next chapter.

A variation on this arrangement occurred in 1729 when Jeremiah Sommering joined the Coke household as a waged footman. Previously he had been apprentice to Messrs Davie, Zaccaria and Johannes Beswilliband, Dutchmen. No travel expenses are recorded for Sommering but Coke paid the Beswilliband brothers £28 over two years to release Jeremiah from his indentures.

The Female Servants:

The housekeeper was an upper servant. Hers was a post first created in the seventeenth century as the number of male servants employed in great households decreased and their places were taken by females. Given the honorary title of Mrs to emphasise her authority, her responsibility was to supervise, control and train the maids. Second only to the lady's maid the housekeeper usually had a maid of her own paid for out of her own purse. Housekeepers needed to be literate and numerate and skilled in all aspects of buying and preserving food, laundry and needlework. They were often the daughters of superior tradesmen or even clergymen.

Over the forty-year span of Thomas Coke's adult lifetime approximately 436 servant names appear in the accounts, of which housemaids make up the largest group, partly accounted for by the fact that three or more were employed at any one time. During this period sixty-seven different women and girls worked as housemaids for varying lengths of time, from over twelve years in the case of Anne Simpson 1730-1743 to the shortest, just two weeks, in that of Hannah Porter in 1742. The average length of service for a housemaid was little more than a year. For a young girl, time spent in an elite household was seen as a form of apprenticeship; many were encouraged by their parents to enter service and learn the ways of the gentry, thus making themselves desirable in the marriage market. An ambitious shopkeeper seeking a wife might well look for an experienced housemaid who would provide him with an insight into the ways and tastes of the gentry and advise him on matters of address and protocol.

The next largest group were the laundry maids. Two at a time were employed. Laundry maids were slightly better paid than housemaids as their work was both more skilful and more strenuous. Their duties included inspecting the wash before laundering it and putting aside any article that needed mending. The heavy work of washing was carried out in hot steamy conditions, in part recompensed by an extra allowance of beer to quench their thirst, a welcome perk. While engaged in washing, the maids all wore pattens to keep their feet dry. After the wash, help was sometimes needed from male servants to work the mangle. This was a large wooden box with rollers, very different from later upright models, much heavier, and requiring considerable strength to start it up and keep it in motion. There are two contrasting anecdotes relating to laundry maids. In the Duke of Chandos's household of 1720 the stablemen were asked to assist with the mangle, but were reluctant to help and excused themselves by saying they were too busy with the horses and had been so for the previous three weeks.[10] By contrast Roger North, a Norfolk friend and neighbour of Thomas Coke who lived at Rougham, disapproved of men having anything more to do with female servants than was absolutely necessary. He pointed out that the laundry should be: ' ... an office wholly of women; and the men, however officious to aid their sweethearts, should not be allowed to frequent there, ... [for] impertinent conversation hinders'. Perhaps he did not own a mangle for in good weather, he continues, the clean washing should either be hung outside in the drying yard or laid on bushes. North advised against hawthorn bushes, as it tore the linen, and neither did he advocate planting box for this purpose because it grew too slowly. For the indoor drying room he recommended an Aunt Sally; he did not call it by this name but the description he gives of pulley, ropes and slats is exact.[11]

When not engaged in laundry work laundry maids were expected to help out in other parts of the house wherever they might be needed and in the evenings to take part in sewing. Like housemaids the average duration of a laundry maid's service was about a year. Exceptions were two laundry maids with the same surname, probably sisters, Catherine and Sarah Hewetson who were employed for five and four years respectively from 1737 to 1742, and Mary Carmen who was employed for seven years between 1748 and 1755.

Johnson's *Dictionary* is delightfully vague on the difference between a laundry maid and a washerwoman. The likelihood is that a washerwoman was involved only with the washing, whereas a laundry maid both washed and ironed; the skill of a laundry maid was certainly put to the test in starching and ironing. Sometimes a woman was brought in to do both. In London in April 1728 Mary Rogers, the upper laundry maid, engaged a woman for three days, two to be spent washing and the third to iron. It was an advantage to have an in-house laundry in London where sending linen out to be laundered invited many risks, from the simple misplacement of articles to the entire consignment being stolen. In 1758 the diarist Mrs Delany lost hers when her laundress owed rent and it was seized in lieu. She had to pay out six guineas to retrieve it. [12]

The female kitchen staff varied. At times it included a cook maid who was essentially a woman cook, sometimes assisting a male cook but sometimes working alone. And kitchen maids who were also often skilled and proficient in preparing meals, plus under-kitchen maids the very lowest paid servants of all, who were there to 'scower', scrub, wash dishes, sweep the floor and generally take on any job they were ordered to do. The term scullery maid was not in use until the end of the eighteenth century.

At Holkham, close by the kitchen was the still-room where the still-room maids prepared and stored conserves. Besides preparing jellies and other desserts, they made flower waters for culinary and domestic use, cordials, spicy alcoholic waters for social drinking and home-distilled medicines. [13]

At some little distance from the house was the dairy, although at Holkham it was not until 1737 that a dairy for the sole use of the house was built. Until then milk, cream and butter was purchased weekly from the wives of the tenant farmers in the parish, Mrs Anger and Mrs Porter. When the first dairy maid, Sarah Staniforth, was engaged it was her duty to provide the house with high quality unadulterated milk, cream, butter, buttermilk, cheese and numerous creamy delicacies. [14] In London dairy produce was purchased from the 'Milkwoman' who according to the household accounts received a garland of flowers each 1st May, often a euphemism for a cash donation.

The remaining female staff in the household were Lady Margaret's two maids, and between 1719 and 1724 a nurse and nurse maid.

In the evenings, between dinner and supper, that is from about 5 o'clock onwards, the maid servants sewed. The great quantities of needlework, 'mountains' as it was often referred to, was done under the supervision of the housekeeper. This work has gone largely unrecorded simply from lack of records, yet it was essential to the running of the household at a time when household linen was made at home. One hundred and forty-five yards of cloth was purchased from Mr Peckover of Fakenham in the autumn of 1720 to be made into twelve pairs of sheets. Hemming and sewing seams made up the bulk of all the work. It is not recorded whether the maids sewed for the male servants though this is quite probable, but they did make simple garments for their own use, mainly shifts. The accounts record purchases of cloth and its intended use, whether for sheets, napkins, tablecloths, towels etc., but not the cost of needles, thread, tape and other necessaries which were purchased by the housekeeper and recorded in her general 'book account' presented once a month to the accountant. She saw to it that all work for the family was marked either by initials or the family emblem, the Ostrich. Irish linen was used for the family's sheets and their visitors, and Lancashire or coarse cloth for the servants.

Clothes worn by the male servants, their livery, breeches, boots, shoes, stockings, hats and greatcoats are well represented throughout the accounts but almost nothing is recorded for the maid servants. None of them wore livery, with the exception of the lady's maids and the housekeeper, for they were never on display. In fact it was hoped to see as little of them as possible; they were expected to perform their duties out of sight of the family using the back stairs to access the various floors of the house. Some of them were occasionally sent on errands in London to collect special purchases from the shops, but usually when they were seen it was outside the house on their way to and from church and on holidays, times when they would be wearing their best outfits. Descriptions of maids in their everyday garb are hard to find. In the opening pages of Richardson's novel *Pamela,* published in 1741, the eponymous heroine is described as wearing a home-spun gown and cotton handkerchief, and twenty years later Mrs Anne Cook author of *Professed Cookery* confirms that maid servants wore home-spun clothes for work, keeping their best gowns for wear only at Sunday church. [15] Young French servant girls in the paintings of Jean-Simeon Chardin are shown wearing plain brown. His under-kitchen maid of 1737 wears an unbleached gown over a grey underpetticoat with a sacking apron round her waist and on her head a plain white cap. Female servants were at a marked disadvantage for not only did they earn less for working just as hard if not harder than their male colleagues, but they also had to pay for their own clothes – as Boswell pointed out. The general imbalance of wages is even more marked when it is remembered that it was as important for maid servants to appear neat and presentable both when seeking a new situation and in retaining it, despite being largely 'invisible'. Appearance was everything.

Funding their outfits was therefore a priority. Traditionally, handing down clothes from mistress to servant, or inheriting from a female relation, had been a reliable source for most, but thrift among all classes meant these well-intentioned gifts were frequently quite worn out by the time they reached the recipient, having been 'turned' and dyed several times. However as the century progressed it appears that many maid servants no longer needed to rely on hand-me-downs, but could afford to buy new, even those working in less prestigious households than Holkham. Research carried out by John Styles found that among the twenty-eight maid servants Robert Heaton employed in Yorkshire between 1768 and 1792, maids spent an average of 86 percent of their wages on clothes, clothing and the upkeep of clothing and were, as a result, fashionable and well turned out. Contrary to previous belief, these girls did not send the bulk of their wages home but experienced considerable freedom of choice when spending their earnings and bought at least one new gown a year. The gowns worn for work were made from cheap worsted fabrics, but others were of printed cotton or linen and cost between 15s. and 21s. each, with the occasional gown of camblet or carpe, a silk wool mixture. The earnings of Heaton's servants were between 31s. and 55s. a year, in contrast to the Holkham maids who earned substantially more, between £4 and £7, so that we may expect them to be equally if not better turned out. [16]

Women's clothes were a series of layers. Next to the skin they wore a shift made of cotton, linen or holland which was washed frequently, very often daily. The cheapest shift cost two shillings according to a bill in the 1720s when shifts were made for the poor at Holkham. Stays were worn over the shifts and laced to emphasize the waist. Stays cost £1 or more and were made by the visiting staymaker who measured his customers in the privacy of the house. To combat the cold, flannel was popular for under petticoats, which might also be made of worsted. These were frequently quilted or wadded both for extra warmth and to give shape and bulk to the skirt of the gowns. Quilted jackets, some with hoods, were designed as outdoor garments but were often worn indoors in winter. Hoops were all the rage by the mid-eighteenth century though servants were not encouraged to wear them. Given the layers of petticoats, a gown made from a light material generally referred to as 'stuff' could be worn on top all year round; gowns were generally bought in either wholly or partly finished. Brown and green seem to have been the approved colours for working gowns. [17] Completing their outfit were handkerchiefs and caps. Handkerchiefs were part scarf, part collar and worn round the neck and then tucked into the front of the dress, some reached as low as the waist where they were held in place by a girdle or belt. They were made from checked cotton or muslin, sometimes edged with lace. A huge variety of caps were worn. Simple linen ones for every day and once again muslin decorated with lace for best. When working in their worsted gowns the maids wore long white aprons which could be hitched up when needed, and these cost about 3s. Stockings were made either from worsted or yarn, shoes cost between 4s. and 6s. a pair, and pattens 1s. Pattens were worn by the laundry maids when working, and for outdoor use by almost everyone else who did not wish to squelch directly into whatever was under foot. The only items of clothing Holkham provided were gloves. Gloves were worn both while working (many of the cleaning materials were abrasive) and for best. Bills from Joseph Baker of Wells show that extra right-hand gloves were ordered since these would have worn out more quickly for example while 'scowering' the pewter, scrubbing floors or blacking grates.

An exception to the above was at times of mourning when the Holkham maids were given a complete set of clothes. When a close family member died the whole household wore black and these clothes were paid for by the master. Women did not attend funerals, but it was expected they should wear mourning when attending church on Sundays or going out; it would have been disrespectful for them to be seen in ordinary clothes at such a time, even in the country. [18]

In 1722, when Coke's brother-in-law Lord Sondes died in the March, and then a few months later his grandmother Lady Anne Walpole, seven maid servants were bought complete new mourning 'suits' and accessories. For Lord Sondes's mourning the accountant Mr Casey records the purchase of twenty-eight yards of Norwich crepe at 2s. 2d. a yard for Mrs Smith the nurse, and twenty-six yards of crepe at 1s. 6d. for her maid Fanny (Frances Lucas). His list continues with a further twelve yards of 'black' at 14d. a yard, nine yards of mantua at 4s. 6d. and two yards of muslin at 9s. 6d. The maids were further supplied with mourning fans, mourning gloves, girdles, buckles and shoes. Each suit of mourning, as it was described, cost 7s. to be made up and the total for each one, material and work came to £9. 9s. Five months later in August when Lady Anne Walpole died, Casey entered a further 136 yards of fine crepe, plus twenty-six yards of 'black', enough to make five suits, as well as stockings and knotts, gloves and girdles etc. as before.

The components of the material and the accessories listed indicates that fashions from the late seventeenth century were still considered appropriate for mourning wear. The plain, i.e. white, muslin entered by Casey was, he says, for their 'head clothes'. The fashion for head-cloths dated from the 1690s; they were worn starched and coffered in three layers above a close-fitting cowl, the final one standing up in a vertically pleated fan. This challenging headdress was achieved by heavy starching and pressing the muslin into crisp, rounded pleats by the use of an Italian iron. Highly skilled work. The alternative headdress, using the knotts he mentions, had been made fashionable slightly earlier in the 1680s; the knotts were wire-stiffened loops of ribbon pinned to a cap with a muslin square over. [19] The mantua was a gown open at the front and shaped by pleating the back and stitching the pleats to fit the upper half of the body, while the skirt fell behind in a train. The 'black' would have been made into a petticoat, which in both the seventeenth and eighteenth centuries was seen beneath and in front of the open gown of a mantua.

It was essential that the material used for mourning should not be shiny or in any way reflect light, but appear sooty and matt. Norwich crepe, or 'crape' as it is more often written, matched this criteria and came in three categories, being made either from a mixture of worsted wool, silk and linen, or silk on its own, none of which was shiny. The muted tones required on occasions of mourning even extended to swords (worn by all gentlemen) and shoe buckles which were specially manufactured to be non-reflective, dark and dull. [20]

It is not clear who owned these mourning clothes, the servants or their masters, it is likely they remained in the family, as the livery clothes did, and were adapted as needed over the years. Lord Sondes and Lady Anne were the first close members of the family to die in the time of Coke's majority, and the provision of these complete new outfits was an exception. When a second brother-in-law, Lord Harrold, died in an accident in 1723, and then Coke's sister Cary Wyvill in 1732 and his younger brother Edward in 1733, there are no entries for servants mourning, none in fact until the death of Queen Caroline, wife of George II, in 1737 when the Wells tailor Richard Hackett made eight livery mourning suits for the male servants only.

Apart from the full-time maids, extra female help was engaged at times when the family travelled between London and Holkham. After the family left either for the country or town, charwomen were brought in to clean and, conversely, they were employed in advance to prepare the house the family was due to move back to. One reason for this was because the maids made these great journeys to and from town by waggon, a slower form of travel than that taken by the main party, who were either on horseback or in coaches. Had they remained behind to clean, it would have been at least two weeks before they arrived at the other end. Consequently a regular supply of part-timers were needed and they were frequently the same people every year. In London Mrs Blinkhorn and Dame Mackdonnel are named as regulars, at Holkham Amy Shultram.

The diversity of work meant that at no time was the household a static entity nor would its members ever find themselves assembled in the same place on the same day. This was true even in early 1719; hardly was the ink dry on the first list of wages than changes took place. The reason for this can be found in the next chapter.

NOTES

1.   Staffordshire Record Office D6 15/P (S) 1/1/5.

2.   Huntingdon MSS 31201. Mrs Larpent [1758-1832] sorted papers to be destroyed towards the end of most years, e.g. in 1811 'sorted the years papers to burn'.

3.   The name Griffiths appears several times in the Holkham accounts, the earliest in 1700: Mrs Griffiths milliner and later Mary Griffiths housemaid in 1746 and John Griffiths footman and baker from 1751-55.

4.   C. Willett Cunnington and Phillis Cunnington *Handbook of English Costume in the Eighteenth Century*, London 1964 p.43.

5.   For examples of the versatility of servants: The Earl of Nottingham's butler John Buckmaster doubled as a baker in 1701. Leicestershire Record Office DG7/1/119 book of wages 1683-1722 and at Wolterton, Norfolk home of the Lord Walpole, where Thomas Doughty was the 'baker in the house' in 1742, among his other duties was gardening, planting trees and weeding and taking the coach horses down to London; when not baking for the family his successor, Henry Bayfield, spent five weeks cleaning the stone steps on the north front of the house. Wolterton Archives Cash Book Estate and Household 1738-49 3/1/4.

6.   *Hary-O, The Letters of Lady Harriet Cavendish 1796-1809,* London 1940 p.208. In 1807 Lady Harriet Cavendish writes how her early morning walks at Castle Howard were halted when her footman became ill. As late as 1853 Anna Maria Pickering wrote that as her footman was in hospital she was 'a sad prisoner ... as I should much like to get out'. *The Letter Bag of Lady Elizabeth Spencer-Stanhope* compiled by Mrs A.M.W. Stirling London 1908 p.303.

7. R. C. Richardson *Household Servants in Early Modern England* Manchester 2010 p.195; J.B. Bird *The Laws respecting Masters and Servants* London 1795.

8. For more about liveries see a lengthy correspondence of Daniel Finch to his father in 1717 in which he discusses price of livery materials (nine shillings a yard), patterns for them, the merits of country tailors, etc. Leicestershire Record Office – Finch of Burley on the Hill archive ref. DG7/Bundle 25.

9. Richardson pp.196-197. Under the terms of the Poor Law pauper apprentices could be directed into service from as young as six, the parents either agreeing or risking forfeiting their poor relief paid for by the parish. Pauper apprentices could expect to stay tied to their employer until they reached the age of twenty-one. Those at Holkham, who had no means of paying apprenticeship fees and were charity cases, do not appear to have been subjected to such a lengthy servitude, most had some previous connection to the household.

See also *the Correspondence of Lord Fitzwilliam of Milton and Francis Guybon his Steward 1697-1709* eds: D.R. Hainsworth and Cherry Walker Northampton Record Society 1990 pp. xv, 16, 19, 38, 39, 75, 87 and 191.

Despite their tender and impressionable years the boys' progress was not always satisfactory as Lord Fitzwilliam of Milton, writing to his steward Francis Guybon in the last years of the previous century, describes. In 1697 two young foot boys joined the Fitzwilliams' London household and were duly sent to school every morning. However the temptations of the city were too great and the first, the son of an innkeeper in Peterborough, took to drink and theft. The second, after a bout of the smallpox, grew idle, skipped his duties and was labelled 'a careless fool'. Lord Fitzwilliam [1643-1719] was a tolerant employer; he had not wanted the father of the first boy to know how hardened his son had become and worried that the second boy would be too badly scarred by the smallpox to be engaged as a servant, 'for I would not have unsightly servants. He nevertheless employed him as a foot-man. Some years later Fitzwilliam warned the young man against quitting his service without another place to go to, fearing that 'he will be press'd to go to sea as they take up all loose fellows out of service and many servants also'. To no avail; the lad left anyway and died just five years later at Bath, cause unknown.

The risk of being press-ganged was very real, many years later in 1755 a Holkham footman was 'pressed' at Wells, but Coke's secretary Mr Mitchell was able to release him for the sum of five shillings; the man must have been out of livery at the time.

10. Huntingdon Library, Stowe MS ST 44. Household Regulations for Cannons 1721.

11. *Of Building: Roger North's Writings on Architecture* ed. Howard Colvin and John Newman, Oxford 1981, p.94.

12. *The Autobiography and Correspondence of Mary Granville, Mrs Delany,* ed. Lady Llanover, London 1861, series 1 vol. 3 p.482.

13. *The Country House Kitchen 1650-1900* ed. Pamela A. Sambrook and Peter Bears, Gloucs. 1996 p.129 passim.

14. Pamela A Sambrook and Peter Bears p.164.

15. Samuel Richardson, *Pamela* , London 1741 and Anne Buck, *Dress in Eighteenth-Century England,* London, 1979 p.113.

16. John Styles *Servants and their Clothes in Eighteenth-Century England* Textile History vol.33 No 1 May 2002 p.13, as to the lowering cost of materials, Holkham paid 9s. 6d. a yard for muslin 1722, while forty years on the Heaton maids paid 3s. 8d..

17. John Styles *The Dress of the People, everyday fashion in eighteenth-century England* Newhaven and London 2007 p.294 shows an illustration of a housemaid in 1801 wearing a green gown, and it is worth recording that Mrs Lybbe Powis in the account of her journey to Norfolk in 1756 says that all the maid servants at Weasenham Hall, where she was staying, were given a length of green camblet cloth to be made into a gown as a reward for good behaviour every Christmas by their Mistress. *Passages from the Diaries of Mrs Philip Lybbe Powis 1756-1808* ed. Emily J. Climenson, London 1899 p.4.

18. *The Correspondence of Lord Fitzwilliam of Milton and Francis Guybon his Steward 1697-1709* p.63 and Mrs Delany Series 1 vol. 2 p.276. In 1743, when Lady Westcombe died, she wrote: 'Six weeks mourning for my mother and three for us, but as she (the deceased) was not known in Staffordshire, I think it is of no consequence to put it on there'.

19. Peter Bears, *The Complete Housekeeper, A household in Queen Anne's times* Wakefield 2000, p.106 and p.103.

20. Information supplied in person to the author by the late Pamela Clabburn in 2006.

CHAPTER 5

An Addition to the Family – Pregnancy and Childbirth

When Thomas Coke and his bride returned to London in late February 1719 Lady Margaret was five months pregnant. At Thanet House the news that a baby was to be born in a little under four months time meant that no sooner had they finished their master and mistress's unpacking and introduced themselves, than the servants could expect new faces below stairs. It was an auspicious time for the young bride, since pregnancy was all too often regarded as a period of ill health before the quickening (at five months), and after that, little better than a condition to be endured. During the first three months Lady Margaret appears to have been perfectly healthy, even unaware of her condition, for at Longford there are accounts of her riding out on her own pad (horse) and walking out (a servant given a vail for finding her clogs), besides paying numerous visits in the neighbourhood. Then in December Dr Chalinor had been called in to bleed her. She may still have been unaware of her condition, for an inexperienced girl the detection of pregnancy could be a considerable problem. The competent authority for this state was considered to be a married woman, rather than a member of the medical profession, but at Longford Hall there were no married women to consult. [1]

Within a week of their return to London Sir Hans Sloane, the most prominent Whig physician of his day, was called in to attend to Lady Margaret 'when ill'. Politics really did matter when it came to doctors as there were significant differences of medical opinion and practice between the Whigs and Tories. Tory doctors were opposed to inoculation, a project promoted by Sloane, and were unsympathetic to the foundation of Lying-In Hospitals, being less tolerant of unmarried mothers than were the Whigs. [2] Sloane was to visit Thanet House often in the coming months; he had not far to come but needed just to cross the road from his house on the south side of Great Russell Street. To provide some experienced female reassurance for his wife, Coke re-engaged his old nurse, Smith. After a month's rest Lady Margaret had recovered enough to go out and about in London both during the day and after dark in her sedan chair, which she continued to do until two weeks before her child was born.

The rituals of pregnancy and childbirth in the early eighteenth century were still very much the domain of women. Many considered it unlucky even to inform their family of their condition until 'all fears of miscarrying being past' which they believed to be the five month mark. 'I shall long to hear you are well past that Danger', wrote one of Sir John Newton's sisters to another. [3] And characteristically there were low expectations of enjoying pregnancy; as a Kentish acquaintance of Lady Margaret's Mrs Mills wrote to her sister-in-law Mrs Lee Warner at Walsingham, when they were both pregnant, she felt herself to be 'as well as most people do in that State but to be sure it is very fatiguing at best'. [4]

A first episode of childbirth was seen as important since there was a firmly held belief that if a young wife could get through her first pregnancy success-fully and produce a healthy child, then the chances of subsequent pregnancies being equally fruitful would be greatly increased. To achieve this, supersti-tious practices were not uncommon. [5] Lady Margaret may not have had much time for such beliefs, but she could not avoid the strict old fashioned procedures when her own confinement arrived. The very word confinement gave some hint of what was to come.

Meanwhile there was still much to do at Thanet House; chairmen were sent with wheelbarrows to collect paintings and books from Sir John Newton's house in Soho Square, goods that Sir John had purchased on Coke's behalf at the time of his parents' sale in 1707. Mr Vanstraten came back for a second visit to clean them and new pictures were bought from a Mr Hay. A 'great picture' with its straining frame was delivered from Somerset House where it had been under the care of a Mr Walton. A Smyrna carpet was bought, an eight day clock, ivory dice and backgammon sets, a tea table, a large linen press, and more china and glass.

New animals were purchased giving the household more than the whiff of a menagerie – a second mastiff dog, a macaw and two smaller birds. Nine guineas, the entire annual wage of a footman, was spent on buying a cockatoo. Both the mastiff and the macaw went missing almost as soon as they arrived, the dog must have already had a collar with a name on it, for he was soon brought home by a street porter. The macaw only got as far as next door's garden where the Duke of Montagu's under-gardener was rewarded with a guinea for catching him. A few weeks later a monkey was purchased and kept on a wire chain. These animals were, of course, chiefly cared for by the servants. One can almost hear them muttering 'Nasty smelly things'.

As Lady Margaret prepared for the birth of her child she spent lavishly; each item was entered in the accounts under the heading of Nursery and the total cost came to £370. The bedroom where the birth was to take place, was hung with blue harriteen, with window and door curtains of sprigged persian. Mrs Gameron, who had provided Coke's embroidered wedding clothes, was paid the vast sum of £101 for embroidering a quilt and a pillow. Childbed linen and lace purchased from Mrs Gill came to £130 and Mrs Ashcroft's bill for quilts and the cradle £48.

In keeping with the custom of the time the lying-in chamber would need to be completely dark and draught free. The daylight was shut out by curtains and extraneous air was excluded by blocking up the keyholes, hence the 'confinement'. Candles lit by day and night produced a soft glow that was soothing and calming and created a timeless capsule. [6] For the actual birth the expectant mother was attended by female midwives only. Dr Sloane and Mr Serjeant Dickens the surgeon were hired by Coke to be on hand if needed for the baby, but they would not be directly involved with the labour or the birth, unless there were severe difficulties and then only as a last resort. At this date childbirth was not officially part of medicine and only became so later in the century with the appearance of male midwives. In 1719 it was strictly an all female affair and had been for as long as anyone could remember. Women friends were admitted to the room once the labour began; some were explicitly invited and attended in a not dissimilar way to the modern custom of a birthing-partner, but with a secondary purpose. They were there to witness the birth not only as friends and companions but to affirm identification at the child's subsequent baptism. [7]

How did this affect the household? Over the period of her incarceration Lady Margaret's three personal footmen were in abeyance and new servants were taken on, namely the midwife and her assistants. The term midwife meant 'with-woman' and as that implies she was there to look after the mother rather than the child and as such would have been giving advice on the management of the pregnancy for a few weeks prior to the birth. The head midwife was a Mrs Jane Dotchen whom Lady Margaret would have remembered from her childhood, for on two occasions Mrs Dotchen appears in Lord Thanet's accounts visiting Hothfield in 1709 and 1712. [8] And it was she who had attended Lady Margaret's sister Lady Salisbury in her confinements. [9] It was vital to employ a trusted and experienced midwife as, for the term of their employment, midwives assumed a role of total command.

They alone were entrusted with the right to touch the mother's 'privities' which no doctor, not even Dr Sloane would be. [10]

Once the child was delivered the ritual lying-in commenced. For the mother this could mean remaining in bed from anything from three days to a fortnight while the room continued dark. In total she would spend a month in this, her own space, away from the conjugal bed, at rest, treated as an invalid and recovering gently.

'Little Master', as he was recorded in the accounts, was born on 22nd June 1719, five days after Coke's twenty-second birthday and four days after Lady Margaret's nineteenth. Immediately, the footman Abraham Blaumer was sent to Hothfield to Lord Thanet's 'with ye News of my Ladys being brought to bed of a Son which happened this Morning at ½ past 8'. Edward Smith the accountant recorded this in his book. Mrs Dotchen was paid 10gns for attending Lady Margaret. For their attendance during the lying-in month which then ensued (the confinement) two nurses, Nurse Pharaoh and Nurse Wetheral, received 2gns each. Nurse Smith was given a gift of 10gns by express demand of Lady Margaret and Nurse Key, the wet nurse, was given the same. [11] Nurse Key was further presented with satin to the value of £4. 11s. It was customary to employ a further woman to sit up each night of the lying-in, a task often undertaken by one of the existing servants, but in the case of Lady Margaret, a Mrs Chandler was paid £3. 10s. undertaking this over seven weeks. [12]

On 3rd July the Little Master was christened Edward by Mr Batchellor the vicar of St Giles in the Fields. There is no evidence in the household accounts to show that any celebration was held for the servants at the birth of 'Little Master', no entry for money to drink anyone's health, but some may have been paid directly by Coke from his own pocket. However Edward Sherwin the butter man provided the house with twice the usual amount of butter and eggs that week, sixty-one pounds and two hundred eggs. William Warner the pastry cook was paid £3. 10s. for two plum cakes and a bill of £2 was paid to Mr Edward Lambert the top confectioner of his day. After the birth, Coke gave his wife a diamond ring costing £100.

The employment of a wet-nurse was standard practice for all those who could afford it. The most understandable reason for this was exhaustion or sickness after childbirth, but many women feared that a child tugging at her breast might be detrimental to her figure and render her less attractive to her husband. For much the same reasons some did not welcome being tied to a routine of feeding but wished to be free to re-enter the social sphere as soon as possible and be able to accompany their husbands on outings and resume a full married life, though it is possible this course of action was not always the woman's choice. [13]

Traditionally it is believed that babies were sent away to live with the wet-nurse at her house but this was not so where the family could afford to accommodate an extra servant. The accounts show that the baby remained at home in Thanet House from the time of his birth until he was three months old. He was considered delicate. Mr Serjeant Dickens the surgeon sent in a bill for £26 for attending him between 13th July and 11th September. In September, just as his parents were preparing to visit Holkham, the great Dr Sloane pronounced that low-lying place to be too unhealthily close to the sea for a delicate infant. Instead he recommended somewhere inland away from sea frets. Consequently a visit to Lord Thanet was arranged and accompanied by his wet-nurse Key, old Nurse Smith and Frances Lucas his nursery maid Master Neddy, as he was now known to the servants, set off to Hothfield and remained there until his parents returned from Norfolk in December. Re-united with his mother and father for a brief moment, Dr Sloane examined him once more, tut-tutted and advised that as the baby continued to show signs of illness he should immediately be dispatched to Kensington gravel pits. The site of the gravel pits to the north of today's Kensington Gardens was judged to be a desirable spot free from any vestige of damp and popular with invalids of all ages. It must have been almost spa-like or at least resembling a sanatorium; many who went there were seriously ill and were never to return.

Dr Sloane was almost certainly responsible for this move. The child and his party lodged in the house of a Mr White in 'healthy' Kensington. The lodgings cost £5 a month and there he remained for three months 'when ill' as Edward Smith recorded it. Master Neddy was visited by Mrs Jenny, Lady Margaret's lady's maid, more than once on her own and it is hoped on other occasions with his parents. By the time he returned to Thanet House in March 1720 he was nine months old and already weaned. In February the wet-nurse Key was paid her final wage of £29 for 'nursing Little Master for seven months'. Lady Margaret had been concerned about the correct time to start the weaning, but bowed once more to Sloane's superior experience and advice. The weaning process, literally the changeover from breast-feeding to a spoon, was an abrupt business where a wet-nurse was involved. In August

1733 Mrs Mills wrote to her sister in Walsingham how she managed to wean her daughter who, by the age of ten months, had two teeth which her mother took as a signal, despite the fact that 'she was so fond of suckling that I had terrible apprehensions about it, but it proved better than I expected, she took her weaning mighty well and is not the least fallen away from it'. This child had been fed by a wet-nurse. [14] Some years later the Duchess of Leeds (whose husband was cousin to Thomas Coke) wrote to her sister about weaning her son: 'The Child is weaned the day I received your letter and [it] was literally speaking just as easy without sucking as if he were seven years old, he was a little harder to get to sleep the first night than usual, but then he has never been good at going to sleep since he was born, he is to have some boiled chicken minced very small with some crumbs of bread'. [15]

Lady Margaret went on to have four more pregnancies, but was not to be so successful again. None produced a child that lived longer than a month. In early April 1720 a child described as 'Abortive' was 'deposited' in the Church of St Giles in the Fields; a third child, another son born in 1721, lived just long enough to be christened 'Little Master Thomas Coke; who dye'd immediately after'. On both occasions Mrs Dotchen was present and a footman, first Abraham Blaumer and then William Shadbolt, was sent to Hothfield to tell her father the news. In the autumn of 1721, pregnant for the fourth time in as many years, Lady Margaret remained in London during the hunting season while Coke went to Holkham taking with him most of the servants including the cook and the housekeeper to cater for his house party. Left in London 'Mrs Blinkhorn acted as Cook for my Lady' at Thanet House. Mrs Blinkhorn, mentioned at the end of the previous chapter, was an occasional charwoman who regularly featured in the London accounts from 1719. Sometimes she is entered as a char, sometimes she worked in the laundry, but always as casual labour paid by the day and not, on the face of it, a likely person to 'attend as a cook'; but looking into Lord Thanet's household accounts for some years earlier, it is found he engaged a Robert Blinkhorn as cook and paid him £25 a year. [16] Mrs Blinkhorn may have been his daughter, more likely his widow. She cooked for Lady Margaret for several weeks that autumn of 1721 and continued to work part-time at Thanet House until 1730. In January 1722 Lady Margaret gave birth to her fourth child, another boy, who was once more christened Thomas. Mrs Dotchen was again present at the birth and received her usual £21. This child lived for a few weeks but on 19th February was 'sent away to be buried in Tittleshall' in the family vault. His father was still in Norfolk 'a-hunting' and presumably arranged and attended the funeral, returning to London soon afterwards.

Lady Margaret's fifth and final pregnancy ended in October 1723 while staying at Minster Lovell, their Oxfordshire estate. This time there is no entry for a christening in the accounts, only for a shroud, the grave diggers bill and money paid to midwives. Back in London there is an entry for a churching, 15gns paid to the Chaplain of St Giles in the Fields, for reading prayers and 'churching my Lady'. The churching of women after childbirth, even if the child had not survived, was largely a form of thanksgiving, a ritual that had hung-on from pre-reformation days. It derived from the belief that women needed to be 'cleansed'; for women with their bodily fluids were considered tainted and after the messy business of giving birth, it was thought they required to be purified spiritually as well as physically. As far as the Church was concerned churching was a necessity if the woman was to continue to attend church services and be acceptable in the eyes of God. Midwives often accompanied the mother to this ceremony, which generally took place twenty-eight days after the birth, and marked a final end to the midwife's care. After 1723 there is no evidence of further pregnancies, the old adage of a successful first pregnancy resulting in further live births had not held good for Lady Margaret. In 1723 she was only twenty-three years old.

Throughout the pregnancies and childbirths, those two shadowy people, Lady Margaret's woman and her chambermaid, remain as elusive as ever.

Young Edward was, therefore, to be an only and much cherished child. Nurse Smith continued in charge of him, assisted by the nursery maid Fanny Lucas. Fanny was discharged in May 1724 shortly before his fifth birthday and in her place Betty Lloyd was employed. She is entered in the accounts as Mr Coke's maid. By the following year, when only six, Mr Coke had his own footman, John Marguerat. Six is a very tender age to command a footman, but at the time the family were in Bristol and a footman provided necessary protection in town when going for treatments at the Hot Wells not in the company of his parents. A good relationship must have developed between John Marguerat and Edward, for Marguerat (possibly a Frenchman) continued as his footman until 1737.

For the first ten years of his life the boy was taught at home by a series of tutors. [17] Later when boarding at Westminster School and travelling 'alone' between London and Holkham, he was entrusted to the care of Coke's valet, then Mr La France, who made the journey to fetch him home for the holidays.

Edward Coke appears to have been a relatively healthy child, bearing in mind that the slightest sign of illness would have been pounced upon.

In April 1728, the year before he entered Westminster school, the brave step was taken to have him inoculated against the smallpox. This was a risky and expensive procedure, but one championed by both Dr Sloane and Dr Friend, the brother of the school's headmaster. The cost of the inoculation itself was £21. Lady Mary Wortley Montagu had famously brought the procedure to public attention in 1721 after having her own son inoculated. That had been a success, but many children did not survive. Careful management after the initial treatment was paramount and often the patient was removed to a house of isolation in the hope of getting the best result. To lessen the chances of contamination, patients were required to bring their own wine, tea, sugar, and chocolate. [18] An entry for providing the boy with these provisions, and a set of pewter plates, a basin and a chamber pot, suggests he endured the treatment in a house apart. (The pewter items, engraved with the Coke crest, would have later gone with him to school). Claude Amyand, the royal surgeon who had successfully inoculated Queen Caroline's daughters, performed the procedure and a Nurse Bateman attended him for the three weeks he was away and received 3gns for her care direct from the hand of Lady Margaret. [19] He recovered well and the following month was taken to the play by his tutor Mr Bennett. Asses milk had been recommended as a restorative and the boy drank it in great quantities. The milk was purchased from a Mr Gittos, another member of the greater family network. A postillion named Edmund Gittos had been taken on by Coke in 1721 who, like Davies and Shadbolt, came from Hatfield where his father had been writing-master to the young Cecils. [20] Mr Bennet, Edward's tutor, may also have had Hatfield connections though these have proved hard to find other than the presence of the name.

The survival of just one child was unusual. All too often young wives of the elite tended either to die in childbirth or carry on to have ten or more children. From the point of view of inheritance the absence of a string of daughters meant Coke could leave his estate entire to his son; the ideal way to increase wealth was not to have too many children. What it says for the relationship between Coke and Lady Margaret cannot be known, only that Lady Margaret became a wife upon whom Coke could and did depend. She ran his house efficiently, took a close interest in the estate and in his career, on occasion writing letters of business on his behalf, and supervising all that touched Holkham. As for the servants, the ones who cared must have thought it disappointing that Master Neddy remained the solitary offspring, but the presence of children in a house was not of paramount importance, the working conditions, wages, care and opportunities were of more immediate concern and the next chapter deals with what servants employed by a family who aspired to greatness could expect.

NOTES

1. Anne Laurence, *Women in England* London 1995 p.75.

2 Adrian Wilson, *The Making of Man-midwifery* Massachusetts 1995 p.152.

3. Lincolnshire Record Office, Newton 7/13 folio 121 and 7/14 folio 59.

4. NRO Lee Warner Box Letter 25. Despite a long correspondence over several years during which both women went through several pregnancies, and did not stint on advice and the progress of their children, there is never any mention of how their labours went.

5. In 1716 Sir Strenysham Master, father of Coke's schoolfellow and companion in Angers, supplied his pregnant daughter with an 'Eagle Stone' which was 'to be tyed to the thigh to cause an easy delivery'. The stone had been acquired by Sir Strenysham in India. In offering this to his daughter, either consciously or unconsciously, Sir Strenysham harked back to pre-Reformation days when pregnant women wore holy relics, girdles, skirts and coats, kept for the purpose by many religious houses which it was believed would reduce the pangs of labour. See Lady Newton *Lyme Letters 166?-1760* London, 1925 p.281 and Keith Thomas, *Religion and the Decline of Magic* Penguin edition London 1991 p.31.

6. Wilson p.26.

7. Wilson pp.1–3 and p.25. Wilson says these customs probably dated back many centuries. By the seventeenth-century the women invited to the birth were friends known as 'gossips,' a corruption of 'god-sib' or god-sibling' meaning a witness, but subsequently became a term used by men in a derogatory sense when women got together either for a childbirth or elsewhere.

8. Kentish Studies U 455 383 A/2

9. Hatfield Archives Bills 485 and 450. In 1715 Mrs Dotchen attended the birth of the future 6th Earl of Salisbury and was paid £26 for her trouble, see Bill 485 and again in 1721 £52 to 'attend the birth of Bennet Cecil Esq., deceased'.

10. Wilson p.26.

11. Mrs Wetheral may have been the wife of, or related to, Josiah Wetheral plasterer and carpenter who was often employed at Thanet House.

12. Mary-Anne Garry, *'Seduced by the Devil' Divorce in 18th Century Norfolk* Norfolk

Archaeology Vol. XL1V Part 1V 2005. The Lockwood case, where Mary Owen sat up twelve nights but refused to do more.

13. Those mothers who wished to breast-feed but were unable to do so, fed the child with a spoon or risked a bottle; both methods were perilous. Feeding bottles did exist, with teats made from animal membranes but were difficult if not impossible to keep free from germs. Consequently those who could employed wet-nurses rather than risk the alternatives and made do with respectable women recommended by word of mouth. The wet-nurse would be employed until the child was old enough to be weaned at anything from eight months to three years.

14. NRO Lee Warner Box 8 441x2 Letter 13.

15. BL MSS 33066.

16. Kentish Studies U 455 383 A/2.

17. Various tutors appear in the accounts, the earliest in 1724 Mr Brereton 'Schoolmaster to Master Neddy 4gns' and later Mr Perrin who taught maths, Mr Elliott dancing and drawing, Mr Hogwood writing and Captain Bedford riding. Mr Disbrowe was paid £10 for the quarter in 1726, and in 1727 Mr Laplace received £36 a quarter for 'boarding and schooling'. Where Master Coke boarded with Laplace is unknown, though he was with him for at least a year before entering Westminster School. At Westminster he lodged with Mrs Glymm. All the while Master Coke had with him his footman John Marguerat.

18. *Norwich Mercury,* an advertisement placed in 1766 by Mr Framingham of Swaffham saying he had two houses for the purpose of inoculation in Dunham, 'being more isolated'. A treatment cost 5gns for a 'bed to themselves' and each person was required to provide his own wine, tea, sugar and washing.

19. Amyand is spelt Amiance in the accounts, but it would seem likely he was one and the same. Again the issue of inoculation was a political one, championed by the Whigs, it was violently opposed by a leading medical Tory, William Wagstaffe. The bill for Master Coke's inoculation was paid in April 1728. Reference for Amyand, see Isobel Grundy, *Lady Mary Wortley Montagu* Oxford 199 p. 215 and for Wagstaffe Grundy p.215.

20. Hatfield Archives Bill 463 George Gittos was a writing master. He taught the page boy and ran the Poor's School founded by Anne Countess of Salisbury. See also HA household accounts the postillion Gittos accompanied the Coke party to Bath in 1723 and rather than ride the lead horse, as he should have done all the way, he jumped up beside the coachman (Frank) on the box and promptly fell off and broke his leg.

CHAPTER 6

Servant Experiences and Expectations

What were the experiences of those servants who worked at Holkham beyond washing, cooking, cleaning, waiting and answering bells? Regular meals, a comfortable bed and with luck convivial co-workers was a reasonable return for the mainly mundane and repetitive work that servants did. But what might they expect besides? Were there perks? What were the chances of promotion? How well were they really looked after? This chapter will attempt to answer this question and to do so involves a journey to Norfolk.

In 1719 the setting of the old Hill Hall at Holkham was purely agricultural, the ancient village still stood round and about. A measure of this can be seen in the 1720s when creating the lawns to surround the mansion involved compensating Widow Carter for the loss of her turnip field, which had been 'taken in'. [1] Contrary to later belief, probably made at the time when the land was cleared to form the park and was lying bare and 'neglected', the parish lands of Holkham were highly fertile. Crops grew abundantly in soil well manured by sheep over-wintered on the land. [2] A mile to the north, but still within the parish, was a further cluster of houses, where the long-disused staithe had once provided access to the sea. The parish church stood, as it still does, a half a mile to the north west. In the distance, glimpses could be had of the sea, generally referred to as the Ocean, 'that great Sublime object' as a later diarist called it. [3] For many of the servants, coming from afar, a view of the sea would be their first. Enchanting and fascinating as it was, it also underlined the distance they had travelled from town to the edge of the world.

In the early 1720s Humphrey Smith the Holkham steward was still resident in the old Hill Hall and it was his responsibility to prepare the house for the Cokes' annual visit. Thomas Coke's election to Parliament in 1722, (for Norfolk, a prestigious county seat) necessitated several appearances in Norwich and on these occasions he took lodgings for himself and his servants. Ab.Thomas his valet, Mr Grundymore the cook, James Davies the under-butler and two new footmen, Philip Bender and George Roth. Abraham Blaumer the footman from the Savoie had quit the previous year and Andrew Griffiths had been promoted to butler. There were also his liveried coachman and postillion and young Tom Robinson, the apprentice. A great deal of entertaining was done at the Angel Inn in Norwich, food and bowls of punch on offer to many. Freeholders, encouraged to vote for Coke, were carted in from the countryside by twenty-two carriers who were rewarded with a free breakfast and a generous 2s. 6d. each for their dinners. Bells were rung at St Peter's and St George's, and if that did not draw enough attention, then the town waits were paid to blast out rhythms on trumpets and drums. A poem was commissioned and read out and the various deserving poor were given five shillings, despite the fact that they were not entitled to vote. Coke was carried through the city streets in a chair bedecked with flowers from which he gave out nosegays and favours left, right and centre, to the porters at the city gates, to messengers and link-boys, to the criers of the court and the four swearers-in. Four clerks each received a guinea.

The election, like so many, was uncontested and the event somewhat reminiscent of the wedding, but with a larger crowd to admire the finery. It cost Coke £103, not a large sum, and for the impressionable servants, if such they were, the election at Norwich was an exciting time. Experiencing the hustle and bustle in a cheering crowd of supporters, most of whom were there for their master, who from now on would be a Member of Parliament, gave them, if nothing else, a fund of anecdotes to tell the servants left at home. The status of your master, no matter how wealthy he might be, was important. Coke's was further enhanced three years later, in May 1725, when he was knighted by George I and made a Companion of the Most Honourable Order of the Bath, followed in 1728 by elevation to the peerage as Lord Lovell and finally, in 1744, Earl of Leicester. All three of these honours bestowed by the King took place, by tradition, in the merry month of May and involved considerable outlay in fees, clothing, entertaining and embellishments, and in excess of £120 on new livery suits for the servants.

The London (parliamentary) season began in late January and ended in July – by September, hunting beckoned all sporting landowners home to their estates. Smith's orders back in 1707 had been to keep the house aired but not to undertake much else beyond essential repairs. Not that there was a great deal to care for, as most of the contents had been sold off in the sale. Coal was burnt for warmth, but for airing the rooms a wood fire was preferred. To prepare Hill Hall for a first visit by Coke was a challenge; no records of furniture being purchased have survived, but presumably this happened. In fact most arrangements were not left to Smith but to a housemaid Anne Radford. The Longford parish registers record many Radfords, and links between Holkham and Longford were to remain constant for the next two hundred years, until 1920 when it was finally sold. After the death of the guardian Sir Edward Coke in 1727, Longford became home to Coke's younger brother Robert. Being a Longford man himself it is likely that Humphrey Smith recommended Anne Radford. Anne certainly travelled *to* Holkham via London. Her orders were to make good the house for Coke's party of family and guests, which she duly did, arriving in January and staying on until April to oversee the installation of her successor Catherine Lines (or Loines). Catherine was to remain at Holkham for the next five years acting as quasi-housekeeper, though her wages were no more than any other housemaid, £5 a year. She purchased soap, mops and other necessities, engaged charwomen and organized the thorough cleaning of the house. She paid for the sweep to clean all the chimneys and stocked up the larders and curing houses. There were always a number of non-domestic servants based in Norfolk, the stable workers, and in the early days these included the brewer and the farrier who both boarded in the house. It was Catherine's job to see that meals were provided for them and to cater for Audit meals held twice a year when the tenants came to pay their rent, for which she bought in a quantity of butter, milk and bacon.

An indication of how sparsely Hill Hall was furnished is shown when Coke wished to bring down 'twelve more gentlemen', five were to sleep in servants rooms and two on field beds in the attic rooms. The servants were moved out or more likely slept in corridors and passageways, a not uncommon inconvenience.

Sport continued to be of paramount importance to Coke, as much for entertaining his friends as for his own pleasure. He kept hounds at Beck Hall in Billingford where his grandmother Lady Anne Walpole lived until her death in 1722 and where he installed a man to feed, exercise and train the dogs, although the huntsmen themselves and all stable workers lived at Holkham. Stag-hunting took place within the confines of Elmham Park close to Beck Hall. Coke employed a park-keeper who wore semi-livery and whose duties were to keep the grass mown and made into hay to feed the deer, to keep the pales (railings) repaired, to flatten mole hills and other related tasks, including sending cuts or whole carcasses of venison packed in baskets as gifts to various of Coke's acquaintances. The park-keeper employed men to cut drains, shoe horses, mend the carts used to carry feed for the deer and horses and, since the river Wensum ran through the park, undertake the swan-upping. His wages were commensurate with those of an upper servant at £24 a year and as a resident of the parish of Elmham he paid parish taxes and poor rates. The fox and the hare, however, were hunted all over Norfolk, and from time to time the fox hounds were quartered at Godwick where Coke kept an apartment in the old hall. [4] When hunting, Coke took with him his valet, who was expected to join in the chase, and his footman cum groom William Holland to look after the horses. If it seemed likely that the chase might end far from home, necessitating a night spent at Holt or Lynn, as did happen, then his cook was brought along to ensure a decent dinner.

Long before any building work was begun on the new house at Holkham, the gardens were laid out. Throughout the 1720s a large amount of landscaping work was undertaken. Levelling of the 'lawns' entailed ploughing by a 'Kentish plow' and a new kitchen garden was created. In 1721 Mr Collings was the head gardener with James Allen, a local man, as under-gardener. Collings was paid £25 per annum but only stayed two years. He was replaced by Mr John Aram from Nottinghamshire who came from a gardening dynasty and was to remain many years at Holkham. At first Aram was paid board wages which suggests he lived in the Hall, catered for by Catherine the housemaid. Later he was given a house in the village rent free.

In contrast to their lives in London, when at Holkham most servants were confined within the bounds of the house and farmyard. In London, even for those who did not often go out, all town life was a mere stone's throw away, impossible not to be aware of its sights, smells, opportunities, glamour and danger. At Holkham on the other hand there was little or no contact with the outside world and as the majority of the servants originated from homes far from Norfolk, the kitchen and laundry staff in particular saw virtually nothing of the house beyond their work quarters. A tradition allowed the Norwich and Lynn carriers to be fed in the servants hall whenever they had business at Holkham, which was once or twice a week; otherwise there was just the gardener bringing vegetables to the kitchen door and the stable and estate workers, the latter surely lingering to get a glimpse of the London servants. It was only when the building of the new house commenced in 1734, that a myriad of builders, skilled and unskilled, lodged in the vicinity; even then it was a world of restricted boundaries. At Holkham, in common with every other country house of a similar size, the servants experienced the true taste of belonging to a 'family'. Their virtual imprisonment, dictated in part by the distance of the house from the nearest conurbation, might result for some in consolidating the sense of family and enjoyment in the company of their fellow servants. For others the home-sickness brought on by isolation led to them wishing to quit their service as soon as possible, and many did so either on returning to London or before.

Their year was divided in two. The usual pattern for the family was to leave London in July and be at Holkham in time for the Audit (at which the servants acted as ushers as well as producing meals and refreshments for a large number of tenants), after which they could 'look forward' to a stay of several months before returning to town after the New Year's Audit in the following January. Gradually the old house Hill Hall was improved, a new servants hall was built in 1729 and every year quantities of furniture and other goods too were sent to Holkham either by waggon or by ship via Wells.

In 1731 the pattern of spending half the year in town and half in the country was altered. That year the family left London slightly earlier than usual, in June, and were to enjoy an unusually protracted stay at Holkham of an uninterrupted nineteen months. Shortly before leaving town it is recorded that Coke spent five guineas on a 'Measuring instrument'. He then purchased a 'Drawing Table, a T and a Level' and set off for Norfolk, taking a circuitous route via Petersham where the Earl of Burlington had recently designed a new house for Lord Harrington, and Beaulieu, the Hampshire estate of his London neighbour the Duke of Montagu. On finally arriving at Holkham the family was not to budge for over a year and a half and it is now that Matthew Brettingham makes his first appearance in the account books along with a copy of Palladio's *Four Books of Architecture*.

These books were a practical guide to building a classical house, inspired by Greece and Rome. The first one is devoted to building materials needed and techniques, the second plans for private houses. They had not yet been translated into English though they were to be in 1738. Brettingham [1699–1769], a builder from Norwich, was also a draughtsman; he was to become the clerk of the works and in time would supervise the building of the new mansion. It is also generally conceded that he had a hand in its design. No-one can be sure which or whose plans were used.

Did they owe something to Coke's early memories of Tittenhanger, or Culverthope his grandfather's house in Lincolnshire, built 1679, of which he was so fond? Or were they the plans Coke had studied on his Grand Tour, brought back to England by his late brother-in-law Lord Harrold? When Lady Harrold, Lady Margaret's sister, visited Holkham in the winter of 1731, did she bring the plans with her? The death of her husband in an accident early in their marriage followed by that of his younger brother had disheartened the Duke their father who never built the intended Palladian mansion at Wrest. Were the plans of Holkham approved or improved by Coke's friend the architect Lord Burlington [1694-1753] or were they an amalgam of many? At all events some twenty-five months later, in 1734, the first foundations were dug and it does seem probable that the long séjour at Holkham with Brettingham was spent in lengthy discussions and measuring the ground.

During this absence from London William Tomley the house porter was in sole charge of Thanet House, along with one well trusted housemaid Anne Simpson. They received board wages for their food at the rate of a shilling a day.

The servant turnover which had begun with the departure of Sarah Howard in 1718, even before the Cokes had settled in to Thanet House, was followed the next year when the housekeeper 'Mrs' Johnson, left to become Mrs Shaw, and carried on unabated despite the family being in the country from June 1731 to early 1733. Each year saw different names appearing and disappearing in the servants lists, and being in Norfolk for a length of time made very little difference. Jane Flavellen, a kitchen maid, left in the autumn and then, in March 1732, Coke's valet Mr La France who had been in this post for three years. The reason for his departure is not known, but it appears to have been amicable for he was taken to catch the Norwich coach by Joseph Johnson the brewer. The journey to Norwich and back by horseback took Johnson two days and Coke paid the expenses, 6s. 8d. Abraham Thomas was still in Coke's employ working as a secretary and stepped into the breach left by La France, a role he had filled already once before. In July 1732 Roquette the French cook had his place in the Lynn coach bound for London, booked and paid for 'when he was to have gone away', but whatever grievances he had were smoothed over, at least for a few months, for he stayed until the October when he finally went with 10s. 'to bear his expences upon the Road' back up to town. John French a stable worker took him to Lynn. The same John French (who was to be discharged himself a month later) had ridden to Peterborough with a horse in April to fetch a new kitchen maid, Elizabeth Berry. She had been hired to replace Mary Wallis who had been dismissed with her expenses paid back to London by waggon. Elizabeth Berry came from Garthorpe a few miles to the north east of Peterborough and rode from there to meet John French on her own hired horse and thence, having left it there, rode pillion behind him from Lynn to Holkham. The cost of this journey including her hiring a horse was 19s. 7d. She stayed for nine months and on leaving she was given 10s. 6d. towards her journey home.

The terms on which a servant left his or her post differed in the way they were recorded. Sometimes their names simply fail to appear in the following year's list of wages, in which case they must have agreed to leave at Christmas, as many did; some choose to quit mid-year but agreed to stay on until the eve of the Family's departure for Holkham or on the return to London. This often happened. The servants wages were always recorded in detail and the amounts owed them worked out precisely. If a servant lasted less than a year then the exact number of days, not just the weeks that they worked, were added up and they were paid for each day. This scrupulous accounting reached its zenith in 1752 when the Georgian calendar was introduced and the servants had eleven days wages docked 'for the Alteration of the Stile'.

The word 'discharged' was the one most often employed when any of the servants left, with its implication of dismissal, though dismissal was not necessarily the case. On receiving their final wages the servants were handed a voucher stating how much was due to them, their name and the date, ending with the words 'I say received and discharged' which they then signed. In this manner there was no coming back later and making a claim, on either side. Their employment had been a contract and with this phrase signed and witnessed, if only with a mark for those who could not write their name, the contract was over, null and void. [5] Reasons for wanting to quit could be marriage, being homesick, failing to get on with their fellow servants, drunkenness, 'sawciness', believing they might do better in another household or changing their occupation entirely. There is no evidence that any of the Holkham servants were discharged as a consequence of pregnancy or for other sexual reasons, though doubtless some were. Specific reasons for their dismissal were not recorded, with the sole exception of Mary Strain who went 'away ill' in 1720. Suspicions do arise when two servants are discharged on the same day, especially if one is male and the other female. Exceptions to this were those who came as a pair, such as the coachman and postillion. They were engaged and discharged on the same days because they worked as a team. The same applied to laundry maids and male cooks. Over the period six pairs of laundry maids were hired and when they quit it was always as a pair, they would leave together on the same day. Among whom were the Hewetson sisters who worked at Holkham from 1738-1742.

Sometimes the word discharged is recorded and followed by 'a month's wages paid for non-warning', as in the case of Mary Wallis a kitchen maid. This implies that either one or other of the parties, or both, were eager to resolve a troublesome situation. Carolyn Steedman in her study *Master and Servant* records that magistrates adjudicating disputes between employers and servants in the early eighteenth century consistently allowed the servant his or her *time*. [6] This explains the extra wages, which gave the dismissed servant time to find a new employer. And of course, as a magistrate himself, Thomas Coke was hardly likely to refuse. If this happened at Holkham then the cost of the journey back to London was also paid; it was best to be rid of an unhappy servant as soon as possible. Between 1722 and 1759 just nine servants, seven maids and two men, were discharged with 'non-warning', the majority of them (seven), before 1735. Often the day chosen for a servant to leave was a matter of convenience, the day before the family departed for the country or the day after they returned to town, as already described. Since at this period the vast majority of servants had been engaged in London, it was only reasonable that they should wish to be there again at the end of their service. Some were employed for a fixed period only (cooks fall into this category) or on trial, but others were dismissed for reasons we can only speculate about. The inconvenience of losing more than one servant on the same day, unless expected, would have been avoided if at all possible. But it did happen occasionally and sometimes with the most unfortunate consequences. One reason could be the arrival of a new housekeeper. When Mrs White took up her duties in 1741 thirteen servants left shortly afterwards. A further upheaval came about in 1745, when twenty-two servants quit out of a total of twenty-eight. An all time record. Mrs Neville had been the housekeeper since 1742, but in December 1744 she married the estate steward Ralph Cauldwell and continued as housekeeper for a further twelve months. Her newly elevated status did not go down well; the servants who quit were hastily replaced.

Meanwhile in June 1731, with the family enjoying their prolonged stay at Holkham, John Bey a new footman arrived from London by the Lynn coach, but he lasted only until September. Another new footman Edward Lorrington arrived a month later to replace him. Mary Ailsworth, a laundry maid, left in November. Sarah Keen, also a laundry maid and possibly Ailsworth's working partner, had been equally anxious to leave but hung on until the family left for town in February 1733, at which time her fare home to Norwich was allowed her. She was one of the very few Norfolk maid servants employed at this time.

The accounts allow glimpses into various events taking place at Holkham during this period. A second pet monkey was acquired and lived at least part of its life at the end of a wire chain. The dog Doney ran off and was eventually found somewhere the other side of Walsingham, game was shot and consumed, cowslips gathered in the spring and made into wine and two 'great dogs' arrived from Longford described by Lady Margaret as 'Wolf Dogs'. Coke attended the Assizes at Norwich and Thetford, and the Quarter Sessions at Walsingham where he sat on the bench with Mr Lee Warner his old chum from the Grand Tour. Social visits were made to Lord Hobart at Blickling, Sir Robert Walpole at Houghton, Lord Walpole at Wolterton, (who gave the Cokes presents of truffles), Sir Henry Bedingfeld at Oxburgh, Mr Edward Spelman at Westacre, Lord Townshend at Raynham, Mr Nelthorpe at Lynford and rather further afield to the Duke of Grafton at Euston. Spelman must have had a particularly fine table, for twice his maid is recorded coming to Holkham 'to dress a Particular Dish' for Lady Margaret. Westacre is some twenty-eight miles to the south of Holkham and was in the owner-ship of Edward Spelman a relation of the Narborough Spelmans.

The widowed Lady Harrold and Mr Edward Coke, Thomas's brother, visited among other unrecorded 'company'. Sir Henry Bedingfeld gave Coke the most generous present of a Chaise. John Neal a footman was sent more than once to fetch Dr Hepburn from Lynn involving an overnight stay at 5s. a time. The fiddlers of Burnham came to the house to play on New Year's Day, harvests were marked and people 'went about' on May Day.

To record the servant changes year by year would be of doubtful inter-est. Throughout the 1720s and 1730s the changes were 'steady' amounting to on average six or seven a year, enough to give interest to those servants remaining but not enough to disrupt the smooth running of the house-hold. Employment agencies did exist in the eighteenth century but were not much used by the elite. Servants usually came by word of mouth, were recommended by friends and relations, by bankers, superior tradesmen and clergymen, or they made direct approaches themselves. Some came from neighbours in London; Mrs Hinckley was housekeeper at both Montagu House and Thanet House though she did not last long at either. In 1745 Rhoda Ford a housemaid moved just a few yards in the other direction when she quit in favour of the Duke of Bedford's household; she was probably related to Cornelius Ford a bricklayer who had worked at Thanet House and lived nearby.

The overall number of indoor servants, between twenty-five and thirty, did not greatly change between 1718 and 1759, although the list differs in some respects as the years passed. By the 1740s the turnover increased to an average of eleven new servants a year, rising to the exodus of 1745 and sixteen in 1746 (exceptional years of unrest, exacerbated by the threat of a Jacobite invasion, not just the new housekeeper), before reverting to an average of eleven for the remainder of the 1740s and into the 1750s. In 1744, the year Coke was created Earl of Leicester, two new outdoor servant positions were introduced. The first was the master of the horse, a role Edward Smith had filled at the time of Coke's wedding, but which had long since lapsed. Thomas Wilkins was engaged for this post in the April 1744 and as a liveried upper servant was paid £30. It was not strictly necessary to employ a master of the horse, except for finery and show; previously and subsequently, the family got along perfectly well without one. It was also in 1744 that a menagerie man first came to Holkham. For many years 'old Mary' had looked after the fowls, collecting eggs and presenting the occasional bird for the table, and from 1736 the dairy maid filled this role. The menagerie man was engaged to breed a selection of birds including pheasants and ducks, though one might imagine there was no need to rear ducks, the marshes being home to plentiful wild ones, but these were not popular for eating due to their reputed diet of frogs and spiders. Previously ducks for the kitchen had been sent from Norwich, indeed the first time Mr Brettingham is recorded at Holkham, the entry reads that he came from Norwich bringing with him eight ducks and mallards and a quantity of pickled herrings.

A menagerie was rather grander than a mere chicken run with birds pecking in the dust, and was far removed from any hint of the farmyard. The beginnings of the Holkham menagerie date from July 1738 when a man was paid for bringing 'the Storks' which, along with other unspecified birds, were kept 'in ye Garden' and fed cannibal style on chopped plucks and offal. In 1744 the first menagerie man as such was employed to care for the flock, which by then included hens, storks, ducks, pheasants, partridge, pigeons, turkeys, and, when the family was in town, the parrot, a white peacock and various canaries. In 1750 a Chinese pig was added. The menagerie itself consisted of an enclosure made from fox-proof wire, inside which were several thatched buildings, where the birds slept at night, and a pond lined with clay where the waterfowl swam by day. Like the gardener, the menagerie man had his own small house, two rooms downstairs and one bedroom above; his wages were a generous £41 a year.

From the 1750s there were two house porters, one in London and the other at Holkham and a new indoor servant; a groom of the chambers was introduced in 1757. By this date the mansion was nearing completion and Mr Kreeger, who worked for Mr Paul Colombine of Norwich, the city's leading upholsterer frequently employed at Holkham, was offered and accepted the post. His duty was to care for the furniture and furnishings and his wages were £30 a year, £10 more than Coke's valet.

The role and number of female servants changed little. There was always a housemaid who lived in London and another full-time at Holkham, with three more who travelled between the houses and two laundry maids. New additions were a still-room maid in 1731 and a dairy maid in 1736.

Numbers of domestic servants were necessary for the comfort of their masters, but their constant presence could also be irksome. For the Cokes and their friends privacy was elusive and solitude almost impossible; temporary escape for a few hours to a temple or cottage *ornée* in the grounds held an understandable attraction. Even at mealtimes the chaplain and the librarian, the Rev'd Mr Springold and Dr Ferrari, shared the main dining table with the master and mistress. Liveried footmen hovered, at the front door the house porter noted down all who came and went, in the background cooks and kitchen staff worked long hours, as did the maids, the dull hum of work hardly ceased; all were needed to cater for the creature comforts of the family.

Servants who married

For female servants marriage meant an end to their employment. A married woman's place was in the home. But before she could make this change permission to marry had to be obtained from the master and mistress. If they approved then they would be expected to provide the wedding party with white ribbon favours and to give the couple a wedding dinner, to be eaten in the steward's room, with music and dancing afterwards. Just eight marriages are recorded, of which six happened within the household, three footmen married three maids and in London a housemaid married one of a chairman who was also employed to guard the house when the family were away. At Holkham the gardener William Aram married a housemaid and Mrs Neville the housekeeper became Mrs Cauldwell the wife of the estate steward.

Some servants were related to one another. After the departure of Charles Wright there do not appear to be any who were kin of the Cokes, but Humphrey Smith for example worked alongside his son Edward. It is not possible to link Humphrey Smith with Nurse Smith, but they may well have been related, as they were all natives of Derbyshire. Nurse Smith was a cousin of Mr Casey the accountant. Likewise Abraham Thomas was probably related to Edward Thomas another sometime accountant. There was a definite familial tie between Abraham Thomas and Anne Neal, who as Anne Coates was a housemaid from 1729-1732; at his death she is described as his sister and executrix.

A further twenty servants shared a surname. Two lots of footmen, the Sommerings and the Rutleys, were brothers, and Mary and Sarah Staniforth sisters. There were four maids by the name of Simpson. The two Hewetsons were laundry maids. Not all were engaged in the same category for example Anne Philpot was a kitchen maid and Elizabeth a laundry maid, Hannah Broughton a dairy maid and Margaret a scullery maid. In London, among the casual help, Mrs Mackdonnel worked alongside her daughter Elizabeth and husband [?] Soloman who guarded the back buildings of Thanet House. In 1746 Sarah and Mary Griffiths both worked in London, probably related to Andrew Griffiths who had set up the accounting method.

Servants who were taught musical instruments

Many footmen played the fiddle and many huntsmen the horn, for example Thomas Annis huntsman who was asked to give his opinion of a French horn in 1724. There were also purchases of bassoons and fiddles and money given to passing musicians, e.g. 'a German that played the French horn at Holkham' and a soldier the same, both given 10s. 6d. In 1728 Jeremiah Sommering a footman was bought a fiddle £1. 6s. and his brother Hiero a bass with bow and set of new strings. The footboy Robinson was taught to play the straight horn as was Philip Bender a footman. French horns were sold by Mr Christopher Bennet in London who also kept them in good repair and 'Anthony' was paid for giving the servants lessons. All members of the family danced, both the Cokes and their friends and the servants. Servant dances were held on twelfth night and on other celebratory occasions such as the wedding anniversaries of Thomas and Lady Margaret and on their birthdays. The Cokes owned harpsichords and possibly a harp, there are bills for tuning and repairing harpsichords and payments to people for playing the harp. The latest country songs were always popular, easy both to learn and dance to, but generally it was 'classical' music of the seventeenth century, such as Coke would have been taught to play on his flute and Lady Margaret on the harpsichord. Some people did send for the latest Handel opera to be hammered out and sung along to in the privacy of their own houses at this date. [7] This may have been the case at Holkham; opera books were purchased, including those of Handel, although there was never a Music Room per se at Holkham.

An entry in 1720 is for Coke paying Mr Smith 'the musick writer' £9 to write out the singers and instrument parts of an (unnamed) opera. A further £18 was laid out for four violins, a bass, a lute, 'a Hautboy' and two tenor singers. This provided a musical performance as part of the entertainment at a grand ball given by the Cokes in London. It was not unknown for some members of the elite to employ professional musicians as part of their permanent household. Sir Jacob Astley of Melton Constable (Norfolk) had a Mr Whitely who played the harpsichord and who, among others, came to Holkham in 1740 to play at the coming-of-age party held for the Coke's son Edward. Lord Salisbury listed musicians among his servants, as did the Duke of Grafton whose players gradually metamorphosed, around 1726, into the first permanent theatre company in Norwich, and were later known as the Norwich Company of Comedians. [8]

Servants who went to the Play

As a schoolboy Coke had been fond of the theatre, and in London he paid annual subscriptions to the box-keepers at Lincoln's Inn Playhouses (which flourished between 1660 and c1732) to Drury Lane Theatre and to Covent Garden. Further payments in the form of Christmas-boxes were paid, 10s. 6d. to each box-keeper and 7s. 6d. to the bill-stickers. The opera appears to have been as much in need of additional support as it is today. He subscribed to 'ye Call for the use of the Operas' generally £50. It is unclear precisely what this was, it was an amount given annually. A season's Silver Ticket was £21. Then there were subscriptions to particular operas, generally those of Mr Handel, at 10gns a time and various payments to actors either on their Benefit nights or individually (£22 in 1720).

From 1720 Coke paid for certain of his servants to attend the theatre. On 4th June that year four upper servants went to the opera. The cost was only 13s. but it was a grand occasion, the premiere performance of Scarlatti's opera *Narcissus*. Five guineas were given as a gift to 'Signor Castrucci'. A week later a second bill was recorded for servants seeing 'ye Opera' which this time cost Coke £1. 7s. and was described as being 'His Honour's Gift'.

Subsequently there are annual entries for upper servants going either to the play or the opera. In 1722 when the Holkham steward Mr Appleyard was visiting London, Mr Lee, Coke's valet, Mr Abraham Thomas and Mr Casey accompanied him to the opera *Griselda*. Appleyard was in London once more in 1730 and went to the opera, and again in 1733, that time in the company of John Aram the Holkham gardener. A visit to the opera was both a reward and a treat, we cannot know how often the servants bought their own tickets but contemporary accounts suggest that it was not out of the ordinary to see servants in the theatre.

One December at Holkham a barn was rented and lodgings paid for a company of players 'by my Lord's order', but it was not until the 1740s that servants in the country, both upper and under, went regularly to the play. This came about by the holding of the Quarter Sessions in Walsingham. It was an event which drew the local gentry into town; Thomas Coke was on the Grand Jury, and the opportunity was taken to offer entertainment to the visitors. The earliest published notice for a Walsingham Assembly, a dance held once a month to coincide with the full moon, appeared in the *Norwich Mercury* in 1742. After dark, travel was easier if the moon was full, providing it was not too cloudy. The first entry for Holkham servants going to the Walsingham playhouse came four years later, in 1746. For the enjoyment of country people the Norwich Company of Comedians, whose season at Norwich ended in April, travelled throughout Norfolk and Suffolk during the summer months performing in improvised venues and were invited to those towns where the Quarter Sessions were held.

The first year, 1746, thirteen Holkham servants went to 'the Play at Walsingham', their tickets cost £1. 6s., and a further 4s. for their stable bill. Walsingham is only a few miles from Holkham and they probably travelled there by waggon. In later years the numbers of servants going to the play increased. In 1748 twenty-two went over two nights and in 1751 twenty-three enjoyed the added treat of supper afterwards at the Black Lion Inn. The Norwich Company of Comedians visited Walsingham every other year and on two occasions during their visit in August 1753 and 1755, 'Players from Walsingham' appear in the Holkham Wine Books being given a quart of port. That year the season began on 1st July and ended on the 18th. On the first night six upper and four under servants were bought tickets and their supper, and three days later tickets and supper for three more upper servants and twenty-two under ones. The plays they saw were *'The Beggar's Opera'*, *'The Lying Valet'*, and *'Barbarossa'*.

In the summer of 1757 the company was at Walsingham for over a month. They opened on 16th July with *'Romeo and Juliet'* – 'altered' from Shakespeare to have a happy ending. It was the first of a variety of plays on offer and the servants went to the play on five different evenings. On one of these thirty-eight attended a performance and must have half filled the playhouse. Not all of them were strictly speaking servants but included people working on the house which was in the final stages of completion. A couple of weeks earlier seven upper servants had attended a performance of *'A Wonder! A Woman keeps a Secret!'*, one of whom is named as 'Mr Clarke the Master plasterer'.

On the days of performances the playhouse at Walsingham opened its doors at 6 p.m. and, according to advertisements in the *Norwich Mercury*, the interior was arranged with boxes either side of the stage 'to render the House cool and agreeable'. In 1757 the gallery was enlarged 'for ease'. Seats or places *on* the stage and in the pit cost 2s. 6d. each, the ones in the gallery 1s. 'Seats on the stage will be formed in a commodious manner as possible and contrived so to render it as airy and agreeable ... ' the advertisement read, encouraging people to fill them, but one imagines they would not have been a first choice.

As in London the theatre programme consisted of a play, a farce and songs, and sometimes dancing, space permitting. Mrs Hill (possibly the widow of Aaron Hill dramatist), was the chief vocalist. The main play of the evening was often requested or rather 'desired' by local dignitaries such as the Cokes, the Warner family of Walsingham or Sir Jacob and Lady Astley of Melton Constable who in 1748 asked for *'The Universal Passion'*, originally by Shakespeare but 'altered by Mr Miller of Wadham College, Oxford'. Shakespeare's plays were very popular but frequently had their endings changed. This was done either for reasons of politics or, as in the case of *Romeo and Juliet*, to provide a happy ending. *'Henry V'* had added scenes to show 'The Conquest of France by the English'. It is not certain how Coke's valet of the time, Monsieur André, would have enjoyed this, or for that matter Monsieur Beaupré, the cook. Both are named among the upper servants in the audience.

Plays by Susanna Centlivre, who had acquired her French surname on marrying Queen Anne's cook, were also favourites at Walsingham. *'A Wonder! A Woman Keeps a Secret!'*, and *'A Bold Stroke for a Wife'*. First staged in London in 1714 and 1718 respectively, both featured servants and were unashamedly biased towards Whigs. *'The Lying Valet'*, another play with a servant theme, as many were at this date, was a two-act farce by David Garrick adapted from Pierre Antoine Motteaux. First staged in 1741, it was often performed at Walsingham. Operas with classical themes were for London; plays extolling patriotism and fidelity, wit and loyalty were better suited to rural audiences – of all classes. However, the most popular of all, as 'desired by the Gentlemen of the Town' of Walsingham, were *'The Merry Wives of Windsor'* and *'The Beggar's Opera'*, neither of which carried so obvious a message. In June 1770 the Lynn Company visited Walsingham. Mrs Turner wrote, they 'open'd the Theatre (commonly called a Barn) on Wednesday last and propose acting three times a week during their stay which ... will be at least a Month'. [9]

Servants made Freemasons

Freemasonry was established, or re-established in England in 1717, and many young men of the elite became members. Its ideals of moral and spiritual values fitted comfortably with the oft-repeated four great aims of the age, politeness, improvement, progress and reason. In the early 1700s Freemasonry was not the secretive sect it was later to become; the freemason's hall was conveniently close by Thanet House in Queen Anne Street and in 1725 Coke's friend the Duke of Richmond was appointed a Grand Master. Thomas Coke was a Freemason and on one occasion chose to extend this privilege to three of his upper servants. As far as the household accounts allow us, we know this happened only once, though he may have paid for others out of his private funds. The entry in the accounts reads:

London 13th March 1731 'Ab. Thomas, Mr La France the valet and Philip Bender a footman were made Freemasons'. The cost to Coke was £20. Abraham Thomas was a faithful servant who had worked in the Coke family from the early years of the century; Philip Bender's full history will be related below. In 1731 he was about to be promoted to a far more responsible post than that of a mere footman. M. La France was the exception; he worked for Coke for just three years and left during the long period spent at Holkham in 1732.

Foreign servants

'Let his house be a pleasant Babel of all Tongues and Nations ... ' wrote Jonathon Swift in his *Directions to Servants*. Tongue firmly in cheek, he recommended a fashionable man should employ a Swiss house porter, French cook, German valet, Dutch butler, Swedish coachman, and Austrian or Hungarian footmen. J. Jean Hecht asserts that this 'picture is not overdrawn'. [10] However from servant lists of the period I would suggest it is, even though most peerage households, like Coke's, employed one or more foreign servants, or servants with foreign ancestry. About 10 percent of the servants employed at Holkham were foreign. As Hecht concedes, at the start of the century some servants with French surnames may have been Huguenots, though by the 1740s there are accounts of large numbers of French servants arriving in England, mainly cooks, valets and lady's maids. [11] The fashion for all things French did not abate until the start of the Napoleonic wars. Until then a number of young men (and other travellers) came back from the Grand Tour with a foreign servant or two, just as Thomas Coke had done, and with a desire to employ French cooks when they set up house. Jean-Baptiste, groom, and Abraham Blaumer, footman, had been engaged in just this way and returned to England with him.

In 1729 Coke paid to release Jeremiah Sommering, a Dutch footman, from his apprenticeship with the Beswilliband brothers. Whether Jeremiah was already in England is not made clear. In 1726 and again in 1746 two pairs of French cooks were sent for direct from Paris. Coke paid their expenses both ways at £25 a time. These cooks would have been procured though the good services of the British Ambassador to France, who in the 1740s was the Duke of Richmond.

Even before the Napoleonic wars French servants were deeply unpopular among the middle and lower classes in England, especially in London where they were looked upon as usurpers and spies, and papist ones at that. Many foreign visitors record being addressed as 'French dogs' as they walked about the streets of the capital. Prejudice against foreign servants was worse in the first half of the century, especially as they tended to be skilled upper servants. [12] How they were seen by their fellow workers within the family adds a further dimension to the tantalizing, but unanswerable question about servants at this period, which is, how did they understand each other in an age when regional accents were far more pronounced than they are today, quite apart from actually being foreign? When this disparate group of people from Kent, Hertfordshire, Derby, London, France, Holland and Switzerland worked together, what problems of communication did they encounter?

As for servants from beyond the boundaries of Europe (which consti-tuted the known world as far as most of the populace was concerned) there is just one in the accounts. In August 1737 Kouli-Khan was baptised at Holkham as George Culican and described in the parish register as a black.

As a footboy (which Kouli-Khan was), his clothing and education expenses would have been paid for directly from Thomas Coke's or Lady Margaret's pocket, rendering him as 'invisible', as were Lady Margaret's personal maids. The little we know about him is that he fell ill in 1742 when the cost of his care was recorded. Fish was purchased to tempt his appetite, he was carried by Sedan chair to a healthier part of London and given Acton water to drink, but in vain. He died and was buried December 5th in the churchyard of St Giles in the Fields. Kouli-Khan was of course, as every eighteenth-century schoolchild knew, a famous Persian general and later Shah of that country. [13] The boy who lived in the Coke family for over five years was more likely to have been African than Persian. It is even probable he was not a slave, but an apprentice, as Tom Robinson and others had been before him. The evidence for this is based on a donation made by Coke in 1729 when he gave three guineas towards the Redeeming of Slavery, a cause promoted by his friend and neighbour the Duke of Montagu who played a large part in repatriating Africans. [14] There are several more entries for money given out as gifts to 'Poor Blacks' recorded in the accounts. How the boy came to live with the Cokes is not known but it may have been through Captain Nathaniel Uring, a Walsingham man who brought rum from the West Indies via Lisbon to Holkham in the 1730s and whose own 'Black' was given five shillings for delivering goods on his master's behalf.

Forty-two foreign servants were employed during Coke's lifetime, most of whom were cooks, valets or footmen. The cooks tended to be French or Swiss, the valets French and the footmen Dutch or German. Two German house stewards are listed; one Mr Grimmerstein was known by his fellow servants as 'Mr Grimestone'. Two of the housemaids were French, but not the lady's maids.

Servants who invested money with Coke

The practice of a new servant bringing with him a sum of money as security has already been described, and the Holkham accounts show that many servants had money invested with Coke in return for annual interest. The initial amount was repaid in full on the departure, with some exceptions. A few chose to leave their money invested with Coke even after they had quit their service, e.g. John Neal and his wife Anne, and Josey Sommering a housemaid. While the servants were in his employ Coke had the use of their money. In 1730 this amounted to a total of £263, in 1740 it was £270 and in the 1750s somewhere in the region of £435. The amounts appearing in the Audit Books can only be seen as a guide, but, however incomplete, they demonstrate a system which benefited both parties and was a better solution for all than keeping money under the mattress, or locked in a box. The older the servant the more money they would have accumulated. For example Gilliard, Coke's valet for ten years from 1742 had £200 to invest. Others equally well qualified for service might have wished to save but had obligations which prevented them. Some got into debt, borrowed from each other or pawned their valuables, such as watches. There are numerous entries for servants of all ranks receiving part of their wages 'on account', that is in advance during the year rather than waiting till December, which after 1727 became the month for payment. The impact of these investments on Coke's income was minimal. At any one time the amount varied between £300 and £800 whilst the total of his domestic disbursements for a year fluctuated between £4,000 and £6,000 plus. However it was still encouraged and worthwhile, with even the most lowly taking advantage of the opportunity. In 1733 Joseph Johnson a stable worker had £10 invested with Coke and William Harriot the coachman £26. Mr Springold, the vicar at Holkham, invested £150 and Dr Ferrari the librarian £350. The interest paid was 5 percent, an excellent rate in the 1730s when more often it would have been 4 percent, and for those servants who invested over many years the rewards were substantial. James Davies, the footman from Hatfield who worked at Holkham for twenty-two years, left with £524. 15s. 6d. in his pocket. It was not unusual for a servant to have in excess of a £100 with Coke, which would add £5 in interest to their annual wages.

Servants in sickness

Smallpox continued to be the most feared disease throughout this period. There are no entries in the accounts for servants being inoculated against it but there are some for them being cared for when they either had, or were suspected of having the disease.

The first occurred while Thomas and Lady Margaret were still away on their honeymoon in 1718 and the maid Sarah Young displayed the feared symptoms. Mr Casey the accountant arranged for her to leave the house and gave orders for her bedding to be thoroughly cleaned, especially the blankets. After six weeks she had made a complete recovery and returned to Thanet House. The next case came the following year, when another housemaid,

Elizabeth Lish, one of the maids originating from Hothfield, became ill. She was sent away in a sedan chair to be nursed by Mrs Forster at Kensington. Lish was only fully recovered and able to resume her duties after four and a half months away. The cost of her illness, paid for by Coke, was made up of her wages paid while sick £1. 5s., the cost of the sedan chair 2s. 6d. and £4. 18s. for the nurse, food and lodgings, plus the wages paid to her replacement Anne Brown, a total of £8. 15s. A considerable expense when taking into account that as a housemaid her yearly wages were only £5. Lish continued to work for the Cokes for a further three years.

It might be thought that the care shown towards Lish was exceptional and had as much to do with its timing, the last months of Lady Margaret's pregnancy, as with concern for the girl, although in theory the housemaid would have had no direct contact with her mistress. However, the danger was too great a risk in any circumstances and similar vigilance was shown to all the servants who contracted, or were thought to be in danger of contracting this disease. An example came only a few months later (as recorded in Chapter 1) when Jack Lee, a postillion, who would only have come into the house for his meals, was sent away to be nursed for a fortnight by the same Nurse Forster: 'in a Distemper, supposed to be the Chicken Pox, but was first thought to be the Small Pox'.

Fear of disease was almost as contagious as the disease itself. When the household first moved to Norfolk in September 1719 the reputation of Holkham as a place of ill-health, with its flat coastline and lingering sea frets seems to have entered the consciousness of the entire servant family, for no sooner did they arrive than many of them were laid low. Within days the cook William Stephenson succumbed to a long unspecified illness, and he was rapidly followed by the cook maid. For the next two months Mr Godwin, a local cook, was engaged to take his place, with a local (unnamed) woman to help him. Then it was the turn of others; two nurses were paid for a period of twenty-eight days at 6d. a day to nurse the 'indoor servants, and another for sixteen days to nurse the stablemen. Mrs Johnson the farrier's wife helped out, sitting up all night with those who were especially poorly, as did Mrs Walker the wife of John Walker, a Holkham groom. John-Baptiste the French groom was one of those most badly affected. Several replacement housemaids were hired to do the work of those too sick to leave their beds. It was an inauspicious start to country life despite having brought a waggon-load of 'wholesome' goods from London. The remoteness of the destination, the inadequately equipped house (Edward Jarrett was sent out to buy chamber pots, coal baskets, lanterns and a quantity of earthenware and brooms) together with the illness that struck so many down, did not make for a successful stay.

The next month, February, a housemaid Mary Strain who had not gone with the main party to Holkham but remained at Thanet House, returned to her native county of Kent. It was recorded that she 'went away ill'. Again concern was shown for her, for although she left her employ several weeks before Lady Day (March 25) her wages were paid up to that date, plus 12s. for a place in the Canterbury coach, 2s. for meals on the journey and a further 5s. 'to defray her expenses upon the Road'. Unlike Sarah Young and Betty Lish, Strain did not return. Cases of smallpox occur only twice more in the accounts. In 1729 Robert Mays, the brewer at Holkham, recovered after a month when he was tended by Nurse Willis and thirteen years later in London, a housemaid Betty Kemp contracted it. Like Young and Lish more than twenty years previously, Kemp was sent away in a sedan chair, this time to Knightsbridge where she was lodged by a Charles Pawley and nursed by him and Henrietta March at a cost of £6. 16s. Her illness lasted from July to October, by which time she was well enough to join the family at Holkham, travelling there by waggon.

Another though less serious condition which necessitated the patient being isolated, as far as these accounts are concerned, was the itch. Scabies was thought quite rightly to be highly contagious. Footmen seem to have been especially prone to it. For several weeks in 1742 two of them were lodged and attended to in London by Elizabeth Macdugall and a third went for a week to be nursed by Anne Taylor. William Wheadon, also a footman, suffered a bout in 1744 and was lodged in London for two weeks by Elizabeth Barrenger who was paid 8s. 'for his Bathing'. At Holkham in the autumn of 1748 two more footmen (unnamed) were lodged and nursed by Frances Rutley for the best part of a month 'with ye Itch', and when the apothecary eventually cured them, his bill and cost of nursing and baiting (feeding) them came to over £3.

The servant household, though large, was a tight ship. Almost every time a servant was unwell and unable to perform his or her duties a temporary replacement was immediately hired. This was especially true of housemaids and kitchen staff; whereas one might be able to rub along with only one footman for a day or two, this did not apply if the number of more lowly workers was reduced. As already noted the female staff worked a full day even to the evenings spent sewing. Any gap in their ranks was quickly filled. Those engaged to replace the sick servants are recorded as 'extra' in the accounts for purposes of wages and other expenses. Before 1730 their names are sometimes recorded, but seldom after that date. In the 1720s Mrs Blinkhorn, as we have seen, was one such, and Elizabeth Macdugall, named above, another, but for the most part they are anonymous. There were always cleaners brought in for the week or so after the family moved to the country and vica versa, and these presumably came from the same source as those who worked in the house when 'ye Maids was ill'. This suggests that some London servants may have specialised in working on a casual basis, ready and able to fill the gaps in households of the elite when needed, for even in times of emergency care as to who was employed would have been taken. Their wages varied, being paid more in town than in the country, but not substantially so; in the main they were paid no more than the permanent servants. In the country local women, especially wives of the estate workers or tenants, took on this role as they had done on the first visit made to Holkham in 1719.

When Catherine Lines a housemaid fell ill at Holkham in 1722 she was treated with wine and lemons. The value of lemons for their cleansing and refreshing qualities was already well known; wine was seen as a tonic. Of the medicines on offer from the local apothecary, one of the most frequently prescribed was bark, a form of quinine taken from the Cinchona tree, ground into powder, mixed with water and taken as a febrifuge, to take away or reduce fever. The taste must have been especially unpleasant for when the Holkham servants took bark, they were usually offered a generous measure of port 'to take the Bark in'.

Apothecaries and surgeons bills appear in the household accounts and were paid as part of the general expenses. In 1729 Andrew Griffiths the account-ant had a small accident, which he did not describe, other than noting that an apothecary Mr Barnard was paid five shillings for 'physick and bleeding when I hurt myself'. When someone was needed to nurse a servant, Coke always paid for this. In 1725 James Davies, a footman, and John Large, a postillion, were nursed at Holkham by Frances Harrison. Substantial sums were paid for nursing servants; when John Magnis a stable worker was ill and nursed by Margaret Pickford at Holkham in 1737 and again by Margaret Turner in 1739, it cost Coke over £3 each time. On both occasions Magnis is described as being nursed 'in his sickness' and not, as was more often the case for stable workers, as a result of an accident. In July 1749 Mary Peck nursed the coachman for twenty-six days and in October the same year Mr Middlestroff the house steward. That summer Middlestroff had paid for a man to bleed six of Coke's servants while they were staying at Sir Henry Bedingfeld's at Oxburgh and a week or two later at Euston, the Suffolk seat of the Duke of Grafton. This was inconvenient but of course servants could not be expected only to get ill at home. The head groom, Richard Essex, had his first serious bout of sickness at Brandon while en route for London, resulting in apothecary, house and stable bills (for his horse) totalling £4. 9s. A few years later, when John Williams, a footman, became ill at Greenwich, his illness cost £3. 7s. The bill was made up of the apothecary's attendance plus a nurse for twelve days and provisions for them both.

The amount spent on treating servants in illness, or as a result of accidents, was fairly steep when considering that in the main they made do without the attention of a physician, although apothecary-surgeons were called in to set broken or dislocated bones and to administer drugs. Since 1704 apothecaries who worked outside London had been eligible to dispense medicine without any regulations and many learnt the skills of a surgeon; some were not just bone-setters or 'curers' of wounds, but adroit (and trusted) enough to bleed Thomas Coke himself. [15] In the country, apothecaries were more numerous than doctors and one or two could be found in each market town. Dr Hepburn, the Cokes' own doctor, lived twenty-five miles away in King's Lynn and charged five guineas to visit Holkham, plus the expense of the Holkham servant sent to fetch him, a two-day journey there and back. Which is not to say the doctor was never summoned to a servant's bedside; in 1729 Dr Hepburn made a visit to Holkham for the sole purpose of treating Dr Ferrari the librarian and Mr George Appleyard the estate steward. But this was an exception and seldom repeated, despite Dr Hepburn attending Thomas Coke and Lady Margaret at Holkham in excess of thirty years. Hepburn, who had previously held a distinguished post in London, died aged ninety in 1759 and is buried in St Nicholas' Chapel in King's Lynn. [16] Dr Holland, who probably came from nearby Walsingham, was far cheaper at a guinea a visit, and was called in four times in 1729 and twice the following year when he attended Mr Dupuis the cook. However after 1732 he does not appear again. [17] A Dr Shouldham attended Mr Aram the gardener and in 1741 came to treat Robert Webster a groom, and in 1742 and 1746 Mr Kemp the farm bailiff. Otherwise, with the exception of Mr Appleyard who died in London in 1742 having been treated by Dr Mead, the Coke's London doctor (the successor of Dr Sloane), the servants, both upper and lower, made do with apothecary-surgeons.

Apothecaries made good livings, often earning more than physicians. They submitted their bills annually, unlike physicians who were paid each time they visited. When Mr Graham, the apothecary most frequently called upon in London, presented his bill for the year 1733 it was for £82, though the amounts fluctuated; in 1744 it was a mere £48 and only £14 in 1751. The average for his year's attendance was normally in the region of £40. In Norfolk the Cokes employed Mr James Jones, apothecary and surgeon, of Fakenham. [18] Fakenham is a good ten miles from Holkham and apothecaries expected to have their travel costs paid for on top of their fees, as well as being provided with refreshments for themselves and their horses. Thus in 1737 two guineas was added to Jones's bill for 'his journies and attendance' and £5 given to his successor Mr Haylett for making forty journeys to Holkham in 1743. Many country apothecaries doubled as vets; the frequently employed Mr Haylett of Wells, who took over after Jones moved on, and later his successor Mr Fassett of Walsingham, attended the whole family, the Cokes, their servants, their horses and their dogs. On one particular occasion Fassett cured Robert Garret, a labourer, of a wound in the thigh which happened when sliding down a hayrick and landing on a fork. Fassett did not confine himself to medicine; on the occasion of Edward Coke's coming of age he sold Holkham a quantity of mugs and glasses. Jones's annual bills were on average £23, Haylet from £36 to £50 and Fassett £20. Several other apothecaries were used in Norfolk, for example Mr Harvey of Lynn, Mr Gibson of Wells and Mr John Curtis, so that the overall bill for the greater family frequently came to more than £100 a year. And this did not include the lodgings, nursing and drugs bought from other sources, the quantities of remedies, cordials etc. made in the still room at home and the port from the wine cellar. Whether Lady Margaret inherited her mother's skills in dispensing medicines is unknown, there is only one entry for 'Physick for ye Poor', but if she did, money for this was more likely to have come direct from her own pocket and gone unrecorded in the house steward's book.

Thomas Coke was not an exception in bearing the expense of his servants indispositions, it was a philanthropic tradition in most peerage households. [19] Employers of every class were encouraged to see servants as people 'of the same Nature with our Selves' and to treat them with fairness and humanity. [20]

To engage a servant was to take him or her into the family and educate and care for them; the law required their wages be paid, but the provision of support in sickness depended on whether the employer was rich and generous enough to supply it. In the case of Holkham the servants could be sure of support and care when ill and this continued into the middle of the nineteenth century when insurance was first introduced.

The combination of eighteenth-century medicine and the natural span of life meant a number of deaths took place among the servants. Regardless of their financial circumstances the servants could expect a decent funeral with shrouds, coffins and all expenses paid for by Coke. Some died in the fullness of their years, Mrs Smith, Ab. Thomas, Mr Appleyard and Dr Ferrari. Others such as Francis Smith a footman were young; after his death his outstanding wages were paid to his father. The account books reveal that Coke paid for the funeral expenses of eighteen servants between 1722 and 1755. The estate carpenter made the coffin and, depending on the position of the servant within the household, some payments included a sum for mourning. When Caton the menagerie man died in 1747 his coffin cost 8s. 6d., his winding sheet 5s. 6d. with 2s. 6d. paid to the curate for burying him. Caton had been nursed in his last illness (4s.) and like Francis Smith must have been a young man for wages were paid to his father. The coffin for Middlestroff who had been a house steward cost £1, that for William Otter a stable worker 10s.

Servants who worked for the Cokes could therefore rely on being well cared for in health, and when ill receiving a generous amount of care and consideration. This was in the main due to the mistress of the house, Lady Margaret, whose father had instilled in her a benevolence towards those for whom she was responsible. The house and its inhabitants were largely the woman's domain though there is no reason to believe that Thomas Coke was not in accordance with how it was run.

NOTES

1. HA In the 1730s the whole of Mr Anger's farm was taken in to become part of the park.
2. Christine Hiskey's chapter *Hill Hall and its Estate* in *Holkham* London 2005 p.54.
3. Huntingdon Library HM 31201 Journal of Mrs Larpent for September 1806,

her description of the sea at Aldeburgh Suffolk.

4.   Godwick Hall was part of the Coke estate in Tittleshall, it was pulled down in the early twentieth century but its moated site can still be seen.

5.   Raynham Archives RAC Box 30/5 Earl of Northampton's papers.

6.   C. Steedman *Master and Servant* Cambridge 2007 p.74.

7.   Dorset Record Office D/WCL /AF1 Mr Weld of Lulworth purchased 'favourite songs in Alfonso and Rodelinda' and the whole of *Semele* in 1744.

8.   Hatfield Archives Bill 528 1725 and Trevor Fawcett *Music in Eighteenth-Century Norwich and Norfolk* Norwich 1979 p.21.

9.   Adverts for plays at Walsingham from the *Norwich Mercury* various years and the HMC *Manuscripts of the Marquess Townshend* London 1887 p.410 Mrs Turner of Warham to Lady Townshend.

10. J. Jean Hecht, *Continental and Colonial Servants in Eighteenth Century England,* p.1

11. Hecht p.6

12. Hecht pp.14–15

13. Staffordshire Record office D615/P (S) 1/310A In the same year 1749 as the Cokes visited Shugborough Lady Anson wrote to her husband about making a Cat's Monument, she called it 'Kouli-Kan's Monument'.

14. Vincent Carretta, *Ignatius Sancho*, London 1998, introduction p.x.

15. Roy Porter *The Greatest Benefit to Mankind* London 1997, pp.288-289, following the House of Lords ruling in the Rose Case of 1704 apothecaries might prescribe and act as doctors.

16. Sir Robert Walpole made Hepburn, his Norfolk doctor, Surgeon's Mate at the Chelsea Hospital c.1715 J.H. Plumb *Sir Robert Walpole, the Making of a Statesman* London 1956 p.205.

17. The Jones Family of Fakenham were 'Welchmen and Maltsters' according to an advertisement in the *Norwich Mercury* of 1735, but others were lawyers and surgeons. Thomas Jones practised as a Surgeon and Man-Midwife in Lynn and later in Norwich; he had moved there by 1738. Mr Daniel Jones was an attorney in Fakenham employed by Thomas Coke since the 1730s.

18. Meldrum p. 91.

19. The sentiments of John Tillotson in 1694 and William Fleetwood in 1737 as quoted by Steedman p.137.

CHAPTER 7

Provisions

Though employed by and answerable to the master, the day-to-day care and welfare of the servants fell to Lady Margaret since it was the convention of the times that, if she was willing and able, the wife should supervise all matters concerning the house, both inside and out. Women of Lady Margaret's class were educated to 'get up accounts'; most kept records of their personal expenditure and many, from royalty downwards, the household accounts. These accounts were to be shown to the master of the house if he was inclined to study them, or left entirely to the mistress as her responsibility. General anxiety about the honesty and reliability of servants, together with a natural desire to know how the 'Domestic Disbursements' were being spent, explains this custom. [1] In 1733 Sarah Duchess of Richmond [1706-1751] wrote to her husband about their accountant Mr Sedgewick: 'I really sometimes think him honest at least I have a great mind he should be so ... '

Her feelings towards the other servants were much the same. She had had occasion to speak severely to their steward Richard Bruckner (whose wife was the housekeeper), their butler and the cook *reminding them all of their duty.* 'I hope they will perform it and that you will be well served'. She continues 'this is quite a letter of business but I have my head full of it at present'. The Duchess was very fond of her husband whom she addressed as 'angel' but worried that they lived in a style they could not afford ' ... if we don't save this summer we are undone I assure you' she wrote, 'consider my angel and take a resolution to reduce your servants and other expenses ... I am always at a great deal of trouble in collecting all the little notes in the quarterly bill and in the book of weekly expenses'. The Richmonds were friends of Coke and like them had two houses, one in Whitehall, the other still building at Goodwood in Sussex. [2]

Curbing an extravagant husband was a further reason for keeping a close eye on the accounts; Duchess Sarah was the daughter of a spendthrift and feared her husband might be of a similar mould. Lady Margaret had some reason to believe her husband could also be in danger, though he was more prone to carelessness than gambling. In the same year, 1733, as Duchess Sarah was writing to her husband and imploring him to cut back on their expenditure, Thomas Coke, by now Lord Lovell and Postmaster General, wrote to the Duke at Goodwood. His letter was opened by the Duchess in error, since it had been incorrectly addressed, as she wryly noted: 'Lovel the Postmaster ought to know how to direct but does not ... ' [3] The culprit confessed a few years later 'I am generally in too great a hurry to dispatch business', confirming that he was more slapdash than he should be. [4]

Impulsive husbands and lack of confidence in accountants and house stewards combined to make it all the more desirable that a wife should control the domestic expenditure. From the surviving account books it can be seen that Lady Margaret had been supervising the kitchen expenses from at least 1723. Williams, one of the accountants employed during the 1720s, kept a cash book in which he recorded the weekly amounts spent on food. These were paid for by funds he received from 'my Lady'; each page was inspected by her and signed in the bottom right hand corner M. Coke. [5] Lady Margaret did not merely read through what Williams wrote, but checked the amounts he recorded against the vouchers received, on occasion writing 'No Bill' beside a particular entry where the voucher had gone missing. The bills varied greatly in how they were written; some had engraved and elaborate headings with the purchases listed in a perfect hand, but on the whole tradesmen selling perishable goods scrawled the goods and the amount due on scraps of paper. These were then folded carefully and handed to the steward. He then checked them and handed them on to the accountant.

A rare survival in the archives is a letter from 1725 which confirms that matters domestic had long been in Lady Margaret's remit; when writing to the lawyer Peniston Lamb of Lincoln's Inn she asks him to pay a bill of £25 due to Edmund Peckover of Fakenham, grocer and draper.

In 1729 the Earl of Thanet, Lady Margaret's father, died and as a result the Cokes inherited the remainder of the Thanet House lease. A few changes were made within the household, one of which was that the money for the 'Domestic Disbursements' ceased to be paid to the accountant or to the house steward *via* Lady Margaret but is entered in the Audit Books as being paid directly by her. Coke was made Lord Lovell the following year and from 1730 she is referred to by her new title of the Rt. Hon. Lady Lovell. It is also from 1730 that Lady Margaret's Household Account Books have survived, written in her own hand, where she listed the weekly expenditure under headings which cover a wide range from food to travel, hounds and hunting, servants wages and liveries, wine, music, library (purchase of books), furniture, linen, silver, Thomas Coke's clothes, sedan chair hire, vails, board wages, gifts, charity, nursery and later Mr Edward Coke's laundry, doctors and miscellaneous expenditure entered as 'Necessaries' or 'Extraordinaries'. From at least 1740 and probably long before, Lady Margaret kept a Day Book in which she listed items to be later entered in the Account Books. For example in February of that year the house steward, Mr Bradshat, refers to 'her Ladyship's Day Book' when recording £80 spent on 'several sorts of Irish linnen' purchased from a Mr Guybon. Lady Margaret in her Account Book of the same week lists these purchases in detail: diaper for the Stewards' Room table, tea napkins, sheeting etc., and her total differs from Mr Bradshat's (£86) because she includes the charges of the cord, box and shipping from Ireland, 'ye difference of ye Exchange'. Bradshat's reference to the day book is the only evidence that such a book existed, but it comes as no surprise when we see her initials on various vouchers to do with the building of the house and the meticulous details of her own household accounts. The work involved in listing each day's spend, and to check and record it was considerable. She was equally vigilant when overseeing the butler's wine books; these she examined every five days writing her initials in the margin, and often at the foot of the page as well, whereas her husband, who was presented with these accounts for his inspection, only occasionally signed them and then with a flourish – L. One can almost imagine him asking, 'Where? where?'.

With the death of Thanet one of his titles, that of Baron de Clifford inherited from his maternal grandmother Lady Anne Clifford, fell into abeyance. In August 1734 as one of her father's co-heirs the abeyance was terminated in Lady Margaret's favour and by patent she was made Baroness de Clifford. It is not known exactly why Lady Margaret, as a younger daughter, should have had a right to this, and indeed it seems to have mystified her contemporaries; Horace Walpole, with typical asperity, decided it must have come about because she was the only one of the earl's daughters to have married a commoner and therefore her children would need a title! Even this did not make complete sense as by 1734 Coke had been Lord Lovell for the past four years. Whatever the explanation, from that date and for the next ten years until Coke was created Earl of Leicester and she became a Countess, Lady Margaret was entered in the audit books as Lady Clifford. [6]

The eighteenth century is often seen as an age when the elite enjoyed a large amount of extravagant entertaining, with French cooks preparing faddish dishes to be consumed by those who remembered such food from their

Grand Tour. Thomas Coke was probably one of those who really did enjoy French food, after all he had spent his formative years on the Continent and judging by his weight in middle years (eighteen stone) was certainly a gourmet, possibly a gourmand as well. However lavish the food might be, behind the scenes it was all carefully recorded. Even so, choice was king, the tables were set with a variety of dishes to choose from, several at each of the three courses, followed by desserts. Inevitably many of the more sumptuous menus of the period have been recorded and commented upon, set out as a guide for the aspiring middle classes and taken to be typical of their times. Only more rarely have records of everyday fare survived. An idea of what constituted an average meal in a house of the elite can be found in the Hatfield archives of Lady Margaret's brother-in-law Lord Salisbury. A daily dinner for just the family had two courses with four dishes in the first course and four at the second.

A dinner of three courses began with a haunch of venison, a dish of fresh fish, a patty of pigeons and a dish of boiled chickens, followed by dishes of rabbits, tongues, tarts and crawfish, while the third course was largely sweet, salvers of syllabubs, jellies and custard. [7]

The precise instructions for buying food and its consumption were recorded by Lord Salisbury's accountant. When in their London house five stone of meat was allowed each day, made up of beef, mutton, veal or pork (costing about £1) and a further 30s. 'to be laid out daily for other provisions such as lamb, fowle and fish, butter, eggs, herbs [vegetables] fruit, flour, cheese etc. and this not to be exceeded'. The steward watched while the meat was weighed and checked all the provisions brought in so that he 'may have a certain check upon the bills. That the account of every week's expense may be made ready against Friday 6 of the clock in the evening ... That the doors be shut up while dinner is bought up and not opened till the servants have dined. And that the porter shall wait at the first two tables. That all the servants resort to their respective tables and nobody suffered to carry out victuals up to chambers on pretence of business or any other account whatsoever unless of sickness, not then without the steward's knowledge and order'. [8]

Similar house rules were drawn up by James Bridges first Duke of Chandos in 1721. His 'Regulation of Provision', shows exactly how much food was to be allowed. Each servant was allowed just three ounces of bread at breakfast, six at dinner and three at supper: twenty-one ounces of mutton at dinner on

Mondays and Fridays: the same of beef on Tuesdays, Thursdays and Sundays and fourteen ounces of pork at dinner on Wednesdays and Saturdays. [9] For of course most of the food in these great houses was eaten by the servants and the larger the household the greater the need for supervision. The prescribed amounts of meat were before cooking, boiled till the goodness 'comes out' as many a recipe advises; beef being cheaper than mutton was the most frequently used. Despite this workhouse approach, there was a clear understanding of the value of a good diet and the importance of feeding servants to keep them in good active health.

When the Coke family were in London, the weekly deliveries of meat were measured by the stone and appear in the accounts simply as meat, with no break down into divisions of beef, mutton or pork. The amounts average out at between forty-five and fifty stone a week, which is the weight of a modern bullock. The cost, 2s. 4d. a stone, or 2d. per pound, varies hardly at all over the period to 1759. The second item on the list 'Meat by Hand' were the more perishable parts, sweetbreads, liver, tongue and other offal.

During the first years, meat in London was supplied to Thanet House by a Mr Chamberlain, who was almost certainly the same 'Mr Chamberlain butcher' who appears in the accounts of Lady Margaret's father Lord Thanet. [10] There were cattle in the fields behind Great Russell Street with a pound in the parish until at least 1736 and a slaughter house where two hundred and sixty beasts were killed in the first half of 1740. [11] Chamberlain may well have rented space to set up his meat stalls in the shambles of Bloomsbury Market. The custom was that food was delivered to the house once an agreement had been reached over the price. Lord Ashburnham describes in his diary how on his arrival in London from Sussex at the start of a lengthy stay, his butcher called on him and he offered *her* a price for her best mutton and veal. His offer was seven groats a stone, an old fashioned amount equal to 2s. 4d.; the butcher said '*she* would consider of it, but we did not then agree'. The following day 'my butcher', as the noble lord calls her, presented him with a side of lamb, but it was not until six days later, on a Sunday, that they fixed the price, the same seven groats he had offered her in the first place. The price of meat in the Holkham accounts fluctuates from the same 2s. 4d. a stone to 3s. depending on the meat, mutton being more expensive than beef. By the 1750s it occasionally rose to 4s. for mutton and beef and 3s. 6d. for pork. [12] Beef always made up the majority of meat bought in the country and stayed at 2s. 4d.

Poultry came from the Nichols family who ran a large enterprise in Parsons Green. They supplied all kinds of poultry including larks, and sometimes, but not always, eggs and butter. Chickens, geese, ducks and pigeons were popular and were occasionally delivered ready larded, spit ready. On the rare occasions when Lady Margaret was on her own she ate only white meat, veal and poultry; veal was always entered separately as a delicacy. [13]

Game and venison was sent from Norfolk, any surplus venison being given away as presents as was the custom, but surplus game was sold, a single pheasant could fetch anything up to 9s. Until the advent of a menagerie man and the intensive breeding of pheasants they seldom cost less than 4s. each. Game not needed for Thanet House was sold to the poulterer Mr Nichols. As Lady Margaret noted in April 1741 he owed her for fourteen partridge and eighteen woodcocks, and in the following July for twenty-eight woodcocks, thirty-eight partridge and nine pheasants.

Fish was not eaten very often in town; barrels of pickled herrings came later in the century. This may have had something to do with personal taste or the abundance of fish available at Holkham, although fresh fish was on offer at Bloomsbury Market, and for the dining room table a favourite dish was turbot with lobster sauce. The bill for fish over a three month period in 1732 came to just £6 while that for meat was £77.

Butter came from a variety of suppliers and varied greatly in quality. Breakfast pats were the most expensive and Cambridge butter, heavily salted, the cheapest. Cambridge butter was only resorted to when local butter was in short supply, usually in January and February. Up to fifty-four pounds of butter was consumed each week, nearly two pounds for each person in the household. That good old staple butter 'eaten alone with bread' was especially popular in East Anglia. Fresh sweet butter was stored in pots and used as a sauce to spread over vegetables. It was further invaluable for potting meat — a welcome change from preserving meat by salting it. Butter for the table was commonly known as 'Breakfast butter', being eaten mainly at that meal, spread on rolls that were made from 'Breakfast flour'. It was also fashionable to carve or mould butter into fanciful shapes, orange-flavoured butter was popular and was also spread on French 'Rowls' baked by Eustace Tomlin after Mr King disappeared. Tomlin, possibly a Frenchman, was *the* baker of his day and like Mr Nicolls had a clientèle all over London from Bloomsbury to Piccadilly. He, or his minions, baked loaves of all kinds and weights, he also sold oatmeal, bran and flour. Judging from the number of

French rolls consumed each week at Thanet House, in excess of a hundred, it is likely that they were eaten by the upper servants as well as by the master and mistress. Bread in London was always bought in. In the country it was customary for one of the footmen to double as baker.

Although ducal in style and wealth, Thomas Coke did not have his own live-in confectioner. Along with many others in London he relied on Mr Lambert the best known and most skilful of the time. Mr Lambert travelled to Norfolk in 1731 when he (and his servants) were hired to go to Houghton to work in Sir Robert Walpole's kitchen, an event important enough to merit a paragraph in the *Norwich Mercury*. In the late 1740s Coke employed a Mr Tricotte who came to Holkham in the summer to make ice cream and 'assist in setting our desserts'. Confectioners were sometimes French or Italian but not always. A contemporary of Lambert's, equally well known and patronised by the peerage group, was Richard Robinson of Bond Street, who may have been related to William Robinson who could be found at the Greyhound and Kings Arms in Fleet Street selling tea, coffee, chocolate, hartshorn and all sorts of drugs, including, as his printed bill adds as an afterthought and in a different typeface, snuff. Both Robinsons appear in the Holkham accounts.

Desserts were served at the end of the meal and were a real chance to show off for the confectioner, whose skill was to make elaborate sugar sculptures as centre pieces. White damask tablecloths were used at dinners in the eighteenth century, generally covering oak or walnut tables. But when the fashion for mahogany took hold and the elite purchased gleaming shiny tables, the cloth was removed after the main dinner was over to set off the desserts to better advantage, mirrored in the highly polished wood. The Cokes bought a mahogany table in June 1728 from Mr Seehousen.

In the absence of a confectioner desserts could be made up by cakes, pastries, fruit tarts, sweet chocolate pies, cheesecakes, muffins, macaroons, biscuits of all kinds, even something called a meringue. All these could be bought ready cooked in London. In the country, sweetmeats and jellies made in the still-room were eaten as dessert and, in the summer, fruit.

The presentation of food in the eighteenth century was an art as skilfully accomplished as any painting or sculpture; fruit was of paramount importance and like certain vegetables it was a status symbol. To be able to offer fruit to your guests, ripened and fit to eat ahead of its season, was the goal of many. Fruit was of course one of the great experiences of the Grand Tour. Many young men were struck by the intense flavours of fruit grown under a

Mediterranean sun and attempts to recreate the taste, sights and smells led to the building of heated glass houses. Oranges were the most popular; bright of colour, they symbolized the Glorious Revolution of 1688 and the securing of Protestant England, an event much fêted. At Holkham Coke built a new kitchen garden over three acres with an orangery and hot walls for grapes. Here several different species of plums, apricots, peaches, nectarines, figs, cherries and melons were cultivated as well as pears and apples. His instructions to the gardener in 1748 fill five double pages. All soft fruit was immensely popular, pottles of strawberries, raspberries, gooseberries and currants, with apricots the particular favourite at Holkham. However, pineapples were the ultimate. Known for more than two hundred years, the first one grown in England and deemed edible was said to have been by Matthew Dekker in 1720. At this date they were more usually known as annanas and at Holkham a special house was built for them at a cost of £64. While it was still under construction the precious plants were cared for by Mr Scott, Lord Burlington's gardener at Chiswick, 'until a proper time to send them down to Holkham'. When that time came the pineapples travelled by sea, packed in baskets and accompanied by Mr Scott himself, who saw them installed in their new home in the July of 1736. The total cost came to £100. 9s. 3d., an indication of their desirability and the wow factor they had on guests, besides the fun and challenge of growing them at all. In winter the annanas house was covered by a sail cloth. An equal amount of effort went into establishing the melon ground.

The fever to produce the first fruit of the season, whether bought at Covent Garden or sent from your own hot house, was second only to the other great passion – asparagus. Asparagus appears each year in the Holkham food accounts from early February onwards when the family were usually in London. It was so prized that it is one of the few items that might be bought 'at the door' a hundred or two hundred at a time. Baskets of asparagus cost 6s. It was steamed and eaten with butter or vinegar, that of a lesser quality being made into soup. Most other vegetables are not named, but entered simply as greens or herbs, and were supplied by the fruiterer-cum-herbman Luke Rose in nearby Silver Street, or viewed and chosen in Covent Garden market. Artichokes were almost as popular as asparagus; other 'herbs' available were 'colly flowers', spinach, celery, onions, garlic, peas and beans, cos lettuces, cucumbers and broccoli (eaten cold as a salad). It should be noted that this was a largely pre-tomato age; they were not yet widespread, even in Italy.

Potatoes were on offer, but at a price; the Townshends had paid 1s. a pound for them in 1685 and they continued expensive. Imported from Spain it was believed at first they could not be grown in the cool English climate, they were a rarity, very few being eaten before 1760. [14] On the whole London vegetables were cheap; the bills varied between 6s. and 18s. shillings a week.

In town, milk and cream was sold by the same milkwoman for many years, a Mrs Howard who was given a garland each May Day. On average the household consumed 30 pints a week and a gallon of cream.

Cheese was bought from Mr Bennet who sold Gloucester and Cheshire cheese, butter, bacon, and candles. Norfolk cheese was bland and not well thought of. Hams came from a firm of grocers, Messrs Burton and Lyde, who also sold the best Wiltshire bacon and sausages. Although Norfolk hams were cured at Holkham, those purchased in London were usually preferred; in fact York hams were often among the food stuffs sent to Holkham. Burton and Lyde sold all sorts of spices, salt, mustard, capers, olives and truffles, as well as almonds, lentils and vermicelli, and those particular favourites of the time anchovies and gherkins. But they were first and foremost English grocers, known as 'oyl men', also selling a selection of non–edible household items such as silver sand, black lead and other cleaning materials and rape oil for lamps. Lamps, both interior and exterior, were widely used, being cheaper than candles.

Some supplies were purchased from the Duke of Montagu, their neighbour. His steward was paid for French cheeses, vinegar, and wine on a regular basis. Much of Coke's wine was stored in the cellars of Montagu House and, even after the Duke moved to his new abode by the river in 1735, the arrangement continued.

Other imported foods were obtainable from Italian merchants. The delightfully named Mr Pastacaldi being the most frequently patronized, with Mr Lucera at the sign of the Orange Tree in Air Street, Piccadilly, a close second. Both sold olive oil from Lucca (then as now the best), pasta, parmesan cheese, anchovies, capers, olives, gherkins, turmeric, pistachio nuts, cinnamon, cloves, rice, sago, currants, and raisins. The Italians were also importers of Mediterranean plants, specializing in roses, and were suppliers of orange trees to Holkham.

One item that increased greatly in the amounts purchased over the years was sugar. Very little was bought in 1718 but by 1748 an average of ten to twenty pounds a week came into the house, supplemented by the occasional bulk purchase. In March of that year room was made in the store cupboard for 176 lbs of loaf treble refined, 140 lbs of double refined, 314 lbs of single refined (for servants) 100 lbs of lump sugar, 28 lbs of beet sugar, 14 lbs of brown sugar and 24 lbs of sugar candy. The bulk of this was sent to Holkham. Sugar decreased in price further still in the 1750s when coloured sugar became fashionable, but the quantities purchased remained much the same.

Chocolate, that popular 'stimulating' early morning beverage, was first bought as coco nuts and sent to Mr Bland to be made into chocolate. Later in the day, tea and coffee were drunk; Mr Twining was certainly well established by the 1730s, but at this period he was eclipsed by Mr Collet Mawhood who held the monopoly, supplying tea and coffee to all the peerage group without exception.

A few of the more unusual food items purchased in London were mangoes and Indian sweetmeats, pomegranates, wafers and ice cream in summer, and on one occasion in 1753, listed between orange flower water and anchovies, a quart bottle of Japan soy which cost 6s.

Dozens of bottles of mineral or spa water were drunk by Coke and Lady Margaret, rather more than in some households. The mineral water was purchased direct from a merchant at the spa rather than from a shop in London; a letter written in 1775 records a Mr Field writing from Cheltenham (a spa of increasing popularity) confirming that he would send the water to 'Mr George Cowls gould smith opposite the Roil Exchange ... he dos Bisness for me in London, I will send it fresh from the well'. [15] The majority of the mineral water purchased by the Cokes came from Bristol, but also from Scarborough and Bath, and something innocently called 'Barbados water' cost a guinea a bottle, enormously expensive.

Although Norwich was well able to provide most of the provisions on the grocers' lists, when the family were in Norfolk almost nothing was bought there. At the beginning of this period, 1718, prices in London were marginally cheaper, though this is less likely to be the reason, rather that the London shopkeepers were known to the family. From the first, non-comestibles such as candles and earthenware were sent from London to Holkham by the waggon along with groceries; in 1720 these included sugar, nutmeg, black pepper, ginger, almonds and rice. Prunes, raisins, currants, Jamaican coffee, mace and nutmegs were all purchased from Mr Wells, a London oilman, to be packed and sent on the hundred and thirty mile journey. As mentioned above, bacon, ham and cheese, both English and foreign were also ordered from London mercers to be consumed in Norfolk. In May 1749, at the start of a five-month stay, the waggon was packed with twenty-four hams, 460 pounds of bacon and sixty-two pounds of Gloucester cheese, plus ten pounds of mustard, forty pounds of chocolate and a large quantity of other food stuffs.

In Norfolk all food, apart from that produced in the kitchen garden and after 1736 in the dairy, was bought in and paid for. Even the park-keeper at Elmham was paid for his game and this was to change very little. Meat was purchased from the three tenant farmers at Holkham and from the butcher in Wells. Fish from Richard Wortley and for over twenty years flour and wheat from Thomas Beeston, a tenant of Horatio Walpole in the adjacent parish of Burnham Thorpe. [16] Before the building of the dairy, butter, milk, cream and eggs were bought from tenants' wives and supplementary fruit and vegetables at market. Norfolk samphire is mentioned, though it is unclear who actually ate this 'poor man's sparrow grass'. The nearest town, Wells-next-the-Sea, had no market, but to the west of Holkham lies the village of Burnham Market where the housekeeper and the house steward bought weekly purchases of yet more butter, eggs and lemons. In winter, barrels of Cambridge butter arrived from Lynn to supplement local supplies; once some came from as far as Newcastle. In the early years tea was bought from the Holkham vicar the Rev'd. Springold, an interesting source but one for which there is unfortunately no further information. Gradually the Wells grocers grew more sophisticated and stocked tea and coffee, then ginger, nutmegs and saffron and were able to deliver regular amounts of raisins and currants, mace, biscuits for the parrots, and by 1749 even bottled capers and olives. Despite this London grocers continued to supply the bulk of dry foods used.

Edible gifts were frequently sent and received. Fruit and venison, as already mentioned, and presents of salmon are recorded, though these were more likely to be sea trout, an even more delicious fish but one not greatly popular with the locals. At an outdoor village feast in 1751 it was recorded that the venison and herrings were eaten with great gusto, but the salmon left untouched. [17]

The 'meat' coming into the kitchen each week, the equivalent of a bullock, would have been the mainstay of the servants diet. The presence of the great jack in the kitchen and the employment of a roasting cook shows that large cuts were roasted having been larded to prevent them from drying out. An equally large amount of meat would have been boiled with vegetables to make pottage thickened with rice and other grains, then garnished with dumplings, fried pigeons, forcemeat balls, sausages or even toast. Yet more meat found its way into pies; these were usually made with poultry, chickens, pigeons, turkeys and hares but also with the more dubious parts of the bullock, first roasted and then hashed. The considerable amount of raisins and currants bought each week were the ingredients of many a boiled pudding eaten in the servants hall. Plum puddings were eaten on days of celebration, puddings made with smaller quantities of dried fruit such as 'spotted' dick were for every day. While the Cokes ate 'frenchfied' food in their dining room, the fare in the servants hall was far plainer roasts and stews. Even so there was generally a choice with two dishes on offer. The menus for the upper servants who ate in the stewards' room was somewhere between the two and reflected those of their master, not unreasonably as some of them were foreign, as were the great majority of the cooks. Servants ate dinner, their main meal of the day, at about one o'clock, before the family, and were served by the kitchen maids. Kitchen maids, when their turn eventually came, got no choice but were given just one dish. The hour for those in the dining room was four o'clock, making the most of daylight hours for hunting and outdoor pursuits and leaving enough time for indoor pleasures of cards and dancing afterwards.

In London the left-overs were never wasted but given to the 'Poor at the Door'. There is no record of this happening at Holkham but it may well have done; there were still many mouths to feed in the country both human and animal.

The cost of feeding the greater family was in the region of £18 a week in the 1720s, rising to £23 by the 1750s, although the size of the household remained largely the same. These sums include the beer and ale drunk by the servants but not the wine. It is reasonable to conclude that the servants were well fed, for a replete servant was more likely to be contented and do his duty than one who was forever peckish. The attitude to size was quite different in the eighteenth-century, when to be well covered, at least for a man, was a sign of being prosperous. Holkham, in common with many another grand house, had a weighing scales upon which people sat, which is how we know what Thomas Coke weighed. It was not so for women, many wished to retain their slim figures and dieted.

Wine was drunk every day; one is tempted to write at every meal. The cellars at Holkham held huge amounts. In March 1739 there were 102 dozen bottles, most of which were bought from merchants and traders in Lynn, one of the major English ports trading in wine in the eighteenth century. The majority of the table wine and fortified wines (port, brandy and Madeira) came either from or via Lisbon, as the frequent entries for ships' captains in the wine books testify. Captain Nathaniel Uring, a Walsingham man who travelled across the Atlantic several times, once in the service of the Duke of Montagu, wrote his memoirs, first published in 1726, and a few years later appears in the household accounts supplying Holkham. Mr Aram the gardener went to Lynn on one occasion in 1737 to pay the expense and duties on two pipes of wine sent by Captain Uring from Lisbon; another time wine was delivered direct to Holkham by 'Captain Uring's Black'. Uring supplied rum from Jamaica and a popular Portuguese wine known as Methuen, named after a British Minister at Lisbon who in 1703 had negotiated a preferential duty between England and Portugal. Wine was also bought direct from other ships' captains, Captains Southgate, Hamilton and Price, or else purchased through the Lynn merchants, which included Messrs Hogg, Brown, Nuthall, Robinson, Steward, Allen and Pealing. These men imported French, German and South African wine. Cape wine dates from the mid-seventeenth century. Presumably supply and demand dictated whether to buy direct from a ship's captain or to go through a wine merchant. Most wine was delivered in casks to be bottled at Holkham. Wine was given as a present and received as such; in the country Sir Henry Bedingfeld gave Coke some French white wine and something that perhaps he had distilled himself, 'Pine Apple Rum'. Lord De La Warr sent Coke champagne, Lord Ravensworth Tokay and so on.

The daily wines on offer at 'My Lords table' were claret and Lisbon, a white wine. Claret was, on the whole, reserved for Coke, his immediate family and his guests; only very occasionally did they drink burgundy. When entertaining, in addition to claret and Lisbon, champagne bought from Underhills in London was offered, along with old port, arrack, Tokay, Madeira, rum and Rhenish. On the occasion of the birthdays, all three of which fell in June, Lady Margaret's on the 16th, Coke's the 17th and their son on the 21st, port and brandy was offered to 'several persons of account' to drink their health. When Edward, the son and heir, was twenty-one in June 1741, an immense party was given at Holkham to mark the occasion with a display of fireworks and extra servants brought in. Mr Warner of Walsingham loaned his cook maid, Lord Hobart from Blickling his butler, cook and three footmen and a Captain Morden (possibly a misspelling of Mordaunt) his butler. [18] On a daily basis those at the steward's table drank Lisbon, port and rum, or punch made with rum or brandy. These would be the upper servants, the estate steward, Mr Appleyard, and his successor, Mr Cauldwell, Dr Ferrari, Mr Brettingham, clerk of the works, the gardener Mr Aram and Mr Coke's tutor Mr Shelvocke. Much the same choice was on offer to visiting tenants, superior tradesmen such as Mr Blyford who supplied large quantities of material for the upholstery, Mr Hill the watch and gun-maker from Walsingham, the captains of ships bringing materials to build the mansion, the doctors and apothecaries, the Fakenham lawyer Mr Jones and visitors' valets.

The housekeeper entertained mainly female visitors, for example Mrs Appleyard in her widowhood and Mrs Harvey her sister, offering them home-made elderflower and ginger wine, but also Lisbon and a choice of port, rum or brandy. In the still room she used wine to preserve fruit to put in jellies. The kitchen used wine in sauces and for 'washing' cheeses. The sweet white wine Lisbon was the most often drunk in the country and Calcavella, a similar one also from Portugal, in London. Servants were given wine as a tonic when they were ill, and presents of port or rum were given as gifts to certain poor people. There seems to have been a firm belief that wine helped servants to recover from illness, judging from the generous amounts they were given, six dozen bottles in 1739 were allowed for 'Servants in Sickness'. Thomas Coke, who suffered from poor sight, had 'eye water' made with rum. Wine was even given to animals, especially horses, as a cure all, and to birds in the menagerie, in fact it would seem to almost anyone who asked.

The twice annual Audit Days were occasions for a great deal of cork-popping. At the New Year Audit of 1749 the tenants drank twenty bottles of rum, six and a half dozen of red port and eleven bottles of Lisbon. Did anyone bother with ale, beer, cyder or cowslip wine when stronger stuff was on offer? In those days of re-cycling all the bottles were later washed out by the under-butler and used again.

The brewery at Holkham produced enough small beer and ale for all the household. The method of English brewing was to use a single charge of malt for two or three mashes, rather like topping up a teapot with a second or third lot of hot water. Ale was the strongest, small beer made from the third mash contained very little alcohol and was the everyday drink, even for children. Brewing was a seasonal business; Robert Mays, brewer from 1730 to 1759, worked between six and nine months a year, and was usually paid 1s. a day with a helper. He had first joined as footman and became under-butler in 1729, but from 1733 worked in the brewery only. When not engaged in this work, that is during the summer months, his given occupation was that of fisherman. Whether leaving behind the world of livery and swopping it for the mashing of hops was a promotion or demotion is hard to say; it was his choice of work and it is impossible to compare the two occupations. In some years he earned as much as £25, easily on a par with a footman.

Other occasions when alcoholic refreshment was provided date from the 1730s when 'Companys' came to see the house. Many of these had begun visiting Holkham long before the foundations were laid in 1734, for building work had started first on the Obelisk and then on the gardens, plantations (woods), the lake and new kitchen garden which resulted in a great many 'People of Fashion' being drawn to Holkham curious to see the progress. The frequency and numbers of 'Companys' could present a problem, interrupting a quiet morning of letter-writing or sketching, but it was acceptable for the family to excuse themselves even from people they knew. Louisa, Countess of Pomfret records in her diary of 1748 how, when a party known to her arrived to view her glorious house at Easton Neston, she and her family 'removed out of the Gallery for them'. [19] But on the whole the owners of the houses visited liked to show them, especially if they were brand new mansions like Holkham. However the sheer numbers who descended made this difficult. Despite the remoteness of Holkham in 1748 twenty 'Companys ' of people visited with up to ten or twelve people in each company. This increased over the years culminating in 1755 when sixty-seven 'Companys', a possible one thousand three hundred people, descended on Holkham between June and December. In the summer of 1741 when the Cokes were on a tour of Devonshire, a total of four dozen bottles of wine were offered by servants to the curious by way of hospitality, in return of course for vails. Then the visitors had a choice of Lisbon wine, rum or port besides many non-alcoholic refreshments. It became an expensive business, though one advantageous to the servants who received an increased amount of vails for serving the sightseers. As the numbers increased the 'Companys' were limited to drinking Lisbon rather than the more costly port. 'People to see the House' came every year, the only requisite being that they should give their names. From 1760, the year after Coke died, his widow Lady Margaret, ever the practical organiser, placed an annual advertisement in the *Norwich Mercury*: 'Holkham Hall in Norfolk is allowed to be seen every Tuesday, but no other day. No persons will be admitted that do not tell their Names'. According to Mrs Poyntz, staying with her son Charles the Rector of North Creake in 1766, Lady Margaret held a Public Day on Thursdays in summer, in addition to the Tuesday sight-seeing. A public day was one for entertaining friends and acquaintances, a sort of open house, in this case left over from the days when Thomas Coke was an M.P. and courting voters. Writing to her daughter Lady Spencer Mrs Poyntz recommended a visit to Holkham saying: ' ... it is her delight to show the house, she told me if my Lord and you ever come to Norfolk, she flattered herself she should see you some Thursday; you will find a very elegant good dinner, for she is very well served, and there is no fuss'. Mrs Poyntz said that Lady Margaret was something of a recluse and hardly ever went visiting, but 'she does great good, keeps many families, but is beloved only by the poor, and will not mix with the people here'. [20] This last remark confirms Lady Margaret's dutiful stance to those less fortunate than herself, servants included.

Finally board wages, that is money allowed the servants for their food while the family was away or travelling. This should be straightforward, but how it actually worked is far from clear. For example in 1754 when the Cokes went on one of their longest tours to Newcastle and were absent for several weeks from July to September, nine servants travelled with them leaving three behind at Thanet House and approximately ten at Holkham. During this time the amount of meat bought into the kitchen at Holkham hardly changed from when the whole family were present. The wheat to make bread, the raisins and currants, sugar and butter was delivered as before and paid for as usual out of disbursements. However, the other regular provisions were much reduced. No fish appeared despite it being summer, no lemons, four rabbits but no other game, no veal, chickens or any other white meat, no eggs, no fruit or bacon nor any cheese. The only luxury was a pound of tobacco and twenty-four pipes. From this it appears that the servants left at Holkham were allowed the basics of their requirements, meat and bread free of charge and bought in the rest themselves, despite being paid the same rate as those left at Thanet House who enjoyed no such perks. Different amounts were paid to individual servants according to their position in the hierarchy. The upper servants were allowed 10s. a week, liveried servants 7s. to 8s. and maids 5s. to 6s. The principle of board wages was in theory to curb extravagance; the temptation to run up tradesmen's bills or help themselves to their master's cellars was great, especially when the servants were left in town. Supposedly many were tempted to live the life of the absent family, if one of the most popular plays of the eighteenth-century, *High Life below Stairs* written in 1752 by Charles Townley, is to be believed. Board wages did give the servants some freedom, namely the choice of how to spend this allowance, whether to be frugal, get themselves invited to meals in other servants halls and save that way, to eat entirely on their own or co-operate with their fellows and pool their funds. Carefully managed board wages gave them an opportunity to entertain fellow servants, though this would have been overseen by either the house steward or housekeeper. Despite this, board wages remain something of an enigma; it is not known how or when they were paid, was it in advance or on the return of the family? Did each servant receive coins and then pay them to the cook or cook maid in return for their dinner, or was it done by voucher? Whichever method was used (or a completely different one), board wages made up a considerable part of the annual expenditure on the housekeeping, e.g. £46 in 1734 and £48 in 1745.

In so large a household catering for an average of forty people in three different dining rooms, a strict 'method', another favourite eighteenth-century term, was employed. Lady Margaret's accounts show that there was the minimum of waste and the detail allows an accurate comparison of prices during the years she kept them, from 1730 and 1759. It is also believed that she inspected the kitchen and adjacent rooms frequently, for cleanliness was paramount. Once the kitchen in the new house was built, no servant not engaged in food preparation was allowed in. There was a hatch in the wall connecting the kitchen to the corridor and at meal times food was collected from here and then carried to the various eating rooms.

Thomas Coke was fortunate in his diligent wife; while nothing was stinted and their entertaining in London and Holkham was on the grandest scale (and the servants well fed), each egg, each pat of butter, each and every morsel was counted and recorded. The tradesmen appear to have been paid promptly, it was known exactly what was owing to them and it was up to them to send in their bills. Some London tradesmen only produced bills at the end of the season with the result that they were not paid until the start of the following one. This was common in many households, but like the annual payment of servants wages, it was Holkham practice to be regular in settling what was owed. An incentive to pay promptly was the discount offered by many suppliers, five percent (on a previously agreed price). The evidence suggests the whole 'family' was well fed and though there may have been instances of theft or pilfering in the kitchen none are recorded. Wine and other stimulating drinks were offered frequently to all, tobacco and pipes given to the servants and hospitality experienced on a daily basis.

NOTES

1. In some households in the early eighteenth century the house steward and housekeeper controlled the 'Domestic Disbursements' between them, preparing the accounts ready to be inspected when called on, although these were sometimes neglected for months or years on end. But in other houses the mistress took these duties upon herself, checking and double checking the accounts weekly and monthly and disciplining the servants both male and female when necessary. For housekeepers left to run a household on their own see Lyme Letters, also the Earl of Pembroke's housekeeper Elizabeth Edsall who paid all the food bills and had charge of the 'ready money' in c.1733 and subsequently her successor Sarah Bayly who had 'all the Tradesmens bills 'under her Direction'. This seems to have been a tradition in the Pembroke family. See Swindon and Wilts Record Office A 5/1. By contrast the Duchess of Marlborough, the Duchess of Newcastle and Mrs Windham of Felbrigg in Norfolk kept a close eye on domestic expenditure: Mrs Windham wrote to her newly wedded son in 1709 ' ... very glad you design to let your wife manage, it is much the best way, the Housekeeper I mentioned can neither right [sic] nor read more than her bills'. Norfolk Record Office WXC 7/21 Letter 18. Louisa Countess Pomfret records in her diary of 1748, when at Easton Neston Leicestershire, she ordered groceries from London from a Mr Rawlinson who also supplied Holkham ref. Leicestershire Record Office RO DG7/4/12a.

2. West Sussex Record Office, Goodwood Archive no 102 Correspondence folios 15 and 20. The correspondence shows that the Duchess was also privy to estate matters. The Duke frequently deferred to her, asking her advice on the subject of mortgages and sending her his winnings from the card table to pay the more pressing estate bills.

3. West Sussex Record Office Goodwood Archive no 102, Correspondence folio 5.

4. NRO WLS XV1/1 410 letter no 131 written c.1740 when Thomas Coke was Lord Lovell to Thomas de Grey of Merton Norfolk, the father of the 1st Baron Walsingham.

5. HA A/10.

6. *The Complete Peerage* and *Horace Walpole his Letters*, Cunningham vol. 1, p.255. 'My Lady Clifford got her barony so in preference to Lady Salisbury and Lady Sondes her elder sisters who already had titles for their children. It is called a title in abeyance'.

7. Hatfield Archives no 58/391.

8. Hatfield Archives no 77/404.

9. Huntingdon Library Stowe MS.ST44 folio 21. Regulation of provisions.

10. Kentish Studies U 455 383 A/2.

11. Woburn Archives. Mr Joseph Willoughby's rent book no 12 for 1740; the meat must have been sold at Bloomsbury Market, a Bedford enterprise.

12. East Sussex Record Office, Ashburnham MSS ASH 932. Diary of John 1st Baron Ashburnham [1655-1709]. Book Two entries for December 1686.

13. NRO MF/234. Mrs Harbord of Gunton, in her recipe book, fricassée of veal.

Thin slices stewed with white wine, eggs, parsley and cream and served with veal meat balls, herbs and bread, or minced mutton wrapped in vine leaves described as a Turkish dish, a favourite was collops of veal cut thin and fried with shrimps and bacon. And for supper bacon and eggs, sometimes as a form of garnish accompanying cold meat, sometimes on their own.

14. Joan Thirsk *Food in Early Modern England 1500-1760* London 2007 p.102.

15. Staffordshire Record Office D615/EH/56, Field to Mr Anson 20 May 1775.

16. Wolterton Archives Estate and Household Accounts 3/1/4 1750. Thomas Beeston tenant of Lord Walpole at Burnham.

17. *Norwich Mercury* 2nd September 1751.

18. HA £38 was spent on musicians at Edward Coke's coming of age celebration; there was a firework display by Mr Palmer, plus a number of bonfires, tents in the garden, the greenhouse lit up by tiny oil lights, crawfish from Fakenham, and extra men engaged to help out in the stables for the visitors' horses etc.

19. Leics RO DG/4/12a Diary of Louisa, Countess of Pomfret for Friday June 10, 1748.

20. Mrs Poyntz quoted by James pp.293-4. Mrs Poyntz was née Mordaunt and the grandmother of Georgiana, Duchess of Devonshire.

CHAPTER 8

Travel

At first glance a chapter on travel may not seem either especially relevant or interesting, but the accounts of journeys made by the greater Holkham family are among the most evocative. There was no more foreign travel after Coke's return from the Grand Tour, with the exception of Edward Coke, the son and heir, who embarked on his tour lasting two years in 1738. But many places in England were visited which give an insight into the customs and interests of the eighteenth-century traveller. It was of course essential for Coke to spend time in London, for although he is chiefly remembered for building Holkham Hall, equally important to him was his time as an M.P. and later a member of the House of Lords. When not attending Parliament or Court it was the custom to visit friends and relations both near and wide, though usually staying no more than two or three nights with each. These journeys were opportunities to visit other gentlemen's seats, besides the wonders of nature ('Ye Peak') and the growing manufacturing towns. Tolls were payable at certain places, but when the Cokes were young, turnpike trusts were a new invention and hardly existed outside Middlesex. Roads were often little more than tracks, rough and rutted, generally limiting distances covered each day to twenty-five miles. When E.M. Forster lamented the loss of rural England in the late nineteenth century he spoke of a countryside we can still just imagine, already criss-crossed with railways. How much greater must be the leap back another hundred and eighty years? According to the weather and the time of the year travelling between London and Holkham, a distance of a 130 miles, took from four to five days. Comments about the conditions of travelling are easy enough to find, but none relate whether the travellers enjoyed the actual business of getting from one place to another. Probably not. A day's journey was just about bearable, but five? However, as it has become increasingly clear even to the present day, people are prepared to put up with a great degree of discomfort in order to visit places.

The popular image of travel in the eighteenth-century is of a coach and four dashing along a chalk path bordered by moorland with perhaps a distant sparkle of the sea, footmen clinging on at the back for dear life and the coachman swaying on his box as he urges his horses on. Generally there is no sign of a postillion – or much else that is accurate.

Many travellers were unable to afford anything other than their own steam. They walked. Long distance travel was hazardous and it was all too easy to lose your way, for at this period large swaths of England were still uncultivated heathland. When a journey of more than a few miles was undertaken, it was sensible for foot travellers to attach themselves to a carrier's waggon, which afforded protection and guaranteed that the correct route was being followed.

If funds permitted, a speedier method of getting around was by horse. A horse could be hired for a shilling a day plus the cost of its feed en route and secure stabling at night, costs which were nevertheless in excess of a modern car and its fuel. If unlucky, the horse might need shoeing or even have to be left behind having fallen lame. More expensive still was to take the stage coach.

When the family, that is Thomas Coke, Lady Margaret, Master Edward and servants, moved between London and Holkham, all three forms of travel, stage coach, horseback and walking were used plus Coke's own coach and his chaise. The chaise was much lighter than the coach; it was designed mainly for pleasure and usually drawn by only one horse. A chaise was capable of carrying two or more passengers, and on these long journeys was sometimes used to transport the upper servants. Moving a party of about twenty-five people was a small-scale military manoeuvre and needed considerable organisation.

In London Thanet House had no stabling of its own and due to the high cost of keeping horses in livery stables they seldom remained in town longer than was necessary. Once they had safely completed the journey from Norfolk, they were rested for a day or two, before being taken back to the country. Only saddle horses were kept in town. It was not strictly necessary to have coach horses in London; six were needed to pull the coach over country roads but in urban surroundings two were sufficient and easier to manage in crowded streets. When a coach was needed in town it was easy enough to hire a pair. The chaise and the coach itself, the Berlin, possibly the same Coke had purchased in France, remained in London while the family was there. After a four or five days' journey, it was often in need of repairs and repainting, work carried out by a coachmaker named Budworth, surely a relation of the Longford vicar.

The area around Great Russell Street was part of the Bedford estate and in 1719 Mr Morton, the tenant of the nearby Blue Boar Yard, charged £15 for Coke's saddle horses standing at livery from June to September. The rent of the two stables and the coach house with chamber above, where the coachman and postillions slept, was a further £9. This sum did not include

the feed for the horses or other incidentals. Morton's bill for corn came to
£23 and he added £5. 3s. for the use of twelve forks, twelve shovels, five
wheelbarrows, six halters, brooms and cords; he even charged for a sack. On
top of this bran for the horses was purchased from Mr King the baker, a cost
of eight guineas in 1727. Ten years later Morton's bill had risen substantially
(and this in a century of low inflation); by then he was charging £57 for
three months and the stable rent had doubled to £18. Then as now, London
stables (garages) were at a premium. When Morton's lease expired in 1742,
Coke was paying for coach house rent only and hiring saddle horses when
needed from a Mr Miller. From 1744 an arrangement was made with the
young 4th Duke of Bedford; Coke paid him £61 for a thirteen year lease of
stables and no more is heard of Mr Morton.

Many grandees either owned or rented small estates near to London where
their horses could be grazed without the need to make a long journey home.
It will be remembered that Coke's great grandfather the Duke of Leeds had
such a place at Wimbledon, his grandfather Newton at Richmond and his
own parents at Tittenhanger in Hertfordshire. These 'suburban' estates were
a welcome treat when their owners wished to escape for a few days from
the 'fowl' air of London. At this date Coke's estate was made up of parcels of
land scattered throughout England, but none were near to London. However
there is some evidence to show that in the early days of his marriage he had
contemplated repurchasing Stoke Poges where, in the sixteenth century, his
illustrious ancestor Sir Edward Coke had lived. Casey records journeys to
Stoke in 1721 in the company of William Talman the architect, but nothing
came of it. Instead, and in common with other families whose estates were
far flung, the horses were returned home. [1]

Therefore, before the family travelled from London to Norfolk, it was
necessary to send a messenger to Holkham with an order to bring the horses
to town; he returned with a groom and as many as twelve or fourteen horses.
The image of this, one or two men riding alone with a string of horses over
four or five days like cowboys in the wild west, reinforces our view of the
trust invested in the servant and of his skill and knowledge in being able to
fulfil this mission. The groom was entirely responsible for the upkeep and
safety of the horses, and each night he paid a man to look out for them while
he slept. He was trusted to take the most direct route and to deal honestly
with the considerable amount of money he needed to cover the cost of
the journey. (He was probably further charged with informing the various

inns along the way that shortly the family would be travelling and booking rooms in them). Two such trusty grooms got through the best part of £7 when leading horses from London to Holkham. The Cokes were fortunate in their head groom Robert Webster who worked for them from 1719 to 1741, he remained at Holkham until his death eight years later and was paid for looking after the dogs.

Once a date had been fixed for the family to leave town and the horses sent for, the servants began to prepare for the great exodus. The family silver was sent to the bank for safe keeping, extra watchmen were engaged to 'lye across the back buildings', and the servants set to organising what should go by waggon. A waggon was always needed to transport the main bulk of the luggage and any heavy goods, from furniture to kitchen provisions. By the time the waggon was packed and the grooms and horses had arrived in town the party was ready to set out. Farewells were said and the 'Poor at the Door' given their charity money to help sustain them till the family returned. This was given in lieu of the food generally distributed at the kitchen door twice a week: ' ... fragments from the several Tables in Baskets ... with the Broth the Meat is boiled in' was customary. [2] Many poor families depended on hand-outs in excess of the parish rate they received; they were 'the deserving poor' known by name to Mr Casey, the accountant, who listed five recipients in London, all of whom were women, some with children.

Consideration was shown to the servants for their extra work in preparing for the journey; before they began the long trek to Norfolk, alcoholic refreshment was handed out to keep their spirits up. One for the road. They were each given a measure of port to help them on the way, and were rewarded with more on arrival at Holkham – 'to the servants coming off their journey port and Lisbon wine'. Supplies of wine were also sent in the coach for the Cokes to drink at the different inns they stopped at en route.

The master and mistress travelled in the coach with their son Edward and Lady Margaret's maids, with the footmen and some of the male servants as outriders. According to the season the main party could expect to spend three or four nights on the road, the first at Leystonstone, the next at either Bourne or Hockerill in Hertfordshire, the third at Brandon and the fourth at Swaffham, each approximately twenty-five miles apart. There was also a halt in the middle of the day for a meal. To ensure comfort the Cokes had travelling beds and their own cutlery and plates, though many country inns offered a good standard of accommodation. Those on major routes aimed to please their elite clientèle and the servants who worked in them were often of long standing.

After leaving London the route more or less followed the modern M11 and was bordered by largely featureless heathland or sheep walks, relieved only by passing through private grounds at Newport (south west of Saffron Walden) for which they paid 1s. 6d. This empty landscape could be confusing if there was little traffic, for there were no signposts and few milestones. North of Newmarket the common at Brandon was a particular hazard and necessitated hiring a guide at a shilling a time, as the shifting sands of the Breckland often obliterated the road. Mrs Lybbe Powis was certainly struck by this fact in 1758 on her way to Norfolk: ' ... those well-known dismal sands' she wrote in her journal, 'not but we had books, packs of cards ... and I think two or three rubbers of whist were played'. [3] Once in Norfolk and past Fakenham, the route to Holkham digressed from that taken today, branching off west via Dunton and then north towards the Creakes, approaching the southern end of the parish over yet more heath and then straight ahead, after 1739 passing through the Triumphal Arch and into the park.

Not all the servants travelled with the main party. The Holkham house-keeper (Mrs Smith from 1725 to 1740) almost always went by stage coach, first taking a hackney coach from Great Russell Street to the Bell Inn at Holborn from where the Lynn stage departed. It was acceptable for gentlewomen to travel alone this way and there is some evidence that in general more women than men used stages coaches, [4] though on occasion she travelled in the company of one or more of the other upper servants. A place in the stage coach between London and King's Lynn cost in the region of 18s. and was reserved at least a week in advance by paying an 'earnest' of 10s. 6d. plus vails (tips) for the coachman and ostlers at the inn. On arrival at King's Lynn the servants were met either by a Holkham stableman, or by a man employed by one of the tenant farmers, with an extra horse or a small cart. Since the distance between Holkham and Lynn is twenty-five miles this man would have set out the previous day, as Robert Webster the head groom did in 1729: 'his expences with two horses bringing Mrs Smith from Lynn to Holkham 6s. 6d.'. A week later the architect Colen Campbell took the stage coach to Lynn, also on his way to Holkham, the cost of reserving his seat was 10s. and that of his servant 5s. From this record we can see that Mrs Smith and Mr Campbell would have travelled inside the coach, and Campbell's serv-ant outside. In the winter of 1739 the Lynn stage coach was hired for the exclusive use of the Holkham servants, plus several boxes and a portmanteau, and on this occasion, on arriving at Lynn, they hired a man and five horses to bring them all to Holkham. There was no hard and fast rule; sometimes upper servants travelled in the chaise with the main party for some of the way and then took the stage coach for the remainder, or vice versa. In May 1743 the new housekeeper Mrs Neville and Abraham Thomas the secretary took the stage coach from London to Norwich; they had possibly left it too late to book places in the Lynn coach. Norwich is a good ten miles further from Holkham and their combined journey cost a princely £5.

The housemaids and laundry maids followed with the waggon at a slower, walking pace taking up to six days to complete the journey. At the beginning of this period the waggon was hired from Mr James Large of Swaffham, who first appears in the Holkham accounts in 1707 running a weekly service to the Bell at Holborn and back again, and extending to Holkham, Walsingham, Binham and Holt as required. In common with other waggon owners, known as carriers, he was an innkeeper with a chain of connections along the route; his son George kept the Crown at Barton Mills. The waggons were pulled by six or more horses, not in pairs, but in a line, one behind the other, with passengers sitting on the waggon if the roads were not too bumpy, or else walking beside it. For the journey the Holkham maids were given board wages to cover the cost of their food and lodgings, 1s. a day for food and 1s. 6d. for lodgings. These journeys afforded them a degree of freedom away from the beady eyes of the housekeeper and house steward, and one might imagine some high jinks and flirtations took place along the way. However, they appear to have been remarkably responsible; there are no accounts of any of them absconding or other misdemeanours, yet there was no hierarchy among them, except that imposed by themselves. In the early years one or two of the 'Boys' travelled with them, either a kitchen or footboy, and once or twice the baker or a footman. But the men usually rode; riding horses was considered more manly than sitting on a waggon or inside a stage coach. Also travelling with the maids, and in their care, were the smaller family dogs and, prior to the building of the menagerie, the parrots. (The monkey does not appear to have lasted long). The large dogs, the mastiffs and others, travelled with Coke; those who went with the maids were mainly spaniels, Dutch dogs (poodles?) and several 'little black dogs' (dachshunds?) one of whom needed physick on a journey in 1741. The waggoner's man drove the horses and the maids travelled unsupervised, walking or riding twenty miles a day and lodging in inns at night or, perhaps to save money in warm weather, sleeping out under the stars. In time the carrier Mr Large was succeeded by Mr Framingham until 1743, after which the estate steward Mr Cauldwell provided a Holkham waggon.

As the waggon travelled at a slower pace than the coach party, the maids always arrived a day or two later than everyone else. The housekeeper was occasionally sent on ahead but the maids were not, nor did they stay on behind to clear up after the family left. Charwomen were hired by the day to fill these gaps, working under the supervision of the resident servant, the house porter in London and the maid-in-residence at Holkham. In 1747 an 'Irish Carr' was purchased which was a lighter faster waggon and the journey time was cut from six days to four. But the carr was disposed of after just two years, being perhaps too light and insubstantial. After 1750 maids occasionally travelled in the chaise with a footman to drive it; in 1753 a maid made the journey between Holkham and London by this means in just three days.

The average number of servants who made this long journey twice a year between London and Holkham, was twenty-five, and the total cost in terms of turnpikes, lodgings, meals and guides was in the region of £25 to £30. The hiring of the waggon was an extra expense, on average £45 a year.

Over the years a good deal of furniture and other large, heavy and delicate goods made their way to Holkham, including many of the works of art acquired by Coke on his Grand Tour. The majority travelled by sea. A regular service ran from Brown's Wharf in the Thames to Wells Harbour. Bills for freight, as goods conveyed by water were listed, appear frequently in the accounts. Sending goods by sea was cheaper than by waggon and the risk of them breaking or being damaged in transit was less, so long as the ship reached port safely. A number of entries for charitable gifts made to men whose boats had been lost, and of sailors washed up dead on the shore, are recorded but the large proportion of the raw materials needed to build the new mansion were sent by ship and arrived with little or no loss. The various captains of what were known as the 'Stone Ships', i.e. bringing stone to embellish the house, were entertained in the steward's room where their favourite tipple was port. Servants also took the sea route from London to Wells occasionally; in 1730 Abraham Thomas and John Pepper, a footboy, travelled to Norfolk this way at a cost of 10s. Possibly they were sent this way to ensure against any pilfering. As both the old house, Hill Hall, was improved and the new mansion begun in 1734, the bills for carriage and freight increased as a stream of building materials, furniture and furnishings were despatched to Holkham.

Whichever form of transport was taken, the journey to Holkham from London was a lengthy one, though it should be remembered that for any eighteenth-century traveller going almost anywhere of any distance took time and involved overnight stays on the way. Even the journey to London from Kent, where so many of the first servants came from, took three days. [5]

The hazards of travel were remarkably few; horses going lame, falling sick or straying were the most frequent problems, but these were solved by hiring post horses. Repairs to the vehicles are not often mentioned, possibly because they were simply kept in good condition and well serviced before setting out; only two instances record the wheel of a coach needing attention. The sole accident serious enough to be entered in the accounts took place in the winter of 1722-1723 when the coach carrying Thomas Coke turned over at Holkham and Mr Tubbing the Burnham surgeon was sent for to see to Coke's shoulder which had been badly damaged.

Incidents of another kind, encounters with 'gentlemen of the road' were also relatively rare. The valet Abraham Thomas was held up by a highwayman in 1723 and robbed of three guineas, his own money; later Coke reimbursed him. The only other encounter also involved Ab. Thomas when he was robbed of 14s. in 1739. This was the occasion when the Lynn stage coach had been hired for the Holkham servants, and Mr Perry the house steward was also robbed, of 5s. That year a single highwayman had twice robbed the Norwich and Lynn coaches near Newmarket, first in February and again in November 'between four and five in the morning and rode off towards Bury'. This may have been the same coach hired for the exclusive use of the Holkham servants; the report says the man took rings and money to the value of £7. The Norwich coach was robbed again a month later. Possibly the 'gentleman' in question was one John Robinson known as 'Nastiface' who was caught and sentenced to be executed at Thetford Assizes the following March; he was hanged there in April 1740. [6]

Coach travellers were more likely to be robbed than horse-riders, as they were something of a sitting duck for a highwayman who chose his place and time carefully, and before 1750 many coach drivers did not carry firearms or guards. Most reported hold-ups took place near to London. [7] No more incidents of this kind affected the Holkham family personally, though there was an indirect episode involving two highwaymen in January 1749. The

Swaffham post boy on his way to Thetford, where he would have met up with the Norwich Coach to hand over the mail bags he had collected from Rougham, Holkham, Wells and Fakenham, was stopped by two masked men and robbed. News travelled with surprising speed, for when it reached Holkham, Mr Banks the house steward set out immediately in the company of a soldier, and possibly others, to join the 'hue and cry' with hopes of retrieving their property. One of the searchers found the scabbard of a sword and was rewarded with 2s. Later the highwaymen were arrested and held at Walsingham where the post boy was sent to identify them. Two months later, again at the Thetford Assizes where Coke would have been on the Grand Jury, the men were found guilty and soon after executed on Castle Hill in Norwich. Death by hanging was the standard punishment for highwaymen and they were only rarely reprieved, in contrast to other criminals, but 'took their leap into eternity' in public, watched by crowds.

For the majority of the population the cost of travel was far more of a deterrent than the dangers. Many longed to explore the countryside beyond the bounds of their parish, and while servants were not at liberty to choose where they went, there was some compensation in the variety of places they visited when going about their master's business. The servants essential to journeying, the coachman, postillions and valet and footmen had to be ready to leave at short notice, for some visits to both Holkham and London were made on the spur of the moment. In a letter to Mrs Lee Warner of Walsingham written in January in 1746, Lady Margaret tells how they had left Holkham for London 'at one days notice' that year; there was some urgency for Coke to be in town due to the 'late Actions in Scotland'. [8] Despite the journey taking a minimum of three or four days, on occasion Coke travelled to Holkham staying there for a week or less before returning and similar brief visits were sometimes made to London.

Within the confines of London male servants enjoyed many outings. They accompanied their master and mistress to masquerades and to the theatre, where footmen went on ahead to reserve seats, to the opera, to Ranelagh Gardens and Vauxhall, and to Court, as well as to numerous private houses. Being sent out on errands had a particular attraction for servants as this was usually a chance to add to their fund of vails; they could earn 6d. fetching items from shops, delivering letters, or calling for a sedan chair. Considering the servants were in their master's employ it is curious that they were given vails for carrying out these orders. The majority of these tasks were not open to the maids, though it was not unheard of for the housekeeper and maids to do some shopping on behalf of the family, even taking the coach on occasions to transport large items such as chairs. The valet and footmen accompanied Coke to Parliament and wherever he went in town (almost daily use of the sedan chair) and on the many expeditions to places close to London, e.g. Hampton Court, Blackheath, Greenwich, Chiswick and Windsor. Coke often visited Lord Harrington at Petersham, where he virtually lived in the spring of 1745, hunting almost daily in Richmond Park. Further afield he visited Guildford, Hatfield and Hothfield with Lady Margaret and her maids, and went into Sussex to Suffield (Lord Delaware) and to the Duke of Richmond at Goodwood. The Duke of Montagu, their neighbour in Great Russell Street, had a house at Greenwich and one at Ditton near Hounslow, where Coke mixed in the Duke's circle among those 'Men of Feeling', who discussed sensibility long before that sentiment became fashionable and discussed the merits of Gothic architecture. [9] Longer excursions were made from London to another of the Duke's estates at Beaulieu in Hampshire and several to his great house, Boughton, in Northamptonshire. Most of these journeys necessitated staying overnight, especially when hunting was involved, and a minimum of three or four servants made up Coke's party.

All involved a degree of organisation, if only to have enough ready cash to pay the increasing number of turnpikes. Horses had to be kept well shod, harness in good repair, bags packed and liveries brushed. When visiting his friends' houses at Colebrook, Chiswick and Richmond, that is near to town, Coke's servants were given board wages and slept at inns, where the bills and stabling for the horses were paid for by his personal footman, who also paid the turnpikes. The vouchers were kept and later presented to the house steward and the footmen re-imbursed. There were soon turnpikes on every road leading from London and the price depended on the number of horses and type of vehicle, one horse and its rider might expect to pay 6d. to get to Chiswick, the whole family travelling to Holkham 9s. 2d. When staying at more distant destinations, such as Beaulieu and Goodwood, the servants were found beds in the house or stables, and the horses stabled free.

Male servants were also sent out of town on solo missions; William Holland the footman went from London to New Hall in Essex at least four times in the early 1720s, probably to do with horses and gifts of venison, and more than once to Hammersmith and Kensington. William Harriott the coachman was sent to Acton, Andrew Griffiths to Holkham and an unnamed footman to

Norwich. Matthew Brettingham, who became clerk of the works at Holkham and from 1732 was in charge of the new build, travelled more than once to various destinations paid for by Thomas Coke to 'observe', among them Ditton and Gunnersbury near to London and then further afield to Lincolnshire and Yorkshire. [10] Similarly the gardener Mr Aram in 1732 was reimbursed for 'going to London and back and seeing several places thereabouts'. This shows that the majority of male servants travelled in and around London with a considerable degree of independence and knowledge, for they were expected to know the way to all these places and not take wrong turnings or be late. At Holkham the footmen had maps in their bedrooms. [11]

The servants also made many journeys when based in Norfolk. Coke attended the Assizes at Norwich and Thetford twice a year, social occasions where much sport was enjoyed at this period, especially cock-fighting. Among his stable or outdoor servants Coke employed Mr Topley, at £15 a year, who was in charge of his fighting cocks. The cocks needed as much care and preparation as did hounds for hunting, and there were a great many of them — an announcement in the *Norwich Mercury* for October 1729 advises its readers of a match to take place at the Anchor in Thetford between Thomas Coke (by now Lord Lovell) and John Thurston of Hoxne with thirty-one cocks on each side. Two years later it advertised a match with forty-five cocks a side and presumably there were more in reserve at Holkham. William Sadler, an employee described as a cock-feeder, was sent to Derby to fetch cocks in 1730. The Duke of Montagu, a virtual vegetarian, known for not wanting to kill cattle for food but waiting until they died naturally, was nevertheless a fan of cock-fighting and met Coke at Thetford on more than one occasion to 'enjoy' a match or two. He travelled with the usual number of servants including his cook and confectioner. [12]

In the country, servants were sent on errands from Holkham to Lynn, and sometimes to Peterborough, either to meet the stage coach, to welcome a servant or wave adieu to a departing one, to collect boxes, deliveries of wine and a myriad other things. Periodically a servant was sent to summon Dr Hepburn from Lynn, and apothecaries from Fakenham. A few went further afield to Longford in Derbyshire, Lincolnshire, Nottingham and Yorkshire on a variety of missions fetching gamekeepers, dogs, horses, and waggon-loads of goods.

In Norfolk the coachman drove Coke and Lady Margaret to pay social visits to Houghton, Raynham, Narborough, Rougham, Oxburgh, North

Walsham, Gunton and Wolterton. It was the custom to visit, even if they had recently seen each other in London. According to Mrs Lybbe Powis the Houghton Walpoles, the Cokes, Townshends and Jacksons of Weasenham 'used to meet almost every week at each other's houses'. [13] In 1730 there was an expedition to Sheringham by boat from Wells. Opinions about the merits of sea air were gradually changing in its favour and it would appear that the family, with servants, were keen to test this out for themselves. Occasionally détours were made on the journeys to and from London to stay at Oxburgh with the Bedingfelds and at Lynford where the Nelthorpes lived, both close friends of Thomas Coke.

Visitors coming to Holkham in their own coaches were frequently met at Swaffham, Brandon or even Saffron Walden, out of courtesy, to show the way. While a schoolboy, Edward Coke travelled home for the holidays from London in company with his own footman and his father's valet or William Holland the footman or both, and after Holland left, by Mr Longstreth junior. They too were met along the route by the Holkham coach or chaise, sometimes at Saffron Walden, more often at Brandon.

In April 1721 the Cokes made their first visit to Bath, where they stayed for two months. They took with them the housekeeper Mrs Thomson, two lady's maids and eight other servants including the cook. They returned to the west country in 1723 and again in 1724, each time spending three months at Bristol. The Bristol Hot Wells were supposed to suit Thomas Coke's health better than the waters at Bath, though Coke went to Bath one last time in 1734. Each journey took in a number of other places on the way, including stays at Minster Lovell and visits to the Bicester and Oxford races. Once more William Talman the architect was engaged to go with them part of the way on one of these journeys. However if Coke had any plans for Minster Lovell, a damp spot with the Windrush lapping at the walls, it would seem they were not carried out. Wherever the Cokes travelled, the most was always made of local sights and interests; short stays were the norm, never more than two or three nights with friends or in a lodging so that a large number of places could be fitted in. As curious as the next man, Coke had purchased two bound books of 'Gentlemen's Seats' in 1722 at a cost of 6gns. These were surely the first two volumes of Colen Campbell's *Vitruvius Britannicus*; the third would not be published for another three years.

Lady Margaret's favourite sister Lady Harrold was widowed in 1723 and lived thereafter at her quaintly named house Bill Hill in Berkshire, which today enjoys a panoramic view of the M4. Over the years the Cokes visited Bill Hill five times, and after Lady Harrold's second marriage to Lord Gower, a childhood acquaintance of Coke's and an equally passionate fox hunter, they journeyed twice to Trentham, the Gower seat in Staffordshire. Not all diversions when travelling were recorded in the accounts; for example in 1749 when they were at Trentham no mention is made of a visit to Shugborough (or the amount of vails given to the Anson servants) but Lady Anson records in a letter to her husband that the Cokes spent a day visiting her. She describes how the party arrived in the morning and were shown the house and the newly built Chinese Buildings in the garden, assuring her husband that despite Coke's love of 'Italian architecture and French Meaubles' their visitor was quite won over and declared a preference for the Anson's Pagoda over the Obelisk at Holkham. [14]

These occasional tours of England were undertaken in the summer months. The first was in 1736 to Yorkshire by a circuitous route that took in Derby to see the silk mills, Chatsworth and doubtless Longford among many other stops. In 1741, following the celebrations for Edward Coke's twenty-first birthday, his parents took him to Plymouth via Brighton (on the cusp of becoming fashionable) and Weymouth; part of this journey was made by sea. Accompanying them were the cook, four footmen, the valet, Lady Margaret's maids and the coachman, groom and postillion. The inclusion of the cook and bills for washing the cook's aprons, and for meat, show that many nights were spent in lodgings. This was a two-month excursion and the list of places visited fills several pages of the account books. The object was to introduce their son to the parts of the estate he had hitherto not visited. In common with other 'tourists' in the peerage group, advantage was taken of seeing as many sites as they could, including Lulworth Castle in Dorset, home to the Catholic Weld family. At some places, such as Goodwood and Wilton, they stayed with friends. On the return journey a night or two was spent at Minster Lovell and then home via Rousham, where William Kent had begun work on the house and garden three years earlier. [15]

In 1744 another lengthy tour was made, this time once more to Derbyshire and Yorkshire, and in 1754 a 'Tour to the North' lasted two months, travelling via Birmingham, York and Durham to Newcastle. Of added interest was to see at first hand the emerging industrial centres. Passing through Sheffield in 1736 they stopped to look at the 'wyer mill', the mill for 'splitting nails' and 'several manufacturers there' and made a number of purchases. Mr Roblau the house steward as usual carried the purse and from it paid for twelve razors, two kitchen knives and forty-eight knives and forks. The latter cost only 10s. which suggests they were without handles which would be added later. At Birmingham in 1754 they bought a number of 'toys', nutcrackers, candlesticks, tinder boxes and toothpick cases. The silk mills at Derby were of particular interest having been founded by a Norfolk family, the Lombes. [16] The last journey of any distance that Coke made was in August 1758 when he and Lady Margaret set out from London to Holkham via High Wycombe, Longford and Chatsworth.

Shortly before Coke was created an earl in 1744 he added a master of the horse to his family of servants. This man appears in the stable accounts only and is never recorded in the list of servants wages though he was an upper servant and addressed as Mr; he earned between £25 and £30 a year. He was primarily a status symbol, a suitable appendage for an earl; when travelling he took over from the coachman and paid all the bills to do with horses and stables. Doubtless he looked very grand in his livery, but his remit was humble; he purchased boots and spurs, a new cap for the postillion and gave money to the footmen to pay the turnpikes. He was sent to Norwich to meet a cook off the Norwich stage coach, to fetch a new landau carriage from Hertfordshire, to deliver a set of horses to Swaffham to be collected by Lord Delaware's groom; he took mares to be covered and once accompanied a sick servant to London. The first man appointed stayed two years, the second only two months. Mr Marcham arrived in 1745 and after he left in 1750 a Mr Pountney was taken on in his place, but he is only recorded for one year and thereafter the position was once more left vacant.

Reading through the travel expenses it becomes clear that travelling played a central part in the life of a Holkham servant whether male or female; even if they were not travelling themselves they were in constant contact with others who were. In the first half of the eighteenth century long journeys were far from comfortable, whether in a coach, chaise or on horseback. Even less so on foot following a waggon, yet a servant accepting a post in a household of the elite would have been prepared to accept that some travelling would be involved. Having already made the break to leave their village or town in exchange for London it was a condition of their employment to undertake journeys accompanying their master and mistress when moving from one house to another, or carrying out commissions. Occasional travel, despite its discomfort, surely relieved the boredom of repetitive manual labour which most servants endured and for the upper servants travel offered opportunities for a wider experience than that of their own household.

NOTES

1. Wolterton Hall Archives 3/1/1 and 3/1/4. In 1738 Edmund Wright was paid extra 'for going up to London with five horses via Attleborough and Barton Mills, and what he paid for a shoe and nails £2. 0s. 9d.' and in 1750 'going to London with the coach horses etc. £3. 5s. 6d.'. Further examples can be found in the Raynham Archives RAD/C4 2 and 3.

2. Huntingdon Library, – Stowe MS.ST44. Household Regulations for Cannons 1721.

3. Lybbe Powis pp.1–2.

4. Dorian Gerhold, *Carriers and Coachmasters* Sussex 2005 p.93.

5. Kentish Studies U 455 383 A/2 Lord Thanet's Book 1706–12.

6. Reports in the *Norwich Mercury* 1739-40.

7. Gerhold pp.100–101.

8. NRO Lee Warner Box 7 441x2 letter 33. Lady Leicester to Mrs Lee Warner from London dated January ye 23rd 1745/6.

9. Stuart Piggot *William Stukeley* London 1958 p.119.

10. The gardens he visited in Lincolnshire and Yorkshire are not recorded but perhaps Culverthorpe and Castle Howard are possible – the Aram family came from Knaresborough originally.

11. HA INV/8.

12. There are no records of Thomas Coke ever going to Newmarket despite it being on the way to London. He lost a huge amount of money at the time of the South Sea Bubble, and did win some back through gambling, see Parker pp.12–20. This must have been at the card tables or at cock-fighting matches.

13. Lybbe Powis p. 4.

14. Staffordshire Record Office D615 /P (S)/4/1–3.

15. Col. James Tyrrell employed William Kent in the early 1730s at his house Shotover in Oxfordshire, Thomas Coke either knew Tyrrell and/or visited Shotover in 1723 when there is an entry in the accounts for a payment to Col. Tyrrell's groom.

16. The Derby silk factory was built for John Lombe a member of the Norfolk Lombe family in 1717; he had studied silk weaving in Italy. It was highly successful. John Lombe met a mysterious death in 1722 but had already made a large amount of money which he left to his half brother Sir Thomas Lombe.

CHAPTER 9

Four Case Histories

In the absence of servants dairies, memoirs and correspondence, it is not possible to follow the individual careers of the servants other than those who stayed with the Cokes for many years. Any attempt to fill out a life must consequently be restricted to one of those long-serving kind, hardly the average servant, but nevertheless worth studying. A number employed by Thomas and Lady Margaret Coke remained in their employ to the end of their lives, for example Mrs Smith, Ab.Thomas and William Tomley the house porter. The four servants cited below were also at Holkham for many years, Jeremiah Sommering for at least twenty-nine, Sarah Staniforth thirty-five, Philip Bender twenty-seven and John Neal twelve. They have been chosen not only for their long service but for their change of role within the household, demonstrating what opportunities a servant could be offered.

Jeremiah Sommering – Footman to House Porter 172 to at least 1759:

Jeremiah Sommering and his brother Hieronymous, known as Jerry and Heiro, both footmen, were almost certainly Dutch. Of the two, Jeremiah was the longest serving. Although there are no entries in the accounts to show that Jerry was a footboy-apprentice, this is likely to have been the case as in 1727 Coke paid £8 to Mr Johannes Beswilliband for 'turning over his [Jerry's] apprentice one years salary beforehand'. A further two payments of £8 were made and in May 1729 a final agreement with Mr Davie Beswilliband was for Jerry to be employed as a footman by Coke at £10 a year. Entries for Jerry in this capacity follow a familiar pattern; he bought food for the monkey, paid for mending Coke's shoes, accompanied him to Houghton and Norwich, to Sir Andrew Fountaine's at Narford and in 1734 to Bath. That year his wages were increased to £12. In February 1735 his brother Hiero joined the family as a footman and was also paid £12 a year. Heiro stayed for six years, leaving in March 1741, by which time Jerry had married one of the housemaids, Josey Simpson, and was about to be promoted to house porter in London.

Jerry's bride, Josey, was not just any housemaid but one of four with the surname Simpson listed in the accounts during the 1720s and 1730s. Simpson is a name found among the Earl of Thanet's servants in Kent, and they may have originated from there. After the death of the earl in 1729 and the final break with the previous generation, the Cokes decided that a more efficient way of running their two homes, London and Holkham, would be to appoint a housemaid-in-residence in each, a maid who would remain there throughout the year and be responsible for engaging charwomen to clean the house after the family left and have it ready for when they returned. The housemaid-in-residence at Holkham would also look after the dog Negroe and the two parrots who appear to have lost their popularity somewhat as they were no longer taken to London. At Holkham her duties would include catering for the Audit, buying in enough beef, mutton, veal, bread and fruit to feed the visiting tenants over the two day period that the Audit lasted. Josey Simpson was appointed to this post in 1729 with Anne Simpson at Thanet House. For the next eight years Josey was in charge of all domestic matters at Holkham when the family was away. As the foundations of the new mansion were dug out in the early 1730s Josey catered for Mr Brettingham the clerk of the works and in 1734 she entertained the freeholders in the house at the time of the election.

Although they took on many of the responsibilities of a housekeeper, the maids-in-residence were to enjoy no increase in wages which remained at £5 a year with board wages at 5s. a week.

Since Josey was promoted to this post the year Jerry finished his apprenticeship it would seem she was a few years his senior and with Josey permanently at Holkham she and Jerry saw each other only when the family was in the country. Nevertheless a bond grew between them and in July 1737 they married. They could afford to do so as by this date Jerry already had savings of £74 invested with Coke, a remarkable sum when taking into account this was his first job and gives some indication of what a footman might pocket in vails. The dog Negroe and another, aptly named Cupid, were given into the care of Mr Aram the gardener when Josey left her employment to embark on her new life as a married woman. The Sommerings were to have several children and in 1740 were living in a cottage at Holkham paying a rent of £2. 10s. Jerry of course continued as footman and as such was absent from Holkham for long periods, either in London or accompanying his master on journeys. When in December 1741 William Tomley retired from his post of house porter at Thanet House (he died just a few months later) Jerry was appointed to succeed him and by 1743 Josey and the children had joined him in London. His wages remained unchanged at £12 a year, but opportunities for vails increased as he was allocated more and more responsibility.

His tasks as house porter were many and varied; some were regular, such as supervising the cleaning of sinks, measuring the coal and posting and receiving letters and parcels. He dealt with the hampers of venison that arrived from Norfolk to be forwarded and also with the Swaffham waggoner, booked places in the Lynn coach and paid gratuities to the box-keepers of the various playhouses. When visitors arrived from Holkham and Thanet House was full, he booked lodgings for them at the Sparrow's Nest and the Blue Boar. These visitors included Mr Cauldwell, the estate steward, and Matthew Brettingham whom Jerry accompanied to Ditton (the Duke of Montagu's) and Gunnersbury, a Palladian villa designed by John Webb in 1658. Brettingham paid at least six visits to Gunnersbury, once with Jerry's predecessor William Tomley, who had been instructed by Coke to show Brettingham doors that closed by themselves and were covered with green baize, i.e. doors that separated the living quarters of the family from those of the servants. [1] There were occasional unsolicited callers at Thanet House, such as Elizabeth Ware, who must have known the people within were linked to her native county; she was given 10s. 6d. 'being poor, to help her down to Wells in Norfolk where she belongs'. Tomley had done the same in 1737 giving a guinea to a poor woman from Lynn, with Coke's approval.

In June 1743 Jerry appeared as a witness in a case at the Old Bailey; at the time of the trial the family had departed for Holkham, although the crime must have taken place while they were still in London. The accused was Catherine Chaplin, who Jerry describes as being 'Servant to Dr Feraro, who lived at my Lord's' charged with stealing a silver spoon, scratching the crest off it with a file and then pawning it. This was Dr Ferrari who had been with Thomas Coke on his Grand Tour and since the mid 1720s had been the family's librarian. It is interesting to note that in her evidence Chaplin said she had lived five years at Thanet House where she had her own room, which Jerry confirms, but with her wages paid for by Ferrari out of *his* wages, she is invisible, never appearing once in the household accounts nor in a servants list. In the 1720s the Cokes had a coachman named Richard Chaplin whose daughter she may have been, for she claimed the spoon belonged to her father. In court Jerry could not swear to the spoon as the crest was filed off, but admitted that they had lost four spoons last winter. Two character witnesses testified on her behalf and it was confirmed that Mr Gardiner, the house steward, or 'clerk of the kitchen' as he is referred to in the transcript, assured her, should she confess, he would plead for her with Lady Margaret who would be merciful. But she 'made no confession till she came before the Justice'. Found guilty, her sentence was transportation for seven years, which meant America at this date – Australia had yet to be discovered. [2]

When Thomas Coke was created earl in May 1744, military music featured as part of the celebrations. That month Jerry's bill, besides the customary five shillings to the 'milkmaid's garland', listed payments to three regiments of 'Foot Guard Drummers' and the drum major of the Horse Grenadiers. As house porter he was entrusted with considerable sums of money and either commissioned to go and buy goods, or else have them delivered at the door. These included a number of books and periodicals, copies of the *Female Spectator*, the *True Patriot*, a *History of Shah Nadir*, a.k.a. Kouli-Khan [3] and two books claiming to be a new method of teaching Greek. He also paid for prints, some of the new earl in his robes, and views of Chatsworth, Trentham, Dunham Massey and a plan of York.

The menagerie at Holkham was created in 1744, perhaps at the suggestion of Lady Margaret to mark Coke's elevation to the earldom. Birds to stock it came from near and far, most travelling to Holkham via London where they rested momentarily under Jerry's care. Throughout the 1740s Jerry lists the carriage of geese, larks, canaries, pigeons, turkeys, and bird cages, 'sending the Fowls etc by Sea'. Once he had care of some fawns, also to be despatched to Holkham. Then there was always a dog or two at Thanet House. In January 1744 Jerry gave Lord Raymond's servant a guinea for 'bringing home the dog Turk who had been lost some time'. Meat for the dogs appears in every one of his bills. In 1749 he paid for bleeding the dog Peter and buying physick for him, and a few months later did the same for Chloe and later for other dogs. The 'dog doctor' did the bleeding and another man was paid for 'teaching' dogs. In 1755 10s. 6d. went towards a nurse for Pat's puppies.

Many goods destined for Holkham went through London; Jerry hired carts to carry them to the wharf on the Thames where they were loaded onto boats bound for Wells. Porterage, Wharfage and Sufferance are frequent entries. Sufferance in this context could mean inconvenience, extra payment in the course of the work, or simply permission. From 1750 the building of the new mansion at Holkham accelerated and an increasing quantity of materials needed for its construction and decoration arrived in London to be sent on to Norfolk. Marble from Italy landed at Plymouth, was transferred to another boat and thence up the Thames to be redirected by Jerry onto the vessel for Wells. In 1752 he was at the wharf supervising the loading of 'Statues from Italy' and again in 1753. In 1754 eighteen cases of marble arrived, together with pictures, paint, locks and a number of mahogany doors. On this occasion the goods were taken overland by waggon from London to Holkham with Jerry accompanying them. Having seen them safely delivered, he returned to town by stage coach. In 1756 more pictures and chimney pieces went by sea; another time twenty tons of lead and, in 1758, 'capitols' (columns), all consignments overseen by Jerry who paid the expenses of their transport and dealt with the Custom House matters.

Not all his business was directly connected to Holkham. In the same way that servants were sometimes 'borrowed' when their masters were entertaining, so too were they 'lent out' on other matters. In 1753 Jerry appears in Brettingham's account books liaising with Mr Mixon, one time mayor of Lynn, and Brettingham over the payment for deals to build, or re-build, part of Euston Hall in Suffolk belonging to the Duke of Grafton. The sums involved were £100 and £120, with another £80 paid to a Mr King in 1756. [4] (See below John Neal who also worked at Euston with Brettingham).

Jerry paid the wages of watchmen and for a man 'to lye across the back buildings' when the family were away, protecting Thanet House from the open fields to the north of Great Russell Street. From 1748 this was a Richard Jones who married the then housemaid-in-residence Susan Cowley in 1752.

During Jerry's time as porter at Thanet House there was a fairly frequent change in the post of housemaid-in-residence, eight in total, far more than the two at Holkham over the same period. He may have been a martinet, a hard task master or simply had bad luck.

It was certainly a life of contrasts being a house porter in London, one day dealing with the King's groom of the chambers, another buying bottles of 'Elixir for the Teeth', then riding to Greenwich with a letter or, as listed in his bill of October 1754, paying the fees for a christening. In 1732 William Tomley had stood in for Thomas Coke at the christening of the daughter of Mrs Archer, Coke's Aunt Sue, and again for a child of Lord Pomfret's in 1734. On both occasions Tomley, on behalf of Coke, had given ten guineas, the standard gift from a godparent. The christening where Jerry stood in for his master was that of Thomas William Coke, the future heir to Holkham. Once again ten guineas was given.

Jerry continued as house porter until 1759, when Thomas Coke died, and the same year that the registers of St Giles in the Fields record the burial of one Judith Sommering. Was she Josey? Thanet House was given up shortly afterwards; whether Jerry went with Lady Margaret to the house she took in Hanover Square is unknown, but there was no vacancy for him at Holkham where, since 1755, there was a full-time porter, one James Brierly from Manchester. By 1759 Jerry must have been in his late forties, having worked for the family all his adult life. His savings had increased, not as fast as in his bachelor days of course for he had a wife and at least two children to support. Nevertheless he had a bond of £100 with Coke. [5]

Mrs Sarah Staniforth — Dairy maid to Housekeeper 1737-1772:

Sarah Staniforth's promotion from dairy maid to housekeeper is unique in the household annals at this period, for generally housekeepers were born not made. It was not merely a question of trustworthiness but of education in great houses such as Holkham.

It all began in 1736 with Mr Oliver the plasterer being diverted from his work on Family Wing and paid £10. 4s. 10d. for 'making a new Dary'. Up until then dairy products had been purchased from Mrs Anger the wife of a tenant farmer in the parish, but this arrangement came to an end in 1735 when Mr Anger was persuaded to give up the lease of his farm as it lay adjacent to the new mansion and was needed to form part of the park.

Once the new dairy was ready, a number of cows with their calves were purchased; these were initially kept and cared for under the supervision of the estate steward. All that remained was to engage a dairy maid. The position of dairy maid fell half way between farm worker and house servant; these girls enjoyed an amount of independence and were traditionally regarded as attractive, even seductive, for a cool dairy with its refreshments on offer, swigs of milk and cream, nibbles of cheese, was always a lure. According to Mrs Stirling the biographer of Thomas William Coke, who was to inherit Holkham in 1776, as a boy at home he had always made his first journey of the day to the dairy and coaxed the maid to skim off the cream into which he dunked bread. [6] By virtue of their employ dairy maids were considered healthy and clean, with good complexions, fresh breath and all that went with a general air of desirability. They needed to be selected with care, especially where there were young men in the family.

Sarah Staniforth came from Yorkshire and must have been recommended to Thomas and Lady Margaret while they were visiting Lord Malton at

Wentworth in the summer of 1736. (Lord Malton was a relation of Lady Margaret and an acquaintance of Coke – they had been ennobled on the same day in May 1728). The Staniforth family had long been established in the Sheffield area; one of the earliest members recorded was William Staniforth, cutler, who died in 1659. By the early 1700s a branch of the family 'of Darnell' were styled gentlemen; others made the journey across the Pennines to become merchants in Manchester and Liverpool. Quite where Sarah Staniforth fitted into this clan is unclear, it is only known she had two sisters, Mary and Anne, and two brothers, Thomas and Samuel. It would appear that they belonged to one of the less successful branches as she came to Holkham engaged to take up the humble post of dairy maid. We may be sure that she came from Sheffield via London for the cost of her journey and board wages while on the road are recorded, £1. 6s .6d. for 'twelve days in ye waggon, seven from Sheffield and five from London'. Her journey to London was carefully timed, arriving in town shortly before the family were due to travel to Holkham. The house porter, William Tomley, recorded paying 8s. in expenses 'about Sarah Staniforth' and a guinea to Joseph Wright for 'ye sd maid's expen from Sheffield to London and to Lord Malton's steward 2s. and for Sarah Staniforth's expenses in Town 3s. 6d'. The family set out for Holkham on 18th June with Sarah and the other maids arriving there on the 23rd. She was allowed some time to settle in and be shown around – in addition to her dairy work she was also to look after the poultry, chickens, ducks, geese and turkeys. Her wages as dairy maid commenced from 22nd July. Sarah had been a good choice and all went smoothly; her time in the Holkham dairy was successful and productive. She was capable of meeting all requirements for after her arrival there are no more entries in the accounts for the purchase of dairy goods, with the exception of some butter in the winter months. She continued as dairy maid for five years until 1741.

1741 is a significant date in the history of Holkham Hall. This was the year the Cokes moved from the old house, Hill Hall, into Family Wing (as it is always known), the first part of the new mansion to be completed and the year their son came of age. The new house was to consist of four wings with a central block; Family Wing was on the west side closest to Hill Hall and at this time was linked to it by a passage. Family Wing was different in almost every respect from the old house. No longer lined with wainscoting, the new rooms were lighter and airier, and needed to be cared for with the utmost skill and respect, especially the library. Such work could not be left to the usual run of young housemaids. The need for an experienced maid led to a break with tradition. In the servants

173

quarters (still in the old house) the year 1741 was further marked by a marriage. Anne Coates the housemaid-in-residence married John Neal a footman, and rather than retiring, as would have been customary, she continued to oversee the maintenance of the new splendour. In addition she had the dogs to care for, seven of them, Miss and her puppies, Negroe and Paris, plus a bustard, the macaw and two parrots. It all proved too much, perhaps with Mr Brettingham, the clerk of the works, breathing down her neck, full of advice and admonishments, for we find that in the following year, 1742, Sarah Staniforth leaves the dairy. With an extra £1 added to her wages she joins forces with Anne Neal as a housemaid, while still keeping an eye on the dairy.

For the next two years the housemaids, Neal and Staniforth, continued at Holkham and though their annual wages remained unchanged, their board wages were increased from 3s. to 5s. a week. By then, having sufficiently initiated Sarah into the role of housemaid, Anne, with her footman husband John Neal, left her employment and Sarah Staniforth was appointed in Anne's place as housemaid-in-residence. The work in the new mansion was demanding and as always there was a continuing need for reliable housemaids. In 1744, when a new one was sought, Sarah sent to Sheffield for her sister Mary, who arrived the following April and, after what we must presume was a successful interview, was engaged. From then until 1750 the two Staniforths were in residence at Holkham all year round. Working at a time when there was so much building activity was testing. The mess, dust, wood shavings, to say nothing of the builders themselves, seems to have caused some difficulties. When the family housekeeper arrived from London to take charge after several months absence, between 1744 and 1750, there was a brisk turnover in housekeepers; five came and went.

For most of their married lives, from 1723 to 1740, the Cokes had been fortunate in their housekeeper, a 'Family retainer', Mrs Smith. She had been an efficient and reliable person holding this post until her death and was hard to replace. Successive housekeepers stayed barely a year, the longest-serving (two years) left to marry Mr Ralph Cauldwell, the estate's steward. It was now that Lady Margaret took the decision to appoint Sarah Staniforth to this role. Despite being mere housemaids, it is entirely possible the Staniforth sisters were gently born but had been left unprovided for. If this was the case it would go some way to explain Lady Margaret's action. [7] No other maid was thus elevated. However, since Sarah Staniforth had been acting as quasi housekeeper for some years at a time when the house and grounds were swarming with builders, her capabilities must have been clear to all. Cautious at first, Lady Margaret engaged a second housekeeper for London, a Mrs Williams, but this woman like the others lasted a matter of months. From 1750 Sarah Staniforth became the sole housekeeper and accompanied the family to London for the season. Once again she proved most satisfactory and retained this post as Mrs Smith had done, to the day she died, in 1772.

A measure of the responsibility housekeepers were entrusted with can be seen when the family was away visiting and they were left in charge at Holkham. As described earlier, many 'Companys' of people came to see the house throughout the year at all seasons, though most chose to view in the summer. Thus it came about that 'Mrs' Sarah Staniforth was the housekeeper mentioned and praised, though not named, on the day that Mrs Lybbe Powis and her party visited from Weasenham in September 1756.

Mrs Lybbe Powis, who at the time was still Miss Girle and only eighteen, was staying with Mr Jackson of Weasenham Hall (not yet owned by Holkham) and wrote an account of her Norfolk tour at the request of her father who had not accompanied them. Their party, that visited Holkham, was made up of young Mr and Miss Jackson, Mrs Lybbe Powis and her mother; old Mr Jackson their host being too infirm to travel. Mr Jackson had told her that when he and the late Mrs Jackson visited Holkham, they had generally stayed for week at a time and that on one occasion, rising early and taking a tour around the outside of the house, he had looked in through the windows and seen Lady Margaret in her kitchen at six in the morning, 'thinking all her guests safe in bed I suppose'. There seems to have been some misunderstanding about this anecdote, for although Mrs Lybbe Powis includes the new kitchen wing in her description of Holkham ' ... such an amazing large and good kitchen I never saw, everything in it so nice and clever', Mr Jackson must have been referring to the kitchen in the old Hill Hall which had been in use until 1757. When Mrs Lybbe Powis visited the kitchen wing, on the east side of the mansion, it had only been completed the previous year and in any case its windows are far too high up to allow any one to see in. The dairy on the other hand had been going some time.

'Her dairy' as Mrs Lybbe Powis refers to it, meaning Lady Margaret's: ' ... is the neatest place you can imagine, the whole marble; in Norfolk they never skim their cream off, as in other places, but let the milk run from it; these things here are all too of marble, so that it all looks so delicate and the butter made into such pretty patts hardly larger than a sixpence'. After an extensive tour of the house she continues, 'We breakfasted at Holkham, in the genteelest taste with all kinds of cake and fruit, placed undesired [i.e. unasked for] in an apartment we were to go through, which, as the family were from home, I thought was very clever in the housekeeper, for one is so often asked by people whether one <u>chuses</u> chocolate, which forbidding word puts, as intended, a negative on the question'. We must be grateful to Mrs Lybbe Powis for mentioning the housekeeper as generally servants were ignored in visitor's accounts; Marchioness Grey for example who visited Holkham in 1750 described the house in some detail but made no mention of either the family, servants or refreshments. [8]

The well-judged hospitality offered by Mrs Staniforth would have earned her a monetary reward, for all visitors were expected to leave vails and the accumulation of these vails (tips) on these and other occasions would have gone a considerable way towards the £1,000 plus that Mrs Sarah Staniforth left when she died in 1772. However humble her origins she became a superior servant. Over her long service of thirty-five years Sarah was paid a total of £500 in wages, out of which she funded her maid, clothes, shoes and other personal items. Her outgoings need not have been large, for she was fed and housed in some comfort by her employers, who also met any medical expenses. But as expected she did indulge in some little luxuries such as 'all my rings' which she bequeathed in her will, to Miss Elizabeth Cauldwell, the daughter of a previous housekeeper. Sarah's savings may have been invested by Coke, as was the custom, and thus earned her interest, but her death falls in the period when the account books are missing so this cannot be checked. Even so the total is such as to suggest her accumulation of vails was considerable.

In her will Mrs Sarah Staniforth is described as being 'late of Holkham and now of St George's, Hanover Square'. After the death of Thomas Coke, Lady Margaret moved from the house in Great Russell Street and took another in the more fashionable parish of St George's, where we see that Mrs Sarah Staniforth was still with her. Sarah left her money to her brother, sisters, niece and Staniforth nephews with just £10 for her old acquaintance Mrs Blackbourne, a haberdasher in London.

Her sister Mary, who had been sent for to be a housemaid, died in 1787. She had left the Holkham family in 1756 having succeeded her sister as housemaid-in-residence and held this post for sixteen years. At the time of her death she was living in the parish of St Ann's, Soho, a respectable address at that date, lodging in the house of Elizabeth Sadler and her four daughters, to whom she left a ring each. Mary Staniforth had close to £400 in cash to be shared among her near relations, plus a gold watch and large silver cup which she left to her great nephew and godson Samuel Staniforth. To Mary Bennett 'who lives servant with Mrs Buttall residing in the same house with me out of respect for the kindness and attention she pays to me' she left a two-guinea piece. This gives a small glimpse into the world of an elderly single woman, a retired servant; her somewhat solitary life in a London lodging house was presumably her choice and preferable to returning to Sheffield. Both sisters counted Ralph Cauldwell, the Holkham steward, and Thomas Hill of 8 Lincoln's Inn, Coke's lawyer, among their close friends. [9]

Philip Bender – Footman to Park-Keeper 1722-1745:

Philip Bender's origins are not known. Bender is not a common name and searches have proved unsuccessful apart from John Bender, a London biscuit-maker and vendor of orange chips and dried apricots in the 1740s. The name Bender could be of German or Dutch origin. Philip was engaged as a footman (always known by their first names) entering Coke's service in February 1722 at £8 a year. The following year he accompanied Coke hunting buck at Minster Lovell and it was soon apparent that he was more at home out of doors than serving in the house. Recognising this during the annual stay in London, three guineas were paid for him to have lessons on the French horn, which would be played out hunting. He was taught by a member of the Covent Garden opera house and the cost and frequency of the lessons suggest that he was a beginner; he had further lessons in the spring of 1726. Two years later his aptitude for the sporting life was recorded when he and Coke went shooting with the entry for 'mending Philip's gun 8s. 9d.'. Subsequently, when at Holkham, he was paid for killing hawks and weasels, earning himself an extra 19s. one year. His talent for catching vermin, mainly by luring them into nets and traps, was valuable at this time when the employment of a gamekeeper was still in the future. [10] In 1729 Philip's wages rose to 12gns a year and from then until 1733 there are numerous entries for his sporting activities, though he remained first and foremost a footman.

At this date shooting was done on horseback, not on foot, and most of the game shot were partridge, remarkable when taking into account the inaccuracies of guns at that time and the size of a partridge. Hitherto partridge (who always travel in families) were more often caught in nets. From August

1731 Philip kept a weekly list of game shot at Holkham. In a typical week in October he recorded nineteen partridge, two woodcocks, two quail, two rabbits, five wild ducks, four snipe, two redshanks and a hare. Rather like a French hunt they killed anything that moved. Pheasants were still rare in the 1730s and were to remain so until the advent of the menagerie. To encourage him further, Philip was given presents of a guinea, a pair of strong boots 'to shoot with', an allowance for flints and cleaning his guns, plus his own spaniel dog who wore a brass collar. Later he was to have several dogs including a 'Trufile' dog for which he paid four guineas.

As Coke's personal footman, Philip travelled with his master, to Norwich and Thetford for the Assizes, to the races at Holt and 'for sport' to Boughton. In March 1731 he had been one of the three servants made a freemason. The following year he is entered as having his own servant, a boy named Richard Dow who was resident at Holkham and took care of the sporting dogs. The Dows were a local family; Richard's father William was a labourer in the garden and stables. Elizabeth and Margaret Dow were employed in the house as casual workers. How Philip performed as a footman is not recorded, but, since his talents clearly lay elsewhere, when the post of park-keeper at Elmham became vacant in 1733, Coke appointed him to this place.

Elmham Park some twenty miles south east of Holkham was an enclosed area of 413 acres where deer mingled with a number of cattle. For Philip elevation to park-keeper was financially very advantageous, he already had savings of £93 invested with Coke and now his wages increased from 12gns to £24, with another nine guineas given him as a perquisite. At the time of his appointment one of the stable helpers, William Pickford, took Philip, the boy Dow and the dogs to Elmham in a cart. At Elmham, Philip was responsible for paying all expenses connected with the Park, an expenditure which came to £32 in the first year and included paying the land tax, the poor rate, the window rate and the constable's rate, as he was now a resident of Elmham parish. He paid out for repairs to the house he lived in and to the park fence, for mowing the hay in the park, making a hay stack and thatching it. The final item of 6s. was for swan upping on the River Wensum. The next year he put in a bill for 17s. for killing moles, and more for cutting drains, hedging and spreading muck. Feeding the deer and cattle were also within his remit, as well as caring for his own horses; he bought oats from the Holkham farmers and hay from William Leeds at Billingford and Charles Boutell at Castle Acre, both Holkham tenants. As it was the custom to send venison as gifts, part or whole carcasses were dispatched in hampers as ordered by Coke, which Philip sent to London by the Norwich coach. Any surplus game in the way of birds was also sent to London and sold by Lady Margaret as described in the previous chapter along with large quantities of crayfish from the Wensum, although most of these went to Holkham.

Records of Coke's visits to Elmham have not survived, but, known for his great love of hunting, he must have gone there frequently. The hunting season began earlier than it does nowadays, in August, and it is recorded in August 1740, when Coke took a party of friends to hunt and dine at the park, Philip's maid was given vails of 10s. 6d. and Philip sent in a bill for the food 12s. 6d. and ale 9s.

In 1745, after twelve years in the post, Philip Bender left Elmham Park and Coke's service, with no hint of a reason why. He had been twelve years a footman and another twelve as park-keeper. The approved phrase is 'he then disappears'.

John Neal – Footman, Gilder and Painter 1731-1743:

John Neal began his service in the Coke household as one of Lady Margaret's footmen on 16th April 1731. His wages were £8 a year, and it is possible he was a Norfolk man, even Holkham born and bred; if this was the case then he would have been the first liveried servant to be engaged locally. In 1733 when he had been in service less than two years a 'Frock' was bought for him from the tailor Richard Hackett of Wells costing 9s. 6d. to 'wear while painting'. The objects John painted were in the garden, benches, tubs, wheelbarrows and chairs. Francis Middleton is entered in the accounts alongside 'helping John Neal to paint'; this is somewhat ambiguous. Had Middleton been helping in the modern sense it would be usual to find the word 'assisting'. Helping in this context may have meant instructing, although painting was not seen as especially skilled work. House painters were not held in high regard; Robert Campbell writing in 1747 advised parents against apprenticing their child for seven years to a trade that may be learned 'in as many hours', claiming a house may be painted by 'any common labourer'. [11] And for this reason there is some evidence that DIY was not unknown in houses of the elite with both master and servants wielding brushes on occasion. [12] It is certainly the case that John Neal was given no extra wages for painting at this stage. However by 1738, when the roof was on Family Wing, John earned 5gns in addition to his footman's wages for painting and gilding in the library, and in the following year £19. The colours used came from Mr Harding in London and Mrs Harding supplied thirty-eight books of gold leaf costing a total of £62. The accounts record that some professional painters *were* employed at the house; Francis Sturgeon and his son spent three months painting in the new wing the same year and conceivably taught John Neal to gild. Gilding was a semi-skilled job. When gilding on wood, gold leaf was used. On metal, 'wet gilding' was the method and was not without its dangers; gold was ground with mercury to form a paste which was then painted on the article and heat applied to vaporize the mercury. The Sturgeons continued to work at Holkham painting and decorating until 1741, though there are no further entries for John Neal painting until after he was discharged as footman in 1743. It seems unlikely that no more was done by him during these five years, for there was plenty of opportunity as the new house grew and, more importantly, in view of Neal's subsequent career.

In 1740 John Neal married Anne Coates, the then housemaid-in-residence at Holkham. Her name first appears in the servants lists of 1729, two years before that of John, when she was engaged as a housemaid and remained as one until Josey Simpson married Jerry Sommering and the post of housemaid-in-residence at Holkham fell vacant. It was offered to her and she accepted. She and John Neal worked together in the same household for nine years before they married – and Anne continued working after marriage for some time, as already described in the account of Sarah Staniforth. Then three years later in 1743 both she and her husband were 'discharged', a term that once again belies the friendly arrangement this must have been, for they did not go far but rented a house in Holkham village until at least 1752 at £1. 10s. a year.

In April 1744 they had a son Thomas baptised at Holkham. Shortly after this child's birth Ab. Thomas who had worked for old Sir Edward Coke at Longford and for many years at Holkham, died. Anne Neal was his heir and as such received the wages due to him on his death £16. 6s. 9d., together with the capital bond he had had with Coke of £170. [13] If it had been their intention that John Neal should set up a business as a decorator then this inheritance was well timed, though presumably not foreseen. The following year John Neal re-appears in the Holkham accounts once more but no longer as footman or servant of any kind but paid for painting and for another more unusual task. It was now 1745 and Norfolk was seen to be in considerable danger of being invaded by the Jacobite forces of Bonnie Prince Charlie. As a precaution John Neal was given £3. 18s. to buy gunpowder and shot, and set about cleaning the guns. But as summer arrived and the threat withdrew, he once more donned his frock and began painting in the kitchen and pleasure gardens and in both the old and new houses. He also gilded a palm and a coronet providing the gold leaf himself. Soon John Neal had £100 of his own invested with Coke.

Once embarked on his new career of decorator there was no stopping him, he painted chairs, a 'Floor Cloth' (oil cloth painted to look like carpet), the vane on the Tower, seventeen buckets for the fire engine, and yards of work inside the new house. He both mixed and ground colours, which he had purchased himself, and provided brushes and linseed oil. In 1750 he was painting sash windows at a 1s. 4d. a dozen, and 'wrote 209 letters at 1s. 6d. each'. Unfortunately there is no record of what these letters were, but they may have been on boards of servants rules or mottos. In 1752 he agreed to go to London to work on Thanet House charging 15gns for his time and trouble, but this was modest in comparison with what was to come. Back at Holkham he painted the four tower rooms, one at the top of each wing, charging 1d. a yard (116 yards), labels for the butler, the greenhouses and the farmhouses of tenants at Wellingham, Dunton, South Creake and two farms at Holkham. 1755 found him painting and gilding in the new dining room at Holkham, the gallery and the west corridor, and so it continued, gilding leaves, plaster friezes, balustrades, the staircase. His bill for that year was a little over £254. By this time he must have had a team working under him, for the amount paid to him was considerable. John Neal painted and gilded the state rooms at 3d. a yard, the kitchen wing, the body of the house, all the doors in the house and outside, the gates to the laundry and to the kitchen courts. His bill for work done in 1756 was a massive £1,066. In 1759, the year Thomas Coke died, John was gilding picture and table frames, chairs and settees and the woodwork in the state bedchamber and he continued working on the mansion until at least 1765. A feeling based on nothing more than the fact he continued working so long, suggests it may have been jolly both for Lady Margaret and her husband to have had their great mansion painted by a mere footman, one can imagine a joke or two and a tease when they met.

John Neal was not the only footman who wielded a paintbrush at Holkham. In the 1750s the two Rutley brothers also painted in the house, though not on the same scale as John Neal. John Neal was twelve years a footman and in excess of twenty-two years a skilled painter and gilder. By the 1740s he had £200 invested with Coke which continued to bring in interest, while his wife Anne had cashed in her bond in 1753. [14] Neal's work was not confined to Holkham; like Jerry Sommering he appears in Brettingham's account books working at Euston Hall in 1756 gilding the dining room which earned him £24. Knowing that John Neal worked at Euston along with two others who had helped to build and embellish Holkham, Elliott the bricklayer and Clark the plasterer, it would seem likely that John Neal also worked with Brettingham at other houses. [15]

Conclusion

In excess of 519 people were engaged as servants by the Coke family in the forty-one years between 1718 and 1759. Their names are recorded in the household accounts but this total does not include Lady Margaret's lady's maids nor every casual worker (mainly chars and washerwomen) which are in the region of a further thirty-four. Nor does it include the servants of the Coke's son and heir Edward until his death in 1753 or those of Edward's wife Lady Mary, who spent time at Holkham and was to be financially supported by the Holkham estate until her death in 1811. Dr Ferrari's maid and others are still invisible. *Nor* does it include the garden labourers or those, numbered by the score, who worked on the house, repairing the old and building the new. During any one year the number of people working in and around Holkham would have been enough to populate a moderately sized village.

Great care was taken over the choice and engagement of each and every servant; letters of recommendation and references were sent, received and studied and for those engaged it was with the hope and expectation that they would prove satisfactory. [16] The constant changes, an average of eight to ten servants leaving each year and their replacements arriving and settling in, cannot have been a positive factor. Yet the concept of the household as a family persisted throughout this period. It was a term used by the master and mistress until at least the early years of the nineteenth century, though by then it was giving way to a more contractual term of employment. Serving in a noble household continued to hold attractions; first of all it was employment pure and simple when work choices were limited, a roof over one's head and food on the table every day. For many it was preferable to work as part of a large team rather than in a smaller household where social intercourse was more restricted and there was little or no opportunity for promotion. In a large household the work was certainly hard, but perhaps less than in a small one. Bettering their lot was a strong motivation for many as they moved from one employer to another. On the whole wages were higher in households of the elite and the wages at Holkham better again. Holkham had a reputation for fairness and for paying their servants wages on time, which is more than can be said for some other establishments where the servants waited for three or four years and were then only paid on quitting. The physical labour continued to be onerous, the hours extremely long, privacy largely non-existent, possessions few, no more than fitted into a box under the bed, and the rewards variable. Yet, on occasional journeys home to their own families, servants frequently found the way of life they had left behind fell far short of the standards they had become accustomed to and were anxious not to stay too long; an upsetting experience for their relations and a disagreeable surprise to find how much they had 'grown apart'. [17]

NOTES

1. HA Brettingham Letters no 8.

2. Old Bailey trials on line ref t17430629-8.

3. Shah Nadir 1688-1747 Shah of Iran and considered by some to be the last of the great Asian conquerors, he fought under the name Kouli-Khan.

4. TNA C108/362.

5. TNA Prob 11/990 – George Sommering's will was proved 21st July 1773. George lived round the corner from Thanet House in Little Russell Street where he leased two houses; he lived in one and sub-let the other to Robert Simpson a barber. His occupation is given as working in the Government Post Office (Coke had been Postmaster General) and he had a wife, Mary. They had no children but he mentions a nephew and niece Thomas and Mary Sommering; these could be the children of Jerry and Josey as the Holkham registers record the baptism of their son, Thomas, in 1739. This George Sommering could even be Heiro with an anglicized christian name, a change he may have made when he converted to Methodism, which we know this man did this since he asks to be laid to rest in the chapel yard, or chapel itself, of the late Rev Mr George Whitfield in the Tottenham Court Road. Methodism was jointly founded by Wesley and Whitfield. Further, George Sommering's wife Mary could be Mary Simpson the Coke's housemaid who quit her service while in London in February 1740, related to both Robert Simpson the barber and to Josey. Two brothers marrying two sisters? The co-incidences seem to point to this, though it cannot be proved at present.

6. Stirling vol. 1 p 81.

7. The third Staniforth sister married a Mr Francis Crofts see Sarah Staniforth's will TNA Prob 11/980.

A William Staniforth married Mary Marco [1719-1775] of Little Haugh Hall, Norton near Bury St Edmunds – their heir was their niece Elizabeth Staniforth [1760-1838] one of the Darnell Staniforths. She visited Suffolk and married John Patteson [1755-1833] of Norwich. see pp.28-29 *The Great Tour of John Patteson* 1778-1779 ed D.Cubitt, A.L. Mackley and R.G. Wilson, Norfolk Record Society vol. LXV11 2003.

8. Mrs Lybbe Powis: According to the wine books in the Holkham archives the Jackson party visited on Friday 3rd September 1756, Mrs Lybbe Powis confirms this, she says they visited Holkham on a Friday – the Cokes were in residence but as no mention is made of them and in view of the Jackson friendship they may have been out for the day. For the account of the visit see *Passages from the Diaries of Mrs Philip Lybbe Powis 1756-1808* pp.8-11 and for Marchioness Grey see Bedford and Luton RO L30/9A/6.

9. The two Staniforth wills, Sarah's proven August 22, 1772 TNA Prob 11/980 and Mary's proven April 5, 1787, TNA Prob 11/1152.

10. It was not until the 1753, three years after a law was passed necessitating the registration of gamekeepers, that one was employed full-time at Holkham.

11. Quoted by James Ayres *Building the Georgian City* Yale 1998 p.211, R.Campbell, *The London Tradesman* 1747 pp.103-4.

12. Ayres p.212 quoting William Salmon *Palladio Londinensis* London 1755 p.63.

13. Anne Coates /Ab.Thomas relationship – it has not been possible to trace Ab.Thomas's will but it is likely that he had been married since a Mrs Thomas appears frequently in the London accounts buying washballs and ribbons. She could have been born a Coates, and thus Anne's sister, and predeceased her husband, or Anne may have been born a Thomas and widowed, Mr Coates being her first husband. The first scenario seems the more likely.

14. HA In the Audit Book A/AU 30 for 1753, Anne Neal's money is entered as 'her principle of £150 with interest £162.1.0'. It was then ten years since she had been employed at Holkham and thirteen since she married. The money appears in her name; it was not uncommon for legacies to be left to a married woman for their sole use.

15. TNA C108/362.

16. Alice Fairfax-Lucy, *Charlecote and the Lucys* London 1990 edition p.211. See for example Lady Chetworth's letter to the housekeeper at Charlecote in the mid eighteenth century about a housemaid she enquires:' ... whether she drinks, her nose and face being very red, or whether it is a humour. Whether she is good–natured and will bear a fault ... I intreat you, Madam, not to veil any of her faults ... '.

17. William Lanceley *From Hall-Boy to House-Steward* London 1925 p.23. 'Our cottage homes and food were no comparisons to what we left behind'. Although this was written in the 1870s it equally applies to the previous century when servants acquired many of their Master's habits such as blowing their noses on handkerchiefs rather than sleeves, using forks for eating, moderating their language and drinking tea.

INTERLUDE

1760-1783

Despite a spurt in the building following the death of his son and heir Edward six years earlier, the mansion was still unfinished in 1759 when Thomas Coke, Earl of Leicester, died. Edward had been a severe disappointment to his parents, whether indulged too much as an only child, or not enough, it is not known. Although taught by some of the greatest names of the day, men such as Dr Desaguliers, a philosopher-scientist, and sent on a Grand Tour with his tutor George Shelvocke, a man who had voyaged round the world [1], Edward lost his way and almost certainly became an alcoholic. He died aged thirty-five at Shelvocke's house in Greenwich to which his parents had been summoned from Holkham: 'Early drawn from this vain and troublesome world' was the *Norwich Mercury's* tactful comment. The cause of his death was given as 'dissipation'; he had been married but there were no children. Without a direct heir, Coke left the house to his wife for her lifetime with the wish that she should complete it. He asked her to oversee both the remaining build and the furnishings, proof further, as if it were needed, that she had been closely involved in all stages of its creation. It was unusual for a widow to inherit in this way. The more conventional arrangement was for her to move out and for the next male heir to move in. As it was, Lady Margaret continued at Holkham for the next sixteen years and only at her death did the estate pass to Wenman, the son of Coke's sister, Anne Roberts. [2]

Thomas Coke was buried in the family vault at Tittleshall. The funeral charges came to £500, most of which went on mourning cloth for suits and accessories. The pulpits and seats of both Holkham and Tittleshall churches were covered with black baize and serge. The male servants were given mourning clothes, but not the female ones.

Immediately afterwards four of the servants were dismissed; they were Conrad Andrée who had been Coke's valet, John Claude Beaufré the cook, Daniel Kreeger (or Krugar) the groom of the chambers and George Mitchell the secretary. All four received their wages, legacies and travel expenses to London. As was the custom, Coke left legacies to all the servants who had been in his employ for more than a year; they totalled £385. 10s. One new servant appeared in the list of legacies, Andrew Sheils described as 'a Sargent' at £12 a year. Little is known either about this man or his duties, only that he was married; Mrs Sheils is entered in the accounts helping Mr Kreeger in 1758.

The remaining servants stayed in situ, since there was no question of down-sizing or moving out. There was no need for any further changes. Lady Margaret engaged a new cook, a Frenchman and a Catholic [3], and lived on in much the same style as when her husband had been alive, but it is thought in a more reclusive manner.

In her widowhood Lady Margaret took care to make inventories of both the London house and Holkham. Wenman was no favourite of hers so that she was at pains to leave an accurate account of the contents of both to avoid any future disputes. The inventory for Thanet House was signed by her in March 1760 and the house cleared shortly afterwards. The bound books from the library went by sea to Holkham in April and the manuscripts by waggon in May. Many items of furniture followed, including forty-six chairs, fourteen tables, three four-poster beds (and their damask hangings), three cabinets, three chests and sixty-four pictures. Eight of the pictures were thought too bad to be hung at Holkham and sent to Beck Hall instead. Thanet House was thoroughly emptied; looking glasses and chimney glasses were taken down and carefully packed, but one broke in the process and another later in the waggon. Even the grates in the fireplaces were removed; anything and everything which might have a further use was removed and despatched to Holkham – lesser pieces included an old clock destined for the menagerie and irons for the laundry. This work was overseen by Jerry Sommering, the London house porter, who paid the last of the London bills: to Mr Dawson the carrier, the rent of the New River Water to Midsummer £4, the pews in St Giles's Church 3gns and cleaning materials for a final sweep. At the end one may imagine him standing in the dusty echoing house, all trace of occupation ended.

Meanwhile Montagu House next door, which had lain empty for some years, was undergoing a face-lift and change of use. Renovated, it opened its doors that year, born anew as the British Museum. The collection of the Cokes' erstwhile doctor and neighbour Sir Hans Sloane formed the nucleus of the 'curiosities'. A museum was a new phenomenon and like a private household it had its own staff of a porter at the front door and four housemaids. [4] Some time later Lady Margaret took a house in Hanover Square. As London spread westwards this had become a more fashionable location. Planned directly after the accession of George I and named for him, Hanover Square (spelt in the English way with only one 'n') was built in the 1720s. The houses were large and 'inhabited by persons of distinction', they had three bays and were four storeys high, not so very different from Thanet House. Later in the eighteenth century the square became a favourite home for learned societies and clubs. [5] Unfortunately, for reasons described below, the household accounts are missing for the period from 1759 to after Lady Margaret's death, so that nothing more is known about this house, either how it was furnished, the number of rooms or what servants lived there.

By 1764 the building work on the great mansion at Holkham was completed and the house furnished. Lady Margaret took an inventory of it the following year, recording exactly what was in each room even to the 'box under bed'. [6] During her widowhood she had purchased a quantity of furniture and furnishings, mostly paid for with money left to her by Coke, but she also spent in excess of £3,000 of her own on yet more furniture and items she considered necessary, as she noted in the inventory. Later she was to stipulate in her will that if Wenman disputed any point, then the furniture placed in Holkham by her should be removed. The mention of Lady Margaret's 'own money' may have been that left to her by her maternal aunt the widow of the 1st Duke of Montagu (father of Coke's neighbour). This aunt, the daughter of a duke and the widow of two dukes, died childless in 1734 leaving £23,000 to each of her six nieces. [7] In 1755 Lady Margaret had used her own money when she built almshouses at Holkham for six people, in two rows either side of the road through the village, by what is today the north entrance to the park. As a married woman, although paying for it out of her 'own separate money', she nevertheless had to go through her husband to achieve a legal indenture. She gave £1,250 towards the enterprise which would raise £50 a year, enough to support it, together with a further sum for erecting the building itself. Today a plaque records the fact that as a daughter of the Earl of Thanet she caused the almshouses to be built, continuing the charitable tradition of her great grandmother Lady Anne Clifford whose title she bore.

Thomas Coke's finances had been extremely complicated in his lifetime. He had suffered badly at the time of the South Sea Bubble and been obliged to borrow heavily from a variety of people, paying off a little by his winnings at the card table and resolving never to have any further dealings with the stock market. R.A.C. Parker described his position in the late 1720s as 'uncomfortable'. [8] However things slowly improved, rents from the estate rose, and from 1729 he derived an income from the Dungeness lighthouse, approximately £1,000 a year as part of his wife's dowry, realised after the death of her father that year, and in 1733 he became joint Postmaster-General with a salary of £1,000 a year. Even so, Coke did not stop borrowing money, 'at a hectic rate' as Parker says, sometimes small sums from the Holkham shepherd or a bricklayer, sometimes larger ones from Daniel Jones the lawyer in Fakenham and brother of the apothecary. His confession of being always in 'too great a hurry to dispatch business' and its consequences are clearly shown in this study. The cost of building the new mansion, estimated to have been a massive £90,000, was made possible by the length of time it took to build. In theory it could have been paid for out of income, for as Parker states it was certainly not built 'as a consequence of overwhelming prosperity'. [9] After Coke's death the trustees, Matthew Lamb the lawyer and Ralph Cauldwell the estate steward, set about paying off some of his debts. In order to do so they raised a mortgage for £30,616 in 1765, the same year that Lady Margaret completed the Holkham inventory and the year after Holkham Hall was acknowledged to be finally finished. This mortgage was lent to the trustees by four people: the Hon. Charles Yorke, Charles Cocks and Philip and William Pynder. Lady Margaret continued to invite guests to enjoy and admire Holkham on occasion, one of whom was Charles Yorke. He visited Holkham in the summer of 1767 with his servant a man named John Hine who, going down to the sea and being unaware of its dangers, got into difficulties and was drowned. This was not to be the only time a visiting servant met such a fate As the seaside became fashionable so it lured more and more people to admire its might.

In 1774 Mrs Delany recorded a letter describing a visit to Holkham from her friend Mrs Boscawen. The wife of the admiral and something of a blue stocking, Mrs Boscawen had been invited to Holkham because her daughter had recently married Lady Margaret's nephew. The visit took place in November in company with Lady Gower, Lady Margaret's sister and mother of the groom. Mrs Boscawen wrote to Mrs Delany: ' ... volumes might be fill'd with what I see daily in this magnificent palace, but I am unequal to the description and more likely to tell you how I wander about it, <u>loosing my way</u>. Lady Leicester is often so good as to be my guide and today shew'd me a new egarement [another way to wander]. When I am bound to the library I find a Bedchamber, in short I walk many a furlong (I had almost said mile) that I did not intend, but everywhere such objects present themselves

– such pictures, such statues – that I willingly halt on the road ... I think it is curious to see my Lady Leicester work at a tent-stitch frame every night <u>by one candle</u> that she sets upon it and <u>no spectacles</u>. It is a carpet she works in shades – tent stitch. Lady Gower and I walk out every day at noon, often Lady Leicester is of the party and seems to be a very good walker. They are both vastly kind to me ... ' [10]

The finished house had twenty-seven guest bedrooms and beds for thirty-two servants. The core of the house, between the four wings, contained the state rooms on the main floor with a servant's bedroom next to the state bedchamber. Below, on the rustic floor, were bedrooms for the housekeeper, house steward and butler. In Family Wing, which housed the library that Mrs Boscawen had such difficulty in finding, were the bedchambers used by Coke and Lady Margaret, and those for the valet, lady's maid, footman and one housemaid on the floor below. Strangers Wing, used mainly for visitors, had nine bedchambers on three floors with one footman's room and another two marked as servants rooms, and underneath these on the lower floor was the house porter's room. Chapel Wing, where Lady Margaret moved after her husband's death, contained her chamber, two attic rooms for maids with seven beds in them and, on the rustic floor, rooms for her personal maid and one other servant. Finally Kitchen Wing: here was the cook's room, three rooms for footmen, three more bedrooms and in the attics a further three.

This shows there was no purpose-built servants wing with the housemaids sleeping on one floor and the footmen on another, but their bedrooms were dispersed throughout the house. This arrangement was determined by the vast distance the valet and lady's maids would otherwise have had to cover when summoned. The servants quarters were certainly comfortable. Good working conditions attracted 'good' servants, or so it was believed, and this was the reputation Holkham gained. A housemaid's room was furnished with her bed, a feather bed or mattress, two pillows, three blankets and a quilt, the same amount of bed coverings as everyone else, the Cokes and their visitors included. Servants sheets were not of the same quality as those of the family, but their furnishings, curtains, chairs covers etc. were of cotton, a new and desirable fabric, cheerfully checked blue and white or green and white. Each housemaid had a chest of drawers, and the share of a table, dressing glass and three chairs. The footman in Family Wing had the same, plus a writing table with drawers and three maps in frames. All the servants rooms had a looking glass, so there was no excuse to appear dishevelled. The maids had fireplaces in the rooms, the footmen not always. As there were seventy fire-places in the house, some open and some with stoves, it is questionable how often the servants, other than the upper ones, actually had their own fires lit. To complete the modern look several of the upper servants bedrooms were wallpapered. Wallpaper was as rare and expensive as cotton. [11]

The mansion house, for all its great size, was up-to-the-minute in design and somewhat ahead of most in technology. Not only was this to be found in the kitchen, but Coke had had a bathroom with two baths, one lined with lead the other mahogany, and a 'biddea'. Close stools were still in use, but there were at least nine water closets in the house which flushed into sewers that carried away the effluent. One of the closets opened off one of the inner courtyards and so was available to the upper servants. To allow these to function, water was pumped into cisterns in the roof of the house by means of a horse walking a circular track, in an 'engine house' at the east end of the mansion. There was even partial central heating from a furnace below the Marble Hall; hot air passed along brick flues and rose through grills in the floors of the hall and neighbouring rooms. [12] Bells hung from wires (another innovation) that stretched along the 'furlongs' of corridors to summon servants, and insulated cupboards, heated by small charcoal stoves, kept food warm in the distant dining room. There was little the Victorians would add to these basics.

Lady Margaret, while admiring, tweaking and improving the great house, continued to keep a close eye on the running of the estate, attending the Audits in the company of Ralph Cauldwell the Holkham steward. This man, the son of a Vicar at Knightley, part of Coke's estate in Staffordshire, had begun as a clerk in the office at Holkham in 1732. He married the housekeeper Mrs Neville, and later wormed his way into a position of absolute indispensability, even managing to is get himself made a trustee of Coke's will.

In 1772 an incident involving the Holkham servants appeared in the *Norwich Mercury*. The story went that on Tuesday 12th December the office at Holkham had been broken into and two bags of gold coins worth 145 guineas were stolen, along with a quantity of silver. The newspaper recorded the crime in some detail: 'On discovery of this Robbery, it was thought necessary that every Servant should be examined before a Magistrate; upon which, one Thomas Huggins, the second Gardiner (who committed the Robbery and had buried the Money in the Garden) immediately absconded himself, and went to Wells, where he took a Post Chaise and proceeded to Lynn, at which

Place he hired another Chaise: several of the Servants were sent in pursuit of him, who overtook him at a town called Dennington near Grantham in Lincolnshire, and being brought back, he was carried before Henry Lee Warner Esq of Walsingham, where he confessed to the Fact, and was by that Gentleman committed to Norwich Castle, in order to take his Trail at the next Assizes. Eighty Guineas was found on him, and in his Confession he said that being very much in Liquor upon the road, he was robb'd of a considerable Part of the Money by one of the Post Chaise Boys. Search is making upon the Boy'. With such a large amount of money to be recovered the servants were doubtless well rewarded for their pains and some, having travelled that road between Holkham and Grantham more than once with their master and mistress, would have been familiar with the route. Huggins was tried at Thetford Assizes in March 1773, sentenced to death but later reprieved, as so often happened, and transported to America for seven years instead.

Lady Margaret died in 1775; in her will she left money for mourning clothes for her servants, seventeen men and thirteen women. These included the bailiff, steward's clerk, the gardener, menagerie man, a gamekeeper and the keeper of Elmham Park, the butler, cook, baker and eight livery servants. The men were to have a mourning suit of black cloth and a frock of raven grey, hats, stockings and buckles, all materials to be made with the customary matt finish, even the buckles. The women were each given a gown, petticoat, cap, handkerchief and ruffles. Few of these servants are named. In one of the inventories she recorded Richard Skipworth as the menagerie man 'who came to serve me February 1771', otherwise only Mr Humphrey the butler, the cook Mr Martinet [sic], housekeeper Mrs Lemon [13] and chambermaid Jane Baad are named. Just two dated back to 1759, Samuel Brougham the steward's clerk and Kirle the baker-cum-footman. Jane Baad was left £30 and all Lady Margaret's clothes, linen and lace, as was the custom.

Holkham now passed to Wenman Coke, the eldest son of Thomas Coke's sister Anne. Though born Wenman Roberts he changed his name to Coke on inheriting the Longford estate from his uncle Robert Coke, Thomas's youngest brother in 1750. Having no direct heirs of his own Sir Edward Coke, the guardian, had settled the Longford estate on Coke's younger brothers in turn, and if they lacked heirs to their sister Anne Roberts. Little is known about Wenman other than that he had been twice married [14] and was heartily disliked by Lady Margaret. He appears to have had a reputation for bad temper. Mrs Delany recorded at the time of his inheriting Holkham that he grumbled about the lack of cattle and cart horses there, which she found distasteful for a man who 'comes into the finest and best furnished house in England'. Mrs Stirling disagreed and said he was a bookish, gentle man. He was M.P. for Derby for many years before being persuaded to stand for Norfolk in 1768, but failed on that occasion. Subsequently he succeeded and was the member for Norfolk at the time of his death. [15]

On moving into Holkham he sent for a new housekeeper Mrs Severn who must have come some distance as her travel expenses were £5. Apart from her, only two other maids are named during the fourteen months Wenman was master. These were Lydia Sizeland assisting in the laundry and Susan Lack, both surnames local to Holkham. A horse was purchased for his wife's chaise, but apart from a few payments for coals, flour, apples and walnuts no record of household expenses has survived. Wenman Coke certainly had plans for the estate; in this year an old malthouse was pulled down at Burnham Overy, and a new farmhouse and premises built at West Lexham. For Holkham he spent £33 at Wedgewood's London shop, ordered a large quantity of garden seeds and plants, engaged an upholsterer, paid Ainger Lack for making servants liveries and bought two volumes of Parkins's *History of Norfolk*. However, Wenman's life was cut short; he did not live to see a second summer at Holkham but died in April 1776 aged fifty-nine. Mrs Severn the housekeeper was paid and discharged and the servants given their wages and board wages which came to £126. 19s. 3d. During his brief time at Holkham Wenman Coke kept up the payments for the Almshouses, forked out £22 for meat and corn for the poor at Christmas and paid Mr Girdlestone the best part of £39 for medicines and for attending the family and servants. He replaced Lady Margaret's chaplain the Rev. John Coe by the Rev. Mr Roberts, perhaps a relation, who continued at Holkham until May 1778.

The heir to Holkham was Wenman's eldest son, Thomas William Coke. Like his great uncle Thomas William succeeded to one of the finest estates in England at a very young age. He was twenty-one and also untitled, for the earldom of Leicester had become extinct on Thomas Coke's death. But unlike his great uncle there had been no period of minority allowing astute guardians to present him with an estate in credit, for although he inherited 30,000 acres in Norfolk alone and a considerable amount elsewhere, his inheritance came with considerable debts. [16]

1. George Shelvocke junior had been a passenger in his father's ship which set out from Plymouth for Brazil in February 1719 (new style) and returned to London via China in August 1722. See Captain George Shelvocke *A Voyage Round the World* published London 1726.

2. Of the five children born to Coke's parents, Edward and Cary, all had died before 1759 and only Anne left any descendants the eldest of whom was Wenman. Wenman changed his name to Coke on inheriting the house at Longford on the death of his uncle Robert Coke in 1750.

N.B. remarkably Philip Roberts, Wenman's father and the grandfather of Thomas William, was still alive in 1776; he was to live for another three years but nothing is heard of him.

3. Catholic Record Society *Return of Papists 1767* Vol. 2 ed E.S. Worrall London 1989 p.124 notes one unnamed male cook, aged 36, resident in England for the past fourteen years.

4. David M. Wilson *History of the British Museum* London 2002 pp.30 –31. These first servants bore names found in both the Coke and Montagu servants lists, Markland, Chaplin and Stanley.

5. *The London Encyclopaedia* eds. Ben Weinreb and Christopher Hibbert London 1983 pp.372–373.

6. H/Inv 8.

7. Berkshire Record Office D/EMP f2/2.

8. Parker p.22.

9. Parker p.23

10. Delany series 2 vol. 2 p.60.

11. H/Inv 8 The housekeeper's bedroom had wallpaper as did the porter's room, house steward's, groom of the chambers and the two lady's maid's. Three further 'servant rooms' also had wallpaper and were probably intended for the servants of visitors as one was in Strangers Wing and another in the Body of the House near the State bedroom.

12. Christine Hiskey, *Journal of the Construction History Society* vol. 22, 2007 pp.3–15.

13. Mrs Lemon re-appears in a letter from S. Cottam to the Countess de Grey of Wrest Park Bedfordshire in c.1777. Cottam writes of Mrs Lemon's Integrity and Care as well as her skill in making cakes, jellies and sweetmeats and says she is in good health and strength – apparently she was recommended with an excellent character to Lady Margaret by Lord Jersey, having previously worked for Lady Anson. After 1775 she was at Sir Robert Clayton's. Letter in the Bedford and Luton Archives and Records Service: Lucas L30/11/79 quoted by Pamela Sambrook *Keeping their Place* Gloucs. 2007 p.27.

14. *The Complete Peerage.*

15. Delany series 2 vol. 2 p.116 and Stirling, Vol 1. pp.75, 83–85 and 149.

16. Parker p.70.

Part Two:

In the time of Thomas William Coke,
1st Earl of Leicester,
1782-1842

CHAPTER 10

From Derbyshire to Norfolk

Thomas William Coke was born in London in 1754 four years after his father Wenman had inherited Longford. [1] His childhood was spent between the two, London and Longford, with his parents, two older sisters and younger brother Edward. A glimpse into his Derbyshire life has survived from 1769, when Thomas William was fifteen, recorded by the Rev'd Mr Abdy. In December of that year Abdy had been summoned from London to Longford to officiate at the wedding of the eldest Miss Coke, Thomas William's sister, with a Derbyshire neighbour Sir Henry Hunloke of Wingerworth. The Rev'd Abdy brought with him his small diary in which he recorded his stay. [2] Thomas William and his younger brother Edward get only a brief mention, for on arrival Abdy records they were away hunting for two days with Lord Vernon's hounds. When they returned and they had spent a little time together he wrote: 'They seemed very good tempered young men, lively and spirited as schoolboys, yet exceedingly polite in their behaviour, they and I were thicker than Mustard together before half a day was over ... ' This is all too familiar when recalling life at Longford sixty years earlier when young Thomas Coke had spent every moment he could with Mr Vernon and his foxhounds at Hilton. [3]

As to the household at Longford, Abdy says he was met at Derby by Wenman Coke's chaise with two postillions and that they 'cut a prodigious dash' from thence to Longford. On arrival the front door was opened by a butler 'out of livery'; it was twelve noon and the butler still engaged in his housework duties. Ushered (his word) into the drawing room Abdy was greeted by Mrs Coke and was then taken upstairs to her 'elegant dressing room' where the bridesmaids, two Miss Bradbournes, were being fitted for their new 'night-gowns' by the Derby Mantua Maker. Abdy was offered hot chocolate and then shown to his room. Soon after, he was summoned downstairs again and met Mr Coke (Wenman) and the bridegroom, and shortly afterwards Miss Hunloke the bridegroom's sister, the bride Miss Coke herself (Margaret), and her younger sister Elizabeth and finally Mrs Roberts who shook him very heartily by the hand. This last person was Wenman Coke's sister Anne, she was unmarried but the title of Mrs was bestowed on her as a woman of maturity. No sooner were introductions made than a bell rang and the butler, presumably now changed into his livery, summoned them to dinner.

Abdy was impressed, as well he might be in mid-winter, to see the selection of fruit on offer for dessert: apples, pears and oranges, besides peaches and cherries in brandy. At the conclusion of the meal they drank coffee from white Dresden china cups and repaired to the drawing room once more, where tea was later served with cake, wafers, french rolls and butter. Immediately after 'the removal of the Tea Table cards were ordered ... ' Abdy was apprehensive when he learnt what high stakes the party played for and worried that if he lost he would not have enough to pay his journey home. However he neither lost nor won, though some of the party did, especially Mrs Roberts; 'the noise and uproar was prodigious'. At exactly nine o'clock they were called to supper, 'only fifteen delicate little Plates'. Throughout the card session refreshments had been on hand so that they were not exactly ravenous at supper time.

As it was a special occasion the clerk of the kitchen stood behind Mrs Coke's chair during supper wearing a fine outfit with ruffles and a laced waistcoat, the very height of an affluent get-up for a servant. He was there to explain what everything was, as they tasted this and that and admired the skill and contrivance of Monsieur Triadeau the man cook and his pastry art in 'making things exactly contrary to what they really are'. There followed a small dessert of sweetmeats and a few jellies. The evening concluded with singing 'till my throat ached'.

The account of this and subsequent days shows that while country hours may have been slightly earlier than town ones, essentially the pattern of meal times and entertainment was unaltered. Family breakfast was between nine and ten, followed by outings, exercise, church and visits until dinner. The immediate family at Longford was no larger than six; Wenman, his wife and four children plus seven or eight visitors, all of whom had servants with them. Abdy says that Mrs Roberts had two of hers with her at prayers one morning but 'with my old Ned [they] were the whole of the congregation'. During the entire account of his journey to and from Longford and his stay of seven days, Abdy's servant, old Ned, gets just two mentions – once at the prayers and later when Abdy ordered him 'to try his interest with the Man Cook for a Copy of the Bills of fare for both the [wedding] Dinner and Supper'. Of the Longford servants, the French cook Monsieur Triadeau had been engaged for the Christmas season only, but there was no shortage of others, for on the wedding day Abdy says 'the Domesticks, to the amount I believe of fifty, assembled in the Church'. This goodly crowd shows how customs had not changed since 1718 when Thomas Coke married Lady Margaret at Hothfield and the servants had far outnumbered the family and guests.

An unusual aspect of this marriage was that the bridegroom Sir Henry Hunloke was a Catholic, a fact which Abdy first mentions at dinner the night before the wedding. The day was a Wednesday but it appears that some abstinence was in order. The dinner was of two soups, 'one of them Maigre for Sir Harry and his Sister' but other dishes though suitable to abstinence were feasted upon liberally by Abdy, while observing that the 'Maigre dishes of a rich Papist were of a very high Regale were I confined to these, I imagine I should of course detest them'. The following day the Hunlokes were married in the parish church of Longford, by Abdy the Church of England vicar, but on the return to the house there was a second ceremony in the drawing room 'in the order of the Romish church and when that was over mutual congratulations were made upon the happy occasion' and the festivities commenced. Abdy mentions the presence of a 'guest' at the wedding, a Mr Hardwick, but tactfully does not say who he is; in fact he was Hunloke's Catholic chaplain. [4] A few days afterwards, when Abdy preached a sermon at Longford, Hunloke did not attend the service but Thomas William Coke led his sister into the church 'in his stead'. And, as Abdy says, 'her Ladyship's Protestant Servants all attended'. This shows that many of the Hunloke servants were Catholics, which would be the norm, since servants appear to have changed religion to fit in with their masters. In parishes where the lord was a Catholic the registers show a high proportion of the population to be of that faith, yet when a change occurred, the lord moved, or the family died out, the locals reverted to Protestantism with apparent ease. The church visitation submitted by the Rev. Samuel Pegge in 1773 stated that about one fourth of the parishioners at Wingerworth where the Hunlokes lived, were Papists. [5] On Christmas Day itself Abdy noted Hunloke went out in his coach and six to Derby to 'attend his Devotions in his own way' which was presumably a shorter journey than to his own chapel at Wingerworth.

There is much that is engaging in the account of Abdy's stay at Longford; he describes how one evening he danced with 'three different Partners', Mrs Roberts, Mrs Coke and the eldest Miss Bradbourne. Mrs Roberts he says, after two or three 'trips', sat upon the sofa and 'in a quarter of an hour or so was so abominably stiff, that she could not rise from it without the greatest difficulty'. Mrs Roberts cannot have been more than forty-nine at this time. The music for these jollities was doubtless provided by the servants as tradition dictated. They would have enjoyed the marriage celebrations with as much enthusiasm as their employers and some indication of the freedom of servants at such an occasion was noted by Abdy when he was reprimanded for the length of his sermon by Miss Bradbourne's maid. She may well have remarked on this in semi-private to her mistress who then related it to Abdy; in any event the comment was considered sufficiently amusing to be recorded in the diary. The general impression of Longford left by Abdy is of a family who enjoyed high-spirited entertainments with a degree of tolerance and extravagance. That young Thomas William and Edward his brother had been off a-hunting for two days suggests they were brought up to savour independence and make the most of their love of sport, though they would have been accompanied by a groom and possibly a footman. There is no reason to suspect that their childhood was anything but happy.

In common with other boys of his background, Thomas William Coke was sent away to school, first to a small preparatory in Wandsworth and then to Eton (which must have been losing its Tory stigma by this time) after which a spell at university was planned, but not taken up. Lady Margaret, his great-aunt at Holkham, (who had not attended the Hunloke wedding) took a dim view of universities, at least for young men from elite backgrounds, and offered him £500 to go on a Grand Tour instead. This was accepted, but little is known about his tour other than that he was away for three years in France and Italy where he was considered a handsome milord, having inherited his grandfather's good looks, for which Philip Roberts had been famous.

Soon after his return to England, his sister Elizabeth married a childhood friend, James Dutton later Lord Sherborne. And, in the following year, 1775, Thomas William Coke married Dutton's youngest sister Jane. This union was a break with tradition, for it was not an arranged marriage but a love match and one that was not altogether popular with some of his family who felt he was too young, and had he waited, could have done better. By now he was heir to the Holkham estates, for Lady Margaret had died earlier that year when his father Wenman succeeded.

At the time of his inheritance the following April, Thomas William Coke was a month short of his twenty-second birthday; he and Jane had been married six months and were awaiting the birth of their first child. Thomas William knew little of Norfolk; he had visited Holkham during the lifetime of his great-aunt, when she had offered him the opportunity of a Grand Tour, but subsequently had considered a parliamentary career representing Derby, for he expected, during the life-time of his father, a man supposedly blessed with a strong constitution, to live at Longford. Now he was persuaded to stand for Norfolk in his father's place, and this he did and was duly elected on 8th May 1776. Visiting Norfolk he found himself fêted, whether at a political dinner at the King's Head in Lynn [6] or at the races at Swaffham. Twenty-five miles to the south of Holkham, Swaffham had recently built new Assembly rooms following a fire which had done great damage to the town. In October 1777, when: ' ... we had a great deal of company at the Races', Mr Coke was there opening the ball 'in a minuet with Miss Glover'. The Rev'd Henry Spelman of Narborough (a Tory) described this event in a letter to his mother and continued: 'many of the best Families in the county came out of compliment to Mr Coke'. He went on 'the Harbords, Sir John Rouse [sic] and Mr Coke etc etc were at Sir Henry's ... ' (almost certainly Sir Henry Bedingfeld of Oxburgh). A measure of the sophistication found at Swaffham was the outfit worn by Miss Glover which Spelman described: 'a Cassian robe with a small black hat ornamented with diamonds rather in the style of the Opera dancers'. [7]

From 1776 until 1782 there are no surviving household accounts and very little is known of the Cokes' personal lives other than the advent of children and visits to Norfolk. The first pregnancy was rumoured to have ended in a still-born son, [8] a second produced a daughter Jane Elizabeth, and the third another daughter, Anne Margaret, who was baptised at Holkham in 1779.

At Holkham Ralph Cauldwell continued to run the estate assisted by his clerk, Samuel Brougham, and Isaac Riches, clerk of the works. Riches was paid £40 a year to oversee all building repairs on the estate. In the Audit Books Cauldwell recorded just one domestic servant, Mr Banks, who after Wenman Coke's death in 1776 was 'to carry on the Country disbursements'. A house steward named Banks, who had been employed by Thomas Coke between 1749 and 1752, is possibly the same man. He also noted that Richard Skipworth, the menagerie man, was living rent-free in a cottage in the village, and in 1782 a Catherine Skipworth appears at the mansion as housemaid in residence. When the Audit dinners were held Mary King and 'another' were paid for cooking them with Henry Proudfoot assisting. The need to employ these part-timers suggests there were few if any other kitchen staff.

Between 1776 and 1782 it is unclear how much time Thomas William Coke spent in Norfolk; it is likely he preferred Longford, his childhood home, when

The temple in the woods where the Cokes often ate in the summer. It looks north towards the mansion and the distant sea.

The dining room showing the partly concealed door in the recess through which the servants entered and left. Behind this door is a plain wooden room in stark contrast to the lavish décor on the other side. Food was carried from the kitchen and up a staircase to this service area where it was kept warm before serving. The staircase is rather wider than most used by the servants, allowing adequate space for carrying large dishes.

Examples of the cornices and ceiling decoration in the state rooms gilded by the footman John Neal and cleaned from time to time by housemaids on ladders.

A view of the main kitchen ...

... while in the basement of Kitchen Wing further cooking took place. Bread ovens and flour bins on the left and a charcoal 'hob' on the right. Charcoal was widely used as it gave out a steady heat. (These pictures show them in an unrestored state).

Thomas William Coke, Earl of
Leicester 1754-1842,
as a young man.

... and older, but still a spaniel lover.

Mrs Jane Coke née Dutton
1755-1800, Thomas William
Coke's first wife.

Lady Anne Coke née Keppel
1803-1844, his second wife and
mother to the 2nd Earl.

Central heating grate in the floor of a corridor.

The corridor with pegs where the tenants hung their coats on arriving for the bi-annual Audits.

Plus ça change – a gardener delivers vegetables from the garden for the day's use in baskets, unchanged in design from the 1700s, and is greeted by the cook who holds lavender and other herbs in her hand. August 2012.

not in London, for each year he ordered copies of the Audit Books to be sent to him from Holkham. It was Samuel Brougham, Cauldwell's clerk who copied these out, the first one in 1778. Audit Books recorded the whole estate, both in Norfolk and other counties, with the rents, repairs, improvements and leases entered in detail. From the evidence contained in them, and information from other sources, T.W. Coke (as he will now be referred to) began to suspect Cauldwell of dishonesty and in 1781, in order to straighten this matter out, Cauldwell was ordered to take boxes of accounts, inventories and leases to London for closer examination by lawyers. At this juncture Cauldwell described his clerk Samuel Brougham as '*his* agent residing at Holkham to transact the necessary business of the Trust's estates in Norfolk two years ended at Christmas 1781' thus wriggling out of some of the responsibility. In fact Brougham was also summoned to London to be examined and gave evidence in the ensuing Chancery case. The result of the enquiry was Cauldwell's dismissal at the end of 1782; he nevertheless managed to survive his 'trial' with some success, emerging with an agreement that T.W. Coke should pay him an annuity of £400.

The high esteem in which Thomas and Lady Margaret had held Cauldwell, and his true friendship recorded by the Staniforth sisters, questions whether in his later years Cauldwell had not simply succumbed to temptation, left with so much power at his disposal that he had been unable to resist fraud. He had certainly given himself a pay rise from £200 to £300 a year. Aspiration may also have played its part for in 1765 Cauldwell had purchased an estate at Hilborough south of Swaffham which may have been an over-ambitious commitment, and a curious one as he had no male heir. He had long since been a widower; his wife, the one time Holkham housekeeper Mrs Neville, died in 1747 some months after giving birth to a daughter and he never remarried. [9] Despite his dishonourable discharge from Coke's employ and the slur which went with it, Cauldwell managed to hang on to Hilborough, where he built a stylish new house and lived there until 1792 leaving his estate to his great nephew also called Ralph. Hilborough Hall continued in the Cauldwell family (in the nineteenth-century spelt without the u, Caldwell) until it was sold to the Duke of Wellington in 1858, by which time the Caldwells had married into several Norfolk gentry families.

We have Cauldwell to thank for the gap in the run of audit books and household accounts. He took them to London as ordered, to be examined, but they were not returned, and despite subsequent searches have never been recovered.

However, with Cauldwell gone, Samuel Brougham was promoted to steward at a salary of £100 a year and began his accounts on 9th October 1782. His first entry is for paying the wages and discharging Catherine Skipworth, housemaid. Her wages were paid up to 11th October Michaelmas, the same day as she married John Yerham a carpenter. The remainder of Brougham's first page is filled with a list of servants arriving from Longford, along with sixteen dogs. Brougham took some time to get into his stride where the household accounts were concerned, partly due to the family being away from Holkham for prolonged periods. The first stay of theirs that he recorded lasted from October 1782 to January 1783, after which they did not return until May of the following year an absence of sixteen months. Longford was still very much 'home' to the young Cokes and would continue to be so until it was loaned to Coke's brother for his lifetime in 1792. Servants, gamekeepers, horses, dogs and others continued to travel between the two. Pages torn from Brougham's account book at this period testify that he was still not confident as to what he should record though he does include some interesting items such as the preparation and completion of a new melon ground and the lighting of fires in the Temple to air the building. The Temple was a favourite place for meals in the summer months.

The structure of the Holkham household under the new regime did not vary greatly from that which had gone before. The main difference was the presence of the children, Jane born 1777 and Anne born 1779, who required a nurse Elizabeth Fillis whose wages were £20 a year and a nursery maid Sarah Orme £7. Among the upper servants Mrs Coke had two lady's maids, Elizabeth Burton paid 8gns a year and Anne Kent 12gns. The butler was Edward Kent on £84, Samuel Brown was T.W. Coke's valet at £30, John Sewell the house porter £17 and Mrs Mary Bagnell the housekeeper £25. There was no man cook, but a cook maid paid 16gns a year and a confectioner entered as 'Gen:Baron' at 50gns. Not an army man, Gen was short for Genaro – he was an Italian. The annual wages bill for the servants was now £900, a considerable increase from 1759 when it had been £400. In Thomas Coke's time a footman had been paid between £7 and £12 a year, by 1783 he was paid 16gns which was to rise to 21gns by 1810. The inflation of the 1790s, in part brought about by the need to fund the war with the French, contributed towards this, but by 1800 a concerted effort had been made to end the practice of vails by increasing the servants wages. [10] There had long been a general disapproval of the custom as more and more people acquired more and more servants; the sheer numbers of those expecting a tip was getting out of hand. Of course it never entirely went away, the demands made by servants upon visitors continued and it was in the interest of visitors not to ignore them; even today five or ten pound notes are left on bedside tables by prudent guests.

The number of servants employed at Holkham had increased by 1782. Despite the position of house steward and butler gradually merging and fewer footmen being kept, new posts were created. One was a pantry man and another the steward's room man. The latter was the servants servant whose duties included setting the table in the servants hall and waiting on them at meal times. After 1820 he is entered as the steward's room boy, earning between eight and ten guineas a year. By then the boy could be as young as eleven and was often a teenager; gradually this post became seasonal as a steward's room boy was needed only when the house was full of visitors and their servants. Also 'new for 1782' was the 'plate woman' and her assistant. The first one recorded was Mary Lawford who earned 20gns a year. This was a skilled occupation; the under-butler was responsible for buying the plate powder, leather skins and brushes, but it was the plate woman who ordered gold leaf and silver solder. Her work was to repair and clean the more elaborate plate and the extensive gilding with which John Neal had decorated the house in the previous generation. A year after inheriting Holkham, T. W. Coke took the unusual and slightly eccentric step of having the south-facing window-frames gilded on the outside, so that they glistened whenever the sun shone. Perhaps he found the mansion austere. The sight of gleaming window-frames would have caught the eye, gladdened the heart and, if the sun was out, complemented the sparkling lake and glimpses of the sea beyond. The gilding of the window-frames was done in 1777 at an immense cost of over a thousand pounds and lasted into the nineteenth century. It is no wonder that a guide book to Holkham of 1808 makes special mention of them. In 1790 the plate woman was replaced by a plate man who had previously been the under-butler, and was probably taught by Mary Lawford how to care for the gilding. It was a post that continued to alternate between men and women; presumably when outside work on the windows needed doing, a man was engaged. In the early 1800s a new plate woman Mary Hall instructed Anne Sewell, the daughter of the house porter, in the art of burnishing, but she only lasted a year. James Kidder from London took over in 1808 at the exalted wage of £60, but he died the following year at the age of forty-one. Subsequently Luke Park was employed more or less full-time from 1809 to his death in 1817. He gilded picture-frames and furniture, mainly chairs, but the major part of his work was done on the windows, including those on the north and west sides as well as the south. In the eight years he worked at Holkham Coke paid him over fifteen hundred pounds. Inside the mansion sun-blinds were installed to protect the new wallpaper in the north state rooms.

The servants living quarters remained largely unchanged. Mrs Coke's two lady's maids slept in Family Wing immediately below her bedroom with direct access to her closet by means of a backstairs. The valet also slept in this wing, again on a lower floor, in his case below the 'Long Library' and a foot-man had a small room near the staircase, all close by should they be needed. The butler had a suite of bedroom, pantry and plate room at the west end of the south corridor, conveniently close to Family Wing, and at the other end of the corridor slept the housekeeper. Beyond her was the house steward's domain in the north-east corridor; his east-facing bedroom was next door to his office and around the corner was the steward's room where the upper servants took their meals. The kitchen wing contained the servants hall where the lower servants ate and a suite of rooms above where male servants slept. The house porter and his helper had a room near the west front door, where most visitors arrived. Once again the kitchen staff and maids were allocated rooms on the upper floors of both the Kitchen and Chapel Wings. Thus the house was divided into separate apartments as before, with the kitchen servants seldom leaving their wing and the upper servants and footmen sel-dom entering it except to take their meals in the servants hall. The kitchen continued to be out of bounds for non-kitchen staff; all food was placed in a hatch to be collected from there as had been the rule in Lady Margaret's day. The series of bells played a vital role in communication, the bell board being centrally placed between the housekeeper's rooms and the butler's. [11] Bells became a status symbol and by the 1820s many of the more affluent Holkham tenant farmers had bells in their houses to summon servants, an innovation not always encouraged by their landlord. [12]

Some new posts were introduced, these were an under house porter, a confectioner and his maid, and more housemaids; seven, sometimes eight, were kept where previously there had been only three. Now there were both upper and lower still-room maids, an under dairy maid, and scullery maids whose lowly work was to clean up after everybody else. There was also an increase in the number of postillions, grooms and stable workers. By 1811 four gamekeepers were employed at Holkham earning from 25gns to 50gns a year, another at South Creake and a sixth at Warham. The gamekeepers wore livery, a plainer version of that of the indoor staff, their coats being of green cloth rather than blue. In summer they wore plain green coats and in winter green plush with scarlet waistcoats. [13]

The increase in servant numbers was needed for the considerable amount of entertaining that T.W. Coke did and for the number of family members living in the house. Besides his wife and children (a third daughter was born in 1795) several of his wife's nieces either lived or spent large parts of the year at Holkham. Two were the daughters of Charles Lambert and Frances his wife, née Dutton. The elder one, Elizabeth Lambert, married Rose Price Esq. at Holkham in 1798; she was a minor (under twenty-one) and the entry in the parish register said she married with the consent of her mother. Her father was still alive – he appears in the game books as late as 1813 – but he was not in Norfolk at the time. When her younger sister Frances married Earl Talbot two years later in London, she was described as being 'of Holkham'. [14] Then there were the Blackwells, more nieces, whose mother was another of Mrs Coke's sisters. There were at least three of them, with their mother, and all were housed and appeared quite at home in the mansion, staying for as long as the family did, and having with them their maids and other servants. When T.W. Coke's two older daughters married in the 1790s they subsequently made equally long visits to their childhood home, bringing with them their children, nurses, maids and other attendants.

After the quiet years of Lady Margaret's widowhood entertaining resumed at Holkham in keeping with T.W. Coke's political life, helped by the increasing ease of travel. By the end of the eighteenth century turnpike roads had reduced the journey time from London to Holkham from four to two days, or a mere fifteen hours in the stage coach as far as Fakenham, where visitors were met and conveyed over the final ten miles by chaise. The Fakenham coach left the Flower Pott in Bishopsgate Street, London, at six every morning and arrived at Fakenham at nine in the evening, an astonishing achievement compared to the lengthy journeys of the previous generation, although it must be noted that the maids continued to trundle along on foot with the waggon when the family moved to London or Longford. Improved roads meant people could be invited in the confident expectation that they would accept. T.W. Coke was highly social. Charles James Fox, Edmund Burke and Joseph

Banks mixed with dukes and diplomats, amid a vast list of others entertained at Holkham. When in November 1784 the young Prince of Wales, at last free of his father the King and living in his own establishment, was courted by Fox and the Whig party he was invited to Holkham, and accepted. [15] This was to be the first of several visits by the Prince and must have caused great excitement and extra hard work in the servants quarters, rewarded by meeting and entertaining the royal servants. During the shooting season the house was always busy with visitors, although some stayed no more than one night as they moved from one great shooting estate to the next. In the summer it was the same. Holkham held open house to a large number of neighbours and acquaintances each July at the time of the sheep-shearing.

It is not certain when T. W. Coke held his first sheep-shearing, probably soon after he 'settled' at Holkham in the 1780s, though they did not become major events until after 1800. The Norwich newspapers carried no reports of them before 1798. [16] They rapidly became popular and by 1803 or earlier were on a par with those held by the Duke of Bedford, Coke's friend, at Woburn. The house would once again be full to bursting with guests from royalty downwards, all curious to see for themselves the latest farming trends and 'not only enjoy your Society but view your improvements and take a lesson in farming', listen to speeches on the subject and drink toasts to all and sundry. [17] Hundreds of meals were served to these visitors, many of whom stayed in the house. In July 1792 a Mr Boys of Betshanger, Kent observed one evening that there was a 'fine group on the lawn of valets, footmen, grooms, cooks, women and labourers to the amount of sixty persons all busy gathering the hay into cocks'. Was this a publicity stunt or common practice? It must have been a spectacle, a charming sight and unusual enough to be commented on. [18]

T. W. Coke never owned a house in London but either rented one or stayed with relations. There were, therefore, no London-based servants. In the spring of 1791 William Windham records dining 'with Coke: present Fox, Burke, Duke of Portland, Lord Fitzwilliam, Grey, Fawkener, Mr Anson, D. North, Lord Tichfield, Lord Petre'. As Windham is careful to say 'with' rather than 'at', this dinner may have been in a club and not in the house where T. W. Coke was staying. [19] Windham was often in London and saw Mr and Mrs Coke there on several occasions, generally meeting them at the houses of friends such as Lord Petre.

The Cokes were frequently absent from Holkham for long periods and, as in the 1720s, the household accounts were kept by a succession of different accountants, each with his own 'method'. But few of these have survived and unfortunately no sets of parallel accounts to match Lady Margaret's. By the 1780s it was no longer common to find accounts kept by the mistress of the house, especially when the establishment was as large as that of Holkham with substantial periods of the year spent elsewhere. The mistress may very well have examined the accounts, made comments and suggestions, but the majority of women's accounts that have survived, apart from those of widows, are for personal expenditure only. Two such books belonging to Mrs Coke, kept between 1789 and 1800, were preserved by her youngest daughter and contain some references to servants and tradesmen. These include entries such as 'treating ye Servants to the Play'. [20]

During his 'reign' at Holkham (his children called him 'Majesty') which lasted sixty-six years, T.W. Coke's life fell into three distinct phases, each of approximately similar length, but very different in circumstances, as will be described below.

NOTES

1. Thomas William Coke was born in London at a time when his great uncle and aunt were at Holkham. As recorded in Chapter 9, their London house porter, Jerry Sommering, wearing his very best livery, stood in for the earl as godfather.

2. Berkshire Record Office D/EAH acc.6158.45.

3. Lord Vernon [1710-1794] created 1st baron in 1762 lived at Sudbury Hall about seven miles south east of Longford, he was the son of Mr Henry Vernon who had died aged 32 in 1719.

4. Dr D.G. Edwards *The Hunlokes of Wingerworth Hall*, Dr D.G. Edwards, Derby 1976 p.31.

5. Derbyshire Record Society vol. 29, 2003 Visitation Returns from the Archdeaconry of Derby 1718-1824 ed. John Beckett et al. information kindly supplied to the author by Dr Edwards.

6. *Norfolk Chronicle* for April 1776

7. *The Spelman Letters, the correspondence of a Norfolk Vicar 1777-1805* ed. David Turner, Narborough Norfolk 2009 letters 7 and 8, pp.5-6.

8. Stirling vol. 1, p.232. quoting Lady Mary Coke.

9. It is not known what happened to the daughter though she is mentioned in Sarah Staniforth's will of 1771 when she would have been twenty-five.

10. Hecht pp.162-168.

11. *Holkham* ed. Leo Schmidt and others, Munich, Berlin, London and New York no date, Christine Hiskey's chapter *Living at Holkham* pp.181-86.

12. HA E/C1/3 p.166 Letter Book for 1816 to Turner of Castle Acre 'he is to be allowed two bells only to pull from the two best rooms upon the ground floor and ring in the kitchens'. The others he has inherited from the previous tenant Mr Self will be collected by Mr Mann, some to be handed in at Mr Brown's House in Weasenham and the remainder to be brought to Holkham.

13. HA E/C1/11 p.22 Letter Book for 1824, Blaikie to Waller and E/C1/12 p.176.

14. Holkham Parish Registers and *The Complete Peerage*, entry for Earl Talbot.

15. J.H. Plumb *The First Four Georges* Fontana Library ed. 1966 pp.138 and 139 and an unpublished letter in the Spelman collection now in the possession of David Turner of Narborough 'The Prince of Wales have been to make a visit there [Holkham] and I hear Mr Rolfe had the very great honour of being introduced to him as Mr Coke's particular friend'. Dated 4th November 1784.

16. Parker p.116.

17. HA F/TWC 24 Letter from Robert Fellowes of Shotesham to Coke 18th October 1788.

18. Stirling vol. 1, p.283.

19. *The Diary of the Rt. Hon. William Windham 1784-1810* ed. Mrs Henry Baring, London 1866 p.219 [Kessinger reprint 1SBN 0548801959].

20. Sheffield Archives Cannon Hall muniments Sp St 1-270 60651-1. Mrs Jane Coke, her personal account books 1789-1800.

CHAPTER 11

An Expanding Household and a
Servant Divorce 1782-1800

From 1722 Lady Margaret had kept detailed records of those in Holkham parish to whom she gave an annual present of clothes. It was not an automatic gift and some were refused with the reasons noted: 'so idle clothes were not given'; some were struck off 'because they would not go to Service' (church) and others who were found to be cheating. [1] Despite this the lists grew longer with each passing year. By 1754 thirty-five families were receiving hand-outs including Widow Rutley the mother of Thomas Coke's two foot-men. When Wenman Coke inherited, some of the those listed were engaged in work at the hall, mainly on a part-time basis, but by 1782 eight were in full -time employment. John Sizeland was the steward's room man, Proudfoot the brewer, Emerson, Playford, Lewis and Elvin housemaids, Thurston a laundry maid and Esther Earl a general helper. They were all Norfolk people, and this was in marked contrast to earlier times when almost every servant came from or via London. There was still one servant left from the time of Lady Margaret, the house porter John Sewell. A married man, two of his daughters were to become maids and his son William an estate carpenter.

Marriage between servants, and servants marrying estate workers, became increasingly common at this period. Between 1782 and 1800 thirteen servants married, of which nine were maids marrying fellow servants, gamekeepers, a shepherd or general workers. This may, in part, be explained by their shared Norfolk origins but also by the number of female servants, which had risen considerably. There were now six, sometimes eight, housemaids and three laundry maids at any one time, as opposed to four and two previously, never-theless this number of marriages shows that a sizeable percentage of servants became linked by marriage and, as most continued to live in the parish, by family connections. Proposed marriages for the maids were still subject to their mistress's approval. They needed permission to marry, and if the union was approved they could expect wedding gifts, but were still obliged to quit their jobs on marriage. It was understood that motherhood would soon fol-low the nuptials and a woman with small children could not perform both roles. A possible exception to this may have been Mrs Coke's chambermaid

Anne Kent – could she have been the wife of Edward Kent the butler? For an upper, or older, servant the rules do appear to have been mitigated, as will be seen below, when a housekeeper was found to be married. Of the twenty-two maids discharged between 1782 and 1800, thirteen left to get wed. Four others, all with local surnames, Sarah Emerson, Susan Hagon, Susan Wagg and Mary Clarke quit for reasons unrecorded, maybe they were needed at home, wished to work elsewhere, or found their employment uncongenial. Only two, Anne Ray and Mary Hall, were given their fares back to London. Whatever the reason for their departure it can still be claimed that, for a girl, employment at Holkham during those years offered a reasonable chance of making a good marriage so long as she was not too ambitious and content to pass her life in familiar surroundings.

Lord North's tax on male servants had been introduced in 1777, but had little effect on the number of men employed at Holkham. Rather the opposite, for numbers increased towards the end of the century. In 1784 Mr Gordon of Walsingham collected £17. 2s. 11d. in tax for sixteen Holkham male servants, which agrees with the number on Samuel Brougham's list. T.W. Coke had only one footman, Thomas Wilkinson, but for purposes of the tax all male employees were included, the coachmen, stable helpers, gardener, gamekeepers and William Leedham a gamekeeper cum butcher. At the same time Gordon collected a further £14. 5s. 1d. for a half year's window tax. By 1798 thirty-one men appear in the servants list; by now there was a man cook, a baker, a groom of the chambers, a plate man, two more footmen, a master of the horse, two postillions and further outdoor employees, the farm bailiff, grooms, a master carpenter, a glazier and at least two boy apprentices. The wages bill was £1,248 that year.

Christmas was generally spent at Holkham and it was during the 1780s that the habit of engaging a specialist cook for the Christmas season began, to continue off and on into modern times. How this practice was viewed by the permanent cook we cannot know, but it is to be hoped he or she was pleased to have extra help. One of these temporary cooks, named Fenton, spent six weeks at Holkham from December 1785 to January 1786; his wages were generous but not exceptional, one and a half guineas a week, plus his travel expenses. Like Monsieur Triadeau at Longford there were a number of cooks who could be hired for special occasions such as weddings and Christmas. What did these men do for the rest of the year? Did they write books, run pie shops, or restaurants and instruct pupils 'in the art of cookery'?

After the Christmas visit of 1784 the family left Holkham for town in early February. There is no record of where they stayed in London, only that they took a number of servants with them including a laundry maid named Jemima Garne who became ill. She was sent away to be nursed, perhaps to Kensington as of old, and was only fully recovered by July when she returned to Holkham by stage coach. The family meanwhile went on from London to Oxfordshire, where Coke still owned an estate, and from there to Sherbourne, Gloucestershire, where his wife's family the Duttons had their country seat, and finally to Longford arriving there in June. It is unclear whether all the servants who had gone to London with them went on (they would have been needed in Oxfordshire and Longford but not Sherbourne) or returned to Holkham, as Brougham omitted to enter board wages in the accounts that year. While they were absent a new groom of the chambers arrived at Holkham in the April; his name was Francis Crick and he was soon to be promoted, first as valet to T.W. Coke, then clerk of the works, and shortly afterwards to be steward of the entire estate, a post he held until his death in 1814.

Among the upper servants Mrs Coke had her own maids, 'Mrs' Burton and Anne Kent, a nurse for the children, Elizabeth Fillis, and a nursery maid, Sarah Orme. Orme (one of four servants with this Derbyshire surname) stayed until the two elder children no longer needed her, and was replaced by a governess, but Fillis continued at Holkham far longer seeing them into their teenage years. Mrs Fillis was a woman with an interesting background who joined the Holkham family shortly after becoming a widow. She had no real need to work, for her late husband had left her comfortably off. He had been head gardener to the Duchess of Gloucester (the illegitimate daughter of Sir Edward Walpole), caring for the large garden of the Duchess's house, Gloucester Lodge, situated in the vicinity of what is now South Kensington. On entering the Coke household, Nurse Fillis, as she became, invested a sum of £430 with T.W. Coke, which later would produce an annuity of £30 destined 'for her youngest daughter Caroline'. Caroline was estimated to be between forty and fifty years old in 1825 (the year of her mother's death) – meaning she was born c.1780 shortly before Fillis arrived at Holkham. [2] This suggests Fillis may have been engaged as a wet-nurse for Anne Coke born 1779, for which post she would have been eminently suitable. When, after fifteen years, she left Holkham, it was to accompany Anne, after her marriage to Thomas Anson, and become nurse to their children at Shugborough. On her departure the Cokes gave her an annuity of £20, an incentive, if needed, to care for the young bride whom she had known since infancy.

This was still in the future. To return to the 1780s when the Coke's two elder daughters were young, Mrs Fillis, assisted by Sarah Orme, ran the nursery where the children were bought up in spartan conditions. Their upbringing shows an evangelical influence existed at Holkham resulting in the 'plain living' conditions in the nursery, cold baths, hard beds, unheated bedrooms and strict discipline, along with a monotonous diet of boiled meat and milk puddings. It was a regime in marked contrast to the luxurious mansion in which they lived. 'A complete absence of luxury' was how Mrs Stirling described it. They were allowed a fire in the schoolroom but not permitted to step upon the hearthrug It was of course all for their own good, the belief being that by demanding absolute obedience, obtained by exercising rigid self control, they would emerge as adults who would take their future duties conscientiously and conform to the conduct expected from the upper-classes. [3] The nursery regime at Holkham was influenced to an extent by Mrs Coke's reading of Rousseau who advocated that children should learn right and wrong through the consequences of their acts rather than through physical punishment, for there was no doubt as to the love these children were given and the great pains taken over their education. When it came to the engagement of a governess Mrs Coke read with interest a pamphlet by Dr Parr, the headmaster of Norwich School, entitled 'A Discourse on Education'. As a consequence of her admiration for the author, Parr was invited to Holkham and soon became a firm friend of the family. Mrs Coke discussed many subjects with him, including Rousseau, and was pleased to find he was of her mind, though, liberal and outward looking as Rousseau was, they did not *entirely* approve of him. Had the children been boys there would have been no hesitation in sending them to be taught by Parr; as it was, the girls were educated by governesses.

For some time prior to 1784 Mrs Coke had begun her search for a governess which had so far met with little success, but now she was to be aided by her friend Mrs Martin ffolkes Rishton. The Rishtons lived in King's Lynn. Mr Rishton had become friendly with T.W. Coke when they met on the Grand Tour and subsequently he and his wife were often at Holkham making themselves useful, for the Cokes were relative newcomers to Norfolk. More than once when attending the Lynn Assemblies the Cokes stayed with the Rishtons. Mrs Rishton was a lively, intelligent woman who held a fascination for many as she was step-sister and confidante of the popular author, Fanny Burney. Her friendship with Mrs Coke was based on mutual attraction according to Anne Raine Ellis, the editor of Fanny Burney's early diaries, who says that as early as 1777 Maria Rishton 'had *her* Mrs Coke of Holkham, while Fanny has, for a while, her Mrs Thrale'. Ellis continues that when it became known that a governess was sought for the young Miss Cokes, Mrs Rishton suggested asking her step-sister to recommend one. Mrs Coke complied, though she only knew Miss Burney through her novels. Nevertheless, according to Ellis, Mrs Coke wrote to Miss Burney saying that she would take whoever Miss Burney suggested sight unseen. [4] What is definitely known is that Mrs Coke set out her 'requisites for a Governess'.

> *Mrs Coke would wish to have a person as Governess to her Children who had the experience of one Education, & that Education had turned out well, that she should possess the strictest religious, & moral Principles, understand English & French Grammars perfectly, & be able to read, write & speak both these Languages with some degree of elegance & to know enough of Italian to teach to read & understand. – She must be genteel in her behaviour ... [faded word] Tolerably well acquainted with Ancient & Modern History, Heathen Mythology & Arithmetic, & well drilled in Geography. If she were capable of keeping up the children's Music & Dancing when they are in the country, it would be an additional recommendation, as well as her understanding of any ingenious works. – The Governess is to be inseparable from the Children, & is to be with Mrs Coke whenever they are.*

> *She is to rise early to walk out with the Children winter and summer before breakfast when the weather will permit, likewise they are to be a good deal out in the air the rest of the day Mrs Coke being of the opinion that a judicious Governess would be able to convey much useful instruction to her Pupils in conversation during their walks when perhaps it might be better received & retained by them, than when presented in the more questionable shape of a Lesson. – The two Miss Cokes are just six & seven, & are very docile good tempered Children & remarkably healthy. – The salary that Mrs Coke would give a Governess so qualified would be equal to what has ever been given to anybody in that situation.*

> [5]

Two things stand out (besides the need to know about Heathen Mythology): that children would never be free of their Governess even when spending time with their mother, and Mrs Coke's hope that the Governess could teach music and dance during the time they spent in Norfolk. It was the practice when the family were in London for the children to receive music, dancing, deportment, singing and drawing lessons from 'Masters', specialist teachers being unobtainable in Norfolk. The little Coke girls were gifted artists, and later Thomas Gainsborough is said by Mrs Stirling to have spent time at Holkham with the express purpose of coaching the children, though he is not mentioned in the accounts. He may well have taught the children in London. They were true descendants of the 'Artistic Duttons' as anyone who has been to Shugborough will know. [6] The walks before breakfast confirm the Spartan upbringing. In the season, and before 9 a.m., were streets in the fashionable parts of London crowded with children on early morning walks?

Views on governesses were exchanged between Mrs Coke and Fanny Burney. Writing to Mrs Rishton in 1783 Mrs Coke expressed her gratitude to Fanny Burney who was to be aided in the search by Mrs Carter and Mrs Chapone: 'I can add nothing to Miss Burney's idea of Governess, & have therefore only to hope that I may be so very fortunate as that she may discover such a Treasure'. [7] The two women helping Miss Burney were at the core of the bluestocking circle, and belonged to an older generation than Fanny Burney [1752-1840]; they were an impressive choice of advisors. In an undated letter written on the eve of departing for London Mrs Coke said she would call on Miss Burney in town 'as I am quite impatient for the pleasure of her acquaintance' and in the same letter made reference to the many agreeable days she had spent with Mrs Rishton both at Holkham and in King's Lynn. A Miss Wilkie had been proposed, but was not engaged – she preferred to await Miss Burney's recommendations. Not long afterwards Miss Charlotte Atwood and Miss Sybille Vrankin were taken on at Holkham to teach the children. To employ two governesses at a time was not unusual, especially if they were of different nationalities.

The governess's salaries (a subtle distinction, governesses were a cut above waged servants) are not recorded, but both women appear in Mrs Coke's personal account books, buying small items on her behalf and receiving presents from her.

During 1786 the family were again absent from Holkham for long periods, ten months in all. The hall continued to be open 'to Strangers' on Tuesdays as it had been in the days of Lady Margaret, and, as before, on Thursdays in July and August if the family was there. Thursdays in summer were the 'Publick Days'. While T. W. Coke was MP for Norfolk, either serving or hoping to be re-elected, public days were an opportunity to welcome neighbours to see at first hand the happy family at home. Dressed in their finest clothes (and latest fashions) Coke and his wife put on an impressive display, offering a degree of accessibility and hospitality designed to encourage those freehold-ers who attended to vote for him. Very often politicians and society figures would be staying at Holkham, specially invited for these open days, along with writers, artists and even musicians, demonstrating the width of the fam-ily's connections and cultural tastes. [8] Naturally they were a great draw in the county. The Norwich diarist, Sylas Neville, curious to see Holkham and meet its owner, wrote to Mrs Coke in late August 1786 asking if he might attend one such day, only to be told that for that year the family would not be at Holkham but at Longford. She replied saying how much she regretted not having seen him during her short stay at Norwich, but hoped to do so on her return to Norfolk. [9] The etiquette of applying to Mrs Coke as the hostess emphasizes the domestic nature of the 'Publick Day'. Neville tried again two years later in June 1788 and this time Mrs Coke *was* at Holkham, but explained that as Mr Coke was away from home she was unable to fix a precise day for 'the pleasure of seeing Dr Neville at Holkham except during the two months of July and August, every Thursday in which ... ' Undaunted, Neville was determined to inspect Holkham thoroughly. He arrived on a Tuesday afternoon, the day the hall was open to 'Strangers', and spent two hours in the house and admired the view of the church across the lake. On Wednesday he toured the grounds, riding in the park along with 'some of the ladies and gentlemen'. Finally, Thursday the public day dawned and at its conclusion Neville wrote: 'This is one of their public days. 28 at dinner. Two courses of 26 or 28 dishes, 12 or 13 on each side of the parterre. 1st course: Principle dishes, a variety of soups, stewed carp and other fish, all made dishes, one very good. Ox's palates stewed and rolled up with small lettuces between 2nd course: Haunch of Vension, Leverets, Rabbits, Pastry, Blomange [sic], Jelly, Oysters, scallop fashion in a triangular dish. Dined in the Statue Gallery. The magnificent service of plate [silver] engages the attention of every visitor. Some of the pieces are of little use and do not look well upon the table'. [10] As Neville demonstrates, visitors to Holkham could spend three days savour-ing the 'unbounded hospitality', the servants were therefore on their best behaviour and the cooks up before dawn to prepare a spread that would be acceptable to all, though clearly the food did not please everyone. Judging from the description above it was relatively simple country fare although expensive in its choice — no need to engage a French cook.

At these public days, if Mrs Stirling is to be believed, Mrs Coke was as fine an orator as her husband and charmed the crowd with her ardent support of Whig politics. A model political wife, such as Mrs Coke appears to have been, had the double burden of organising the day, meals and entertainments, appearing as a Grande Dame and at the same time being open and approachable to all. [11] Mrs Stirling goes on to say that to support the Norwich shawl industry, Mrs Coke purchased many shawls which she draped over furniture at Holkham at least in 'part of her elegant mansion ... and thus established an industry for which Norwich afterwards became famous'. [12] This can only have been post 1793, for the Norwich shawl was still in its infancy in that year, when Mrs Coke records visiting a Norwich Shawl Manufactory Exhibition held in New Bond Street which was attended by royalty and many of the nobility. [13] What we can be sure of is that Mrs Coke bought a Norwich shawl for Miss Vrankin, one of the governesses, and doubtless Norwich shawls did become popular at Holkham and may well have been worn by several of the female servants.

The servants were called on for an extra special effort in late 1788 when a Grand Fête was planned at Holkham as part of a nation-wide celebration commemorating the centenary of William of Orange's arrival in England. The date was 5th November. By chance this was the day William of Orange had landed at Torbay a hundred years previously and was unrelated to any anti-Catholic stance. Events were planned throughout the country, and the Holkham fête was just one among many, although on a more magnificent scale than most, for it came at a period when T.W.Coke was not in Parliament and provided a splendid opportunity for encouraging voters to support him in future. A list was drawn up with the help of ever keen Mr Rishton and over 1,500 people were invited. It was in essence a vast political extravaganza, weeks in the preparation, and the talk of Norfolk and Suffolk for many weeks beforehand. To be sure that no-one of any significance was left out, the two counties were divided into sections and the clergy and mayors of every town asked to send a list of those local inhabitants to whom 'cards' should be sent. Naturally the plan was to include all the freeholders who had voted for Coke in the past and not to exclude any who might be persuaded to do so at the next election. Mrs Walpole of Wolterton counselled Mrs Coke against thinking only of those who had voted for Mr Coke previously, but to take advantage to 'make as many friends as he can', and she sent lists of names who would be unforgiving if not invited. The choice was eclectic, the nobility were invited along with the gentry, but the bulk were the middling sort with a number of tradesmen and their families, the latter mainly Wells people. At least twenty families were offered beds within the mansion, while others, some of whom lived forty or more miles away were listed under the heading 'To Return Home'. A few were asked from even further afield, notably Mr Nathaniel Kent [1737-1810] from Fulham, and Mr Humphrey Repton [1752-1818] from Essex. Both these men were known to Coke through William Windham of Felbrigg. Repton, about to embark on his career as a landscape designer, had been Windham's confidential secretary and Kent his land agent and agricultural advisor. [14]

Those invited were listed alphabetically in a book with columns against their names where their answers were recorded, accepted or refused. If refused the reasons were noted. The majority of the refusals cited the distance; it was too far from them to travel. The second most common plea was that they were already committed to local festivities. Illness, old age, pregnancy in its latter stages and undisclosed but urgent need to be elsewhere were other excuses, though some felt it unnecessary to give any explanation. Among those who refused, and whom we may miss the most, was Parson Woodforde. However, thanks to him we know that the invitations were printed 'all but our Names' on a gilt-edged card, which invited them to a ball and supper to begin at eight o'clock. Parson Woodforde received his invitation on 29th October, a week before the event. He and his niece Nancy were asked, but as a Tory, living at a distance with only a cart and no carriage, he refused. He remarks that a general invitation had been sent out throughout the county. Even so it clearly stayed in his mind for on 5th November he wrote: ' ... very fine evening tho' cold for the Holkham Jubilee'. [15] Much closer to Holkham, at Burnham Thorpe, Nelson the future admiral also declined. The most eminent guest was to have been the Prince of Wales, but he was summoned to Windsor at the last moment and in a similar fashion Charles James Fox was called away to the bedside of a sick relation. On the other hand many were desperate to attend no matter what, and replied in the affirmative, only warning that everything depended on being able to get hold of post horses, which, owing to heavy demand that day, would have to be booked well in advance. [16] Another wrote offering loans of plate, knives and forks. [17] There were still enough grandees to impress, but inevitably some people were left out. One substantial group not invited were the tenant farmers, not one of whom received a card, the reason being that they could be counted on to vote for Coke and so were not 'needed' to be either persuaded or impressed by finery.

No surprise to find Sylas Neville among those who accepted; having visited in the summer, the invitation could not be resisted. On the great day, 5th November, he records dining at Fakenham and arriving at Holkham at 9 p.m. Along with his fellow guests he entered the hall through the Egyptian Hall, as the marble hall was known, where a painting of the Prince of Wales's feathers 'presented itself' with the motto 'Liberty is our cause'. To compliment this it was understood by most that to wear a Whig 'uniform' of buff and blue would be appreciated, and many of the ladies as well as their menfolk made a point of doing this. The household accounts do not record whether the servants were included, but it would be surprising to find they were not. The Coke livery colours were blue and red, but on this occasion the liveried servants may well have worn buff facings and blue stockings instead of red ones. T.W. Coke stood at the door of the saloon at the top of the marble staircase to greet 'the company'. To accommodate the large numbers the party was spread over most of the house; there was dancing in the Saloon and Statue Gallery and card tables set up in three adjoining rooms, with more on the rustick floor below in the billiard and audit rooms. The library and a few other places were set aside for 'conversation', and all the while refreshments were on offer. [18]

A firework display began at ten in the evening choreographed by Signor Martenelli. The display involved a representation of the Prince of Wales's feathers and motto 'Ich Dien', with an Ostrich, the emblem of the Coke family. Mr Gay of Norwich, writing to T.W.Coke before the Fête, explained that Martenelli was 'extremely anxious to give satisfaction'; he already had the first two displays ready, the feathers and the motto worked out with the help of Mr Gay, and 'I have desired him to try and do what he can with the Ostrich'. Martenelli travelled to Holkham two weeks before the day of the Fête to direct the erection of the scaffolding and to be sure that none of the fireworks would go off prematurely. 'He dares not venture to send any of his works ready charged'. The display was a triumph and contemporary accounts said it could be seen throughout the district. [19]

Supper with hot soup and game was not served until 2 a.m. Neville thought the crush at supper time could have been avoided if the ladies had been allowed to eat first. He records Mrs Coke ate in the north dining room seated at a horse-shoe-shaped table, while the rest was 'confusion'. [20]

Despite the opulence of this event it hardly gets a mention in the household accounts. There is no indication of what extra help was engaged to help cook and serve, nor the amount spent on food and drink. What is recorded is illuminating in a different way. At the time the mansion stood in a park of three thousand acres enclosed by a wooden fence that stretched, as Sylas Neville had estimated, for eleven miles or so, a wooden fence which could easily be scaled – the present stone wall was still some years in the future. With such a vast number of guests, security was paramount. Only those who had been invited were to be admitted and to ensure this the head gardener, John Sandys, and forty of his labourers were promoted to temporary constables and were paid accordingly. In addition Henry Savage, the estate carpenter, and fifteen of his men, Thomas Harris, described as a slater, and fourteen of his, and a further thirty-two men from Tittleshall were called in to stand guard – a hundred and four in all. The local men were paid 2s. 6d. each, and those from Tittleshall 5s. Each was given a cockade to wear in his hat to denote his authority. Indoors the demands on the servants catering for the guests can only be imagined. All we know is that, for whatever reason, three servants quitted their posts five days later including a still-room maid and a housemaid.

The Fête set a standard; the Cokes were already known for their hospitality dispensed in a grand style, but this event in all its lavishness was viewed and experienced by *le tout* Norfolk, and it would be forever remembered by all, those who had attended as well as those who had not.

The following summer of 1789 a Mr Gunter came to Holkham to work as a confectioner and stayed on until 1st December when he was paid £25. At this date James Gunter was already a partner of Domenico Negri and would succeed him in another ten years, inheriting Negri's confectionery shop on the east side of Berkeley Square which would become one of the most fashionable rendezvous in London for generations to come. Messrs Gunter and Co., as it became known, was to supply Holkham with many a temporary male cook engaged for the Christmas period during the nineteenth century.

While Gunter was at Holkham in July 1789 news reached Norfolk of the fall of the Bastille; there were no French servants at Holkham to be perturbed by this, for with the possible exception of Miss Vrankin, all were British. Coke's valet was a man named Atwell and the male cooks also had thoroughly British names, Lochhead, Hurwood and Denson, reflecting the change from French food and forgein servants so popular in the earlier part of the century, to plainer English fare, as described above by Sylas Neville.

The hostilities between England and France began in earnest in 1793 and the threat of an invasion by the French was taken seriously. The Wells sailors who volunteered 'to serve on the Norfolk coast' were given 5gns by T.W. Coke, who also contributed towards the expenses of forming a Provisional Cavalry which consisted of at least seventeen mounted men. Sergeant John Holton of the Prince of Wales Regiment, directed by the Prince of Wales himself, arrived at Holkham from London with his wife and child to take charge of the defences. His board was paid for by Coke and a new military jacket, waistcoat and greatcoat made for him by Haycock the Wells tailor. He was further provided with a pair of doeskin pantaloons (£2) a helmet and a sword. Both Mr and Mrs Coke complimented the Sergeant by wearing military uniforms themselves. [21] Holton stayed at Holkham until April of the following year when he was paid for '40 weeks teaching Military exercise to the Holkham yeomanry corps £21'. He and his family lodged with James Alford the estate plasterer. Thereafter the Holkham Yeomanry were given a dinner with wine on 4th June the King's Birthday. Thus protected from the prospect of armed combat on their doorstep, the possible invasion did not cause panic and alarm among the servants as it had done in 1745 when the Jacobites were at hand and upwards of sixteen servants fled. The main disruption as far as the servants were concerned was James Alford white-washing the house throughout the service quarters, the arrival of a full-time confectioner named G.F. Grantzon (a German name), and the marriages of the Cokes' two eldest daughters.

Both Jane Coke and Anne her sister had their own 'women'. Susannah Lee at 14gns a year attended Anne and Jane had Charlotte Carey at 16gns, both these maids appear in the general list of servants wages. It is generally believed that at this date lady's maids were paid directly by their mistresses from their pin money, which had been the case with Lady Margaret, but from the 1780s onwards they appear alongside the other servants in the general list of disbursements.

The survival of two of Mrs Coke's personal account books show how she spent her pin money. Pin money was given for the private use of the recipient, as part of the marriage settlement. Mrs Coke received £300 a year to spend as she wished, answerable to no one but her conscience. Each year she gave away a considerable proportion of it: to the poor 2gns, the children of the poor 1gn, the Norwich Hospital 5gns and the Abolition of the Slave Trade 10gns. There were annual gifts to her maids (Mrs Burton got 4gns), and at Christmas gifts of 10s. 6d. to other servants: the groom of the chambers, the woman cook, the under-butler, her personal groom, the coachman, her personal footman John Parry, 'the Housemaids in Family Wing' and others. She treated the servants to the Play, as already mentioned, gave money to the people in the almshouse, to the occasional poor woman, the Holkham workhouse, the Poor house at Wighton, the Charity School in Norwich and inevitably to servants at places the Cokes visited. There were also gifts to her relations, 15gns to her Blackwell nieces in 1796, 10gns each time she was asked to be a godmother, more than once 10s. 6d. to James Hunloke her nephew by marriage, all of which did not leave much for herself. Her personal expenses included mending fans, buying peppermint drops, cleaning and dying feathers, buying a Calico gown, 'My Box of Paints', the dentist, and some travel. While outwardly life at Holkham was lived on the grand scale, Mrs Coke's personal accounts show her private life was modest indeed. When in 1794 their daughter Anne married Thomas Anson of Shugborough, T.W. Coke gave his wife a draft of just £20 to pay for the wedding clothes and she gave the bills to him as proof of expenditure. [22]

At the time of the wedding Mrs Coke was pregnant once again. It is not known how many pregnancies she had had in the sixteen years since the birth of Anne their second daughter, only that she had been unsuccessful in providing an heir. That feat was achieved by her sister-in-law, the wife of T.W. Coke's younger brother Edward. They had a young son, also named Thomas William known as Billy, the accepted heir-presumptive. After the wedding and the departure of her nurse, Elizabeth Fillis, who accompanied Anne to Shugborough, Mrs Coke prepared for her next confinement by engaging Ellen Sewell, the daughter of the house porter John, as nursery maid and a wet-nurse, Mary Parker, from London. It was in London that the child, a third daughter, Elizabeth Wilhelmina, was born in March 1795. London was still considered the most suitable place to give birth with the best doctors and midwives on hand. Mrs Coke was forty-one, no longer young, but all went well, the baby thrived and the two new nurses entered the household.

The 1795 list of servants wages, compiled when Thomas Barker was house steward, contains fifty-one names and the sum of their wages came to £1,285. 12s. 0d. Thirty-two of the servants were men, of whom fourteen worked in the house, four were footmen and five others either in the kitchen or in related areas; such were James Denson the brewer and Richard Dodsworth the footman cum baker. The cook was Peter Tanrade. Of the nineteen women three were lady's maids, two for Mrs Coke and one for her daughter Jane; there was a housekeeper, six housemaids, three laundry maids, a woman cook, two kitchen maids, two still-room maids and one dairy maid. A total of eleven people worked in Kitchen Wing. The paucity of the household accounts at this period allows very little insight into the background of the servants; the accountant merely records when they left. One laundry maid, who was paid 8gns a year from 1794, is intriguing, if only for her name, Mary American. Knowing that both Mr and Mrs Coke were great supporters of the abolition of the slave trade, the question arises was she black? She worked at Holkham for twenty years eventually leaving in 1814 with a present of £25 on marriage to John Kidman servant to Mr Charles Lambert (Mrs Coke's brother in law).

During the 1780s and 1790s the household disbursements were generally in the region of £300 a month in the summer and down to as little as £180 in the winter, with the exception of November, when many guests were invited to Holkham for fox-hunting and shooting. There was another smaller peak in consumption at Christmas, according to records in the wine books, but nothing conspicuous. Christmas could, and often did, pass almost unmarked as far as the kitchen expenses went, despite engaging a special cook. The annual disbursements for the early 1790s vary from £6,600 to £10,000. Like his great uncle T.W. Coke was permanently, though not disastrously, in debt. He had inherited debts of about £97,000 which increased at an alarming rate. Buying land partly accounted for this as did spending on politics, but hospitality must account for a large percentage of the rest. In addition were the provisions for his two daughters who each received £20,000 on marriage with the promise of another £10,000 to come. Anne married Thomas Anson in 1794 and Jane married Lord Andover in 1796. [23]

The office staff were not included in the servants wages and are recorded only in the audit books. Like the governesses they were salaried rather than waged. Samuel Brougham the estate steward and accountant from 1782 was paid £100 per annum, assisted by Isaac Riches who superintended the repairs needed on the estate and earned £50. In 1790 Francis Crick, who had previously been Coke's valet, joined Brougham in the office taking over from Riches. He then earned £100 and Brougham's salary was increased to £120. However Brougham's name does not appear after 1792. In 1793 the entry reads: 'The Accountant and his assistant a years salary £250'. Crick had succeeded him but does not record who *his* assistant was.

The greater family, in terms of those whose wages were paid directly by T.W.Coke and were engaged solely by him, was therefore in excess of fifty-seven people in the 1780s and 90s, and was still seen as a family though less frequently referred to as such. The impact of Holkham on the local economy, the extent to which local businesses relied on orders from Holkham to boost their incomes, is hard to ascertain. Although Wells was the nearest town, Walsingham appears to have been the place where it was more likely to find the specialists used by the local gentry, such as clock and gun-makers. The excise man, to whom the taxes were paid, had his offices in Walsingham, as did the local lawyer, the doctor, the apothecary and Henry Burcham who repaired furniture at Holkham and made 'pleasure chairs for the garden' in 1793. Wells had the advantage of a quay where groceries ordered from London were unloaded from the 'Wells vessel'. Mr Foster of Wells was a wine merchant who supplied Holkham, and barrels were bought from John Gardiner of Wells, a cooper. By 1799 Wells had a Book Club to which Mr and Mrs Coke and their daughter and son-in-law, Lord and Lady Andover, subscribed. The shops stocked a wide range of items – they were indeed general stores. Mr Bloom of Wells sold all sorts, from oats and wine to coal. Mr Haycock was another. Mary Alderson ran a draper's and sold cloth for the livery suits, which were then made up by James Emerson who also made clothes for T.W. Coke.

Some work was done in the house in 1795. James Sudbury was paid for wallpapering and putting up new dressing glasses and bed furniture, but the main alterations at Holkham occurred in the park. Robert Walker a brick-layer was paid for three years from 1793 for building stables and walls at Longlands farm near the south entrance, and then for an entire new village 'near Longlands' to accommodate eleven families. The architect is believed to have been Samuel Wyatt. One of the first tenants was Violet Sizeland and his wife Clara née Playford who had been a housemaid at the Hall. It was also decreed that the offices of the estate staff should be based at Longlands and in all probability the estate steward lived there, though both Blaikie, the steward from 1816, and his assistant William Baker, also had rooms on the lower floor of Strangers' Wing in the mansion adjacent to their office.

During this period, to the end of 1799, three servants died and several changed jobs, but it was on the whole a time of relative stability in the household, broken only by the scandal of a divorce. Divorce was still a rare event in the late eighteenth century and largely confined to the upper echelons of society; servants would be more likely to appear as witnesses than to be caught up in a case, but this example shows that servants themselves were occasionally centre stage, for this one involved the Holkham housekeeper, her estranged husband Robert Edwards a valet, the steward Francis Crick and T.W. Coke himself. The most straightforward way to obtain a divorce at this date was to show that adultery, quaintly called 'criminal conversation', had taken place. Previously there had been five means of resolving an unhappy marriage: through the church courts, by Act of Parliament, a private agreement (the most popular choice for most), desertion or elopement, or wife sale. 'Criminal conversations' were argued out before judge and jury with the male parties (husband and lover) being represented by lawyers. The case in question came about as follows.

In early 1793 a thirty-one year old servant named Charlotte Flower, working in the household of a Mr Pierrepoint met and married Robert Edwards. Edwards, a valet, was described as having 'recently returned from India with General Meadows', a relative of Mr Pierrepont's. Charlotte was a good catch for Robert Edwards; he was penniless and she brought with her a small inheritance. Her aunt, Mrs Anne Horton of Tyson Street, Bethnal Green, was to testify that Charlotte had been left £300 by her uncle and £30 by her mother. Further, she had a share in 'some mills etc' in Leicester. Besides her aunt, Charlotte had two other relatives in London, a sister Mrs Smithwaite, whose address was given as Bruton Street, and a cousin, Mrs Horton's son William, a shopkeeper in Newgate Street.

According to Charlotte's later testimony she and Robert Edwards were married soon after they met, on a Sunday, and on the following Friday he left her to return to India. She says she only slept with him for one night. However, they had made plans for their future; once settled in India, Edwards was to send for her and in the meantime she was to seek employment. As a married woman Charlotte would find it hard to obtain a good position if she was to continue as a servant, so they agreed to keep the marriage a secret. Edwards was evidently not able to provide for his wife even for a few months and it was he who arranged for her to go to Holkham as housekeeper under her maiden name of Flower, though quite how he managed this was not disclosed.

Charlotte set out for Holkham to take up the post of housekeeper, arriving in late May with her luggage marked Charlotte Flower. Charlotte's predecessor

Elizabeth Crump had been in the post less than three years, with wages of £25 a year, and Charlotte was to be paid the same. The arrival of a new housekeeper was always an event, especially in this case as the family were absent. By the time they arrived at Holkham six weeks later Charlotte had made a favourable impression with the household and was soon to do so with her employers. This was fortunate since her husband Robert Edwards was 'disappointed' in India and did not stay there long. He returned to England in the following summer of 1794 and went at once to Holkham. On his arrival, Charlotte 'mentioned' the marriage to her employers and this was accepted by Mr and Mrs Coke, who showed considerable tolerance at the deception. Not only did Charlotte continue in her post as housekeeper, but Edwards was invited to stay with her for six weeks. During this time it was proposed that Edwards might take an inn at Fakenham, though the evidence for this is slight. Edwards certainly did not see himself as an innkeeper since, at the end of his stay, it was agreed that Charlotte should carry on at Holkham while he returned to town to seek a post in service. This he did and before too long he secured a place with Lord Harewood.

Before leaving Holkham, Edwards arranged with the Cokes that he would visit his wife once a year, but he did not encourage her to visit him either at Harewood in Yorkshire, or in London. There is no record to say whether Edwards did visit his wife during the following three years as he said he would, but since he repeatedly 'blamed himself for neglecting her' it is probable that he did not.

What happened next was that in the spring of 1795 two babies were born, one as already recorded was the Coke's third daughter, Elizabeth Wilhelmina, born in London. The other was at Holkham a month or so before the Cokes were due to arrive for the summer, and its mother was Charlotte the housekeeper. She gave birth to a son and named him Robert. Contrary to all previous rules about married servants who had children, Mr and Mrs Coke were so well pleased with Charlotte's conduct as housekeeper that they allowed him to be brought up in the house. The Cokes approval seems beyond doubt as an entry in Mrs Coke's personal account book testifies: she wrote in early 1796 in her list of presents 'I have also given out five guineas to Edwards the Housekeeper'. [24]

Elizabeth Wilhelmina Coke flourished but little Robert Edwards did not, and in January 1798 at the age of two and a half, he died. Poor Charlotte, despite the undoubted kindness and sympathy of Mrs Coke, hers would have been an isolated position as a female upper servant. She would not have mixed socially with the other servants, but lived in her own rooms with no companion to share her grief. However, at the risk of sounding like a Gothic novel so popular at this date, there was one person at Holkham who was willing to ease her pain, Francis Crick, the estate steward. Crick, a married man, had been at Holkham since 1786. In 1798, the year baby Robert died, he was forty-three years old and Mrs Sarah Crick, his wife, fifty. They were a childless couple.

One fact is beyond dispute, Crick fell in love with Charlotte and only a few months after her little boy was buried, Charlotte was pregnant again. This time she did not continue as housekeeper but in July 1798 went to London. From here she wrote to Robert Edwards to inform him of her situation, but gave him no contact address.

Edwards was alarmed at receiving her letter as well he might be, but it was not until two months later in September that he wrote to Charlotte's cousin William Horton enquiring her whereabouts and stating that he was very anxious to find her. Horton had long since known of her semi-secret marriage and was disinclined to help Edwards. He simply said that Charlotte was 'comfortably situated', adding that a settlement was to be made on her by the father of the unhappy child, though he did not know who the father was. Edwards wrote back thanking him.

There then followed a protracted effort on the part of Edwards to track Charlotte down. And after some time he succeeded. Softened by his stance as the humble husband who should never have neglected her, Charlotte invited him to her lodgings where she lived with her maid Anne Jordan. Initially all went well until she refused to name the father and he asked to search the house which she also refused. According to her aunt Mrs Horton, who was present, it was a day of high emotion: 'On the whole he seemed to treat her with great affection, but constantly appeared anxious to know who the Father was. She [Charlotte] was greatly concerned, cried much, and Edwards took her on his knee and kissed her'.

Having failed in his objective, it would seem that Edwards was now furious. Next he went to Holkham and rifled through Charlotte's boxes which had been left behind. Although he found a number of letters in them, there were 'none that were material'. After this abortive visit and realising he would make no more headway with his wife, he met up with the Hortons once more and repeated his inquiries as to the identity of the father, but they either could not or would not enlighten him. It was now September 1798 and until April 1801 no more was heard of Edwards, although, as Charlotte stated, he knew where to find her.

From the time of her arrival in London in July 1798 Charlotte had been visited by Francis Crick several times. According to evidence later given at the trial they lived together as man and wife in the house in Islington where Charlotte had taken lodgings in her own name of Mrs Edwards, and where she was seen to be with child. The baby was duly born in London, in January 1799. It was a girl, and named Charlotte. Crick was on duty at Holkham at the time of the birth but sent a letter shortly afterwards. He began by addressing Charlotte as his dearest life, congratulated her on her recovery from pain, and trusted she rested comfortably at night with 'his dear babe'. He had already settled money on Charlotte, with her cousin William Horton as one of the trustees. Over the next two years Charlotte and the baby lived quietly, spending part of the time in Suffolk. It was not until April 1801 that Edwards re-appeared, and this time in a dramatic fashion with no warning or attempt at friendliness, but came banging on the door of the Islington house demanding to be let in. He was accompanied by an attorney, for he had got it into his head that the father was not Crick but T. W. Coke. When Mr Hatton, Charlotte's landlord, protested about the disturbance they were making, the attorney said Mr Edwards only wanted papers concerning an action they were intending to bring against Mr Coke. When Mr Hatton asked if he meant 'Mr Coke of Holcomb', the attorney said 'Yes'.

Charlotte later confirmed that Edwards and the attorney, a Mr Harpur, called at her lodgings while she was still in bed, forced open the door and took away all her letters and papers, among which were letters from Francis Crick, 'but not signed or directed'. She added that they warned Mr Hatton not to trust her, and ended her evidence by saying that Edwards had had between four and five hundred pounds from her. This statement was given two weeks later to Messrs Hanrott and Metcalf, T. W. Coke's lawyers. She repeated that Edwards already had all her money, for she was concerned, with good reason, that a successful legal action against Crick could bankrupt him.

Edwards was obliged to renounce the idea of bringing an action against T. W. Coke: for despite having raided Charlotte's lodgings and read her personal correspondence, he still had no real evidence as to the father's identity. There was no denying the letters addressed to her came from Holkham but they were none of them *signed*. His attorney may have persuaded him that to pursue T. W. Coke with such flimsy evidence would end badly, whereas an action against Crick the steward would at least stand a chance of producing damages. Who suggested to him that Crick could have been the father is unknown, but Edwards now sued for divorce citing Francis Crick, and the date was set for 26th June 1801.

The trial took place before Lord Kenyon in the King's Bench in Westminster Hall, a judge known to be hard on adulterers. Charlotte was not present. Women were always unrepresented even in the tiny minority of trials instigated by wives. Accused of adultery they were powerless to contest their case. The main evidence produced by the plaintiff was one of the unsigned letters written after the birth of the child in which the author referred to 'his dear babe'. Despite its anonymity Edwards now played a trump card. In consequence of reading that letter and because it was not signed, he told the court that he had hired a detective to tail Crick's movements when Crick had been in London. The man had followed Crick to the house in Islington, and seen him emerge some time later arm in arm with Charlotte. By making enquiries the detective discovered that Crick had visited Charlotte in 1798, and that they had lived as man and wife. This proved the adultery.

On Crick's side, the evidence gathered by Mr Dunn of Metcalf and Hanrott did little good. Charlotte's aunt gave witness as to her good character and it was suggested that Edwards had brought about the case for the sole purpose of the damages and that he had neglected his wife and already received all her money. It was pointed out that Crick had settled an annuity of £60 upon Charlotte and should not be punished further. All of this was rather wasted on Lord Kenyon, the judge. He abhorred the fact that the defendant was middle-aged and married. The absence of the husband on business was no excuse, indeed the number of similar cases which had come before him recently only depicted the profligacy of the times and in order to check this 'growing evil' urged the jury to come down hard on the defendant.

In the end Crick got off lightly, he was fined just £400, instead of the thousands he might otherwise have been obliged to find. His salary was only circa £150 a year but he had considerable savings.

The newspapers reported the trial, and the *Norwich Mercury,* a Tory paper, had it on the front page, which was normally reserved for advertisements. Despite the publicity T. W. Coke showed a remarkable degree of tolerance towards Crick, as he had towards Charlotte. Crick was not dismissed as might have been expected, but continued as steward at Holkham until his death in 1814. This is even more remarkable when later he was found by his successor to have been a less than able steward and to have left the estate in a fair degree of muddle. Crick's wife also appears to have forgiven him. Perhaps reconciliation with her was a condition of his continued employment, for in his will he refers to her as his 'dear wife Sarah' and leaves her sufficient funds for 'comfortable support and maintenance during her life'. She lived until 1822. Crick also provided for the daughter of his liaison with Charlotte. He left an allowance for her education and maintenance and in 1814 Charlotte and the child were still living in Islington. It is not known how long Charlotte survived Crick; by 1819 their daughter Charlotte, though under age, was married to a Mr Wall. In the Holkham Letter Books it is seen that Mr Stokes, Coke's lawyer in Fakenham, often failed to send her the annuity left her by her father and letters from her to Holkham about this matter survive to 1854. [25]

Charlotte Edwards was unfortunate in her choice of husband and the death of her son, but not in her employer nor in her lover. Women servants were always vulnerable to the consequences of pregnancy and the numbers of female upper servants who bore illegitimate children and needed to give them up in order to seek re-employment was surprisingly high according to the records of the Foundling Hospital, which suggests that in 1820 they made up 37 per cent of the total seeking refuge. Despite the added scandal of divorce, Crick stood by Charlotte.

NOTES

1. HA Holkham Deeds Bundle 22 lists clothes and food given to the poor of the parish by Lady Margaret between 1722 and 1773. She gave them material, brown serge, duffel, dyed linnen and flannel. This was for both under clothes, shifts, petticoats, waistcoats and shirts as well as for suits and gowns. Tape, thread, buttons and linings were also given. Sometimes they were expected to make the clothes themselves; on other occasions they were made for them, the only items not given were hats and shoes. Each year an average of 21 men were in receipt of these hand-outs, 29 boys, 26 women and 39 girls. They were also given food in years of bad harvests. A regular amount of fourteen pounds of beef and flour per family, and if single nine pounds, was given at Christmas and varying amounts at other times. In 1753 for example 29 people were in receipt of extra food, 54 in 1765 and 67 in 1773.

2. HA E/C1/12 Letter Book for 1825.

3. Stirling vol.1 p.408 and Jessica Gerard *Country House Life, Family and Servants 1815-1914* Oxford 1994 p.44.

4. *The Early Diaries of Frances Burney* edited by Annie Raine Ellis, London 1913 vol.1 p.278.

5. Mrs Coke's correspondence and her Requisites for a Governess holograph are in the Berg Collection of the New York Public Library, pasted into a book catalogued as *The scrapbook of Fanny d'Arbley and Friends, England 1759-1799.* Items nos 32, 33 and 34.

These documents are pasted so firmly in the book as to prevent them from being photocopied, scanned or photographed. Grateful thanks to Mrs Mary Clow for kindly transcribing them.

6. Mrs Coke's family the Duttons of Sherbourne had long held a reputation for being accomplished artists. An example can be seen at Shugborough where a portrait of her three eldest children painted in 1799 by Lady Anson, née Anne Margaret Coke, hangs in the red drawing room. In London the next generation of Cokes were taught deportment, fencing and drawing by Jean Baptiste Tenniel of Huguenot descent whose son later illustrated Lewis Carroll's *Alice in Wonderland.*

7. Elizabeth Carter (1717-1806) was a poet and translator, but one who combined domesticity with learning, famously described by Dr Johnson as being able to make a pudding as well as translate Epictetus. Hester Chapone (1727-1801) was the author of *Letters on the Improvement of the Mind*, an educational book, originally written for her fifteen-year-old niece, it had become an instant success on publication in 1773.

8. Elaine Chalus *Elite Women in English Political Life c.1754-1790* Oxford 2005 pp.174-175.

9. NRO MC7/320.

10. Sylas Neville pp.328-9.

11. Chalus p.175.

12. Stirling vol. 1. pp.235-6.

13. Sheffield Archives Sp. St 1-270 60651-1 Mrs Jane Coke personal account books as above and Pamela Clabburn *The Norwich Shawl* London 1995 p.13.

14. HA F/TWC Bundles 25 and 28 Mr Nathaniel Kent, writer on agricultural matters – Mr Humphrey Repton, landscape architect. The list is an invaluable source of townspeople, 68 in Great Yarmouth, including Mr Cotman senior, and 19 from Swaffham showing the latter to be a fashionable place in contrast to Fakenham which is not mentioned at all.

15. *The Diary of James Woodforde Vol 12 1788-1790* ed. Peter Jameson, the Parson Woodforde Society 2001, p.85 and 88.

16. HA F/TWC 28 Mr Chamberlayne's reply.

17. HA F/TWC 24 Miss Parsons from Wrentham her reply.

18. Sylas Neville pp.330-331.

19. HA F/TWC 24.

20. Sylas Neville pp.330-1.

21. HA A/47.

22. Sheffield Archives Sp. St. 1–270 60651–1 Mrs Jane Coke personal account books.

23. Parker p.130.

24. Sheffield Archives Sp St 1–270 60651–1.

25. For a fuller account of this affair see Mary-Anne Garry 'Seduced by the Devil' Divorce in 18th Century Norfolk *Norfolk Archaeology* Vol. XLIV Part IV 2005.

CHAPTER 12

Widowerhood 1800-1822

The divorce trial of 1801 and its publicity took place in the aftermath of a much darker year, one which profoundly changed life at Holkham. It started with the winter of 1800 being unusually severe. There were food shortages in the parish and extra flour and meat was handed out to the poor. During one of the storms at sea a locally owned ship foundered off the coast with the loss of its entire cargo. The more grave misfortunes began on 8th January. While out shooting near South Creake there was an accident which resulted in the death of Lord Andover, the twenty-four year old husband of the Coke's eldest daughter Jane. Ten days later he was buried in the Coke family vault at Tittleshall with due pomp and the servants in mourning. In the immediate aftermath of her husband's death (there were no children of the marriage) Lady Andover remained at Holkham until March when the family party broke up and the Cokes left Norfolk for Bath. It is very probable that Lady Andover went with them as three of her servants were left at Holkham to live on board wages for the next fifteen weeks, paid for by her father. These were her 'woman' Charlotte Carey (her maid since 1794), footman Charles Pierce and groom William Curtis. Miss Hunloke, one of T.W. Coke's many nieces, was also of the party. She left her maid, Harriet Rotherham, to lodge in the house of John Sandys the Holkham gardener from March until May. Harriet's board wages were also paid for out of the general household disbursements.

This unhappy start to the year was a foretaste of worse to come. Mrs Coke was unwell. The previous year she records being in Buxton with her youngest daughter Eliza to take the waters, and later in London paying a bill to Sir William Farquahar, the Dr Sloane of his day, a society doctor. He failed to cure her and she returned home no better. Her illness was the reason for going to Bath. They were a large party: Mr and Mrs Coke with their five-year-old daughter Elizabeth and her nurse Sarah Johnson, Mrs Coke's sister, Mrs Lambert, and Mrs Branthwayt, the wife of a Norfolk lawyer [1] plus Lady Andover and Miss Hunloke. In Bath another of Mrs Coke's sisters, Mrs Masters, was staying close by in Milsom Street. They took with them a number of servants, but not Mrs Coke's personal footman John Parry who was also unwell. At Bath they were to share the housekeeping expenses with Mrs Branthwayt, which half share for the sixteen weeks came to £290, or about £18 a week, a modest sum. After seeing his wife comfortably settled T.W. Coke left his footman Anthony Dodsworth to wait on her and went to London for the start of the Parliamentary session. Mrs Lambert also left Bath soon afterwards. Bath in the spring was an attractive place to be, but Mrs Coke continued ill; in her personal account book she records paying Mrs Needham £5 'for nursing me' and 2gns to the Bath Hospital.

The 'best' Bath doctor, the renowned Dr Parry, was engaged. He recommended the usual remedies and Mrs Coke was well enough to enter several amounts paid to the 'Bathing woman' and the 'Pump woman'. Meanwhile in London William Windham wrote in his dairy for 23rd April that he had heard that Mrs Coke was dangerously ill. [2] Her symptoms were giddiness and headaches, and finally a 'violent pain upon her temple'. However, one morning in June Mrs Coke was seen by Dr Parry and pronounced better. Later she went out and about paying visits, appearing to be in good spirits. Mrs Branthwayt was with her all that day as well as her two maids, Mrs Burton and Mrs King. On her return home, however, she suffered a 'seizure', was helped upstairs to her bed where she died three hours later. The date was 2nd June. Immediately after her death was confirmed, 'Dr Parry says it was a kind of Fitt', the footman Anthony Dodsworth was commanded to take the news to his master. He left that same evening and was expected to reach London within twenty-four hours, travelling by post horse, only to discover that, unknown to those in Bath, T.W. Coke had set out for Holkham two days earlier. [3] As soon as he did receive the news Coke ordered the Holkham vicar the Rev'd Henry Crowe to Bath to see to the arrangements for the funeral cortège.

Crowe travelled via London where at Coke's request he called on Mrs Coke's sisters, Mrs Blackwell, Mrs Lambert and Mrs Masters (now returned to town) and on the dowager Mrs Coke. Writing from Bath on 8th June Crowe detailed the return route he would take saying that 'the awful scene will close at Tittleshall on Monday'. Mrs Coke was forty-six at the time of her death.

Back in Norfolk Mrs Coke's footman, John Parry (presumably no relation to the Bath doctor) had died at Holkham on 10th May, cause not given; he was just forty years old and unmarried. [4] His funeral was paid for from the household expenses, an oak coffin £2. 7s. 6d. with £7 of other costs and the balance of his wages paid to his niece Anne Ellis. As neither Mrs Coke's nor John Parry' symptoms suggest a contagious disease, their deaths were just an unhappy co-incidence.

The cost of Mrs Coke's funeral came approximately to the enormous sum of £2,000, including the journeys between Bath and Holkham and mourning for the servants. The greatest bill, from Mr Crook the undertaker at Bath, was for £792. 19s., which must have included embalming as it was now summer and two weeks were to pass before she was buried. Mrs Burton who had been Mrs Coke's woman, that is her companion, was broken hearted. She and the chambermaid Mrs King returned to Norfolk. The cortège bearing the body arrived at Swaffham on a Saturday where it stayed for twenty-four hours before proceeding to Tittleshall for the burial service at eleven o'clock on Monday. A mourning coach had been hired from Norwich and two of the grooms and the coachman went to fetch it.

The upper servants had already been given mourning for Lord Andover in January, and now the non-domestic upper servants, that is the farm bailiff, gardener, office assistant and the indoor upper servants who did not wear livery, i.e. the steward, valet, groom of the chambers and cook, were bought coats, waistcoats, silk hose, shoes, knee buckles, studs, silk gloves, muslin for neckcloths, and two cambric pocket handkerchiefs at a cost of 11gns each. Four of them were given mourning suits costing 14gns each. Twenty-nine other male employees from the church clerk to the gamekeepers and cow-men, and two retired servants, Thomas Boyce who had been the coachman and James Cooper, an elderly groom, received mourning suits costing £9. 10s. each. The postillions got new jackets, with silk tassels for their caps. Every servant wore an arm-band of crape or a hatband. Sixteen maid servants were provided with mourning gowns. The cloth was purchased from Alice Alderson of Wells and made up by Anne Hall also of Wells. The new housekeeper Mrs Bell had her mourning bought in London for which she was allowed £8, as were Mrs Coke's two lady's maids and Sarah Johnson Miss Coke's nurse. At this date women did not attend funeral services, which is not to say they were uninvolved. Wearing their mourning clothes they would have taken part in the funeral procession to the church and attended the graveside after the ceremony was over. [5] The church at Holkham and the Mansion Chapel were hung with fringes of black cloth.

After the funeral T.W. Coke left Holkham and did not return for six months until 20th September. A notice in the *Norwich Mercury* announced the cancellation of the annual sheep-shearing festivities. [6] The servants were on board wages for this period, including Sarah Johnson the nurse who looked after the little Elizabeth Coke, who must have been left at Holkham in her care. Mrs Burton was given a year's wages, 16 gns, plus her travel expenses to London to include the carriage of her luggage. The chambermaid Mrs King received the same allowances and her wages of 10gns. They left Holkham for good in July.

In the following year, 1801, the accounts continue to list bills for mourning. In February Miss Alderson of Wells provided black ribbon for the maid servants, nineteen pairs of black gloves, sixteen chip bonnets and forty-two yards of 'Love Ribbon'. In March Joseph Haycock, the Wells tailor, sent in a bill for 'second mourning for servants £382' and another 'for livery hats £26'. The second mourning refers to the suits he made for male servants, who no longer wore the dense 'first mourning' suits he had made them at the time of the funeral, but slightly less subdued ones. The household remained static: only one servant left, William Travis, the groom of the chambers, who had been there little under a year. The great sorrow felt by T.W. Coke seems to have permeated down to the servants who remained in their posts, despite being on board wages again that year for another six months during his absence from 16th March to 28th September. Amongst them were Lady Andover's servants. Three of the Andover servants were Norfolk, if not Holkham, people. The young Lady Andover, herself widowed, took over her mother's duties and saw to the domestic matters in the house. She found plenty to do and as early as December 1800 was ordering mahogany bookcases from George Bailey of Lynn; for the next few years she acted as hostess when T.W. Coke entertained. John Godwin, her footman, was to be one of the longest serving in the household. In 1804 he became footman to T.W. Coke, was promoted to butler in the 1820s and remained as such until his death in 1843.

After Lady Andover re-married in 1806 and moved away, T.W. Coke was 'looked after' by a number of his relations. His sister Lady Hunloke, widowed herself in 1804, was often at Holkham according to the board wages paid to her servants. So too was the eldest Miss Blackwell, a niece, ordering 'sundry Mahogany furniture' to be delivered to Holkham, window blinds and protective covers for the furniture in the state rooms in 1810. Her servants (unnamed) had board wages paid for them. Lady Andover (who retained her title despite being married to a Colonel Digby) was back at Holkham in 1811 ordering £73 worth of linen cloth. The whole family played their part; Coke's youngest daughter, Elizabeth Wilhelmina, was put in 'charge' of the dairy in 1802 when she was just seven years old. The profits from the butter and cream not needed for the house and sold were credited to her account every three months. It was not unusual to find the 'lady of the house' enjoying this perk, many of whom dabbled in making the butter themselves. The fashion for playing at diary maids dates from at least the mid-eighteenth century and was popularised by Marie-Antionette at Versailles where she had a garden and farm laid out for her in the English style. At Shugborough in c.1805 Samuel Wyatt converted the two lower storeys of a park building known as the Tower of the Winds for Elizabeth's elder sister Lady Anson. Here he installed a most luxurious dairy lined with Derbyshire Alabaster, shelves of marble, stained glass windows and earthenware by Wedgwood. This may have been inspired by the Holkham dairy, once the province of Sarah Staniforth, which sadly has not survived. [7]

Young Miss Elizabeth Coke was treated as older than her years as far as having her own servants was concerned. From 1801, when she was only six, she had her own footman John Houseman, and her own groom Francis Browne, besides her nurse maid Sarah Johnson, and governess Miss Atwood. From then until her marriage in 1822 she had five successive footmen and three grooms. The second footman appointed for her was Anthony Dodsworth who had been her father's, and her next groom Joseph Clarke, had been her mother's. Years later, on the eve of her marriage, Miss Coke recorded a letter of congratulations in her commonplace book from Mr Roger Wilbraham of Twickenham, a well known agriculturist, horticulturist, politician and friend of her father's who, she says: 'almost educated me, being very much in love with my Governess, and a great plague at the time'. The faithful governess either did not take a fancy to Mr Wilbraham or could not bring herself to leave a motherless child, for Miss Atwood stayed at Holkham until 1812.

T.W. Coke continued to spend long periods of time away from Holkham, the regular absence from March to July was often extended to October or even November. When in London, more often than not he stayed with his daughter Mrs, later Lady, Anson at the Anson house in St James's Square. However, when he was at Holkham, entertaining continued much as it had before.

The period of inflation in the early 1800s did not greatly affect the increase in wages paid to the servants, at any rate the male ones. The house porter's wages had risen from £17 to £21 by 1810, the man cook to 100 gns a year and footmen from 18gns to £22. With the exception of the housekeeper, whose wages went up from £25 a year in 1790 to £31 in 1810, those of the maids stayed generally unchanged. The housemaids earned between eight and ten guineas, as did laundry maids, the dairy maid 9gns, and Miss Coke's maid, who had previously been her nurse, was unchanged at 16gns.

During this period the majority of the male upper servants continued to come from afar, while the female servants were largely local, at least in the early years of the century, with the exception of the housekeeper. The practice of employing locally born people as indoor servants, begun in the 1780s, must have been judged successful at first, though unusual. Dr Rigby commented on the fact in 1807 when he stated that he was surprised to learn that nearly all of T. W. Coke's establishment were locals. [8]

The servants conditions continued much as before, being cared for in sickness by the local apothecaries, first Mr Girdlestone and later Mr Hugh Rump, who attended the mansion prescribing medicines for all its inhabit-ants. There is no record as to whether they also prescribed for the horses and dogs as their predecessors had done. [9] Two examples show that considerable help was given to the servants when needed. In 1804 one of the game-keepers, John Hawksworth, was taken to London by the footman Anthony Dodsworth 'in his illness' at a cost of £27; they returned to Holkham but Hawksworth died shortly afterwards. He was 64 years old and unmarried, and what makes this payment all the more remarkable was that there was found among Hawksworth's possessions in his room a purse containing over £867. [10] The following year John Harman the gardener was given three guineas as a 'charity' payment towards the expenses of 'having bad eyes and going to London for advice'. When the groom Joseph Clarke was in his last illness (at the same time as another of the grooms, David Haggard, who recovered) they were attended several times by Dr Heath at a cost of £6. 16s. 6d. Joseph Clarke, first Mrs Coke's groom and subsequently Miss Coke's, was only 37 when he died in 1804; the funeral charges came to £5. 14s .6d. paid for by T. W. Coke. Clarke came from a large local family and had begun as under-groom at 12gns a year plus another 2gns for breeches and boots; by 1800 he had been promoted and his wages increased to £23. As a groom he went on numerous journeys, one of the longest in 1795 when he accompanied the newly-wed Ansons to Shugborough and on his return put in his expenses of £12, once again illustrating that servants continued to be trusted with considerable amounts of cash. Besides many entries for his 'sundry travel expenses' at the time of the election in 1789, he had been in charge of buying cockades and decorations for the saddle horses spending over £9 on these. In April 1806 a woman named Elizabeth Herring, not a servant, was employed to attend the footman cum baker Richard Dodsworth for nineteen weeks when he was ill; she received 3s. 6d. a week for nursing him and a further shilling for every night she sat up with him.

Coke's reputation as a fair employer was well-founded by this time; he appears to have been generous in an almost impulsive way towards his greater 'Family' with little regard for detail, very similar to his great uncle. In 1806, £1. 11s. was paid out for medicine and attendance for a labourer, Jonathon Porter, 'by order of Mr Coke' and that same year £11. 12s. was spent on porter (beer) for the poor in the parish and £6. 12s. on mutton. Mutton was still more expensive than beef in 1806 and seen as something of a treat; it was what the gentry ate. The local wine merchant's bill 'wine for the poor of Holkham' from April 1798 to February 1806 came to the astonishing sum of £69. 8s. 8d. Small wonder that Coke was in frequent receipt of begging letters.

Long-serving servants continued to be well treated after they had left Holkham and were generally in receipt of an annuity or annual donation. These donations, or pensions, were a highly personal choice, the subject of a particular affection or circumstance. Thirty-three years after his retirement in 1793 the sister of Samuel Brougham (the steward who had succeeded Cauldwell in 1782) wrote to Holkham from her home in Darlington Co. Durham, to thank T. W. Coke for her annuity of £20, 'paid yearly since the death of my brother'. The widows of upper servants could also expect to be in receipt of annuities long after their husbands had died; it is not always possible to know the exact source of this money, whether it was interest paid from investments or was given as a pension. Until the advent of banks and confidence that their money would be safe, servants savings continued to be invested with their masters, who dispensed financial advice even after it was no longer strictly needed. Some servants were given personal annuities by the Cokes on retirement; one such was Thomas Boyce the coachman who left to be the landlord of the Ostrich Inn in Castle Acre (and to be the eyes and ears of Holkham there). Another was the laundry maid Jemima Garne. Jemima and her sister (?) Hannah, a housemaid, had come from Sherborne in the 1780s, Mrs Coke's childhood home, where their relation was the under-butler. In May 1790 Jemima married William Pierce, a groom at Holkham, and thirteen years later in August 1803, when Pierce died, she returned to

Gloucestershire to live at Bibury on the Sherborne estate, relatively secure in receipt of an annual pension of £20 paid to her via Lord Sherborne. Both Lord Sherborne and his son John Dutton record that they gave her the money in person. Usually she was at home when they called, but occasionally she was absent away on a visit, and then they gave it to their Bibury gamekeeper to give her. In this case a return visit was necessary, in order to obtain her receipt, which was duly forwarded to Holkham. Jemima continued in receipt of this pension for twenty years. Sometimes when the money was late, as in 1819, Dutton paid it himself and was repaid by Holkham. In 1822 a report was received that she had died, but it turned out not to be true. She was simply very ill; the donation having been again late in arriving, she had not been able to tell Dutton and was in great need of funds to pay for medication.

Another Gloucestershire servant was Joseph Wilkins, groom of the chambers from 1801 to 1817. On his retirement he left Holkham to live in Newton Cottage (whereabouts unknown) and kept chickens, until thieves stole them. Although compensated for this theft by T. W. Coke, he retired to live with his brother Richard at the Boot Inn, Tetbury, where he died in 1821. His annual pension in retirement was also £20.

In 1810 a new housekeeper was engaged at Holkham at 30gns a year. Her name was Mrs Mary Greengrass, a woman of mature years and the mother of a grown up daughter named Charlotte. Mary Greengrass was another unfortunate housekeeper, but in a very different way from Charlotte Edwards. Greengrass was a thief; she had sticky fingers and may have been pilfering for years before she was found out – she would have had plenty of opportunity to do so during the time Miss Coke was growing up (just 15 in 1810) notwithstanding the presence of the numerous Coke relatives helping to run the house. What is known for sure is that sometime in early 1815 she contrived a plan to steal a quantity of bedding and curtains. It was a clever choice as these items would have been her direct responsibility – she controlled everything in the linen cupboard – and were far less likely to be missed than some of the more obvious treasures in the house. From her arrival at Holkham Mrs Greengrass had been in the habit of ordering goods on her own account, candlesticks, glasses, earthenware, jugs and £35 worth of bed furniture in 1811. Quantities of crimson cloth, Irish linen, coffee pots and rush-bottomed chairs, tea and coffee all were requested by her, written down and passed on to the appropriate merchants. There is no previous, or subsequent, record of a housekeeper purchasing in this manner.

Mrs Greengrass's housekeeping books were unremarkable. The expenses recorded in them are simple incidentals needed in the house, anything from sewing materials to mops and pans. However, in February 1814 it is recorded that her books had not been settled for the last nineteen months, a total of £186 owing. In theory she should have shown these books to the steward Francis Crick every month and received payment but clearly this did not happen. (Such sloppy practices as the non-payment of servants books for months at a time were part of what shocked Francis Blaikie the steward who arrived in 1816).

Later that same month Mrs Greengrass ordered bed 'thicken', blankets and rugs costing £32, and some of these were the items she wrapped in mats and sent away. A year later the local carrier named Archer confirmed that he had been ordered to Holkham to collect 'three large Matts' labelled for a Mrs King at Wareham in Dorset. In the days before brown wrapping paper and padded Jiffy bags, goods were packed inside woven mats, rolled round and tied with twine. Mats protected the contents and could be used more than once. Mr Seeth the agent for the Archer Waggon Office in London (26 Sun Street, Bishopsgate) confirmed that the mats in question had been collected from Holkham and delivered to the Bull in Friday Street from where they went on by Russell's waggon to Dorset. At about the same time, March 1815, a Mrs Cox who lived at Mr Sheldon's in Jesus College Lane, Oxford, stated that she received two other packages from Mrs Greengrass: 'which she beg'd me to take care of, being unacquainted with every sircomstance [sic] I in course expected to see her'. Mrs Cox and Mrs Greengrass were friends but until a recent meeting in town had not met for six years. Mrs Greengrass may have boasted of her act, for Mrs Cox was aware she was in possession of stolen property, but had every faith that she had nothing to fear from the Bow Street officers 'or any other person' knowing that a line from Mr Coke would 'settle everything'. To add insult to injury Mrs Cox said her brother, presumably Mr Sheldon, had taken the packages in and had had to pay the postage charge of twelve shillings.

Mrs Greengrass was exposed as a thief shortly afterwards and took the dramatic step of fleeing from England. The disgrace fell upon her daughter Charlotte whose address was 80 South Audley Street, London, where very likely she was employed as a servant. Mrs Cox in Oxford commiserated with Charlotte, writing in a wonderfully vernacular English, that she was ' ... indeed very much surprised to here the disagreeable Sittuation you say your Mother as placed you in ... your mother as left you too settle her affairs I think you are the most proper person for me to deliver her property too therefore I think you as better come and fetch them'.

Two days after receiving this letter Charlotte Greengrass wrote to T.W. Coke, a letter worth recording in its entirety, a more educated effort than Mrs Cox's though, like hers, with minimum punctuation:

'Sir/ to express my feelings would be impossible suffice it to say the only way of consolation I have felt since my Mothers misconduct was to hear you say you would not hurt her, judge how keenly I must have felt the contents of Mrs Kings letter that she received from you, God knows I wish every item to be returned to its rightful owner and have done everything in my power to discover where any Package or Luggage mat be but let me beg of you as a Parent not to ask me to give up my Mother I am the only one who knows where she is, picture to yourself her unhappy Daughter on her knees imploring God to dispose your heart to hear her Petition with Lenity [sic] not for her Mother can entreat she is and ever must be an Exile from her Country and Friends that with her own reflections I hope you will consider sufficient punishment and in mercy, think what a task it is for a child to plead for a Parent and that Parent unworthy and pray consider my feelings and alleviate them in some degree by telling me you will hear my Prayer it is me you spare and not my Mother whose fault I know was great and yet I do not think I can survive if she shall be made a publick example of, that you may spare her is the wish and prayer of her most wretched and unhappy Daughter and your most humble and obedient servant Charlotte Greengrass'. [11]

All the surnames in the above episode appear in the Holkham accounts of the period; Francis and William Greengrass were the pump men and well-sinkers, William Cox an apprentice in the kitchens who married a housemaid Dinah Dunn in 1803, and a Mrs King who had been Mrs Coke's maid pre-1800.

The same year Greengrass had been engaged, 1810, the dowager Mrs Coke (T.W. Coke's mother) died. Her funeral was held in Norfolk where she was buried in the family vault at Tittleshall. Having married Wenman Coke more than sixty years previously, she would have been a grandmother in her eighties. Lady Andover, her eldest granddaughter, supervised the mourning clothes for the Holkham maid servants. £38 was spent on cloth from Thomas Tingey of Wells and £37 worth from Mr John Kerrison of Burnham to be made into gowns by Mrs Land. Miss Jickling of Wells provided mourning bonnets for the maid servants; the upper servants and others, including Mrs Greengrass, were given 12gns each to provide their own mourning outfits. These were Sarah Johnson, Miss Elizabeth Coke's maid, Abraham Dunn the butler, Leger Pelteret the cook (a foreigner), Joseph Wilkins groom of the chambers, John Godwin T.W. Coke's valet, Francis Crick the steward and William Baker his office assistant, John Loose the gardener and Miles Bulling the bailiff of the farm. The remainder of the male servants had their mourning made for them by Richard Clarke the tailor in Wells.

The following year an even more distant link with the past was severed with the death of Lady Mary Coke the widowed daughter-in-law of Thomas and Lady Margaret who had married their son Edward in 1747. She had lived to be eighty-four, in an age when such longevity was rare. As a consequence of these two deaths T.W. Coke's income increased, for until then he had been liable for his mother's annuity of £3,000 a year (raised out of the property she had handed over to him in 1803, Hillesdon in Buckinghamshire) and Lady Mary Coke's of £2,000. Together this was enough to pay the interest (£4,000) on the huge debts that Coke owed but did not reduce them. By 1806 his income was £24,000 net after paying taxes, repairs, and improvements on the estate. Parker says that about £9,000 should be deducted from this for servicing debts and other obligations (e.g. daughters' portions), and that by 1822 his annual household and personal expenses were estimated at £16,000. His debts were therefore increasing. [12] But again, like his great uncle without a direct heir, there appears not to have been a great incentive to reduce them.

By 1810 Mrs Lambert one of the sisters-in-law who had spent so much time at Holkham had also died, but Mrs Blackwell and T.W. Coke's daughters and nieces were still on hand to help out with domestic matters. Lady Andover, Coke's eldest daughter, and Miss Blackwell his niece by marriage appear more frequently in the household accounts than does Lady Anson who was mother to a large family of her own. These women continued to help run the house until Elizabeth Coke, the youngest daughter, was able to take her place as hostess for her father and manage the great establishment in 1816.

Throughout this twenty-year period some improvements and changes took place. In 1807 James Groom a stone mason was employed to install Italian marble fireplaces in Strangers' Wing and later to create a paved terrace to the south of the house. Fashionable mahogany furniture, as we have seen, was acquired from time to time and a Mr Martin was hired to 'modernise' some of the old. The upholsterer, Mr Ling from Norwich, lodged at Holkham for weeks at a time every year, much of the work being done at the 'new library'. Many of the pictures and looking-glass frames in the house were re-gilded. Zachary Fenn of Walsingham was paid to paint and wallpaper a number of rooms. In January 1807 he had earned 1gn for gilding a chair as 'specimen of his worksmanship', which evidently did not pass the test as subsequently he was only paid for decorating, 'colouring' the rooms and hanging paper in the breakfast room.

Among the servants the cooks changed more frequently than any of the others, seventeen male cooks in twenty-two years, and thirteen female ones between 1810 and 1822. Admittedly some were engaged for limited periods over the summer sheep-shearing when great entertaining took place, and in the autumn for shooting parties and at Christmas. The changes were particularly frequent after 1810, the year Mrs Greengrass arrived as housekeeper. The male cooks earned in the region of 100gns a year and came from and returned to London, as did the female cooks, who were paid 25gns. The assumption is that considerable friction was caused by having male and female cooks working at the same time. Since T.W. Coke was a generous employer the problem must have been in-built. Elizabeth Glossop for example worked from March to September 1810, Sarah Jones from September 1810 to January 1811 and Anne Rees from October 1811 to February 1812. Between Jones and Rees, Martha Haines was engaged as cook in June 1811 and worked in the kitchen for two months until the family went away, after which, though continuing to receive board wages, she was living in Wells. Some clash of personality must have occurred for her to have moved out and still be paid, for when she was discharged she received money for 'one week's expense at Wells' and her travel expenses back to London.

After 1810 there began a general trend back towards employing servants from London, even the maids. A few came from other places such as Mary Jenkinson from Shugborough, but in this middle period of Coke's life at Holkham twenty-four servants are recorded as having their fares paid to London on being discharged, and thirty replacements came from London including laundry, house and kitchen maids. This was a marked alteration from the first years of the century and the two decades of the earlier one when Dr Rigby had remarked on the number of local people employed. It suggests that both Lady Andover and Miss Blackwell thought that the house could do with tidying up and improving, and also that engaging servants locally was far from ideal. Despite there being no complete lists of servants from 1816, when Francis Blaikie arrived as steward, until T.W. Coke's death in 1842, the trend towards employing London servants and away from locals continued, as evidenced by entries for their travel expenses on being engaged and discharged.

In the grounds a new riding school was built beside the stables, which at this date were at the far side of the lake to the west of the mansion. Riding schools were basically large barn-like structures where horses could be exercised under cover, a desirable asset in an age when riding for pleasure was so popular – shades of Thomas Coke and his manège. Miss Coke rode side-saddle on her own pony and in 1810 was bought a second black one that pulled a cart made comfortable with cushioned seats, which she used for visiting Wells.

But all this paled beside the amount Coke spent on his childhood home at Longford, where his brother Edward and family were living. Workmen were sent from Holkham and close to £5,000 was laid out on 'modernizing the house there' between 1807 and 1813.

Of the seventeen servant marriages which took place at Holkham between 1800 and 1822 ten were maid servants, some of whom were already several months pregnant. With the exception of Charlotte Edwards, the housekeeper, there is no hard evidence to be had regarding those responsible for the maids' pregnancies, only that arriving at the altar in 'an interesting condition' conformed to the national trend which had been accelerating since the later part of the eighteenth century. When in 1804 John Godwin, T.W. Coke's valet married Anne Taylor, an upper still-room maid, she was three months pregnant. John Ransome, plate burnisher and liveried servant, left it later still before he married Amelia Lack who was seven months and John Oliver, a footman, married Sarah Fishburn when she was six months pregnant.

By 1810 John Godwin the valet was a widower, but not for long; he soon married for a second time, and once more to a fellow servant, Sarah Johnson, who had been Miss Elizabeth Coke's nurse and later her lady's maid. Sarah was eight years older than her husband and aged forty-three when she gave birth to their daughter Elizabeth in 1813. Married upper servants were given the opportunity to live out in nearby cottages. When Abraham Dunn the butler married in 1808 he was offered the Octagon Cottage and accepted it. Thomas Wilkinson, footman and later under-butler from 1783 to 1822, married Hannah a one-time cook maid and moved into the West Lodge. John Biller the coachman had a cottage at the Staithe. Thomas Blunt, who succeeded Abraham Dunn as butler, was married with four children when he came to Holkham in 1812, and on his appointment moved into West Lodge, displacing Wilkinson who was offered a cottage in Holkham village. Later John Godwin lived at North Lodge. Even John Favré, Coke's valet married to Sarah, a lady's maid, did not live in the hall. Since the nearest cottage was a good fifteen minutes' walk away this cannot have been very convenient, especially for the valet, but the fact that the offers were taken up shows the respect Coke had for the state of matrimony and the value the servants put on independence. The rent for these cottages was approximately £2 a year.

Francis Crick, steward from 1793, died in 1814 and was succeeded by Mr Bulling the farm bailiff. On his appointment Bulling moved from Longlands into the Hall and lived there until he married a year later. To assist him, Bulling had the services of William Baker, the office clerk who had worked with Crick since 1809, and together the two of them tackled the domestic disbursements and estate affairs until Francis Blaikie arrived on 25th March 1816, Lady Day. This appointment was to be the dawn of a new day in estate management. The newly-wed Bulling returned to Longlands where he continued as farm bailiff for a further twenty-five years.

Francis Blaikie was previously agent to Lord Chesterfield [1773-1815], a cousin of the 4th Earl of Chesterfield whose collected letters had been published in 1774 and read by 'everyone' both in England and on the continent. Blaikie, a scrupulous Scot, came highly recommended. In the early nineteenth century Scottish stewards ('steward and agent' as Blaikie styled himself) had an 'enviable' reputation for toughness and thoroughness in dealing with every aspect of estate matters. Blaikie and his 'energetic management' as Parker has called it, was needed at Holkham where, as already hinted, a certain laxity had crept into estate affairs. For example, Blaikie was horrified to discover that, although T.W. Coke had spent widely on building new farmhouses and premises throughout his Norfolk estates in the 1780s and 1790s, all with the latest fashions such as bells, stoves and marble fireplaces, not one of them had an inventory of the fixtures and fittings i.e. those items that belonged to the landlord and should be left in situ when a tenant departed. These newly designed estate farms impressed visitors with their neatness and efficacy, it was not merely the tenants' successful farming methods, the crops they grew, the stock they bred (and the income they produced), but the gentlemen's houses they lived in. Some were faced with the famous white Holkham bricks and had generously sized sash windows and pediments above the doors, but were often no more than one room deep with offices behind. [13] T.W. Coke's permanent mark on the landscape, apart from his promotion of matters agricultural, were these new farms and their premises. They were his legacy, executed in a manner to compliment Holkham itself – no less than fermes ornées on a larger scale. There is little or no written evidence to substantiate the belief that T.W. Coke got Samuel Wyatt to design some of them, though some of their features suggest that he may have done. One of Blaikie's first initiatives was to visit each farm, describe them at length and record all the fixtures and fittings he found; this exercise served as an excellent personal introduction to the Norfolk tenants.

Blaikie's salary began at an impressive £490 and rose to £650 by 1821, so highly valued were his talents and dedication. William Baker remained as clerk and had his pay increased from 100gns to £155. Francis Blaikie and William Baker comprised the office staff, along with an 'architect'. At first this was Henry Savage who had been a master carpenter at Holkham in the 1780s. He was sixty-five in 1816 and died in harness aged seventy-six; he was succeeded by Stephen Emerson first entered as a postillion in 1793 and later as a servant to Lady Andover in 1801. The architect, or more accurately the clerk of the works, was responsible for all repairs and improvements at Holkham and throughout the estate, a position previously held by Isaac Riches.

Another of Blaikie's innovations was to begin a series of letter books into which every letter both written and received regarding estate business was to be recorded. At least that was the idea and the majority *were* recorded. These letters give an insight into Blaikie's dealings and his character, showing him to be zealous and punctilious in the extreme, a man determined to be fair, but also determined never to be proved wrong. In July 1816, shortly after his arrival at Holkham he entered a memorandum in the letter books recording that William Farley a groom, who had been twelve years with T.W. Coke (in fact he was Miss Coke's groom) had died and was buried two days later. He wrote that the hearse was 'followed by the Servants and principle Tradesmen of the Family, with the exception of H. Savage architect, S. Emerson carpenter, F. Loose glazier, Wm Ballard gamekeeper and L. Loose shepherd'. This record was very much for Blaikie's own benefit, but there was more to come. The very night Farley died one of the garden labourers, Samuel Cooper, broke into Farley's room. At first he had tried to pick the lock, but not succeeding he fetched a ladder and entered the room by breaking the window. The room was above the stables and from it Cooper stole a coat and waistcoat. He was caught soon after and when challenged said it was true he did have a set of 'picklock' keys which he had taken from the blacksmith's shop at Longlands, but that he only used them to take corn from the granary for 'the use of the horses under my care'. Cooper was dismissed, his punishment unrecorded.

Blaikie saw plenty of room for improvement in the running of Holkham Hall and, beginning with the stables, he drew up new rules for their management. John Biller the coachman was to be given £15 to 'furnish the Coach stable' both in town and country with horse combs, blacking, brushes, etc. including tallow grease for the carriages, oil for the harnesses and mops for washing the carriages. He followed this by drawing up an agreement between T.W. Coke and David Haggard the head groom of the saddle horse stables. Haggard was to be allowed 17gns a year to pay for soap, candles, forks, pails, brushes, and other goods to be used both for Mr Coke's servants and horses and for the servants and horses of all Mr Coke's visitors.

Next he made an agreement for a Holkham boy, Charles Lack, who helped with the slaughtering and cutting up of meat. In addition he was to be given 6s. a week to assist the brewer, take his meals in the house with the servants when the family were there, and to have a further 6s. a week board wages when they were not as then no slaughtering would be done. So, Blaikie said: 'by this regulation the expence of a regular brewer's assistant will be rendered unnecessary'. The direct management of the servants was outside his remit, but it cannot be doubted that he would have made absolutely sure that each grain of sugar and every farthing's worth of wages was recorded, checked and double checked and it would have been no surprise to find Blaikie encouraging the employment of more 'trained' (i.e. London) servants for indoor posts.

In late 1816, having recently returned from a visit to the Coke estates in Oxfordshire and Buckinghamshire, Blaikie received a letter from a Mr Lines, one of the Buckinghamshire tenants, who in turn had had a letter from Lady Anson asking him to find her a dairy maid for her beautiful Shugborough dairy. Lines wrote that he had a girl in mind, but was unsure she would suit as she was unable to write or keep accounts. [14] Lady Anson was staying at Holkham at the time so Blaikie was able to discuss this with her personally. She was not put off by the girl's shortcomings and in his reply Blaikie made no reference to the girl's educational limitations but enquired if Lines and his daughter would be prepared to take her in and train her since she was also not 'fully acquainted with the process of Butter making ... that very important art'. Mr Lines replied that his daughter would be delighted but Lady Anson must understand that at this time of year (by now it was early January) the dairy was very low and further his daughter 'does not understand cheese'. This dairy maid was a far cry from the proficient Sarah Staniforth who rose to become housekeeper, but shows how recommendation was preferable to all else and it may be that Lady Anson's close involvement with the dairy would reduce the need for the girl to keep accounts immediately. Educating her could be dealt with in due course.

It became customary to share or exchange a number of servants between the two houses of Holkham and Shugborough, the Anson seat in Staffordshire. In 1803 Anne Lander travelled to Holkham to begin work as a laundry maid where she remained for the next ten years, returning to Shugborough, all expenses paid, in 1813. In 1810 another Shugborough housemaid, Mary Jenkinson mentioned above, joined her but stayed for only two years. An Anson servant named Peter O'Hara was at Holkham as house porter from 1816 to 1821. After he left, O'Hara was in receipt of a weekly pension of 5s. allowed him by Lady Anson and when he died in late 1829, Coke sent £5 towards his funeral expenses. There is no mention of him in the Shugborough records which suggests he was a London servant, stationed at the Ansons' house in St James's Square. Servants were also loaned for short periods; while the Ansons were in Paris in 1817 (with the young Miss Elizabeth Coke) their cook Thomas Moxon spent time in the Holkham kitchens, and later, during the 1830s, George Rennell came from Shugborough on several occasions to act as temporary Groom of the Chambers. Conversely, several Holkham sur-names, such as Middleton and Dodsworth, appear in the household accounts at Shugborough. [15]

Trust continued to be the hallmark of a good servant and much was asked of them. In 1808 Thomas Clarke, T.W. Coke's footman, was sent to London to fetch the plate (silver), and claimed 'travel expenses of Himself and Luggage and carrying the Plate'. The silver fitted into its own trunk, possibly the one Thomas Coke had bought in the 1720s. Both arrived safely back. At the time of the sheep-shearings and the vast numbers of visitors to Holkham (invitations that few refused) servants acted as marshals advising the visitors as to where they could and could not go in the house. Mr Samuel Taylor, a journalist from Ditchingham near Bungay, complained to Blaikie that although he had been able to get into Mr Coke's room every day it was 'by accident with the crowd'; the servants 'executing Mr Coke's orders' had not allowed him into the Statue Gallery and from his place in the dining room he had been unable to hear the proceedings. He was concerned that his report would be 'imperfect', just when he needed to be extremely rigid in view of the competition. 'It is no impeachment of the hospitality of Mr Coke', he wrote, and neither did he blame the servants. Blaikie replied that having laid Taylor's letter before Mr Coke it was agreed to fix a proper place for him at the table next year and the servants would be notified to that effect.

In the first two years of the 1820s the affluent times at Holkham continued unchanged, and the coming and going of Royalty and a stream of lesser visitors with their servants continued despite the economic downturn in the world outside. An agricultural depression, caused largely by bumper harvests and low prices for grain, resulted in many of the tenant farmers not being able to pay their rents. From the estate office Francis Blaikie and his assistant William Baker sent out copious letters to the tenants cajoling, reasoning and finally warning those who had not paid. In the worst cases of non-payment notices to quit were delivered. The hardships suffered by the farmers and others is very evident in the letter books as the 'depression of the times' had a knock-on effect throughout the land. The precarious nature of life was seldom more in evidence; even Mr Foster of Norwich, Coke's lawyer and steward of the Courts on his estate, stated that of the twenty Inclosure Bills in which he had acted as Commissioner almost all had, in his opinion, had a detrimental effect on the poor. He reckoned an average of twenty families per parish had been 'injured'. [16] Several of these bills concerned Holkham parishes. Following the end of the Napoleonic wars, general unemployment was compounded by large numbers of ex-soldiers and sailors who were no longer needed for active service and were often in poor health or suffering disabilities, a toll on many a parish. Their numbers were matched by the widows and children of those who had not returned, seeking to supplement their meagre pensions. Those looking for posts as labourers and domestic servants had never been more numerous.

With many of the Holkham rents either reduced or not paid, Blaikie saw that a crisis of extreme severity was approaching and planned various ways in which to stave off the worst effects. He began by setting an example; he and the office staff took pay cuts. Blaikie's own salary was reduced from £650 to £550 and his assistant William Baker and Henry Savage the architect suffered similarly. Some of the servants were less inclined to accept a cut in their wages and in May 1821 there was a small exodus. That month saw three upper servants give in their notice; they had their month's wages allowed them and their expenses paid to London. These were the groom of the chambers Robert Quin, the cook George Taylor, and the house steward James Brown. None had been at Holkham for more than four years. Peter O'Hara the house porter also left Holkham this month but this may have been for health reasons. Servants were in the habit of leaving in clutches; it had happened in 1812 when seven left between the end of February and early April. There had been no apparent reason for that exodus; the arrival of a new housekeeper or house steward could upset the status quo but this had not been the case then, nor was it in 1821. Nevertheless something was afoot, for another three servants left in May and June. In the absence of a wages list it cannot be known whether this was due to proposed pay cuts or whether those who stayed had accepted one. The times were hard and although T. W. Coke was burdened with debts for much of his life, to the great concern of Blaikie, the immediate condition of those who worked in and around Holkham was largely unaffected; the overall number of servants was not reduced and the pay cuts agreed to by the office staff lasted for only two years.

However an unexpected and far greater change of an altogether different nature was about to take place at Holkham for, in early 1822, at the age of sixty-eight, Thomas William Coke married for a second time.

NOTES

1. Miles Branthwayte was a Norfolk lawyer employed by T.W.C.

2. *The Dairy of William Windham 1784-1810* p.424.

3. Sheffield Archives Sp St 60583 Letters 11 and 15.

4. Holkham Parish Registers.

5. HA copy of Lady Catherine Coke's will 1688: 'my executors to give these five [female] servants named necessary mourning that they may the more decently attend my corps to my last resting place'.

6. *Norwich Mercury* 14th June 1800.

7. John Martin Robinson *Shugborough* for the National Trust, London, 1989 p.86.

8. Stirling vol. 1. p.293.

9. The Veterinary College in London was founded in 1791 by a Frenchman, Vial de St Bel, and trained students from its inception.

10. HA H/X5, thanks to Christine Hiskey for bringing Hawkworth's savings to my

attention.

11. HA F/TWC 34.

12. Parker pp.126–129.

13. See for example the farmhouses built by T.W. Coke: Leicester Square at South Creake and the Wicken, Castle Acre.

14. It is likely however that she could read. Children were taught to study the Bible, but teaching them to write was seen as dangerous for it would give them the means to expound rebellious or revolutionary ideas.

15. Staffordshire Record Office D 615 EH/26 housekeeper's accounts 1763–1823 and EH/29 Steward's accounts 1801–35.

16. J. L. Hammond and Barbara Hammond, *The Village Labourer 1760-1832* London 1911, Sutton edition pub. 1987 p.83.

CHAPTER 13

The Second Marriage 1822-1843

After the briefest of engagements T. W. Coke's marriage to Lady Anne Keppel, a young woman of eighteen and fifty years his junior, took place in London in February 1822. The bride knew Holkham well from visits made during her childhood and in this respect, and that of her birth, she was eminently suitable, but the disparity of their ages and the hasty wedding gave rise to much ribald comment. In late March the newly-weds travelled to Holkham where they spent three weeks over Easter. A new mistress would be expected to make some alterations to the household, if only to introduce her own personal maids, and, despite the brevity of this first visit, changes were made. The still-room maid Anna Beere, and laundry maid Elizabeth Haggard, both left. A new housekeeper was engaged, Jane Dakin a Derbyshire woman from Longford, eased into her role by the outgoing Mrs Scott. An unforeseen change took place when the under-butler Robert Sizeland, who had been absent some time through illness, died on 10th April aged only thirty-three. A married man with two children, he had risen to this post from humble beginnings as an under-groom. William Clarkson was engaged in his place. A few days later the Cokes returned to London taking with them the valet John Godwin, the butltler Thomas Blunt, footman Thomas Steel, the groom of the chambers Edwin Dudley, the male cook William March and the woman cook Mary Richardson. The 'London' house they stayed in was at Dudley Grove in Paddington, then a rural village around a green with a few old houses on either side of the Edgware Road. The house belonged to Lady Anne's grandmother, Lady de Clifford, and they were to rent it several times in the future. [1]

Coke's youngest daughter Elizabeth, now twenty-seven, a life long friend of her new, much younger, step-mother, was shocked at the change of status. No longer the chatelaine of Holkham, she wisely absented herself for the first months of 1822 going first to London and then to Dalmeny in Scotland, the home of her Anson cousin Anne Margaret who had married Lord Rosebery. Miss Coke disliked Scotland as a place, but not her cousins' guests. During the course of her stay she became engaged to one of them, Mr John Spencer-Stanhope, a well-to-do West Yorkshire landowner.

T.W. Coke and Lady Anne returned to Holkham in time for the July Audit and spent the remainder of the year there. As the summer passed and the cold weather set in, another death occurred among the servants, Thomas Blunt the butler died in October aged fifty-six. His place was taken by a J. Robins from London, who arrived the following month 'wearing a bright chestnut wig' which much amused Elizabeth Coke.

That first year Lady Anne found running Holkham a daunting business and her step-daughter Elizabeth recounted how at the beginning of November, when Lady Anne had been married for nine months and was eight months pregnant, she struggled: 'Yesterday I sat with Lady Anne in a crying fit, and I believe it has been the same today. She finds probably what I have found over several years, that this house entails a perpetual sacrifice of one's own feelings and inclinations'. On several occasions during that first winter Lady Anne failed to appear at dinner and when this happened T.W. Coke asked his daughter Elizabeth to take her place, but she declined and it was offered to Lady Anson, his second daughter: 'who will like it of all things ... ' This formality was necessary for the great number of guests present. Mrs Spencer-Stanhope, Elizabeth Coke's future mother-in-law, described the house at that time as being always 'very full, like an Inn'. [2] It did not always go well. Elizabeth Coke described one dinner: ' ... my father having caught cold, Lady Anne with a bad headache and nearly as white as powder ... and the others all dull'. (Dull at this period could mean unwell rather than dreary). Among those staying were Lord Althorp, a widower and frequent habitué and Sir James and Lady Smith, known as Sir James Daffodil and Lady Daisy as he was a botanist, with Mrs Patterson and her sisters the two Misses Caton, and three American sisters famed for their looks. These were the daughters of T.W. Coke's old friend the Baltimore merchant Richard Caton. [3] Earlier H.R.H. the Duke of Sussex and Lord Bury, Lady Anne's brother and an admirer of Elizabeth Coke, had been there – just some of the twenty-six guests staying at Holkham that November 'to talk of mangled hares and missed woodcocks'. [4]

December was also busy. Elizabeth Coke's wedding to Mr Spencer-Stanhope was set to take place on 5th December with the new housekeeper, Mrs Dakin, ordered to make her wedding cake. [5] Lady Anne was due to give birth less than three weeks later. Mrs Mary Humphreys had been considered for the post of nurse but Lady Anne had either heard something against her or disliked her on meeting as she was turned down in favour of a nurse from London, Anne Powell. Mrs Humphreys was given £3 to defray her travel expenses, but did not go quietly, for having left her home in Norwich to set up in Wells with her family, she claimed unfair dismissal. Days before the birth due date Humphreys was finally paid off and given £18 'the balance of a year's wages' though she had not worked one day. Some time later, perhaps funded by 'Another', she published a pamphlet: 'to be had of all booksellers in Norfolk'. In this Humphreys claimed her husband was in the debtors' gaol entirely as a consequence of her rejection by T.W. Coke and Lady Anne; for had she been allowed to take the post she reckoned she would have earned £293. She calculated her lost earnings as £3 for her journeys to Holkham, for which she was paid, wages £21 (she was given £18) with the remainder being expenses of board, washing and loss of a future situation. What really galled her was missing out on the vails; 'it being customary when an infant is baptised, for the sponsors and visitors to make a present to the nurse and for her to receive the baby-linen and other perquisites'. [6] It must have been doubly frustrating to learn that the baby was a boy, a true cause for celebration. She went on to criticise Blaikie the steward who, she said, had started life by running away to become a gardener, perhaps confusing him with Thomas Blaikie [1751-1838] a Scottish gardener who worked in France. She wrote that Blaikie was 'insensible of domestic comforts', a vague jibe but one suggesting it may well have been he who judged her unsuitable to work at Holkham. [7] Doubtless the publication of the pamphlet pleased Coke's enemies and Mary Humphreys felt vindicated. The affair provides an interesting insight into how much a nurse might expect to earn, how attitudes of power were altering, and also how vails had not yet been stamped out.

Baby Tom, the future second earl, was born on 26th December. All went well. He was to be the eldest of six; followed in 1824 by Edward, Henry in 1827, Wenman in 1828, Margaret in 1832 and Francis in 1835. Francis died young but the others all survived to adulthood. A monthly nurse, Elizabeth Golding, also from London, was employed. In previous times the midwife stayed on after the birth of the child to look after the mother for a month, her lying-in period. Now, once the mother was safely delivered and the baby put into the care of a wet-nurse, a monthly nurse took over, her primary function being to care for the mother. Gradually, as fewer wet-nurses were used, it became usual for a monthly nurse to look after both mother and child, but this did not happen until the twentieth century.

According to his daughter Elizabeth, T.W. Coke picked a nurse maid himself in 1827. 'Who do you think Majesty has chosen as nursery maid for

Tom?' she wrote to her husband, 'Polly Fishburn at the Lodge. Mrs Perrot [her nurse] heard the proposal with unfeigned horror'. Polly Fishburn a gamekeeper's daughter was described as a 'veritable Amazon' and was not suited to the position, as soon became clear. There was nothing the matter with the girl, apart from her love of the outdoor life and a wish to follow in her father's footsteps. The engagement did not last long; Polly was dismissed only to be rescued by the Spencer-Stanhopes and taken to Yorkshire where she worked on their estate as a gamekeeper for the rest of her life, dying in her late seventies.

Blaikie thoroughly approved of the Coke-Stanhope marriage. He had explained to Elizabeth Coke what her financial prospects would be and given her a locket set with diamonds as a wedding present. A number of Elizabeth Coke's letters were collected and published many years later by her great-granddaughter Mrs A.M.W. Stirling, who said disingenuously that Elizabeth 'wrote lots of letters, not reproduced, but of great charm'. The whereabouts of these letters is unknown; however, enough were chosen and printed to give a flavour of life at Holkham in the 1820s. [8] Having been mistress of the household until her father married Lady Anne, Elizabeth Coke was experienced in both choosing and engaging servants. '[I] have always been in the habit of writing every character both of the men and women myself, and carefully supervising the dress of the latter, banishing curl-papers and tendency to finery. So well used to domestic troubles ... it was such a task and charge ... '. 'The establishment,' she wrote after Lady Anne had succeeded her, meaning Holkham, 'is altogether quaint, I should have liked you to have seen it in former times ... '. [9] When she had been in need of a new maid for herself, she was famously given some light-hearted advice by her sister Lady Andover in what to look for in a lady's maid. The maid, she said, was to be a paragon, to come at once when called, to have no will of her own, always be good-humoured, eat next to nothing and be a first rate vermin catcher. Elizabeth Coke wrote in 1822 'My poor old nurse has been so ill that I have been reduced to waiting upon myself, however my new maid has arrived, a sober personage of about thirty, with good health'. Mitchell, the maid in question, must have possessed many of the qualities needed, for she stayed with her new mistress into old age. A point in her favour was her agreeing to 'always go on the barouche box' when travelling i.e. to sit next to the coachman and not demand a place inside. [10]

When it came to choosing a housekeeper for her new household Miss Coke relied on her husband-to-be, Mr Stanhope, to find them one: 'Pray do not engage a terrible-looking housekeeper, if she frightens you, she will frighten me more. I want a goody sort of person, who will occasionally make up a mess of broth or sago for the poor people'. She told him that she was sending the daughter of 'our old butler' and asked him to buy her 'some neat caps and banish curl papers etc.'. This would have been a child of Abraham Dunn — the Holkham butler from 1805-11. Miss Coke's new home was Cannon Hall in Yorkshire and on going there she took at least two other Holkham servants, Richard Penfold her footman, whom she promoted to butler and now had to address as Mr rather than Richard: 'I really could not suppress a smile at Mr Penfold's appearance in a new blue coat, the handsomest black silk waistcoat and the thinnest black silk stockings with gold lace buckles'. A year later John Ransome, sometime Holkham burnisher and footman, whom she had some years earlier described as 'our red-headed Holkhamite ... but remember his red head will not show with powder', also joined her household. [11] John Ransome had not been too popular when in the service of T. W. Coke; Miss Coke had had to lecture him 'on making himself out of breath while waiting at table ... Majesty (her father) complained bitterly yesterday that the Servants snorted at him as if they had four nostrils and blew all the powder out of his hair'. [12] Hair powder was evidently still used by T. W. Coke as well as by the servants; Coke continued to wear his hair in a queue, until his new wife, wishing him to be more up-to-date and pronouncing a queue to be a Tory fashion, snipped it off. Even so Coke powdered his head and kept to his knee-breeches to the last. [13] The red-headed Ransome was born at Holkham where his brother James was employed as a tailor; another brother, William, was a servant at Wentworth in Surrey.

Cannon Hall was found to be rather a damp house and by 1825 Elizabeth and her husband, drawn to Norfolk, took Quarles Farmhouse to the south of the Triumphal Arch to be their winter home. There in 1827 Elizabeth recorded further glimpses of the Holkham servantry when John Ransome, their footman, informed them: 'this morning (a Saturday in February) Poor William, the tall white Footman fell into a fit from drinking ... they say he is always going into the pantry, which occasions Majesty to thunder with indignation'. William did not survive his fit for long and died soon afterwards. She continues: 'the poor footman's wife was bought here in a carriage this morning'. The man had been T. W. Coke's personal footman, William Elam, and he was just thirty years old leaving a widow, Mary, and a newly baptised daughter Mary Anne. The temptation to enter the pantry and steal drink may explain some of the other premature deaths that occurred among the male servants. At least two under-butlers, six footmen and a house porter died at this period, all under the age of forty. In the case of William Elam it would have been a significant failure in duty for a butler to have a house servant pilfering drink, but worth noting that the butler, Mr Blunt, died himself later that same year.

Lady Anne Coke welcomed the presence of her step-daughter and family at Quarles. By 1828 they had half a dozen children between them and the Quarles visits were not just confined to the winter months, for Elizabeth describes 'Majesty' bringing her lilacs and the 'old place smelling so sweet with violets and sweetbriar'. Lady Anne provided her with fresh baked rolls 'and the Holkham cow comes up to be milked every night and morning'. [14]

For most people the 1820s and 1830s continued to be a time of hardship and begging letters in many guises arrived at Holkham almost every week. One was received from Mrs Sarah Seaton of Somers Town in London. After reading it T.W. Coke told Blaikie to send her £1 but she should not expect any more, saying that people in and around Holkham came first. This might be seen as harsh when considering that from 1813 Miss Coke's personal footman had been one Thomas Seaton, who had also travelled with Lady Anne Coke in 1824, the last year he appears in the accounts. Mrs Seaton wrote to Coke in February 1827, her exact relationship to Thomas Seaton unrecorded, but in her letter of thanks for the £1 received she and wishes 'you and your Lady and son health and happiness. I do not know of any more children to wish the same, as I knew of only one when I paid a visit to Norfolk'. Her visit therefore must have been in 1824 or before. No more is heard of her. Other appeals came from former tenants fallen on hard times and many from distant members of the Coke family who claimed annuities reaching back several generations or referred to promises made but seemingly not carried out. Blaikie was always at pains to show how fair T.W. Coke was but that a line had to be drawn somewhere. He explained how Coke was entirely reliant on farm rents for his income, which was true.

In the 1820s the keeping of domestic disbursements moved from being the responsibility of the house steward or butler to that of the estate office staff, first Blaikie and then, after he retired in 1832, William Baker and assistants. None of them divided the entries under headings but kept a general list of miscellaneous expenses, adding up the total at the end of each year. This undoubtedly gave the estate steward a better insight into the family's expenditure than he might otherwise have had. Each upper servant continued to keep his or her day book in which to enter any purchases, all vouchers being preserved and presented for payment once a month. The cook was in charge of ordering food unable to be supplied by the estate, and after Elizabeth Coke came of age he took over the dairy business of selling the surplus butter and cream, and the kitchen fat. The latter went to make tallow candles. Seven different male cooks were employed between 1822 and 1835, two of whom were Frenchmen. Following the deterioration of France's finances and renewed revolutionary disturbances in the late 1820s, many French chefs left for England. These cooks did not necessarily attempt to re-introduce French cooking, but did their best to adapt to English tastes while adding a certain panache to the dishes they cooked. One of them, Nicolas Honère, was cook at Holkham for six months at £105, and from November 1831 to June 1834 Philip La Roche at 110gns a year. La Roche lived in a house in the village paying a yearly rent of £4. From the monthly totals presented for payment by the cooks the pattern of entertaining at Holkham can be seen. From the beginning of the century until 1822 the amount spent on food in July and August had been between £250 and £300 a month, two or three times more than was spent each month in the rest of the year. These were the years of the sheep-shearings which ended with Coke's second marriage. From 1822 no more than £92 a month was ever spent, at least not until the autumn and the advent of the shooting season, peaking in October and November, and again at Christmas.

As a result of hard times after the Napoleonic wars and throughout the 1820s and 1830s, wages had risen very little. In 1842, at the end of T.W. Coke's life, the house porter was paid £26, an increase of £5, although the valet's wages had gone up from £42 to 50gns in 1817 and then to £70. Footmen's wages increased by £3 to £25. The coachman did better, £18 in 1810, £30 in 1842. The housekeeper's wages peaked at 35gns in 1817 but went down by 1842 to £30. Housemaids were paid between £10 and £12, where before it was £8 and £10, laundry maids unchanged at 10gns, kitchen maids likewise unchanged at £8, the same as the still-room maids. The graduated payments introduced for the housemaids were new, where previously they had all been paid the same, though the title 1st, 2nd and 3rd housemaid was still some way in the future. The increase in the wages of the male servants, very often over the entire lifetime of a servant, contrasts with the much smaller increases in the wages of the female servants. Maid servants continued to be seen as transient employees, though a minority stayed for many years.

The method of paying tradesmen's bills altered from 1800 with the spread of provincial banks. Between 1800 and 1810 this was at its height and most tradesmen quickly became used to dealing with them, accepting payment by cheque rather than a bond or ready cash, despite the nearest bank to Holkham being Gurneys at Fakenham. Wells did not get its own bank until 1864. [15] On delivering goods the majority of suppliers now sent a bill, often with the promise of a 5 percent discount for prompt payment. To one such bill, 'which I found on the office table', Blaikie replied enclosing a cheque 'on a ten day promise' and asking for a receipt as soon as possible. If the recipient failed to present the cheque at the bank within the ten day limit there would be no payment. Even so merchants as close to Holkham as Wells were accepting payment by cheque by 1815 or earlier. For those further afield the same procedure took place using different banks at which T. W. Coke had an account. First the money was sent to Gurneys in Fakenham, who forwarded the required amounts on Blaikie's instructions to, for example, the London bank of Hammersleys in Lombard Street. When this bank failed, Coutts was used, and always at the same ten days' notice. This was but a variation on a time-honoured practice of using the family's 'London Man of Business'. He would be sent bills (money) and a list of those who should be paid, and how much. There had always been a time limit of a few days imposed on these transactions.

Blaikie took on this role when, on his twice yearly visits to the Coke estates in Oxfordshire, he travelled via London and spent a night or two in the Angel Hotel in the Haymarket. While in town he arranged to pay cash to the various London tradesmen who preferred this method of payment, having written to them in advance telling them to meet him on a fixed day at the Golden Cross Inn in Charing Cross. Non-appearance would mean a delay of 365 days. The tradesmen who chose to be paid in cash were mainly suppliers of comestibles, e.g. Davison and Newman the grocers, Whitfield for butter and cheese, Grove the fishmonger and Paul and Co. for soda water. Among the suppliers of non-comestibles were Barclays wax chandlers, Ridgway stationers and Pearce the coal merchant. 'Superior' London tradesmen, such as Gattie and Pierce perfumers, Hunt and Co. for playing cards and Mr Robert Smith a specialist fruiterer in Piccadilly, posted their bills and were paid by cheque. Just occasionally Blaikie became involved with Coke's personal bills as for example in 1829 when Chalmers, shoemaker of Sherrard Street, Piccadilly, claimed to have sent a bill to Coke's valet 'who would not take the least notice of it'. On this occasion Blaikie wrote back saying that 'Mr Coke's tradesmen's bills are forwarded to me at Christmas always ... '.

Almost all the groceries used at Holkham came from London. The cook sent orders to Messrs Davison and Co. of 44 Fenchurch St or Messrs Howis of Piccadilly and deliveries arrived three times a year, at Easter, summer and Christmas. On the occasion of a visit by H.R.H. the Duke and Duchess of Gloucester, fruit, being perishable, was ordered by Blaikie from Mr Smith of Piccadilly to arrive on two different days in July 1819: 'ten to twenty pineapples and six melons, of the large variety, we have plenty of the small size here' (i.e. in the Holkham hot-houses). For speed they were to be sent by the Fakenham stage coach. Dry groceries on the other hand were packed into hogsheads (large wooden barrels) and travelled to Wells by sea, a cheaper and more leisurely journey. On one occasion in March 1823 while the Wells trader was unloading its cargo onto the quayside, an accident occurred. A hogshead containing sugar and tea fell onto the quay and split open. Mr Croft, the Wells merchant appointed to deal with the goods, wrote at once to Blaikie to inform him, and Blaikie replied the same day, the letters being carried by a messenger. The cook's order had been for £23 worth of sugar of which half was spoilt, a loss of £10. Afterwards Croft managed to sell off some of it cheap to Mrs Rump the surgeon's wife and two other Wells inhabitants, but he was still out of pocket. The matter was put before T.W. Coke who generously paid half of Croft's loss. Blaikie wrote to Croft that since 'Groceries cannot be supplied in the County ... I [sic] have ordered an equal quantity from the same house in London' and told him to look out for the replacements arriving by the next vessel. Although we know from the eighteenth century accounts that Norwich and later Wells shops sold almost every grocery produce that the Holkham kitchen could want, the old habit of buying everything from London persisted.

There was always fierce competition to supply Holkham with non-comestibles. In 1824 a Mr John Pinson of Wells offered to serve the house 'with as good goods and upon as good terms as any other Persons in the Trade', adding that he was a freeholder and also had a vote at Yarmouth; the implication being he would vote for T.W. Coke in return for custom. Coke replied via

Blaikie that he could not possibly deprive the other Wells shopkeepers of 'the little benefits they derive from serving the family', but should one of them decline business he would bear Pinson in mind. By 1830 the Wells shops supplied Holkham with a variety of goods, but apart from William Foster, a wine and spirits merchant, none was for the kitchen or still-room. Leather breeches for the servants and gloves and gaiters for Mr Coke were bought from the Baker family, first Joseph and later Robert; William Elvin sold boots and shoes. Linen and stockings came from Thomas Tingey and William Elgar, baskets and hampers from a Mr Canfer, stationery from Robert and William Mindham who were also ironmongers, cabinet-makers and upholsterers. The Mindhams always had a stock of iron Ostrich crests ready to be attached to the stoves sold to estate tenants. Wells supported several furniture-makers; mahogany chests of drawers and cabinets were bought from Jacob Levi and John Leslie. Coal was purchased from two different merchants. From at least 1782 coal for the offices, gardens and brick kilns had been bought from the Harrrison family and coal for the mansion from Mr Bloom. In April 1829, perhaps a particularly cold Norfolk spring, Lady Anne Coke asked Blaikie to complain to Bloom about the quality of the coal he had sold them. Blaikie duly wrote that the coals had been indeed of 'a very inferior description' and added his own complaint which was that Bloom asked for cash on delivery and more than once Blaikie had paid him out of his pocket 'not having any of Mr Coke's money in the house'. According to the accounts Bloom generally asked for £200 plus, obviously an old fashioned man who did not trust banks.

In contrast to earlier years less and less was bought from Walsingham. Orders for stationery, newspapers, china, shawls, and linen were sent to various shops in Norwich, and upholsterers, carvers and gilders made annual visits from Norwich to work at Holkham. Furniture was bought from Burt and Co., Robert Sewell of Norwich hired out pianofortes at 12gns a year, Josiah Fletcher bound books and J. Knights, an early taxidermist, stuffed birds. His first bill for stuffing a Jungle Pheasant was recorded in 1826; twelve years later in 1838 he is described as a Bird Preserver.

Two regular suppliers of fortified wine, both in Lynn, were Messrs Everard and Messrs Oxley, English and Oxley. The former sent two pipes of port wine a year to Holkham and the latter two butts of sherry, after they had been chosen (i.e. sampled) by the Holkham butler. A pipe held 105 gallons and a butt 108; both were actually delivered in casks. Coke liked to have his wine delivered this way to be bottled by the butler. Corks were purchased from

Mr Mugridge, cork cutter of Lynn, at a cost of about £14 a year and the bottles from John Douglas of Newcastle upon Tyne stamped with the Ostrich crest 'at the bottom'. Breakages were inevitable on the long journey south and extra bottles were always included to compensate. The bottles were of a quart size and ordered in huge numbers, 186 dozen (2,232) in 1830 and 42 gross (6,048) in 1833. Claret was supplied each spring by Mr George Barns of 63 Lincolns Inn Fields, London, who in 1827 proposed sending the last year when the vintage was judged to be good, 1822, saying it needed to be bottled soon. The next good vintage would be 1825 which would not be ready for bottling until 1828. Mr Barns enquired of Blaikie saying he was unsure of how much to send as T. W. Coke, who was in town at the time, did not know the 'state of his cellars'. Blaikie consulted Mr Godwin the butler. He thought they had enough to last the present season. Before his promotion to butler Godwin had been Coke's valet, but acted as butler when the family was in London. For example in May 1824 Blaikie wrote to Mr Barns the London wine merchant that 'Mr Coke's house in London this season will be Lady de Clifford's in Paddington from Tuesday 11th May. Some of the servants will be at Paddington House on Saturday next, and you will please to send there on Monday the 10th 4 dozen Port, 4 dozen Maderia, 4 dozen claret, and 4 dozen of sherry such wine as you think will suit Mr Coke. Mr Godwin who took charge of the wine last year will do the same this year, the butler does not go with the family to London'. Barns also supplied Holkham with champagne and brandy. Wine and champagne occasionally arrived at Holkham from other sources, some from Lord Rosebery, Coke's grandson-in-law, and some from English wine merchants based in France, but these were not regular suppliers. Madeira was still popular but losing out to sherry which was drunk in increasing amounts from 1800. In 1830 whisky made its first appearance at Holkham, supplied exclusively by the Norwich Wine Company – a curious amount, eleven and a half gallons each year. Coke had been to Scotland twice, once in 1817 and ten years later with Lady Anne in 1827. Gin is not mentioned.

The house in Paddington, No 4 Dudley Grove referred to above, was the one belonging to Lady Anne Coke's grandmother, but from 1830-1837 the Cokes rented The Grove House at Old Brompton from a Mr Brett. Here again the setting was semi-rural and the house came with its own gardener. Henry Coke, the third son, remembered being at this house when George IV died. He said the coachman had just driven his mother home and he was watching one of the grooms spin a peg top in the stable yard when the news came and 'in a few minutes four or five servants – maids and men – came running to the stables to learn particulars'. He described the house as being a long way from street criers, quite out of town and completely surrounded by fields and hedges. [16] The months spent in 'London' were not exactly an urban experience for the servants, hardly more than an exchange of views from parkland to gardens and fields. The choice of a suburban London house where the family spent the season, each May and June, may have had to do with Lady Anne's love of gardening, being the months when gardens are at their best. Her hobby was thought to be peculiar according to Mrs Stirling. She created her own flower garden at Holkham with Mrs Mackie and later Frederick Mackie of Norwich supplying nursery trees, shrubs and seeds. The Mackies were a link with the past, being descendants of William Aram gardener at Holkham in the 1750s who had left to set up a nursery in Norwich. Mr William Moore of Dereham was another nursery man patronised by Holkham.

During the months spent in London the coachman dealt with William Harman and Co. of John Street, off Oxford Street, concerning all matters to do with vehicles. Harman is a name often found in the Holkham parish registers and for reasons not at all clear, T.W. Coke did not own his coach but hired one from Harman. The arrangement was renewed every six years, whereby Harman would rent him a chariot and keep it in good repair, even to the extent of varnishing, painting and supplying new wheels, a total cost of £63. In 1819 Coke had added a Landau at 80gns, hired under the same conditions except he would be liable for any damage to the linings and glass in the windows and for any accident that might occur due to failure of adequate greasing or oiling. The tax payable on coaches was not large, a matter of shillings. Coke also hired carriage horses from Mr William Smith of Curzon Street, Mayfair. The cost of four horses for a year was 120 gns, and when Mr Smith could not oblige then horses were rented from Mr Anderson in Piccadilly. The reason for hiring coach horses was to get an exact match. At Holkham there was a plentiful supply of horses, but not apparently four that looked identical and were of the right colour which was grey. The horses were taken to Holkham and used the year round. These arrangements were largely conducted by the coachman, who inspected both the horses and the vehicles, an arrangement that continued for many years. When the Landau was exchanged for a Barouche, the coachman, John Billers, even had a hand in its design. Each year during the London season the vehicles were returned to Harman for servicing, though repairs were only carried out when ordered. In 1824 Blaikie received a bill from Harman for work done to a carriage and questioned the amount, saying that neither Mr Coke nor Lady Anne had any recollection of the repairs needed and the coachman had not given orders for them. In 1826, having a contract with Harman for a coach and a chariot, they decided to return the chariot and order a new Barouche to be built 'according to the pattern described to you ... by Lady Anne Coke'. Harman was upset at having the chariot returned, and he wrote that he had served Coke for two and twenty years and never before had he known of any complaint. The Cokes already hired one Barouche and wished Harman to build another 'on Jobb' (to hire) to accommodate luggage in a more satisfactory way: 'There is a great complaint by the servants of the inconveniences of packing luggage with the present Barouche,' Blaikie wrote, explaining that they were willing to make new purpose-built trunks for the luggage, showing that the coachman was involved in the design of the vehicle. 'At present if Mr Coke and Lady Anne go out in the Barouche to stay a few nights with any of their neighbours the servants cannot possibly take a sufficient quantity of clothes and other necessities. I have spoken to the coachman on the subject ... he says you can make one trunk for the swing board behind, to fix on when the Standards are taken off, another trunk to fix on as before, and above that a swing imperial under the driving seat as in the present Barouche. You had better prepare these trunks now ... if you think the coachman's plans will answer ... there should also be a leather flap to the driving box to fit on occasionally, and that the driving box or Dickey should be sufficiently large to hold two persons, Mr Coke and Lady Anne's personal servants.

William Harman died early in 1831 and, soon after, his possessions were auctioned, including the vehicles T.W. Coke rented. Harman's successor, Mr Willoughby, offered Coke the opportunity of buying the landau and the barouche. After ascertaining that Willoughby would remain in the same premises and rent out vehicles on the same terms as Harman, Coke agreed to continue with him. Willoughby then 'bought' the landau and the barouche at the auction, putting down a deposit of 25 percent for them. Willoughby is last heard of in 1834. Renting coaches under these terms seems unnecessarily complicated and, according to Blaikie, T.W. Coke had long wished to own his vehicles. This was finally achieved in May 1837 with the purchase of a chariot costing £400 from Messrs Fell and Briggs of London, which had been ordered the previous September. Fell and Briggs had previously attended the annual Holkham timber sales, sourcing timber for their business as coach-makers, and when the order went through, Mr Briggs made a special trip to Holkham with the express desire to get things right. While there he discussed the state of an old carriage harness with Lady Anne who told him to patch it up so that it would last until spring when a new one could be made. Very possibly the chariot was partly made from Holkham timber; it was painted yellow and lined with dark blue, with a net to the roof, patent axle, imperial cap case and various other technical details. All would be ready to coincide with the arrival of the Cokes in town for the 1837 season. The coachman told Briggs to deliver it to The Grove House, Brompton.

That year T.W. Coke was created Earl of Leicester and in the autumn the chariot was returned to Briggs to have the coat of arms altered. Until then we must assume that the Ostrich crest was painted on the sides of the chariot, much like a personalised number plate. The arms of an earl were rather more complicated. Baker recommended Mr Briggs to apply to Mr Stephenson of 5 Arlington Street who would have received the new arms from the Herald's Office. Lady Leicester, as Lady Anne Coke now was, had written to him giving him directions. Briggs wrote to Baker in March 1838: 'all the work goes well, except the Hammercloth ornaments will not do again as it is not usual to have both Arms and Crest when a Coronet is worn, the Crest only with the Coronet above, the present Crests are not sufficiently large. We have waited upon Mr Stephenson from whom we have received the drawing of the Arms and who has directed us to write to Lady Leicester on the subject … and include a sketch for her Ladyship's approval … the alterations of the Heraldry cannot be made without new Painting the body, the Crest being too high on the Quarters to admit a Coronet being placed over it and that being the case, we beg to ask whether you would like to have the carriage new painted as well as the body, we beg to observe that the Carriage does not really want painting but we have thought it proper to mention this as the body when new painted will look fresher and of a somewhat brighter colour than the carriage.'. No wonder Coke had wished to remain a commoner. It was said he agreed to the earldom for the sake of his son Tom. [17]

From time to time T.W. Coke made brief visits to London on his own and then stayed in more central locations, at St George's Hotel in Albemarle Street, a rented house in Hanover Square or else with his daughter, Lady Anson, who by 1830 had moved from St James's Square to Curzon Street.

Livery continued to be worn by the footmen, house porter, coachmen and postillions. Livery cloth, breeches and footwear came from Wells as before, and the suits were made up by Wells tailors. Servants livery hats came from William Redfern of Holt until 1824 when Joseph Ashmead of Wells supplied them. The amount spent on hats suggests that new ones were purchased every year, but lack of detail regarding the livery suits and overcoats makes it impossible to know how often new ones were given. In London T.W. Coke's tailor was William Middleton of 61 St James's Street who in 1824 wrote to Holkham to say he was retiring and accompanied this letter with his final bill, £72 for Mr Coke, plus £156 for servants liveries. Blaikie was outraged by this 'sweeping amount' and demanded Middleton should explain it. If he did, his answer went unrecorded and no more is heard of London tailors.

Much of the wool produced at Holkham was marketed by Henry May Waller of Foulsham, who in turn supplied Holkham twice a year with green plush and scarlet livery cloth for the gamekeepers' liveries. Although Holkham ordered and paid him regularly he felt a need in August 1829 to write and say 'do not forget me when green plush cloth is needed, times very hard this year'. He wrote this from Lynn market where he had bought a bundle of pack sheets, sending them ahead to Wells for the Holkham bailiff to have ready for him 'to collect on Monday next'. Presumably the pack sheets were to contain the fleeces. Waller travelled on business to the mill town of Bradford, Yorkshire, from where he wrote in 1831 that the wool trade had not improved and he was very glad to have sold the Holkham wool at Swaffham Fair, for the news from the north was of three large 'failures ... to the value of £10,000'. Waller was also an agent for the Norwich Union bank, but despite his wide-ranging trade interests he continued to be financially insecure and dependant on Holkham. [18]

At the start of the 1830s another new housekeeper arrived, Mrs Hadricke. Jane Dakin had continued in this post after her marriage to Blaikie's assistant William Baker in 1824, another example of accepting a married housekeeper, and each year for several months over Christmas from 1827 to 1831 her brother [?] George Dakin, in the employ of Lady Anson, worked at Holkham as groom of the chambers.

In the school room, despite their tender years, the young Coke boys had had a governess, Miss Antoinette Batton who, in 1828, was replaced by a tutor and passed on to educate the Stanhopes' two young daughters.

The Christmas season of 1830–31 was enjoyed much as any other. Queen Victoria and Prince Albert are generally thought to have initiated Christmas as a time for family gatherings, but for many years before their marriage (in 1840) there had been a tradition of uniting as many members of the extended Coke family as possible at this time of year. At this particular Christmas Lady Anson (a widow since 1818) was present with several of her children including her son Colonel Anson and servant George Dakin. Christmas passed, New Year and Twelfth Night were celebrated as usual by a Ball, and by mid-January the house was slightly less full according to the kitchen disbursements kept by Philip La Roche, the cook. There was only the Audit Day to look forward to before life grew quieter still. At some time during the night of 12th January, the second day of the Audit, after the household had been locked up for the night and all had retired to their rooms, a window was broken on the south side of the house and through this window a burglar entered and made his way to the saloon. After looking around, he took his bag and helped himself to a quantity of silver objects which had been on one of the tables. In addition he stole some teaspoons each with an Ostrich crest and several 'ornamental things likely to be found in Ladies work boxes', gold and pearl thimbles, a gold chain, a silver hunting watch and £55 in bank notes plus a variety of other 'articles of no great value'. George Dakin, acting groom of the chambers, would have been responsible for making sure the house was secured each evening, the doors and windows fastened and the fires dampened down, and in the morning for opening it up. As the last one to bed and the first one up, he later testified as to what had been taken from the saloon and Colonel Anson provided a detailed description of each article.

Although the burglar managed to reach London within a very short time, when he tried to dispose of the booty the man he offered it to, a Mr Goodman, seeing the crest on the teaspoons, was immediately suspicious and informed a policeman and the man was arrested. What concerned Holkham was the ease with which the burglar had entered the house and his knowledge of where to find small but valuable articles. Had there been an accomplice? The burglar was named George Lilley, and it was learnt he had been a servant in Lord Ellenborough's family. This at least would explain his familiarity with the house, since Lord Ellenborough had been married to one of Coke's granddaughters and they had been frequent guests at Holkham, although since divorced. Lilley would therefore also be known to the servants, and indeed George Dakin was sent to London to identify the items stolen and also to speak to Lilley. When confronted with his crime Lilley said he was no more than a receiver of stolen goods, someone else had committed the burglary and had arranged to give him the bag (of swag) at Fakenham for which Lilley paid him £10. He maintained that no one was able to prove he had been nearer to Holkham than Fakenham, but he had reckoned without Blaikie whose comment on this account was to describe it as 'fudge'. Being an able detective, Blaikie was able to prove that Lilley had indeed travelled by stage coach from London only as far as Fakenham, and then, after laying a false trail, had taken the Wells coach two days later, asking to be set down at Holkham Park gates. Blaikie obtained this information by interviewing Brown the Wells coachman. After committing the burglary, Lilley had walked back to Fakenham overnight before getting on the Newmarket coach the following day. The state of his boots when he reached the Crown Inn at Fakenham told against him. They were caked with mud. Elliot, who drove the Newmarket coach, remembered Lilley and said he 'had a bag in his hands containing a square substance of which he took particular care'. Case closed. Both coachmen were ordered to Bow Street to confirm their evidence, their travel and accommodation expenses of 6gns paid for by T.W. Coke. The sharp-eyed Mr Goodman to whom the stolen items had been offered, was rewarded with £5 from Coke and £1 given to Steven the policeman. Mr Henry Stokes, Coke's Fakenham lawyer, who prosecuted George Lilley sent in his bill for £70. Lilley was bound over to be tried at Thetford Assizes.

The trial took place in March 1831. Again both coach drivers were called on to give evidence, also two servants from the Crown Inn Fakenham, Samuel Ellis landlord of the Ostrich at Wells, Mr Goodman, who had reported Lilley (described as tailor and salesman), the Bow Street Officer Stevens, and from Holkham Francis Blaikie the steward, Stephen Emerson the clerk of the works, entered as a carpenter, George Daky, a.k.a. Dakin, Lady Anson's butler and John Williams the house porter. Williams gave evidence saying that there were five outer doors at Holkham of which he, not the groom of the chambers, locked four at six o'clock on the evening in question; the other was open till two a.m. It was the Audit and there were 'many servants besides Mr Coke's in the house'. He said he found all the doors locked in the morning. Emerson had examined the window and said the glass had been removed by taking out the putty. The window was about four foot above the ground and large enough to admit a man. The next morning he had observed 'footmarks, a narrow foot, high heels, square toes, I traced the foot prints across the garden'. Old-fashioned shoes. Blaikie said he had seen the window a little before midnight and that it had been 'whole' at that time. He believed it was a fixture, not an opening. After a very short deliberation the jury found Lilley guilty. His defence lawyer, Mr Andrews, claimed he was a very respectable young man and Blaikie put in a plea here on behalf of Coke requesting his Lordship the judge to spare the prisoner's life if it could be done. The final verdict was that Lilley should be detained at His Majesty's pleasure, to be sent out of the country and to remain a slave all his life. [19]

1831 continued a troublesome year. The summer was cold with rain and gales; many farmers lost their crops. Hard times persisted. Agricultural workers, believing their livelihoods to be threatened by the introduction of thrashing machines, machines that would do their work for them over winter, rose up in a rebellious mob incited by 'Captain Swing'. The pattern was for farmers to receive a warning threat from a man signing himself 'Swing' followed by machine-breaking, setting fire to farm buildings, corn stacks and even labourers' cottages, events recorded at length by Blaikie in the letter books. 'A night seldom passes without ... a diabolical practice'. Sure enough the year ended with riots in nearby Burnham Overy and Burnham Thorpe, T.W. Coke, accompanied by William Baker and others, rode out to quell the unrest and arrested a number of people.

The true incendiaries were never caught, and nor was 'Swing' ever identified, but it occurred to T.W. Coke to send to George Eeles on the Oxfordshire estate where bloodhounds were used for 'running deer in the forest'. Eeles replied that he saw no reason why bloodhounds should not 'turn to run to the foot of a man' for they often helped their masters home when lost among the trees. Blaikie insisted the dogs should be well trained and then, typically, questioned the price. Eeles replied that bloodhounds were very scarce, but he was able to send two, Merlin, twelve months old and Tunefull, a female of two years. He suggested they should be trained every day to follow a shoe dressed with a little oil of aniseed. Being expensive (£14) the dogs travelled from Oxfordshire via London in a locked cage with their collars marked TWC. Normally a dog might walk tied to the axle of a waggon but this was considered too risky. An air of nervousness persisted, for when the family went to London for the season a few weeks later, in early 1832, Mathew Fisher and James Chapman were paid for ten weeks to watch the house. It had never been deemed necessary before.

The following year Blaikie announced he was to retire; William Baker the office assistant since 1810 would succeed him. T.W. Coke would regret his leaving; he himself was to retire from politics after an almost continuous involvement of fifty-five years, and a quieter life lay in prospect. Among the servants, six quit in 1831 and seven in 1832, but that was no more than usual. On taking Blaikie's place, Baker did not prove to have an aptitude for keeping detailed household accounts and his correspondence was rather more sparse than Blaikie's had been. An unexplained incident occurred in 1833 when an under-butler named John Fairbrother was recorded as being paid one month's wages 'on his being discharged from Walsingham Bridewell'. He had been engaged since July 1831 when he arrived from London with travel expenses paid, but nothing was recorded to explain how or why he landed up in the Bridewell. That his wages were paid on his leaving prison suggests that he was not discharged from Holkham, but left of his own accord. The following year a young footman named George Freebury became ill and was sent to the Norfolk and Norwich Hospital where he died. This was the first recorded case of a servant being sent to a hospital. Shortly afterwards T.W. Coke received a letter from a Major Court writing on behalf of his gardener John Freebury, the young man's father. Freebury senior could read but not write; he had heard of his son's illness and death in the hospital and now asked for the boy's possessions, his watch, clothes and any other items. Baker the steward had the difficult task of informing Mr Freebury that his son had pawned the watch for £4 and borrowed money from a fellow servant which, when paid back, would probably account for much of the wages due to him, but he promised to return the clothes and an abstract of what money was due 'which I fear will be very trifling'. George Freebury and his 'fellow servant' had previously worked together in the Duke of Bedford's employ.

On a more cheerful note, 'a new road to the Sea' was built, and named Lady Anne's Drive. Races were held at Holkham and in late September 1835 there was a visit from sixteen-year-old Princess Victoria, accompanied by her mother the Duchess of Kent and a party of ladies-in-waiting, equerries and servants. To cater for the royal visitors a cook was sent for from London, William Temple, who spent nine days at Holkham at a cost of £10. 4s. 6d. and, from Shugborough, George Ronnell arrived to act as groom of the chambers, essentially a sort of major domo. According to Mrs Stirling the Cokes' nursemaid, clandestinely married to the head gardener Hugh Girvan and heavily pregnant, was so overcome by the visit that she gave birth the day the Princess arrived. This event caused great amusement and the Princess asked to see the baby, fortunately a girl, who was later baptised Victoria Jane.

Owing to the paucity of servants records at this time the nursemaid does not appear in the accounts, but she was probably Jane Serman from Kent aged about thirty-four. Living a somewhat isolated life in the nursery rooms she may have formed a friendship with the gardener when taking the children out for their daily walks. All that is known is that she and Girvan married at Lakenham near Norwich some three weeks before their child was born. It was an age when women wore large skirts, but even so it is surprising that she was able to conceal her pregnancy and retain her position as nurse to the children. Hugh Girvan, a Scotsman, was several years younger than Jane. After this traumatic event he carried on as gardener at Holkham for the rest of his life, living with Jane in the appropriately named Gardener's Lodge. [20] At the time of this royal visit the elder Coke boys were away at school, Henry at Temple Grove in East Sheen which he later described as a Dotheboys Hall, made bearable only by the presence of a red-headed Norfolk maid, jolly and round in person and a bestower of 'cordial hugs'. [21]

In July 1836 T.W. Coke's younger brother Edward died aged 82 and with his death Longford Hall reverted to Holkham. Mrs Edward Coke the widow moved out to live at Mayfield near Ashbourne. As soon as he could spare him Coke ordered Baker to Longford, the first of many visits. After a thorough examination of the house and estate, one of the recommendations Baker made was to send a gamekeeper from Holkham, one George Fishburn, 'to acquaint himself with the countryside and get in a stock of game'. Mr Robert Hudson the Longford steward was instructed to look after him and his family on arrival. Baker explained to Hudson that as Fishburn was not used to travel and had only been allowed enough money to get him to Longford, Hudson was to give him more on his safe arrival. Fishburn arranged to send some of his own household furniture to Longford by water (canals?) which Baker disapproved of, though he conceded the expense was probably cheaper than 'buying it anew'.

When the previous improvements had been carried out at Longford in 1809, workmen had been sent from Holkham; this time Derbyshire men were employed, Scipio Rawlstone a bricklayer, and John Rawlinson a carpenter. Re-decoration was to begin at once. Samples were sent to Lady Anne Coke at Holkham who chose the paint colours for the walls, while the woodwork, windows, shutters and skirting were to be painted white 'which will give the rooms a light appearance'. To the consternation of the resident housekeeper Mrs Nokes, Mrs Edward Coke made frequent return visits to Longford and helped herself to many items. Mrs Nokes reported this to Hudson: 'things are carried out continually' to the extent that when the Holkham Cokes arrived she was afraid 'there would not be one useable article left in the house'. Should she put a stop to it? Hudson consulted Baker who replied 'the less that is said about it the better' and thought it must have been done with the permission of Mr W. Coke, her son Billy, who had been the heir to Holkham until 1822. In fact Billy Coke spent much of 1836 quite happily at Holkham; he appears to have inherited the easy-going character of his uncle and continued to be obliging and undemanding. All the same it was awkward for Baker as the Holkham family were looking forward to a long visit to Longford.

This visit did not take place until March 1838; by then they wished to find the terraces cleaned, the conservatory finished and all litter cleared away. Lord and Lady Leicester (as they now were) proposed sleeping in the bedroom and dressing room above the steward's room and the still-room. On the long journey from Holkham to Longford, Lord Leicester had caught a cold, but not a serious one. Lady Margaret and her nurse Mrs Siveman went with them and were put in a small bedroom opposite her parents. As to the refurbishments, Robert Hudson wrote to Baker that Lord Leicester was 'very well satisfied' with the work done so far, and followed this with a request for more money.

The repairs and improvements at Longford Hall were extensive; the entire house had problems with cracks appearing on the interior plasterwork at regular intervals. The following July Hudson wrote that the wall at the end of the kitchen had given way altogether and four weeks later the same happened at the north end of the Hall. It was then discovered that this part of the house had been built without foundations, but Lord Leicester, who was present at the time, seemed relatively unbothered. He called in a Mr Evans to examine the damage and reverted to his new interest – 'intent on being a Derbyshire Farmer'. Later there was trouble with the piers at the entrance gates; new iron gates had been delivered but could not be hung as the piers were crumbling.

Servant problems arose in 1838 when a Longford servant named Sarah Morley quit her position, and in the absence of the family, pestered Robert Hudson to settle her account. Lady Leicester had instructed Hudson to pay her wages but he felt uneasy, not knowing upon what terms Morley, a local woman whose large family lived in the parish, had been engaged. Morley claimed she was owed 'something more than £23' to include board wages. Hudson gave her £20 and left the final settling of the matter until Baker's next visit.

The cost of the refurbishment continued to mount and Robert Hudson's requests for funds became more frequent. 'I have Lord Leicester's interest at heart every much as you do' he assured Baker. Baker went to Longford at least twice, sometimes three times a year, accompanied by his wife Jane, staying a night or two in Lynn with Mr Jarvis a lawyer en route. Jane Baker accompanied her husband as she originated from Longford where her family were farmers and prosperous enough to keep servants of their own. [22] Lord Leicester and party were at Longford again in March 1840 and remained there until the end of September. He was now eighty-six years old (his youngest child Lady Margaret was eight) and thought to be remarkable insomuch as he had 'health very rarely enjoyed by persons of his advanced period of life'. This observation was written by a land agent in Oxfordshire who had known him for over fifty years. In fact his poor eyesight had deteriorated further and his hearing was not keen. Even so, life continued to follow its familiar pattern with no let-up in the number of guests invited to stay at Holkham. Thomas Creevey was one of these in the late 1830s, not always thrilled by the choice of his fellow guests but impressed by the room service: 'I live mostly in my charming bedroom on the ground floor with a door at hand to go out of the house if I like it ... a maid lights my fire at seven punctually and my water [for shaving] is in my room at eight. The attention of my Maid in refreshing my fire thro' the day, almost hourly, is really beyond ... '. [23] Creevey's account shows how well the domestic arrangements at Holkham were run; as in many large establishments the servants would have had a timetable and kept to it, and though it ran the risk of rendering their work monotonous and unvarying, on the whole an uninterrupted routine was preferred. The majority of servants chose to work that way, giving rise to clichés such as the 'well oiled machine'. As part of a household such as Holkham, servants continued to enjoy security, good conditions and opportunity for promotion. As C.V. Butler reported some years later, the rich seldom complained of inefficiency as they could 'afford to pay high wages and insist on good service in return'. [24]

In the family the time-honoured ways endured, in particular the old-fashioned habit of early dining – at four each afternoon they and their guests assembled in the Statue Gallery to await the announcement of dinner. By a quarter past they were seated ready to eat 'a plain but substantial meal' according to Alexander Napier who arrived to live at Holkham in 1841 — soup, roast duck, followed by roast pig and stewed venison with thin watery vegetables. Napier also mentioned side dishes of cutlets, very likely fried in egg and breadcrumbs and accompanied by the renowned 'sauce Reform'. (Coke was a founder member of the Reform Club where Alexis Soyer was chef). [25] They finished up with 'pudding and pies, both excellent'. Napier says they drank port, sherry and 'glorious beer of which the ladies liberally partook'. He was surprised at the absence of wine, and surprises us by saying that the talk was all about eating. After dinner there was no slouching on sofas or playing cards; when Napier wrote this account it was August and everyone went out of doors and rode in the park. At eight o'clock they returned for tea and newspapers, before retiring at ten. [26] Napier, a young clergyman who was to become librarian to the second earl, took a great interest in the catering and claimed that the average consumption of the household was a bullock a week, sixty sheep a month, besides pigs, poultry, game and fish. He also said there were 60 servants in the house. How he came to this number he does not reveal but he understood that the meals were actually ordered by Mr Edward Ellice, especially when entertaining, and that Ellice also chose the wine on these occasions. This was true. Ellice born in 1783 was a politician and prime mover behind the Reform Bill of 1832; related to Earl Grey by marriage and now a widower, he was a particular friend of the earl and countess, even acting in loco parentis for their young family. In November 1841 H.R.H. the Duke of Sussex was staying at Holkham along with numerous other guests including Landseer the painter, and several members of the extended Coke family. At one of the grand dinners given during this time Lady Leicester had a list of all the dishes on offer which she read out to the Duke, but Napier noted Ellice had no need of such a list, he knew all the dishes by heart. Stewed carp, a trout from the river Thames, roast beef, venison and mutton were a few of those on offer. Once again Napier was astonished at how much beer was consumed by the ladies during dinner and how they ate roast pig which upset him; he did not like to see women eat 'such gross meals'. Napier's middle class sensibilities were offended, foreshadowing Mrs Beeton who later wrote: 'The truth is the whole of a sucking pig is delicious, delicate eating; but, in carving it, the host should consult the various tastes and fancies of his guests, keeping the larger joints, generally, for the gentlemen'. [27]

Napier may have disapproved of Holkham table manners but he slowly warmed to Thomas William Coke despite saying that the old gentleman had no interest in anything save party politics and agriculture: 'He knows he <u>has</u> books and pictures etc. and that they are splendid and valuable and this because judges of each have told him so ... he has added nothing to the collection'. Worse still he had depleted it when at least two old masters, one, a Chiari, the must-have artist in the days of his great uncle's Grand Tour, had long since been taken out of their frames in order to accommodate paintings by Coke's daughters and had been left 'rolled up in the long passage'. [28] Napier's father was the editor of *The Edinburgh Review,* a publication read by every Whig and intellectual; Napier noted that at Holkham it was taken but lay largely ignored upon a table in the library. By 1841 Coke's eyesight was too poor to allow him to play cards and he was too deaf to hear sermons, but he impressed Napier by appearing at a quarter to nine each morning for family prayers, with all the household present, and by his attendance at church, though he could not hear a word. He did it for example he said; in the same way his object was to make his tenants happy by being interested in their farms but leaving them to work them independently.

After the acquisition of Longford the pattern of the year changed in one respect. Where previously the Leicesters had left Holkham for London as soon as Easter was passed, they now renounced town in favour of Derbyshire, where in April 1841 they arrived just in time to be included in the first census to record names, thus providing the most comprehensive list of servants since 1814, when Francis Crick died. The Longford party was made up of the Earl and Countess, their daughter Lady Margaret and four Stanhopes, Lady Elizabeth, Coke's youngest daughter by now aged forty-five, her husband and two teenage daughters, Anna aged sixteen and Eliza fifteen. Also staying at Longford, but behind the green baize door, were Holkham servants plus John Stanhope's valet Charles Wray, and Jane Mitchell the lady's maid Lady Elizabeth Stanhope had engaged at the time of her marriage twenty years previously. Eleven indoor servants had come from Holkham, excluding William Baker, the steward, but including his clerk John Lulman. The eleven were Favré the valet, and his wife Sarah who was lady's maid to Lady Margaret, Anthony Warren the under-butler, two footmen, Elizabeth Edwards the cook, Anne Sculfer kitchen maid, Mary Pearson the woman baker, Anne Arnold a still-room maid, and Maria Bacon laundry maid. An unknown name, Jane Gates, appears in this list next to Sarah Favré, most probably the Countess's maid.

There were also at least four more servants living out in the stable cottages, the coachman, postillion and grooms sharing with William Shaw, his wife and small children (and their nurse maid) who were servants of Billy Coke's. The resident servants at Longford were the housekeeper, Mrs Nokes, who had witnessed the disappearance of items from the house whenever Mrs Edward Coke called, and four maids, one of whom, Anne Watson, was to become housekeeper when Mrs Nokes stepped down.

Meanwhile back at Holkham the 1841 census records a further nineteen servants living in the house: the housekeeper Mrs Hadricke, the house porter whose surname was Porter, and his wife Elizabeth, William Mead the plate-burnisher, and John Godwin the butler (who slept in the house during the family's absence), five housemaids, laundry maids and others.

At a time when the servants lists at Holkham have not survived the census returns are illuminating. By the mid-nineteenth century the general servant population had grown and from the census it is possible to see servants living in Holkham parish but employed in households other than the hall. Soon Napier would acquire a cook and housemaid of his own, William Baker, the steward, two housemaids, and the more prosperous farmers five or six servants plus a governess.

The next year, 1842, the Leicesters made their annual visit to Longford where, in June, Lord Leicester died. The death, at his advanced age, was of course not unexpected, but for many the passing of Thomas William Coke, Earl of Leicester, Majesty at Holkham for sixty-six years was indeed the end of an era.

By this date, life among the servants was undergoing a subtle change. Upper servants in general had begun to see themselves in a different light, as professionals rather than members of a family, although this did not preclude loyalty, for many continued in the same household for most of their working lives. Rules and regulations, limits and hierarchy had always existed but now they were adhered to with more stringent attention. Expectations of what a servant in a household of the elite might and might not do were listened to and *faute de mieux* accepted. A footman could refuse to carry coal buckets, hold the ladder while a housemaid cleaned the stucco friezes in the grander rooms, help with the mangle in the laundry or break up blocks of sugar in the still-room. The duties and rules set down by many an eighteenth-century master, in hopes they might be carried out, were now enforced and ironically it was not always the masters who insisted on them but the servants. Demarcation of labour became the norm and no longer did the household always pull together as an entity, and mutterings such as 'It is not my place to ... ' were heard. The number of servants employed at Holkham was set to increase with the next generation, a larger family to look after and more ornaments, indoor plants, carpets, curtains and furniture to care for as the fashion for Victorian clutter took hold. It was by no means the end of a golden age, but the sun may be said to have dimmed somewhat. The Theatre at Walsingham, visited every second year by the travelling comedians and so richly enjoyed by the greater family, is not mentioned in the accounts after 1836. David Fisher, the actor manager, had died a few years earlier and it closed altogether in 1844. Entertainments became more scarce, though there was always the Servants Ball at New Year, the occasional visiting conjuror, bell-ringers and concert parties. The public days were also coming to an end; the park was to become a more private space. Few called to marvel at the mansion, *Italia in campagna*, and the treasures within. Increasingly visitors to Holkham turned the opposite way, down Lady Anne's Drive to the sea shore where they picnicked under the pine trees or on the sands with scarcely a look back to the great mansion in the park.

NOTES

1. Stirling vol. 2 p.284.

2. *Letter Bag of Lady Elizabeth Spencer-Stanhope,* complied from the Cannon Hall Papers 1806–1873 by Mrs A.M.W. Stirling in 2 vols, London John Lane, 1908 vol. 2 p.36.

3. Letter Bag vol. 2 p.39 and p.34, Mrs Paterson was widowed shortly after this visit and later married the Marquess Wellesley; her sisters also married into the English nobility, one became Lady Stafford and the other the Duchess of Leeds.

4. Letter Bag vol. 2 p.57.

5. Letter Bag vol. 2 p.43.

6. HA A/51 and Stirling vol. 2 p.305.

7. Quoted by Susanna Wade Martins in *Coke of Norfolk 1754-1842 a Biography,* The Boydell Press Suffolk 2009 p.87 and p.89.

8. The Letter Bag was published 1908 in two volumes.

9. Letter Bag vol. 2 p.56 and p.43.

10. Letter Bag vol. 2 p.50.

11. Letter Bag vol. 2 p.100.

12. Letter Bag vol. 2 p.76.

13. Stirling vol. 2 p. 334. This is confirmed by T.W. Coke's son Henry 'My half sisters [Lady Anson, Lady Andover and Elizabeth Spencer-Stanhope] wore turbans with birds of paradise in them. My mother wore gigot sleeves; but objected to my father's pigtail so cut it off. But my father powdered his head and kept to his knee breeches to the last'. Henry Coke *Tracks of a Rolling Stone* first published 1905, reprinted by Kessinger Publishing's Rare Reprints no date p. 55.

14. Letter Bag vol. 2 p.122.

15. Harold Preston *Early East Anglian Banks and Bankers*, Thetford 1994, no page numbers but banks by number – no 13 and no 29. Wells got The Provincial Banking Corporation, a bank in 1864, taken over by Barclays in 1918.

16. Henry Coke pp.3-4.

17. By the 1850s and the advent of the railways, the horses travelled between London and Holkham by train accompanied by the coachman. As to accepting an earldom offered to him by the young Queen, T.W. Coke had been in the Whig tradition where titles were not sought.

18. White's directory for 1836, see entry for Foulsham.

19. *Norwich Mercury* March 1831.

20. Lakenham Parish Register for 1835 and Holkham Census 1851 and 1861.

21. Henry Coke, pp.9-10.

22. Longford census for 1841.

23. Thomas Creevey's Papers 1793-1838 ed. Sir John Gore. London 1948. Penguin edition 1985 pp.382-383.

24. Gerard p.199 C.V. Butler *Domestic Service: an Enquiry by the Women's Industrial Council, 1916.*

25. The Reform Club was founded by Edward Ellice, he who spent so much time at Holkham. In her biography of Alexis Soyer, Ruth Brandon made the famous Reform Sauce from scratch, it took her two and a half hours and the result – to her surprise it tasted of 'the world's favourite sauce – tomato ketchup!' Ruth Brandon *The People's Chef* Chichester 2005 pp.101-102.

26. HA C/AN the Napier Letters.

27. *Beeton's Book of Household Management* ed. Mrs Isabella Beeton London 1861 p.309.

28. HA Letter Books for 1846 ref : E/C1/34 p.46. George Barker, on behalf of Earl Spencer, wrote to Baker, saying he knew about these paintings 'long since there ... do not unroll them for fear of paint cracking' and offered the second earl £80 for both, which was accepted.

EPILOGUE

At the time of his death all four of Thomas William Coke's sons were away from home; the eldest was in Scotland – this boy, also Thomas William, was aged nineteen, a minor and even younger than his father had been at the time of his inheritance. In August, three weeks after the funeral, an event which attracted much attention both locally and nationally, Lady Leicester the thirty-eight year old dowager Countess, together with Mr Ellice, took her children abroad for a tour of the Continent. It was understood that when she returned it would not be to Holkham but to Longford which she intended to make her home. It was the house for which she had chosen the decorations and where she and T.W. Coke had spent many months each year in the latter years of their marriage. In view of this, the new earl being under-age for another eighteen months, the trustees appointed to manage the estate took the decision to close Holkham for two seasons, that is until the earl's twenty-first birthday, and to dismiss all the servants.

Consequently each servant was paid his or her wages up to the first day of August 1842, given an allowance of £5 for mourning clothes and, if they qualified, a legacy. The legacies varied greatly – some, like the laundry maid Susan Stimpson, received 5gns, equal to half a year's wages, but Margaret Smith the dairy maid was given 13 gns, considerably more than her annual pay of 8gns, although both had been employed at Holkham for several years. With wages and legacies combined, plus the allowance for mourning, the maids received sums of between £15 and £25 each, the male servants substantially more, an average of £45. Three of the Longford servants were included in this handout.

William Baker was kept on and his letter book for August 1842 bulges with correspondence relating to annuities, donations, subscriptions, household expenses, taxes, office expenses and tradesmen's bills – complicated by income tax having been re-introduced that year to which all the annuities and donations were subject, often to the mystification and concern of the recipients. In preparation for the closure of the house, Baker and his assistants drew up a list of all the dry groceries and candles in the kitchen store cupboards, which would no longer be needed, packed them and put them on board the Wells boat to be returned to the London grocers who had supplied them and would now credit them to the Holkham account. One of the greatest concerns for Baker was what he should to do with the plate (the silver) once it had been weighed by the valuers. Eventually it was sent to Gurney's Bank in Norwich who stored it in their fire-proof room 'under our banking shop ... we will endeavour to take care of it but cannot make ourselves responsible ... '. The trustees were largely absent from Holkham leaving these day-to-day affairs entirely in Baker's hands. A letter written in mid September shows he was not getting as much advice as he would have liked, for he wrote to them asking when he should 'shew the House again', Tuesdays being the traditional day. No answer was recorded.

William Spelman of Norwich and William Beck of Mileham arrived at the latter end of August to take inventories of the Hall's contents and the stock on the farm. An inventory was also taken at Longford where there was some confusion due to the presence of servants still employed by Mr William Coke, 'Billy' the erstwhile heir, and various items bought since the death of Mr Edward Coke. Mrs Nokes the housekeeper was unable to confirm exactly who owned what. The furniture in the Servants Hall belonged absolutely to Mr W. Coke she said, as did the contents of the dairy, but pictures, books and wine in the cellars had a question mark beside them. It was agreed that the 'whole of the lighter Literature in the library' belonged to Mr W. Coke. There should have been no question as to the rest, for in 1836 Baker had made it very clear that since Mr Edward Coke had not been a tenant for life but a tenant at pleasure, the house contents and everything on the premises and estate belonged to T.W. Coke. This confusion exemplified much else that happened after T.W. Coke's death. Several people, including ex-servants who had hitherto been in receipt of donations from Holkham, found these cancelled. The reason Baker gave was that various recipients had not been named in the will, despite at least one of them having money 'in Coke's hands' and therefore the right to receive the interest, will or no will. These claimants were obliged to write to the executors and state their claim, who would inform the trustees. Only slowly was order restored.

In the end, the proposed mothballing of Holkham Hall did not happen. The trustees had reckoned without the young heir's love of sport, for the shooting season in Norfolk proved too great a lure. It was not to be sacrificed. In November 1842, less than six months after his father's death, he, his mother and Mr Ellice assembled a large sporting party – a party which included a Mr and Mrs Whitbread and their daughter Juliana. Impressed by the beauty of Miss Whitbread, Napier, the librarian, wrote to his father that she was the loveliest girl he had ever seen and judged her to be about seventeen years old. He said her father was brother 'to The Mr Whitbread, the famous London brewer'. [1] As to the new earl, Napier wrote of him: 'though a boy in years, he is a man older than I am in manner and as such he takes the lead in the house'. The Earl was also struck by the beauty and charms of Miss Whitbread, so much so that the following March, after a brief stay in London, he travelled to Cardington in Bedfordshire, the home of Mr Samuel Henry Whitbread, where, though still only twenty years old, he married her. Juliana Whitbread was indeed just seventeen as Napier had correctly guessed. From Cardington the Earl and his new Countess travelled to Holkham in time to spend Easter there.

Consequently the closure of the Hall never took place and nor were all the servants dismissed, though changes did take place. John Daniel Favré T.W. Coke's Swiss valet, having inherited his master's clothes and a legacy of £70 and annuity of £20, was living in Grosvenor Square in early 1843 with his wife (previously lady's maid in the household). Later they were at Longford Hall, showing that they were now employed by the Dowager Countess with Favré valet to Mr Ellice. John Porter, the house porter, left to become the landlord of the Ostrich Inn in Wells and two other senior servants died at about this time, Daniel Row the footman in December 1842 and in January 1843 John Godwin the butler. Godwin had been ill for a year and attended by the Fakenham doctor, Dr Parry, an impecunious man, struggling to make a living, who had periodically sent a number of begging letters to Holkham, notably in 1832 the year of the cholera epidemic. In 1842, when attending Mr Godwin, Parry hired a gig for the journey on the understanding that this expense would be re-imbursed. The Godwins lived at North Lodge and Mrs Godwin told the doctor to call at the Hall for the money, which he did, but found no one in the office. A week later he wrote to Baker who sent him his fee of three guineas. After Godwin's death his annuity was paid to his widow, Sarah, who many years previously had been Miss Elizabeth Coke's nurse and later her maid. She moved to Octagon Cottage where she lived for the next seven years, dying in 1850.

With the new era at Holkham, Baker the steward was at pains to explain to the tradesmen that until December 1843, when he would attain his majority, the earl was not able to be pay any bills via the office; all would be passed on to his trustees. However, as the estate was not yet settled, Lord Leicester had a free hand for the time being and he and his bride set about improving Holkham inside and out. The 1842 inventory was the first one taken since

Lady Margaret's death in 1775 and shows that in some rooms virtually nothing had changed. The North Dining Room still had the same mahogany chairs with their red morocco leather seats, three mahogany tables, plate warmers, crimson window curtains, a painted floor cloth, folding screens and two dumb waiters. More recent additions were a Turkey carpet, window blinds and two antique oriental tables. The great majority of the bedrooms were likewise much as they had always been, four poster beds with hangings (curtains) for both the family and servants. The names and functions of some of the rooms had been altered since 1775; for example in her widowhood Lady Margaret's private rooms were in Chapel Wing. Lady Margaret's dressing room had yellow damask windows curtains matching those in her ante room, closet and bedchamber. Her love of checked material (still found in the servants rooms in 1842), extended to her own bedchamber where her bed had yellow and white checked curtains, the servants had either blue or green. Her closet contained a mahogany writing table with a taper to seal letters and in her dressing room a sewing table. The rooms were carpeted and had tables, cupboards, chairs, fire screens, a clock and a hand bell. Some seventy years later Countess Anne's bedroom in Family Wing had a bedstead with carved posts, a blind at the window and a wardrobe, a newish invention where previously clothes had lain on shelves. The room was modest enough, as was her dressing room; only her sitting room near the library shows her youthful and fashionable taste. Here a Bengal carpet covered the floor with a matching hearth rug, two inlaid tables and an inlaid cabinet, a sofa 'full sized', two ottomans and sixteen chairs, two cases of stuffed birds, a guitar in a case, muslin curtains at the windows besides heavy curtains on a brass pole, and numerous other pieces of furniture, including many stands for holding vases and plants. Her daughter's sitting room, adjacent to her mother's, had no carpet but a floor cloth and painted chairs with rush seats; the one extravagance was a grand pianoforte. Nevertheless this room is worth noting for it was in addition to the school room and nursery, yet its occupant was only ten years old. Lord Leicester (T.W. Coke), was also minimalist compared to his wife; both his sitting room and bedroom, also in Family Wing, were simple and functional.

Guided by his mother-in-law, Mrs Whitbread, and by his wife, the new Lord Leicester visited the London shops and ordered samples and patterns of carpets, material to cover the furniture and a quantity of china. He hired guilders to re-guild chairs and sofas, hung or re-hung the shutters and doors on which he put many new knobs and escutcheons. Mrs Ling of the Norwich upholstery firm continued to be employed as of old to repair and restore, but most of the workers and materials came from London. Mr Dowbiggin of Mount Street was one of the main suppliers of the new finery.

Three months after her son's marriage the dowager countess married Mr Edward Ellice (hence the employment of Favré the valet) – this may have been foreseen, even suggested in the life time of T.W. Coke, but it was to be a short lived union ending with the countess's death in childbirth the following year in July 1844. From then on the young earl added the care of his younger siblings to his other duties; his brother Edward went into the army and became a captain in the Scots Guards, Henry was guided towards the church but did not enter it, Wenman was still a schoolboy at Rugby where that 'muscular Christian' Dr Thomas Arnold had lately been headmaster. The youngest child, Lady Margaret aged eleven, went to live with her mother's relations the Keppels at Quiddenham in south Norfolk. The earl and his countess were about to start a family of their own. The first child, born in December 1844, was to be followed by ten more, filling Holkham and requiring a new set of servants to care for and educate them.

Old and retired servants were not forgotten and eventually received their annuities every six months. Miss Charlotte Atwood, governess to Miss Elizabeth Coke from 1789, lived on until 1854 when she died unmarried at Weybridge, Surrey. Miss Sybille Vrankin was living in Bristol in 1832 also unmarried. Mrs Hadricke retired housekeeper died in 1852, Favré the valet in c.1853 and was buried at Longford, and his wife Sarah, once a lady's maid at Holkham, lived on to 1879. Edward Stiles the baker, who must also have doubled as footman in the old way since he wore livery and used hair powder, had left Holkham for another employer in 1834 but received his annuity until his death in 1855. So too did Widow Dodsworth to 1850, the year she died. She had once been a still-room maid, but was long since based at Shugborough. At Holkham Mrs Blunt, the widow of a butler, stayed on to become the keeper of the West Lodge until her death aged eighty in 1859. Several others received donations, a few in addition to their annuities such as Favré, some as an occasional gift and others as regular small payments. John Biller, the retired coachman, was an example of the latter; aged seventy-nine in 1851 he had begun as coachman in 1796 and was now living in a cottage at the staithe. He is occasionally entered as being in receipt of a donation of £1. 10s. every six weeks; at other times he was given £1 just now and again.

Donations were gifts, but some people under this heading were entered in error. For example Mrs Cuff (previously Mrs Wall) the base born daughter of Charlotte Edwards and the steward Francis Crick had money invested with the earl, of which she received an annual payment of £30 which was interest, not a donation. The majority of donations were paid out to ex or retired servants and their dependants, an amount which often totalled £120 a year.

Four servants retired to the Almshouse; James Denson one time brewer was eighty-nine in 1851 and lived there with three retired laundry maids as neighbours, Esther Bacon aged ninety and Sarah Mann and Frances Barnes both well over eighty. Generally life expectancy for servants, especially female ones in a great house such as Holkham, where they were well fed, clothed and warm, was above average. As laundry work was the most strenuous of all it is interesting to note this longevity.

Thus the second earl had considerable domestic responsibilities at a very young age besides the estate business. One of his early acts was to take on the entire household, servants indoors and out, gardeners and foresters, by rail to the Great Exhibition of 1851. During his lifetime the railways, telegraphs, gas lighting, sewing machines, photography and much more would change all their lives.

The Poem

None of the Holkham servants left any writings behind them, at least none are known. But Sarah Biller born 1805, daughter of the coachman at Holkham from 1798 to 1838 and his wife Sarah a kitchen maid, wrote verse. In 1839 she published a volume of poems which went into two editions. The title was *Holkham Scenes of my Childhood and other Poems.* She dedicated 'this little work' to the Earl of Leicester and included a long list of subscribers. The Earl and Countess of Leicester paid for a copy each, Lady Anson for five copies, Miss Blackwell for two, even the young Viscount bought a copy. Among the names are those of Miss Atwood, Elizabeth Coke's governess, a Miss Dakin, Mrs Girvan the gardener's wife, Mrs Hadricke the housekeeper, Mr Baker the steward and agent and Mr Lulman his clerk, Mr Rump the Wells doctor, Mrs Skoyles from the Inn, and many others whose names appear in the lists of servants over the years. Sarah Biller wrote a short Address explaining the common desire among poets to eulogize the place of their birth and as no other had done so for Holkham so ' ... deficient as I am ... I am persuaded'. She states she had little education in her youth and since her 'calling in life requires close application to services of a very different nature ... will be some excuse'. It appears that in 1839, the year of publication, she was living in London. Her publisher was Foster and Hestell of 268 the Strand, otherwise nothing more is known. The book was small in format for there are only twenty lines to a page. The Holkham poem, the longest in the collection, covers twenty-one pages. It is a straight eulogy as she claimed, a description of Holkham. She describes the sea in all its moods, wrecks and tranquil sweetness, the beach, the marshes, woods, fields, the lake, harvest (sometimes gathered by moonlight), winter, the hunt and skating on the lake. The house she describes as a place where treasures have found a proper setting and the library 'feasts the docile mind'. She mentions the chapel and the illustrious visitors who have enjoyed Holkham's pleasures, and T.W. Coke himself cheered by the presence of so many grandchildren. 'Content at home an honoured master lives.'. As to the labourers in the fields and 'stewards, servants, or whate'er their state, likewise who all their master wait, if they with diligence their course pursue, will not go unrewarded ... '. The wealthy landlord 'provident and kind' who gives title to this study. No-one is left out of the poem; Lady Margaret is praised for having built the Almshouse the refuge of the old, 'long since calmly joined the dead, she like a guardian angel from on high, supports their tottering footsteps till they die'. The school, and even the alehouse get a mention, and that well remembered embodiment of a happy rural life the village green. Finally she contemplates the future when Holkham 'the cherished Eden of our valiant land' will yield to the wreck of years and lie covered in ivy like a Roman temple 'more beauteous in its ruin than in its prime'!

Sarah's poem for all its varnish pretty well sums up the parish of Holkham. Both generations of Cokes were lavish spenders who did not worry about the detail and enjoyed the spectacle. Yet they were also considerate employers who looked after their servants, from the furnishings in their bedrooms to food and care in sickness and old age. And they paid good wages. It is difficult however to give any simple reason for the constant turnover of servants, other than the vagaries of human nature. Servants, as we have seen, were not dependant on the local 'big house' at this period, as most came from or via London, but were free to pick and choose just as their masters and mistresses were. Many a high hope was dashed when a bad judgement was made, many a mistake made, and many took it for granted that after a certain time a servant would wish to move on. This can be seen in the characters servants received from their employers. Most were given with no rancour or resentment but with a passive almost detached tact. By contrast some were content to stay for many years. Mrs Lybbe Powis claimed that Mr Jackson's servants at Weasenham had been there an astonishing length of time, the housekeeper for fifty-one years, the butler forty-two and the lady's maid twenty-four. She put it down to Mr Jackson liking people. [2] At Holkham a good proportion continued in the 'Family' for almost as long and probably for the same reasons. As seen in the cases of the housekeeper Charlotte Edwards and others, tolerance and understanding was practiced on an impressive scale. 'Content at home an honoured master lives' Sarah Biller wrote of T. W. Coke, whose household 'if diligent would not go unrewarded' and applied this also to Thomas and Lady Margaret who were clearly not forgotten.

NOTES

1. Samuel Charles Whitbread [1796-1879] MP for Middlesex in 1820 and in 1824 married Julia Brand daughter of the 2nd Lord Dacre. Their daughter Juliana was born the following year.

2. Lybbe Powis p.4.

Index

Egmont, John Perceval 1st Earl   56

Elam, William   footman   256-257

Elgar, Mr William   draper   261

Ellice, Mr Edward   politician   274, 279-281, 283

Elliot, Mr   master bricklayer   182

Ellis, Miss Anne Raine   author   213

Ellis, Mr   schoolmaster   21-22, 24-25, 64

Elmham Park, Norfolk   30, 109-110, 143, 178-179, 191

Elvin, Mr   merchant   261

Emerson, James   taylor   223, 246

Emerson, Mr Stephen   architect   246, 268

Emerson, Sarah   housemaid   210

Essex, Richard   head groom   129

Euston, Suffolk   115, 129, 171, 182

Fairbrother, John   under-butler   270

Fakenham, Norfolk   90, 130, 134, 146, 156, 160, 162, 188, 205, 218, 225, 229, 259, 268, 281

Farley, William   groom   246

Farr, Mr   cook   63

Fassett, Mr   of Walsingham   apothecary   130

Favré, Monsieur John Daniel T.W. Coke's valet   245, 275, 281

Fell & Briggs, Messrs   of London coachmakers   264-265

Fenn, Zarachy   of Walsingham   merchant   243

Ferrari, Dr   36, 40, 42, 50, 61, 117, 125, 129, 131, 146, 169

Fillis, Mrs Elizabeth   nurse   202, 211-212, 221

Fishburn, George   gamekeeper   271

Fishburn, Polly   nurse, later gamekeeper   255

Fisher, Mr David   actor-manager   277

Flavellen, Jane   kitchen maid   112

Florence, Italy   44-45

Ford, Cornelius   labourer   115

Ford, Rhoda   housemaid   115

Forster, Mr E.M.   author   152

Forster, Mrs   nurse at Kensington   126

Fountaine, Sir Andrew   collector   44

Framingham, Mr   carrier   158

Freebury, George   footman   270

French, John   stable worker   112

Friend, Dr   medical doctor   104

Gainsborough, Mr Thomas   artist   214

Gameron, Mrs   embroiderer   59, 99

Gardiner, Mr   house steward   169

Garne, Jemima   housemaid   211, 238

Garret, Robert   labourer   130

Garrick, Mr David   actor   121

Gay, Mr   of Norwich   party planner   218

George the First, King   108, 187

George the Second, King   93

George, Mary   laundry maid   69

George, Prince of Wales, later George the Fourth   2, 206, 217, 220

Germany   47-48, 50, 54

Gibb, Mr James   architect   64, 66

Gibson, Mr   banker   22

Gibson, Mr   of Wells   apothecary   130

Gill, Mrs   draper   99

Gilliard, Monsieur Thomas   Coke's valet   125

Girdlestone, Mr   apothecary   192, 237

Girvan, Mr Hugh   head gardener   270-271, 284

Gittos, Edmund   postillion   104

Godwin, John   T.W. Coke's footman, then butler   235, 242, 244-245, 252, 262, 276, 281

Godwin, Mr   cook   126

Goodwood, Sussex   133-134, 161, 164